ує
7.6.06

First published in the UK and USA in 2000 by
Booth-Clibborn Editions
12 Percy Street
London W1P 9FB
www.booth-clibborn-editions.com

Portrait of Stephen Bayley by Lisa Seligmann, 1986

A Cataloguing-in-Publication record for this book is available from the Publisher.

ISBN 1-86154-068-X

GENERAL /KNOW-LEDGE

Design : GRAPHIC THOUGHT FACILITY
Headline typeface : 'VMR' by JULIAN MOREY
Printed and bound in Hong Kong

STEPHEN BAYLEY

```
* * * * * * * * * * * * * * * * * * * * * * * * * * * * * * *
*  CONTENTS :                                    *
*                                                *
* * * * * * * * * * * * * * * * * * * * * * * * * * * * * * *
```

INTRODUCTION :
5 : I was always a bit of a carspotter

PART ONE :
                    TASTE

12 : Taste : the story of an idea
42 : On the urban plight of the
     swirly numberplate
43 : The chameleon of fashion
46 : Taste sensations unfit for
     human consumption
48 : Luxury - a dated concept in
     the 1990s
50 : A disputation about taste
53 : Outing the closet
56 : The cabinet room
58 : The modern dilemma

PART TWO :
     CULT OBJECTS, STATUS SYMBOLS
          AND TRIBAL HABITS

62 : What turns an object into a cult?

64 : Why it's time to ban the dreaded
     baseball cap
65 : Requiem for the trainer
67 : Fountain pens make a big comeback
     with the smart set
68 : Sloping off
69 : White space
71 : Where there's muck there's brass

PART THREE :
          COMMERCE AND CULTURE

74 : Watteau, art and trade
77 : Reproductions and originals
80 : Goodbye to the avant-garde
83 : Beauty in the beast
85 : The myth of progress

PART FOUR :
               MAKING IT

87 : The sad downfall of the world's
     oldest workshop
91 : Stiffen the sinews - this is war

93 : Did British Leyland throw a
     vital tool away?
96 : Vision that was blurred by big
     business
98 : Zagato's family business
102 : Zen and the cycle of motor art
106 : Robots take over the Boilerhouse
111 : God is in the fast lane

PART FIVE :
     SELLING IT : IMAGE AND IDENTITY
----
115 : The Coca-Cola bottle: the shape
      of the century
123 : Top marques
125 : Brand new ideas
128 : Brand values and Vauxhall
130 : Rooms with a distorted view
131 : The new British Airways
136 : Don't phone the identity man yet

PART SIX :
     THE HUMAN CONDITION
----
139 : Dunne roaming
144 : Come the man, come the hour
145 : Call of the riled
147 : The air fix. Fear of flying:
      the theory and the practice
150 : The power and the gourmet
152 : Creative review
154 : Labour pains and long lunches
157 : Shaking all over
159 : The kiss
161 : E-mission control
163 : Sex in-flight
165 : In defence of my opinion

PART SEVEN :
     OUR CULTURE, THEIR CULTURE
----
171 : The guilty men: John Betjeman
174 : Are the British visually
      literate?
177 : Paradise lost
180 : A nation living at ease with
      itself
183 : French lessons
186 : In this sterile diorama, life
      is but a theme
188 : La Grande Corniche
190 : Milan : fizz, fun and style
191 : Design capitals

193 : Gianni Agnelli
193 : The empire of ideas
196 : In the Japanese style
199 : On the shifting sands of
      Californian design
200 : An office you can't refuse

PART EIGHT :
     MUSEUMS AND MONUMENTS
----
203 : Cars for cathedrals
207 : We don't need our history
      packaged by this Trust
209 : A haven for modern muses
211 : Bauhaus on Thames
215 : So, who is the most stylish
      of them all?
217 : Curators of poor taste

PART NINE :
     DESIGN ELEMENTS
----
219 : On corporate identity cowboys
220 : Metropolitan lines
223 : Design Council : facing the
      scrap heap
225 : On the decline of product
      design
227 : Classic statement
229 : A bird's-eye view of
      automotive aesthetics
231 : On the deadly monograph
234 : Future of graphic design
236 : Exhibition design
238 : Gordon Russell
240 : On a fundamental misunder-
      standing of Italian design
242 : French élitism
244 : The new

PART TEN :
     DESIGN POLITICS
----
249 : Rock Bottomley
258 : A brand-new Morris Marina
262 : Disposable attitude to
      aesthetics
268 : Cool Britannia
273 : The Dome: an open letter to
      Pierre-Yves Gerbeau
276 : Urban shambles
280 : Index

```
*******************************************
* INTRODUCTION :                          *
*                                         *
*******************************************
```

I WAS ALWAYS A BIT OF A CARSPOTTER

The very first photograph of me does not include a teddy bear or a rattle, but the huge reflector of the headlamp belonging to the Talbot car my father owned at the time. I may well, ever since, have had an easier relationship with things than with people. Later, from the back seat of a Ford Pilot, a Humber or a Jaguar, I can't remember which, I first saw a road-going Lotus XI. I suppose this must have been about 1961 somewhere near the Aintree race track. The lean, elegant, aerodynamic shape was unforgettable and gave me an early impression, later to harden into a lifetime's conviction, that at its best, technology offered a sort of perfection usually rare in everyday life. At least as seen from Liverpool.

I saw my first Ferrari in 1965 or 1966, again from the back seat of a car. I think it must have been a 275GTB and I was in, I don't know, perhaps an Austin Westminster and travelling through Herefordshire. The vivid red Ferrari was on a garage forecourt with a sticker price of £6,000, which seemed a lot in those days. Even now, I can remember the intense feeling of exoticism and almost erotic longing this beautiful car exuded. Ordinary life may have been humdrum, but the mere sight of such a machine promised obscure delights, as voluptuous as they were remote.

But more significant in its way than the neat Lotus or the lascivious Ferrari was a car I now recognize as the 1967 Model Year Vauxhall Viva. Again, I recall seeing a pre-production car testing on the backroads of Northants and was very struck by its flamboyant shape with that distinctive Coke-bottle contour line at the hips. Back at school, I was eager to explain sighting this curvaceous novelty to friends. I said it was so modern and interesting, it couldn't possibly be British, must be American. They all wanted to know how on earth I could determine such niceties just from a passing visual appraisal. The belief that nationality, and indeed a good deal else besides, can be read from appearances dates from this moment and has been with me ever since.

Next year, when the Viva was actually launched, I tried to sell an unsolicited piece about its fascinating Coke-bottle curves to, of all places, the *Listener*, then the BBC's thoughtful weekly. This was the time when BBC and intellectual could be used in the same sentence without irony. My story was typed with two fingers on a wobbly, but beautiful, little Olivetti Lettera portable, another device I found to be very satisfyingly life-enhancing. I was 15 and, like so many others of my ventures at the time, this journalistic attempt failed. One reason for this was the hysterical overstatement of my argument (a mannerism that's been with me on and off ever since); the other was that, even in the year of *Sergeant Pepper*, highbrow journals like the *Listener* were not yet ready to consider design, least of all car design, as worthy of scrutiny.

But my first rejected article established a pattern, not – I'm glad to say – of rejection, but rather of belief. Praise for the Vauxhall Viva confirmed my view that: (a) you *can* tell from appearances; (b) industrial design has usurped 'art' as a source of beauty; (c) writing for magazines was something I badly wanted to do.

This last I got from Tom Wolfe, just becoming a significant diversion as I started my A-levels. Given my lazily contemptuous approach to directed study, anything could have been a diversion, but Wolfe (and Hunter S. Thompson and Marshall McLuhan) with their neologisms, street-smarts, sharp suits, seductive high-octane volatile Americana, wit, sesquipedalian sentences, cool cars and irreverent ideas offered tantalizingly vicarious access to a world of values not then being considered by my university officials.

I fast developed an approach to knowledge that was, depending on your viewpoint, heroically eclectic (this was my own perspective on the matter) or exasperatingly undisciplined (this was the teachers'). I read *International Times* (a respectable source of nude photography) under the desk in maths lessons and Marvell and Herrick and the Metaphysicals under the desk in music. In one memorable year, a music report read 'Great silly ass! Grossly incompetent!'. All I learned from this music teacher was how to be promiscuous with explanation marks, but I found that 'had we but world enough and time' worked wonders with girls. I am still proud to boast that, not only can I tell you the first three finishers of the 1966 Indianapolis 500, but I also know the early publishing history of Allen Ginsberg and Jack Kerouac.

The Americans were only one source of inspiration and diversion. You can't grow up in Liverpool and not notice architecture, there's lots of it. Some, the Victorian and Edwardian stuff, powerful, swaggering, impressive and intensely romantic; others, most of the local authority housing, wretchedly tedious and depressing, tearing a huge black hole in the universe's enthusiasm. Again, from the leathery back seat of a comfortable car it was impossible not to want to make telling contrasts and to wonder why the same materials could in one century be the substance of inspiration and in another, the material expression of human defeat.

Nikolaus Pevsner helped me here. In the same year that Graham Hill won the Indy and the Beatles telecast *All You Need is Love* worldwide, Penguin (in fact, Pelican) reissued Pevsner's *Pioneers of Modern Design*. Here was a real epiphany. Pevsner confirmed my schoolboy's observations that Liverpool was a city of astonishing and powerful architectural character: now I could put a name to the world's first iron-framed commercial building (Peter Ellis' Oriel Chambers) and the greatest neo-classical building on the planet (Harvey Lonsdale Elmes's St George's Hall, also the first building in the world with mechanical air management). Long before I had been to New York, I was convinced (and still am) that, in terms of drama, poetry, romantic melancholy, sheer accidental genius of architectural proportions and a bizarre menu of styles, Liverpool's Pier Head is an authentic rival to Manhattan's more famous one. It would be a very dull person who was not immensely moved by each.

But it was Manchester that made me. One of the starting points for my own fascination with everyday design was in a university seminar room nearly 30 years ago. Trademark Mancunian drizzle, industrial grisaille and traffic. A tutor was droning on about fine art matters, when, looking out the window, I thought something like 'this is all very well, but why on earth is nobody telling me about why a great Northern city looks the way it does?' In those days, art history was Florence or Rome. In those days, the study of any post-Renaissance architectural history was a novelty. Baroque was a fringe subject and neo-classicism more so. Victorian architectural history was not quite proper. The Vauxhall Viva had still not had its day in the sun.

My university career was as uneven as school. I more or less refused to consider anything on a list provided by a tutor, but started my own ambitiously autodidactic programme of reading. This confounded the conservatives who took their revenge with bad grades. One distinguished external examiner said 'This boy is either very clever or very stupid', a judgement I still treasure.

On the other hand, the more adventurous tutors found something to nurture. One of these was Jules Lubbock who in his Didsbury cottage generously introduced me to both Josef Albers prints and pizza, thus establishing a link between Italian food and modernism which I have ever since found difficult to eradicate. Jules it was who once gave a lecture about Simone Martini ('the pure effulgence of tooled gold' sticks in my mind) while holding a book on systems theory in the other. This was baffling, but fascinating. He made us read *New Society* where I discovered Reyner Banham. He said to me 'Mr Bayley, just why are you studying history of art? Wouldn't you be better off in advertising?'

The other teacher who saved me from academic catastrophe was Charles Sewter, the owlish and altogether wonderful William Morris expert who had founded Manchester's history of art degree in 1947. Sewter had known Moholy-Nagy and Mondrian in Hampstead in the 1930s and was incomparably generous and indulgent, introducing me to Moholy-Nagy's *Vision in Motion* and Charles Biederman's *Art as the Evolution of Visual Knowledge*. These gave me a good excuse for not bothering to read Heinrich Wölfflin. My first practical experience of editorial work was doing a very bad job of correcting page proofs of Sewter's book on the baroque during a summer in Birkirkara when the ferocious Mintoff had scared away the tourists. Even the benign Sewter could not, however, cope with my using the word 'logo' in a 1972 essay on Bonnard.

It was people like Lubbock and Sewter who taught me that the history of art could have some use outside the privileged parlours of the connoisseurs. There never had been any doubt in my mind that the very best of British High Victorian commercial and public architecture was at least the equal of the Taj Mahal or St Peter's: it was only the *snobbismo* of conventional art historians (who preferred research trips to Tuscany over research trips to Lancashire) that said any different. In the same way, I have no doubt that in terms of artistic value it was not impossible to compare a 1959 Ford Zodiac with a Donatello sculpture. My entire obsession with legitimizing modern design is simply a way of applying the principles of art history to the everyday.

Not much more than five years after having my daring formal analysis of the Vauxhall Viva promptly rejected by the *Listener,* I found myself – entirely by accident – as that magazine's art critic. Here, again, I exploited a nice man's benevolence. This time it was Dick Gilbert who let me write about design. Happily, my style was now improving into a mellow mixture of high aspirations and hack instincts. A wodge of *Listener* reviews helped me to get a serious academic job at the University of Kent and one day walking across campus I realized that it was going to be very difficult to teach modern design without any textbooks, so I decided to assemble one myself.

This was *In Good Shape*, which a slightly bamboozled Design Council published in 1979. It was one of the very first books of its kind, one which took the assumptions of Moholy-Nagy, Biederman, Pevsner and Banham – who established the Holy Writ of design – as a basis on which to proceed. If nothing else, I think the book can claim a first: a picture of a Zippo lighter appearing in a hardback English publication. But its subtitle was controversial. Although Paul Reilly, retired Director of the Design Council, wrote a generous foreword he felt it necessary to explain that 'Style in Industrial Design' my sub-title was a dire symptom of having been brought up in the age of Pop. However, when Terence Conran was looking for someone to help to promote design, he asked Paul Reilly and Reilly recommended me. All the rest, as somebody said, was sociology.

What does all of this have in common? Well, I have a passion for things and for trying to understand them. Objects have a life and a language and, as Henry Ford said, you can read them like a book if you only know how. I have a fascination with well-founded novelty, whether in objects or in expressions. I'm in awe of, say, Tom Wolfe's ability to combine microscopically acute visual observation with a fine ear and an unknowable alchemy of getting the right words in the right cadences and proportions within a sentence to express something that has often been thought, but never said anything like as well. Equally, I find the ability of, say, Ettore Sottsass jnr to know exactly what that little Olivetti portable should have looked like wonderfully exhilarating, even moving. Both Wolfe and Sottsass qualify for Goethe's definition of genius: the ability to put form on the indeterminate. They also qualify for mine: after Wolfe and Sottsass, no one else working in the same field will till that particular soil again. There you have it: the worm of 'progress'.

I love the twentieth century and all the opportunities it has offered, even if some of them are delusions. Equally, I despise snobbish antiquarianism as much as I detest boorish levellers and their scattergun condemnation of élitism. The great adventure of the century recently past is that the best is available to everyone – at least in theory. And, if any relativist reviewing this starts whining about who-knows-what's-best, I'd just say that the doctrine of cultural relativism is philosophically absurd as it carries its own relativist self-denying and self-destructive argument. Mass production and industrial design have the potential to make beauty commonplace and luxury affordable. Granted, there's a way to go, but that's no reason to stop trying. As they used to say in the PCI [Partista Communista Italiana]: the best salami for everyone!

What errant gene made me so obsessive about ordinary things? In a moment of idleness, I made some genealogical enquiries. About as far as it goes on one side is a butcher in Regency Shoreditch, on the other back to an early Georgian gamekeeper at Wilton. Does this explain anything? I can only refer to Edgar Wind's citation of Pico's belief, as expressed in his oration, *On the Dignity of Man*, that man's glory is derived from his mutability. To which might be added Hunter S. Thompson's moment of self-revelation, not in its way dissimilar to my own: 'Holy shit, if I can write like this and get away with it, why should I keep trying to write like the *New York Times*? It was like falling down an elevator shaft and landing in a pool of mermaids'.

Not only have I always been a bit of a carspotter, I've been a bit of a lifter too: it wasn't me who said the original bits are not good and the good bits are not original. But the thing about plagiarism is this: don't do it unless you're prepared to trade up. Which is, of course, why I swapped Vauxhall for Ford.

I do have one passionate belief completely uncompromised by smart aleckry or irony and it is that the world can be made a better and more beautiful place not with less technology, but with more. I don't see any civilized alternatives to dignified and thoughtful progress. While the wretched Dome cost three-quarters of a billion and pleases no one, a modest art gallery in Walsall demonstrates the power of architecture and design to transform cities: for less than 3 per cent of the cost of the embarrassing Millennial tent, a modest, but courageous and uncompromised building will revive both the culture and the economy of a depressed post-industrial area. It was exactly the same with the Guggenheim in Bilbao.

Looking dolefully on the crumbling remnants of the family palazzo, the great Sicilian novelist Giuseppe di Lampedusa remarked: 'If you want things to stay the same, they are going to have to change'.

Quite. Culture means growth. Culture implies evolution. There are few human instincts more likely to be counterproductive than the desire to preserve and conserve. I have my doubts about pedantic preservation, not because it cares for fine old buildings (a taste I share), but because it seems to freeze them at one particular moment in time.

Stewart Brand, author of *The Last Whole Earth Catalog* and *How Buildings Learn* said 'You don't finish buildings. You start them'.

It's true for the entire man-made environment, urban and rural. It's an unfinished job, a work-in-progress. It must change. But not for the worse, for the better.

Everything we value in art and culture has been the product of a revolutionary change. The builders of the great Palladian houses we so rightly admire did not hesitate to raze the fine Jacobean buildings that preceded them on the site. Only now, the rigid desire to preserve at all costs is a symptom of a depressing and timid lack of conviction about the future.

Our present view of landscape is distorted by class and cultural prejudice. The countryside is a factory. The picturesque itself is a foreign import (from Italy). English garden design would lack almost all its most celebrated features had it not been for the influence of the paintings of Claude Lorrain, Gaspar Poussin and Salvator Rosa. It is a confection no less 'artificial' than a sixteenth-century Dutch parterre. The vision of nature as a state of primal innocence is a historically specific one. It is a snare and a delusion.

I think we too readily look back to a golden age. The very idea that a golden age existed is a historically specific idea that comes to us from the eighteenth century (after a longer journey from antiquity). Ever since pioneer decorator Elsie de Wolfe introduced new American money to old French furniture, the eighteenth century has been a reference point. Today, eighteenth-century collectibles still dominate taste.

Be aware that fully three-quarters of what we call 'traditions' are in fact inventions of the second half of the nineteenth century: these include Druids, morris-dancing, most public schools, parliamentary procedure and a beguiling, but utterly inaccurate, view of the Medieval period (the one that so seduced Lord Irvine when he did his Homebase Pugin in Parliament).

If you believe in culture you have to believe that we can make tomorrow's heritage today just as easily as we can live off yesterday's. I am not an advocate of change for the sake of it. Only an advocate of maintaining creative awareness of the idea that excellence takes many forms.

The very many awful modern buildings that scar the towns and the countryside are not awful because they are modern. They are awful because they are… awful. Simply, bad architecture: badly briefed, poorly conceived, badly proportioned, poorly executed, badly maintained. Modernism, remember, is not so much a style (the easily parodied geometric designs with industrial materials), but an attitude. It is, as Frank Lloyd Wright believed, simply a matter of 'making the most of contemporary possibilities'. Remember that the alternatives to progress are not packhorses on the downs, crumpets and honey on the vicarage lawn, but overcrowded roads, run-down services, shabby provincial architecture. The alternatives to progress look much more like the A38/M6 intersection with its litter of rusted prams, supermarket carts, weeds growing through pock-marked tarmac, crisp packets, diesel stains, Coke tins, dog shit and fag ends than a Constable landscape.

What we need is brown-field developments in our ruined and exhausted cities. Of course, I'd like to see the finest architecture of the past, but I don't want it preserved like the body of Lenin in his tomb for the delectation of a humble proletariat. I deplore that self-consciousness about the environment that leads to the death of real culture. I'd like to see the countryside used and lived in, evolving as fruitfully and as beautifully as it did between, say, 1500 and 1750.

To reject the possibility of useful change is to misunderstand the past, to betray the present and short-change the future. But it is significant that the rate of change of progress in fashion and product and graphic design is actually slowing down, at least in the aesthetic sense. With cars, while technical refinement advances rapidly, styling is stable. Successive generations of, say, a Volkswagen Golf or a Lexus deliberately ape their predecessors. In consumer durables, there is a visual stasis that leaves room only for hectic fads or meretricious novelty rather than genuine innovation. In any case, design tends to be inspired by radical technical changes and in, for instance, electronic consumer goods we have had very few. Between 1955 and 1980 Sony managed a radical innovation almost every year. The transistor radio, portable television, cassette and video tapes, high-quality colour monitors, the ineffable Walkman, CDs, minicams, minidiscs. We have had no substantial innovations for nearly a decade and this is reflected in external style. Just as we know what a gentleman's suit should look like, so we now know what a Golf or a hi-fi should look like.

Maybe this is late millennial timorousness. Certainly, in the light of the foregoing and in tense expectation of the new century we have to be especially wary about predictions. Some people, it is said, take no exercise other than jumping to conclusions. Futurology is often hilariously inaccurate. It has always amused me that Thomas Edison saw no future for A.C. In 1901 (two years before it happened) Wilbur Wright saw no possibility of heavier-than-air flight. Rear Admiral Clark Woodward of the US Navy said in 1939 that you can't sink a large naval vessel with a bomb. The list goes on.

Current predictions for the next twenty-five years include:

- genuine e-cash
- computers recognizing handwriting
- remote surgery
- aquaculture
- humans on Mars
- a sober-up drug
- virtual sex
- mag-lev trains
- cell-repair technology
- cryonic reanimation
- self-replicating robots

In the immediate future we will have conservative style married
to radical technical innovations. But the predictors themselves are often
inefficient too. When Kelvin McKenzie of *The Sun* decided to sack his
paper's hopelessly inept astrologer because of the wretched inaccuracy
of the tabloid's horoscopes, he amused himself in the letter by beginning

Dear So-and-So
As you will *already* know…

But we have to remain fascinated by the future: we have no choice
because that is where we are all going to spend the rest of our lives.

```
*****************************************
*  PART ONE : TASTE                     *
*                                       *
*****************************************
```

TASTE: THE STORY OF AN IDEA

Look at Dr Freud's consulting rooms. The great man is sitting in a
sombre Viennese interior. You can see the craquelure, smell the leather
and the polish, sense the aspidistra. Even though it is a black and white
photograph, you can tell the dominant colour is brown. Tomes of grim
Mitteilungen suggest that psychoanalysis has the sanction of the past,
that it is an ancient and respected academic medical practice.

Two things would be different if Dr Freud were practising in New
York or London today rather than in the volatile Vienna of Loos, Schiele,
Klimt and Werfel. One is that his consulting rooms would look very

different: nowadays leaders of the medical profession do not present their seriousness in terms of sombre bourgeois interior design; wealthy professionalism is suggested by black leather and chrome furniture and middlebrow junk art. The other is that the dark corners of his patients' minds would, on inspection, be found to be corroded not by anxieties about sex, death and mother (for nowadays these things are commonplace), but by … taste. This word, which formerly signified no more than 'discrimination', was hijacked and its meaning inflated by an influential élite who use the expression 'good taste' simply to validate their personal aesthetic preferences while demonstrating their vulgar presumption of social and cultural superiority. The very idea of good taste is insidious. While I stop short of believing that all human affairs are no more than a jungle of ethical and cultural relativity, the suggestion that the infinite variety and vast sweep of the mind should be limited by some polite mechanism of 'good form' is absurd.

Everyone has taste, yet it is more of a taboo subject than sex or money. The reason for this is simple. Claims about your attitudes to or achievements in the carnal and financial arenas can be disputed only by your lover and your financial advisers, whereas by making statements about your taste you expose body and soul to terrible scrutiny. Taste is a merciless betrayer of social and cultural attitudes. Thus, while anybody will sell you as much as (and perhaps more than) you want to know about their triumphs in bed and at the bank, it is taste that gets people's nerves tingling.

Nancy Mitford noted in her acute discussion of the term 'common' (as in 'He's a common little man') that it is common even to use the word 'common', which gives double-bluffers rich hunting grounds among the maladroit and insecure. Explicit social class and explicit material taste are a part of the post-industrial reordering of the world and as Nick Furbank wittily pointed out in his book about snobbery, *Unholy Pleasures* (1985), 'in classing someone socially, one is simultaneously classing oneself'. He might just as easily have said 'in criticizing someone else's taste, one is simultaneously criticizing oneself'.

The one certain thing about taste is that it changes. Taste began to be an issue when we lost the feeling for intelligible natural beauty possessed by the Neo-platonists and medieval artists and writers. Nature and art are, in a sense, opposites, and art has been the most reliable barometer of attitudes to beauty. As André Malraux noted at the end of the 1940s, in the modern world, art, even religious art of the past, is divorced from its religious purposes and has become a negotiable commodity for consumption by rich individuals or by museums.

Art was the first 'designer' merchandise and there is no surer demonstration of fluctuating taste than the reputations of the great artists and the pictures they created. Averaged across centuries of first lionization and then neglect, it is clear that these reputations have no permanent value: the estimation of the value of art depends as much on the social and cultural conditions of a particular viewer as on qualities embodied in the work itself.

The reputation of El Greco is the paradigm of this phenomenon. Praised in his own lifetime, he painted in a style, exaggerated even by the standards of mannerism, which neo-classical critics found unsettling. The only way encyclopedists could interpret his attenuated forms and his spooky colours was to claim he was going blind and had gone mad. A century later, French Romantics travelling in Spain, like Théophile Gautier, recognized in El Greco's forms, colours and mannerisms exactly those passions they wanted to versify, paint or articulate. Half a century on, Picasso singled El Greco out for major cultural rehabilitation.

Once El Greco could only be understood in terms of medically recognizable disorders, but by the early twentieth century he was seen in a more positive, less pathological light and hailed as a source of *duende*, the romantic Spanish gloominess described by Lorca. This *duende* inspired Picasso: his *Les Demoiselles d'Avignon*, conventionally held to be the origin of Cubism, was as much influenced by El Greco as by Cézanne and allowed Picasso to claim an earlier Spanish precedent for the movement he invented. As El Greco became a cult, other converts followed Picasso, including his friend Santiago Rusinol, a rich aesthete responsible for the Catalan Renaixenca.

As arbiters of taste are inclined to, Rusinol created a museum, Cau Ferrat, in Sitges in 1894 to vindicate his own preferences. In the opening ceremony, his two El Greco paintings were carried on a float to the accompaniment of a marching band while assistants scattered flowers. By 1898, Rusinol had convinced his fellow townsmen to subscribe to a monument to the painter, which still stands in the Catalan port. At the same time, Picasso's studio was covered with photographs of El Greco, and, in fact, close parallels in both style and subject matter can be seen between Blue Period Picasso and late El Greco. The identification of one with the other went so far that in one sketchbook Picasso scribbled, '*Yo el Greco, yo el Greco*' (I am El Greco, I am El Greco).

El Greco is now established as an 'old master' after centuries of alternating vilification and neglect. Or is he? The El Greco anecdote makes clear that what is fashionable in one generation often becomes preposterous in the next. When Kenneth Clark wrote his first book, *The Gothic Revival* (1928), it was almost as a jeu d'esprit: Victorian Gothic architecture was a lost cause and it was a sophisticated and amusing literary rite of passage for a parvenu aesthete such as Clark to talk it up.

During the First World War, on strolls through Kensington Gardens, the philosopher R. G. Collingwood was shocked by the ugliness of the Albert Memorial. He concluded in his *Autobiography* (1939) that the Albert Memorial was 'visibly misshapen, corrupt, crawling, verminous'. Despite this attack, he found the general effect of Gilbert Scott's design so powerful that he produced a study, *Truth and Contradiction*, which attempted to deal with the perplexing problems, perceptual and ideological, which the curious memorial caused him. A marvellous diversion in the history of taste, it was never published.

The Albert Memorial has often been described as a 'test for taste'. Despite Collingwood's obloquy, the memorial became absorbed into the repertoire of Englishness, while the memory of the cruel and squalid age which created it faded into comfortable nostalgia. The Gothic revival itself, witness the successive editions of Clark's book, became more and more acceptable, until verminous became quaint and quaint became haunting. This process culminated in the founding of the Victorian Society in 1958, a club whose members can also be verminous, quaint and haunting.

Perhaps an even more dramatic demonstration of changing values in art occurs in literature. Shakespeare's reputation as a genius of timeless relevance is a recent one, or, at least, recently renewed. To us he bestrides the narrow world like a colossus. And so he did to Samuel Sheppard, who in 1651 described him as 'sacred', but by 1662 Samuel Pepys thought Romeo and Juliet 'the worst [play] that I ever heard' and described *A Midsummer Night's Dream* as 'insipid' and 'ridiculous'. Half a century later Alexander Pope called Shakespeare 'divine', but there was also a moment in the eighteenth century when he was regarded as a talented barbarian of local interest and little more: Dr Johnson wrote in the 1765 Preface to his edition of Shakespeare that he 'has … faults, and faults sufficient to obscure and overwhelm any other merit.' Voltaire likened Shakespeare's complete works to a 'dunghill'. Thomas Bowdler found Shakespeare so offensive that in 1807 and 1818 he edited the works for family consumption, so that 'Satan's cleverest bait' would no longer drag pure-minded youth towards a life of vice. Bernard Shaw despised him and Tolstoy wrote of 'an insuperable repulsion and tedium' on reading *King Lear*, *Romeo and Juliet* and *Hamlet*.

Civilization has presumably not reached such a degree of global stagnation that the value of Shakespeare might not again be reassessed, and, in an age with different (although perhaps not superior) values, his literary art might be found wanting. The ebbs and flows of history show us that the possibility exists. If great artists and playwrights are vulnerable, what claims can be made for design?

More than mere historical anecdote, this spectre of continuous reassessment suggests an extraordinary dynamism, even uncertainty, perhaps even arbitrariness, in matters of aesthetic judgement, affecting everything from altarpieces to washing machines. Another example: the poet John Keats was fascinated by Hellenism. In a library somewhere in Rome or London he focused on an engraving of the British Museum's Townley vase (or some say the engravings of the Borghese vase in the Louvre) and wrote of his 'still unravish'd bride of silence' that 'Beauty is truth, truth beauty'.

Beauty and truth bring together the formal and the moral, just as the acknowledgement of the existence of taste requires us to judge one in terms of the other: formality and morality might also be used to describe the purposes of modern industrial design. A Bauhaus teapot, for instance, is both a geometry lesson and a sermon.

The apparent universality and implied timelessness of Keats's judgement is made less clear and more poignant by the clutter of metaphor surrounding the poem. In trying to come to terms with the problem of beauty and decay (a concern of other poems, including 'Ode on Melancholy' and 'Ode to a Nightingale'), and, 'saddened by the mutability of natural beauty, he sought consolation in the more permanent beauty of art'. But the perception of value in art changes.

A century and more nearer our own time the pioneer American design consultant Norman Bel Geddes, addressing the spirit of the age, claimed that if Keats had been writing in 1940 he would have said the same about an aeroplane as he had about that old Grecian urn. In the Middle Ages the scholastic philosophers construed beauty to be an attribute of God, rather than of urns or aeroplanes; beauty and art were not necessarily related, indeed the idea of 'art' as a discrete activity was not acknowledged. Keats's neo-classicism, the prevailing taste of his day, required him to admire the Hellenic pot, while Norman Bel Geddes, suffused with the spirit of the twentieth century, was as moved by the plane. In *Design This Day* Geddes's contemporary, Walter Dorwin Teague, apparently without irony, compared one of the Texaco filling stations he had designed to the temples of Greece.

Each age finds its own expression in material things and the faculty we use to identify those we find palatable or repellent we call taste. With the spread of materialism, consumerism and commodity fetishism, minute aesthetic criteria are being established as the basis for general social competition for the first time in civilization. Everyday things we consume are – if perhaps only briefly – acquiring the sombre resonance of great art.

Because it involves everything we do, taste can soon become a neurosis. Just as quality in design is most conveniently explained by the use of moralizing terms like honest, decent and sound, which have their origins in observations of human behaviour, taste is similarly rooted in performance, in that the exercise of it is somewhat akin to manners. The architect Viollet-le-Duc, an eloquent spokesman for structural rationalism in building design, applied the same principles to personal behaviour, believing that, 'Le goût consiste en paraître ce que l'on est, et non ce que l'on voudrait être.'

Semantically, taste is rich and confusing, its etymology as odd and interesting as that of 'style'. But while style – deriving from the stylus or pointed rod which Roman scribes used to make marks on wax tablets – suggests activity, taste is more passive. The old Latin tag 'De gustibus non est disputandum' (there is no disputing about taste) is the oldest formulation of the idea 'One man's meat is another man's poison'. It is primary evidence that since Roman days the matter of taste has involved choice, whether individual or collective. Today, taste means both aesthetic and social discrimination, as well as gustatory sensation. Etymologically, the word we use derives from the old French, meaning touch or feel, a sense that is preserved in the current Italian word for keyboard, *tastiera*.

In English, the term 'good taste', meaning 'sound understanding', appears in the early fifteenth century, but it is not until the seventeenth century that the concept of aesthetic discrimination arrived in England in the 1685 translation of Baltasar Gracian's *El Oraculo Manual y Arte de Prudentia* (1647). In which the term '*gusto relevante*' becomes 'quaint and critical judgement'. Interestingly, this book for the courtier has never been out of print since its first appearance, and, more interestingly still for a book devoted to the professional cultivation of charm, it was made most famous in the German translation of Arthur Schopenhauer.

The metaphorical use of 'taste' to mean judgement began in France, where Gracian's '*gusto relevante*' was rendered as '*le goût fin*'. A literal translation gave a new and troublesome word to English. The salons of France, where art, literature, antiquities and science were discussed in circumstances of considerable comfort and luxury, adopted the word and gave it a capital 'T'.

By the early eighteenth century the word 'taste' was becoming familiar in essays on literature; the major transformation was complete and 'taste' had become synonymous with judgement. A subtle and even elusive concept was born, elements of refinement and restraint attaching themselves to the definition only later.

The Earl of Shaftesbury's *Letter Concerning Design* is a typical marker of the phenomenon. It was published just as critical discernment was about to become an intellectual sport. The Letter was written when art had been separated from its didactic and divine purposes and was well on the way to becoming a consumer product. At this moment, taste did not have any particular values; it was only identified as a part of the human apparatus of discernment; you either had it or you didn't and there was no question of 'good' or 'bad'.

When man replaced God as the chief object of study, it was inevitable that the idea of beauty deriving from divine inspiration was replaced by a more secular, even materialistic, notion of aesthetic satisfaction. La Rochefoucauld remarked that 'Our pride is more offended by attacks on our tastes than on our opinions', an observation which puts into nice equilibrium the forces of cupidity and sophistication which dominate modern consumer behaviour.

But in a culture which had only one class with the economic capacity to make discriminating judgements, the matter of whether taste was 'good' or 'bad' was not so much irrelevant as inconceivable and its characteristics still wanted defining. Early pursuit of precision in this matter began by trying to locate where exactly in the body taste operated. To the Earl of Shaftesbury (1671-1713), having taste was like having an accessory for the soul. To Joseph Addison (1672-1719), as soon as taste was established, vice and ignorance would automatically be banished, presumably from loins and head – in that order.

David Hume (1711-86) – who had said of Shakespeare 'a reasonable propriety of thought he cannot for any time uphold' – defined taste as a 'sensibility' to every kind of beauty or deformity. Hume's view was that standards *could* be established, while Sir Joshua Reynolds (1723-92) upheld this view in the fine arts. Reynolds thought that genius and taste were very much the same thing, except that genius had the added ingredient of execution. To an academic painter like Reynolds, taste was to be found lurking in the same dominion as reason and was, therefore, in his view, equally exempt from any possibility of change.

The *Discourses* which Sir Joshua Reynolds delivered at the Royal Academy between 1769 and 1786 are a *tour de force* of aesthetic conviction; they are also the richest ground for sniffing out the English Enlightenment's attitude both to man-made rules and to God-given genius. Reynolds declared, 'Could we teach taste or genius by rules, they would no longer be taste or genius' (1770). But in grandly stating the case for rules, he made the most persuasive statement ever of the academic principle:

Every opportunity therefore, should be taken to discountenance that false and vulgar opinion that rules are the fetters of genius. They are fetter only to men of no genius; as that armour, which upon the strong becomes an ornament and a defence, upon the weak and misshapen turns into a load and cripples the body which it was meant to protect... How much liberty may be taken to break through those rules... may be an after consideration when the pupils become masters themselves. It is then, when their Genius had received its utmost improvement, that rules may possibly be dispensed with. But let us not destroy the scaffold until we have raised the building. (1769)

Yet, the worm of analysis kept burrowing in the foundation of Reynolds's classical certainties. 'How', you can imagine him always nagging himself, 'do we objectify our preferences?' Taste-makers of the eighteenth century were concerned with whether judgements were based on mysterious, internal forces insusceptible to analysis, or whether there was a standard of taste which was rational and measurable, which could be scientifically determined and from which no reasonable man would withhold his approval. In this transition from the classic to the romantic in art, David Hume suggested that beauty was not solely subjective to the viewer, but may be inherent in objects. This suspicion was reinforced by Immanuel Kant (1724-1804), who reasoned that aesthetic judgements have universal validity. Kant was wrong.

An explosion in production during the nineteenth century opened up consumption to social classes which did not include the President of the Royal Academy and distinguished philosophers; the idea of taste then came to represent not a commonly held view, but the antithesis of choices made in the market-place, which, patronizing experts always observed, expressed themselves in a debased and depraved form. In the fine arts, this meant that painters were caught in the cross-fire between Romanticism and popular culture.

The entire history of painting after, say, 1830 can be understood in terms of the dilemma faced by painters: whether to be society's picture-makers, or to be misunderstood private visionaries. Dostoevsky described this as the choice between lofty suffering and cheap happiness. Similarly, manufac-

turers and designers did not know whether to satisfy existing popular taste, or to lead it by enhancing it. The question has not been resolved in the fine or the applied arts, but one thing is certain: by about 1850 it was very clear that aesthetic judgements – wheresoever applied and by whom – most certainly did not have universal validity. The age of consumerism has no time for Kant.

To account for this popular rejection of severe philosophy, the aspirational concept of 'good' taste began to emerge. Good taste was assumed to be a standard to which the masses would aspire, were they given the chance. The legacy of this underpins our behaviour in every activity from interior decorating to eating and table manners. Art historians have long struggled to understand what Birmingham manufacturers in the 1840s and shopkeepers of the 1980s understand intuitively: the mechanism by which civilizations and their preferences change and evolve.

Cultural historians, in pursuit of meaning in the chaos of history, take refuge in vague structural models such as Hegel's *Volksgeist*, an abstract entity embodying the national spirit, which imparts a common stamp to religion, politics, ethics, customs, arts and science. Marxism substituted economic conditions for the *Zeitgeist*, spirit of the age, but the frigid calculations of the political economists do not clarify the nebulous discussion. Mixed industrial economies substituted 'good' design for Marxist imperatives.

In an address to the Danish Society of Industrial Design in 1970, J. K. Galbraith said: 'As living standards rise – as man multiplies the goods he consumes and the artefacts with which he surrounds himself – we are entitled to believe, or at least to hope, that quantitative measurements give way to qualitative ones.' A vain hope, since economists have no explanation for the mechanism of choice, even if its consequences are the very stuff of economics. How does change in taste affect supply and demand? How does a change in income distribution alter the ability of a market to satisfy certain tastes? But taste itself always lies out there ... it is exogenous, unexamined. In their search for a value-free science, economists prefer to regard taste as a mystery, its nature only glimpsed through 'revealed preferences': choices registered in the market-place. Economists rarely analyse, still less judge, the origins of taste, preferring to leave it to those of us who are less squeamish about the unquantifiable.

Whatever happened to 'good' design

Good design was an inevitable consequence of the invention of taste. And soon after 'good' design got itself a bad name, the word 'designer' was mired in putrid froth. The first signs were to appear on Gloria Vanderbilt's bottom. Indian jeans manufacturer Murjani knew there was no better way to tart up his product than by having a famous name on them, so he pursued and failed to acquire the services of Jackie Onassis. Second choice was mature socialite Vanderbilt, who, in a contract which will form future case studies in business schools, agreed to model the product and have her signature embroidered on the rump. Thus, in one hideous, meretricious swagger of the marketing mechanism, 'designer' jeans were born.

As I write, the editors of the *Oxford English Dictionary* are engaged in tracing the descent of a word that once signified an honourable vocation. While they work, 'designer' declines still further. A lurid concoction of narcotics, hallucinogens and amphetamines was recently and witlessly described by *The Guardian* as a 'designer' drug. Someone recently started calling Perrier, 'designer' water. Now anything offered for sale that is irrelevant, matt black, expensive or just plain freaky weird is sold as a designer this or a designer that. So, a vocational term for a dignified profession, which includes Vitruvius, Christopher Wren, Thomas Sheraton, Henry Ford and Eric Gill, has been debased to a slap-on epithet of no real meaning to join other dead or dying labels like 'de luxe', 'executive' and 'turbo'.

Such epithets are dead or dying because they are stripped of real meaning. When language loses its basis in reality, we are threatened by suffocation in a Babel of flashy values. Car manufacturers of the 1950s and 1960s, cynically refusing to improve the suspension, transmission or engine, added cute bits and big mark-ups to banal products and called them 'de luxe', as though a Vauxhall dealer could sell you a motorized Dunlop-borne pleasure dome instead of an under-engineered barge that droned, squeaked, smelt of plastic and made you feel sick. The ghost of meaning attached to the concept 'executive brief-case' is exorcized as soon as you articulate it. 'Turbo', a word once used exclusively by researchers into forced induction in heat engines, is now liberally applied to anything from chocolate to carpet shampoo, though the sweets and the soap are not fitted with an exhaust-driven compressor.

The absurd debasement of the 'designer' is a fascinating episode in the history of taste, and all the more extraordinary when you consider that only a little earlier this century 'design' began to usurp art in its power to delight and astonish the public. As soon as painters and sculptors ceased to communicate with people and chose instead to create commodities of debatable artistic interest exclusively for dealers and museums, it was inevitable that the public would take its aesthetic pleasures where it could find them: in the styling of cars, the cinema and in popular culture. Put another way, the century of consumerism has moved the entire man-made world into the province of aestheticism.

With the whole of material culture open to scrutiny and painting disappearing up its own art, it was necessary to make some claims for design. One of the first consisted of certain learned people declaring certain artefacts to be in possession of that mysterious and numinous attribute, 'good' design. Good design could mean something as long as there was some identifiable competition in the form of 'bad' design. In Britain and the US in the 1950s and 1960s there was felt to be more of one than the other, and it perhaps meant something because then you found lots of manufacturers competing in the same field, some making good design and some bad. But 'good design' was rarely defined precisely, because what was really being discussed was not so much design of any sort as taste. No survivors of the period are willing to confirm this devastating observation but you can still hear them, like J. K. Galbraith, pointing to bleached ash Scandinavian furniture with webbing seats, products and typefaces in certain reductivist forms, colours of a certain restraint, and saying, with the fervour of the fundamentalist, 'That is good design.' Maybe, maybe not, but what they almost certainly mean is, 'For someone of my age and educational background, that is to my taste.' In other words, 'I know better than you.'

This sort of 'goodness' began to discredit design in the eyes of the public, because it suggested the exclusivity of a remote clique. There is excellence in design, but it is altogether more scientific: you can measure it and weigh it. You know for certain when something is durable, affordable, useful, efficient and – if you make it – profitable. What is less certain is whether you like it, whether bleached ash furniture tells other people things about you which you would like them to know. Does it reveal the social and cultural influences operating on you? Is it sending the world secret messages about you? Does it betray your … taste?

Good design got itself a bad name because of this confusion, and the 'designer' phenomenon is an inevitable consequence of it. Just as the qualifying adjective 'good' was plucked from universal vocabulary to give extra validity to certain products, so nowadays, in the de luxe, executive, turbo tradition, 'designer' has become a tag of dubious cachet. It is, as Marxists will tell you, just one way that capitalists valorize surplus and make you think you want to consume something you don't really need. If, to paraphrase Dorothy Parker, you want to know what God thinks about 'designer' merchandise, just look at the people he gives it to.

But politics and religion aside, the 'designer' fad only survives because of credulous consumers, uncertain of their taste, adrift in oceans of junk. The depravity of the 'design' business is the implied suggestion that only jeans and mineral water and expensive things are designed – that it is rare and exclusive for something to be designed.

Everything has been designed, sometimes well, often badly, and the great challenge for manufacturers, retailers and educators is to learn to speak the language of objects so that more genuinely good design can be more widely available.

Both 'good' design and the 'designer' phenomenon are products of cynical ages, concepts which could only be validated by the continued existence of and demand for the bogus. According to J. K. Galbraith: 'It is said by the exponents of bureaucratic method that they serve the taste of the majority, and that taste is intrinsically bad. It will, indeed, be bad if there is no alternative, but given a choice, people have … a greater instinct for beauty than we often imagine.' With better products in all the shops neither 'good' design nor designer goods would be necessary, or even possible. But how is the individual to determine quality, or is discrimination to be merely a whim?

If we agree with Keats that beauty is itself variable, we are left with the perplexing conclusion that truth too is not eternally valid, but a function of specific social and cultural circumstances. Any dire ramifications arising from this are properly the province of philosophers and priests, but there are also implications for designers and consumers.

Clearly, in any particular age there is a universe of choice in matters of colour, form, style and purpose, yet only certain options are generally considered worthwhile. Standards are always being established by outstanding minds in each generation. In the eighteenth century an oligarchic control of wealth influenced all aesthetic judgements and these aristocratic requirements influenced society as a whole. Nowadays, different forces operate and our understanding of them is impaired by our confusion about the difference between taste and design.

Take any object. If you have access to data you can immediately tell whether it can be manufactured economically, whether it is durable, popular and profitable. These things can be measured in dollars and centimetres. It is the less tangible elements in any design which are the subject of this book. Why do certain designs seem to transcend fashion and achieve a timeless quality?

Is it true that the form of the most admired designs is such that you can immediately understand what the object does? Is it true that in all excellent design there is a harmony and coherence between the overall form and the individual details? Do all admired products, buildings and fashions have a certain equilibrium between the technique employed in the manufacture and the intention of the product?

My intention is not to say that any taste is 'good' or 'bad', but in the midst of arguments that suggest aesthetic judgements are liable to continuous review, can any claim be made for universality? Certainly, the Modern movement can be interpreted as an attempt to restore rules to the theory and practice of architecture after a century and more of eclecticism. For perhaps fifty years of the twentieth century the modern aesthetic, disguised mostly under a veil of 'rationalism' blown stiff by the wind of social purpose, dominated European and American taste.

No one can state better the rules of that aesthetic than the German product designer Dieter Rams. A student of Ulm's austere post-war Hochschule für Gestalrung, the designer whose work for Braun made first the white and then the black box a fetishistic commodity, Rams explained his philosophy of form: '*Einfach ist besser als kompliziert. Leise ist besser als laut. Naheliegendes ist besser als Gesuchtes.*' Perhaps Dieter Rams would not accept that his version of 'simplicity' (*Einfach*), his version of 'quietness' (*Leise*) and his interpretation of 'obvious' (*Naheliegendes*) are themselves determined by aesthetic preference and can make no claim to being undeviating absolutes. The preferences which Rams so artfully and eloquently expressed in his severely beautiful, but very restricted, designs for Braun appliances betray the social and cultural conditioning of the Wirtschaftswunder: they represent the *Zeitgeist*. Or did.

Different times demand different values. Nancy Mitford thought it was vulgar to display any sign of undue haste and therefore sent only business letters by airmail, whereas Dieter Rams travels the autobahns in his very fast Porsche 930. The global electronic village is not yet upon us, but clearly Nancy Mitford would have been very perturbed by a facsimile machine.

With all the past immediately available for consumption and history deregulated by postmodernism, with the world becoming smaller and smaller, taste more than ever is confused with fashion and with design.

Consuming taste

As a metaphor for choice – if not for sensation in the mouth – taste is a peculiarly modern, Western faculty. The hieratic societies of the ancient past and of the Orient did not fret about the finer points of discernment. Even in the European Middle Ages the concept did not exist. Medieval economies were based on survival and subsistence, while medieval art was didactic. The idea of art devoted to the excitement of pleasure is a recent one. Although medieval scholars had a great deal to say about proper social conduct, in a world that was not materialistic, their strictures were largely confined to canons of behaviour rather than consumerist choice.

But there are some interesting examples in the Middle Ages of things being acquired for edification and delight rather than for survival. Museums did not exist, but certain aristocrats acquired collections of curiosities as booty, as symbols of power and as hedges against economic disaster. Intended for private contemplation rather than public education, such collections are not to be understood at all; no great distinction was made between the beautiful and the merely odd. If the inventory is anything to go by, the Duc de Berry seems to have held equal regard for his collection of paintings and his embalmed elephant.

With art and life seen as one, medievals did not distinguish between the moral and the aesthetic content of works of art. Hence disinterested aesthetic experience did not exist and therefore taste had no meaning before the beginning of the world of the consumer some four hundred years later. Beatrice Webb, aware of the modern citizen's preoccupation with being a consumer, described this role as perhaps 'the most pregnant and important piece of classification in the whole range of sociology'.

Taste is in the soul of the consumer, a means of accommodating ideas about art and morality into lives which provide for little of either. Whenever we find that art and morality are in conflict, it is because we are trying to reconcile a modern conception of the moral. The structure of modern society – where consumption of artefacts has replaced the inheritance of them – required a concept of taste so that qualitative discussion, and social competition, could present established values – definite concepts by which performance could be judged and found impressive or wanting.

Taste may be an expression of personal values, but it also identifies an individual with a certain class. Since taste was invented by and for the middle classes, it is always the middle classes who suffer in discussion of it. 'Bourgeois' is French for middle class. Once meaning merely a town person, the word had acquired a pejorative sense as early as the seventeenth century: in Molière's Le bourgeois gentilhomme (1670), being a town-dweller – when the court resided elsewhere – was clearly a social disadvantage. Although the term 'bourgeois' fell into disuse during the French Revolution and was replaced by the less value-laden and more scientific 'citoyen'. British writers preserved the concept for stigmatization well into the nineteenth century.

In his Book of Snobs (1848), slyly subtitled 'by one of them', Thackeray calls snobbishness a 'diabolical invention of gentility', but puts gentility on the spot now and for ever more when he cautions that 'Stinginess is snobbish, ostentation is snobbish, too great profusion is snobbish.' Thackeray immediately identified patterns and preferences of consumption with moral values. Matthew Arnold in Culture and Anarchy (1869) described the middle class as 'Philistines' prey to 'hideous and grotesque illusions' and inclined to seduction by 'worldly splendour, security, power and pleasure', an observation since validated by the glossy magazines and their advertisers.

In 1872 when the Midland Railway decided on a two-class system in its coaches, it was second class that went – first and third remained, the idea being to distance the one and suggest a level of aspiration for the other. Such tensions underpin the neatly constructed world of the consumer. Taste and class are almost inseparable. The greater part of economic activity in the West is devoted either to the pursuit of taste or to the disguise of class. It is the prosperous but unsure middle classes who are the most voracious consumers and therefore the ones most animated by considerations of taste.

To judge by the advertising, taste is at the heart of personal motivation in matters of consumption. Ideas about group membership and group exclusion are either overt or esoteric in most consumer advertising and in the consumption which follows it. An account at Henri Bendel's New York store was once considered a requirement for Manhattan's 'contemporary aristocracy', which New York magazine defined more precisely, if less attractively, as 'small-boned women who lived for style'. When the down-market chain store The Limited took over, that small-boned aristocracy was scandalized. The Jewish princess is perhaps contemporary America's most accurate gauge of taste: deracinated, classless except for levels of consumption, proud by acquisition, a keen supporter of the 'arts and diseases', patron of designers, maker and breaker, arbiter of taste.

Taste and class feed off each other. Both words and concepts, each more impressionistic than scientific, came into being and use at about the same time. In Samuel Richardson's novel Clarissa (1748) class supersedes the earlier 'station' and by the later eighteenth century expressions such as 'of the lowest class' were, so to speak, common. The same semantic shift took place in Germany where Karl Marx, for whom such considerations were a profession, began using Klasse to signify what had previously been known as Stand (estate). Marx said that class could only be understood in terms of an individual's relationship to the means of production (which is to say, as worker, consumer or owner). Taste can only be understood in terms of individuals' relationship to their need for consumption.

The creative people in advertising agencies are unconsciously aware that discrimination is a stimulus to consumption. The account planners are more alive to it. But their taste too is culturally determined, as any anthropologist with a global perspective can explain (or as any review of international campaigns for identical products will demonstrate). But colours, like ways of selling booze and cars, have different meanings in different territories. In Britain, black is culturally associated with death and mourning, while in Venice or Spain it suggests grandeur and the grandee. Yellow is a sacred colour in China, but white is disagreeable for the same reasons that black used to be in Victorian Britain. European normality is merely a local preference. Martini is not in every sense a global product, and the technological criteria which obsess Audi engineers are no more universal a taste than *Wurst mit Rösti*. In his essay 'Reading Things' (1976), Umberto Eco asked, 'If Vienna had been on the equator and its bourgeoisie had gone around in Bermuda shorts, would Freud have described the same neurotic symptoms?' Probably not. Even here in Europe, the history of evolving social taboos, whether bare knees or nose-picking, demonstrates a susceptibility to change. To use Nick Furbank's illustration of the absurdities of discrimination, which make the English upper classes such a rich source for critical observers: 'Lord Beauchamp thought it middle-class *not* to decant champagne. Lord Beauchamp clearly had it in for the town-dwellers.

There are differences in tastes between different territories, as well as between social classes. The French have a more marked preference for offal than the Germans. In Chiavari, Italy, you can eat fish brains in the most expensive restaurants; try to serve them in Cleveland, Ohio, and you would be prosecuted by the Food and Drug Administration. There is also the element of time: taboos about food are in some cases recent. There is more than one nineteenth-century cookery book which gives instructions on how to carve a calf's eyes. With the industrialization of food-processing (and the distancing of the consumer which that process entailed) a taboo about identifiable bits of edible animals evolved: generalized meat of no specific source was safe for middle-class consumption, but an all-too-obvious eyeball, ear, snout or trotter became unacceptable. By an interesting process of inversion, this particular taboo has been reversed, so that steak and chips is, at least in Britain, a proletarian dish and a lamb's pancreas an extremely sophisticated one.

European culture became refined through the practice of such arcane discrimination. Since the Middle Ages, when eating and drinking were even more social spectacles than they are today, conduct at table was a ground for scholars to pontificate. In his magnificent book *The Civilising Process* (1978), Norbert Elias describes medieval texts which feature discourses on socially acceptable behaviour. The scholastics had a definite idea of proper conduct which passed into mainstream European culture as 'courtesy'. As with the word taste, courtesy's cognates in all European tongues have the same meaning: *courtoisie* in French, *cortesia* in Italian and *Hubescheit* in German all signify exactly the same thing. Etymologically, this is 'how people behave at court'.

Manners became a means of objectifying certain taboos and giving expression to the self-image of an emerging bourgeoisie: middle-class, consuming town-dwellers. In exactly the way that the concept of taste was to evolve into a code for accepted gentility, manners became more and more refined so that they no longer meant general conduct, but signified a certain caste's idea of acceptable etiquette. This interpretation of behaviour is not necessarily normal.

We respect cleanliness and order in the social consumption of food but in his *Origin of Table Manners* (1978) Claude Lévi-Strauss observed that respect for eating quietly is a modern European phenomenon. He discovered that the table manners of 'primitive' people (he was thinking of the South American Indians) were not so much the crude fumblings of 'primitives' as an adjustable code which could be used as a language to communicate different moods and ideas. Eating habits are not innocent behaviour, but a method of broadcasting attitudes; some methods are vilified, others approved. As late as the nineteenth century, the French maintained the Spanish custom (alive still in Arabia) of belching after a satisfactory meal to demonstrate a favourable repleteness. Since the Renaissance, eating habits have been acknowledged as a form of non-verbal language.

Table manners demonstrate what Lévi-Strauss

called a 'compulsory message'. Cutlery is just one means of moderating our relationship with the external world. In medieval Europe it was customary to eat out of a common dish. Crucially, for fastidious Westerners, cutlery achieves a distance between self and object. In non-Western cultures, eating implements are intended to preserve the food from the malign influence of the eater. In the West the same implements are regarded as a means of maintaining internal purity and external grace. Health (so-called) is only the latest of an endless line of fads which have dominated European behaviour at table: wine was once denied to children not on grounds of well-being, but because their virulent young spirits might improperly acquire its potency. Health is itself a matter of taste.

Since Baldassare Castiglione's *Il libro del cortegiano* (1528), the first modern book of manners, there has been an element in Western thought which places appearance above feeling. Castiglione's book was full of ideas which marked the beginning of the process, studied here, of interpreting artefacts in terms of behaviour. Castiglione's *sprezzatura* was the first expression of taste in everyday behaviour. A contrived, clever, courtly manner, its very artificiality put it at odds with nature. It was, by definition, artificial.

This form of self-awareness was a modern awakening. Establishing the standards for proper courtly behaviour was a way of structuring the world. From that moment behaviour was understood in terms of good and bad. But while courtiers, philosophers and anthropologists understand art and gestures, they are less certain about how objects and images communicate meaning, Cesare Lombroso, Professor of Psychiatry and Forensic Medicine at Turin (dedicatee of Max Nordau's notorious *Entartung*), took the eighteenth-century idea that beauty has a moral character to an extreme in his attempt to typify criminal types by their distinguishing features, but he was predicting a sort of pseudo-science that the Second World War was to discredit.

In post-war Paris there was a different mood of intellectual speculation. Roland Barthes, Professor at the Ecole Normale des Hautes Etudes, knew his audience: it was a sophisticated one for whom reading was already a nearly sacred rite. French intellectuals of the 1950s were already familiar with Marx, Freud, their own native theatre of the absurd, their own new wave films, the new novel, as well as pre-war surrealism. With the ground prepared in this way, acceptance of Barthes's structural analysis was considerably easier than it would have been in Britain or the United States. Like the other 'new' critics, he was chiefly concerned with literature and language, but, inevitably, his close reading of texts spilt over into close readings of objects. For so athletic an intellectual, it was but a short leap from, say, a stylistic analysis of Flaubert to a structural analysis of the new Citroën, steak and chips, or detergent.

Paradoxically, despite his dedication to explication, Barthes's successive critical works get more and more obscure. In his early collection of essays, *Mythologies* (1957), he writes in an unscientific, lapidary and brilliantly terse and ironic manner. There is a witty revelation on each page. The latter and far more detailed *Système de la Mode* (1967) is perhaps his most powerful and most baffling work. Wit is replaced by algorithms and organograms. He looks at fashion as presented in magazines as a system, a structure in its own right. Fashion is an identifiable set of signs by which society communicates its concerns. Thus Roland Barthes, in his search for interpreted meaning in everyday things, was to the catwalks of Paris 4ème what Lévi-Strauss was to the Polynesians.

Umberto Eco, Professor of Philosophy at Bologna University, has been more successful than Barthes in applying high-falutin literary theory to the everyday world. Eco has been accused of 'intellectual slumming', just as Roland Barthes might have been accused of 'haute vulgarization' in writing about Marilyn Monroe in the same sentence as the Académie Française. Eco defended his assault on the modern world in this way:

Today in Pompeii tourists are visiting murals depicting Romans with huge penises; originally meant as adverts for brothels, they are now considered great art. In the eighteenth century Telemann was thought a greater composer than Bach; in the nineteenth, Eugene Suc a greater writer than Balzac. In 200 years we may consider Picasso inferior to the man currently responsible for the Coca-Cola commercials ... So we should never be afraid to analyse marginal or inferior manifestations of our culture.

Our views on the character of the world itself are equally vulnerable, and our respect for nature and individual countries has varied in the course of time.

In pre-industrial, let alone pre-electronic, ages, nature was not necessarily benign. In medieval chronicles nature is often presented as hostile and menacing. Mountains, quite properly, were once regarded as fearsome. The concept of the sublime in landscape was, as life imitates art, largely influenced by the paintings of Salvator Rosa and developed by Mrs Radcliffe in her bravura accounts of the Apennines. Turner's better Italian pictures capture something of the vastness of the mood. It is significant that a love of nature was accommodated into culture at just the moment when industrial urban expansion threatened it. In this sense the entire Romantic movement was remedial. Sir Uvedale Price and Richard Payne Knight, neighbours in Herefordshire as well as in spirit, and authors of, respectively, *Essays on the Picturesque* and *The Landscape* (both 1794), were among the most important influences on the English picturesque movement – that sensibility which defined itself as art imitating nature and became refined into nature imitating art.

It was an astonishing episode in the history of taste. Price and Knight believed that material things have certain qualities which render them, say, beautiful, sublime or picturesque. Following Edmund Burke, who argued in his Treatise on the Sublime and the Beautiful (1765) that beautiful things have a capacity to relax the nerves, Price contented himself with enumerating the things that contained those relaxing qualities in the highest degree. Price clearly assumed that humankind had a particular sense attuned to perceive these qualities – an apprehension dismissed by William Thomson in his *Enquiry into the Elementary Principles of Taste* (1768): 'there are almost as many different opinions concerning taste, as there are persons who lay claim to

it'. While most eighteenth-century debate on the subject was conducted in these long, slow rallies, as if by accident, Price codified the rules which define and therefore limit our expectations of the English landscape, and which are still with us today.

Just as our relationship with nature is not fixed and determined, one country's attitude to another – now amused, now disinterested, now scornful – reflects changing taste as surely as the fluctuating reputations of great artists.

The British reaction to Italy provides one of the most engaging and revealing examples. Few things seem more evocatively Victorian than the figure of Punch, but Mr Punch, whose features betray it, was originally Pulcinella of the Neapolitan *commedia dell'arte* of 1600. He only acquired his English wife, Judy, in 1818 at the end of a progressive – and unrequited – infatuation of one country for the other.

So complete was the English absorption of Italian architecture, marbles and paintings that when travelling through Italy in 1786-8 Goethe wished he had a 'cultured Englishman' as a companion. Italy was an idea as much as a country, so much so that, despite a generalized assumption among English travellers that Italians were popish, not to be trusted, idle and lascivious, their home country was held in very particular regard for centuries.

A transition occurred in the late eighteenth century, when milordly amateurism sickened into scholarship. Between William Roscoe's *Life of Lorenzo de' Medici* (1795) and J. A. Symonds's *Renaissance in Italy* (1875) there was an explosion of popular books about Italian life, history and culture. Of these books, spontaneous, impressionistic, unscholarly, Charles Dickens's *Pictures from Italy* (1846) was perhaps the best written, if the least influential. F. T. Palgrave's edition of Murray's *Handbook for Travellers in Italy* (1843) was instrumental in changing British taste. Later, the guide book was taken in two different directions: one by John Ruskin, the other by Augustus Hare. Born in Rome, Hare wrote several guide books to Italy and had a natural mother called Italima. These personal details are all witness to the cult of things Italian, which extended to religion and Romanticism. John Henry Newman, an Anglican clergyman, visited Rome in 1833; he left it well on the way to becoming a Catholic. Dismayed and enthralled by the Eternal City, he wrote: 'The first thought one has of the place is awful – that you see the great enemy of God...Next, when you enter the museums, galleries and libraries, a fresh world is opened to you – that of imagination and taste.'

Romanticism, the first democratic, mass-media movement in art, depending for its force on a combination of word and image, which in a sense provides the scriptural origins of pop culture, tended to popularize travel. Byron got his first impressions of Italy second-hand. Of Venice he wrote,

Otway, Radcliffe, Schiller, Shakespeare's art
Had stamped her image in me.

In poetry, Wordsworth, Keats, Shelley, Coleridge and Browning monopolized Italian subjects. In prose it was Edward Bulwer Lytton and George Eliot. Roscoe's *The Life of Lorenzo de' Medici* (1795) was a source for Pre-Raphaelitism, but in a curious way the Pre-Raphaelite Brotherhood rejected Italian subject matter, just as their spiritual forebears, the Nazarenes, had begun to create in Rome from 1809 a style of painting that was entirely German. Thomas Stothard, who drew the figures for the engraved illustrations of Samuel Rogers's influential *Italy* (1830), had never actually been there; a synthetic stereotype was passed on to an entire generation. Although Holman Hunt, Millais and Rossetti had been inspired by engravings of the Pisan Campo Santo when they founded the Brotherhood in 1848, they were all without direct experience of Italy and its art. Holman Hunt explained their reluctance to acquire it: 'In these days men of British blood ... should not subject themselves to the influence of masters alien to the sentiments of the great English poets and thinkers.'

In 1849 Hunt exhibited a painting based on and accompanied by a long quotation from Edward Bulwer Lytton's *Rienzi* (published in 1835 and dedicated to Alessandro Manzoni, author of *I promessi sposi*). Rienzi is shown as the patriotic liberator of Rome. But contemporary Italian painting had no influence on mid-nineteenth-century British art. The Pre-Raphaelite Brotherhood was only one of a number of attempts to capture the purity of earlier Italian art, sometimes through the example of contemporary second-rate English literature. The rehabilitation of Botticelli, which preceded that of El Greco, was typical, as was Alfred Stevens's designs for the proposed new bronze doors of the Geological Museum in Jermyn Street (1846-9), an exercise in higher pastiche.

Another example of a cultish vogue for things Italian was the brief fashion for the Garibaldi blouse, a version of Giuseppe Garibaldi's famous red shirts (which were in fact supplied to him by Thresher and Glenny of the Strand as part of London's contribution to the Sicilian expedition of 1860). The Italian liberator also became a popular model for Staffordshire figures, and a biscuit, still in production today, was named after him.

Inspired by the magnificent example of past Italian art, Sir Joseph Noel Paton – a painter whose *Dream of Michelangelo* (late 1840s) is in the William Morris Gallery, Walthamstow, London – wrote, in an era of copious mediocrity, an outstandingly bad poem:

No, Buonarroti, thou shalt not subdue
My mind with thy Thor-hammer! All that play
Of ponderous science with Titanic thew
And spastic tendon – marvellous, 'tis true –
Says nothing to my soul

The quality of Paton's verse is perhaps appropriate to a taste that went into decline almost as soon as it had finished its ascent. Two such unlikely bedfellows as Karl Marx and Queen Victoria both condemned the Garibaldi cult. The communist dubbed it 'a miserable spectacle of imbecility', while the monarch found herself 'half ashamed of being the head of a nation capable of such follies' (although she did have an Italianate villa called Osborne built for herself on the Isle of Wight). What Byron called Italy's 'fatal gift of beauty' could lead to dismay, and the taste for things Italian became less robust. Browning's lugubrious line, 'What was left, I wonder, when the kissing had to stop?' hints at a mood of disfavour.

Exposure to Italian music was an inescapable fact of life in Victorian Britain. Grand opera, maudlin songs for an accompanied pianoforte, and the itinerant organ grinder offered each of the British social classes vicarious contact with Italian culture. But as early as the 1840s the popularity of Rossini, Donizetti and Bellini was being challenged by the Germans Mendelssohn and Weber. By the time W. B. Scott paid his last visit to Italy in 1873, he found that Italy helped 'decrease my love of painting' and added, 'How does the traveller begin to loathe the Madonna.' In Britain, Italian music was kept alive not so much by composers as by singers and instrumentalists and impresarios (itself an Italian word). This change in status has contributed to the prejudice, still not entirely eradicated, that Italians are amiable buffoons. There is a hint of this in *Mrs Beeton's Household Management* (1861) which declares that 'With the exception of macaroni, [Italians] have no specially characteristic article of food.'

Improved communications were a fundamental influence in turning English taste away from Italy. Familiarity breeds contempt, so for as long as Italy was impossibly remote, artists were happy to provide imaginative confections of Italian scenery and the public was happy to be beguiled by them. Whereas in 1820 John Keats took four and a half weeks to sail from Gravesend to Naples, and in 1833 the painter Charles West Cope (whose picture *Italian Hostelry* – in fact painted in London in 1836 – hangs in Liverpool's Walker Art Gallery) took more than seven days and nights to travel by road from Paris to Milan, by the 1860s the railway had reduced the London–Milan journey to a mere fifty hours.

Mrs Beeton's amused dismay passes straight through to Norman Douglas, although in his case the subject is treated with more exuberance, charity and knowledge than Mrs Beeton could muster. In *Old Calabria* (1919) Douglas revels in curious details: Venose displayed 'a reposeful dirtiness, not vulgar and chaotic, but testifying to time-honoured neglect, to a feudal contempt of cleanliness'; 'one old man ... was wont habitually to engulf twenty-two litres of wine a day'; 'mice ... are cooked into a paste and given to children'.

While there is some mockery in Douglas's account of pre-industrial Italy, there is also an element of et in *Arcadia ego*, which was to be expressed in a new, romantic interpretation of Italy and the Mediterranean stimulated by the privations of the Second World War.

Norman Douglas's ghost stalks the pages of the marvellous cookery books written by Elizabeth David. By the time Mrs David's *Italian Food* appeared in 1954, Italy was overdue for a revival. In her introduction to successive editions Mrs David repeatedly invokes authenticity. The subtext of her descriptions of England in the 1950s is a critique of English life and manners at least as important as that of the more loudly trumpeted contemporary Angry Young Men. Being concerned with sentiment as much as with recipes, the popularity of Mrs David's books proved the centrality of taste to the modern consumer.

Born to shop

The meaning of taste in history has swooped and veered between physical sensation and aesthetic predilection. Wordsworth was worried that a taste for poetry might be confused with something so indifferent as a taste for rope-dancing or for sherry. The same can be said of the Italian word *gusto* or of the French *goût* and the German *Geschmack*. It is a concept at once substantial and suggestive, the metaphorical transfer from passive sensations to intellectual acts of discrimination. Taste with a capital T developed from an abstraction to an attribute. As Raymond Williams noted in *Keywords* (1976), 'We have only to think of related sense words, such as touch or feel in their extended and metaphorical usages, which have not been abstracted, capitalized and in such ways regulated, to realize the essential distinction.'

In 1755 Johann Joachim Winckelmann, a librarian from Dresden, went to live in the Roman palace of Cardinal Albani, taking with him a bag full of rationalist philosophy. He was appointed Prefect of Roman Antiquities in 1763, and his early distinction between Greek and Roman marbles laid the basis for modern archaeology. He also laid the scholarly basis for neo-classicism, a taste in art, architecture and design that became – in an age on the verge of mass production – perhaps the first consumer cult.

Winckelmann found in Greek art a confirmation of his personal theory of beauty. He considered that simplicity, harmony, functionalism (in both structure and adaptation to the local environment) and respect for materials were all prerequisites for the achievement of beauty in architectural design. He did not see that either colour or ornament had any part to play in it. Beauty resulted from a certain arrangement of shapes and forms which were in some way expressive of the ideal. This was what he meant by his demand for 'noble simplicity'.

In providing a theoretical basis for the neo-classical aesthetic Winckelmann was a profound, if esoteric, influence on the history of European and American taste. A contemporary of his, Jeanne Antoinette Poisson, had a more immediate contribution to make to the newly developing European material culture. Known to history as Madame de Pompadour, Mademoiselle Poisson's astonishing career demonstrated the close relationship between social aspiration and modern taste – a relationship which has been more or less inseparable ever since. Pompadour made tangible the elevated idea of 'taste'. It ceased to be metaphorical, and became instead a particular vision of haut-bourgeois style. She turned *arriviste* middle-class snobbery into a minor movement in the history of art, creating 'positional' goods two centuries before the term was invented. Hers was the *'objet du goût'*, her legacy the discretionary part of the market-place, where all modern consumers are adrift between the Scylla of conformity and the Charybdis of error. Madame de Pompadour was the inventor of the consumer product.

Ever the one for the grand gesture, the ambitious young Poisson was pleased to drive, as circumstances demanded, either a pink or a blue phaeton across the path of Louis XV as he hunted or pursued his botanical interests in the forests around Paris. With style, she wore pink in the blue phaeton, and blue in the pink one. The gesture did not go unnoticed by the monarch, who, bored with the queen, had also recently lost his mistress. He picked her up at a fancy-dress ball held at Versailles in 1744. Apparently without irony, Poisson went as Diana the Hunter. She easily captivated the king with her wit and coruscating conversation, her singing, dancing and musicianship.

He gave her an estate at Pompadour and the title of marquise. She gave him everything except her body, an exercise in restraint that in the era before Freud was not properly understood, but which throws into dizzying confusion her willingness to pose enticingly and fleshily in the nude for François Boucher's voluptuous *Toilet of Venus* (1751, once in the collection of the Vicomte de la Béraudière). Her nude portrait, while not without a strong erotic *frisson*, was intended for her own apartments at Versailles, not for the titillation of the king. It is an image designed to confer status, in this case divine, on the sitter. The once humble Poisson had a high regard for her own worth. At court she became notorious because, with true middle-class snobbery, she conducted herself with chilling hauteur.

Jules Beaujoint published this ditty in his *Secret Memoirs of Madame la Marquise de Pompadour* (1885):

> The Birth of Jesus made,
> At court a stir indeed,
> And Louis in a coach drove off
> To Pompadour with speed.
> Said he, 'The Child we'll go and see',
> Said she, 'No, not at all;
> They'd better bring the Child to me,
> I never make a call.'

Madame de Pompadour's exercise of taste was facilitated by ready access to money and is thus a prototype for modern consumerism: it is often said that her collection was the most remarkable assemblage of possessions ever acquired by a French citizen. While Louis XV had the greatest difficulty in getting between her legs, she slid easily in and out of his bank account. Nancy Mitford's *Madame de Pompadour* (1954), based on sources that include de Hausset, Croy, Bernis, Luynes and Maurette, has her saying, 'He doesn't mind signing for a million, but hates to part with little sums out of his purse.'

She bought house after house to decorate for the king: Crécy near Dreux; Montretout at Saint-Cloud and La Celle nearby; others at Compiègne and Fontainebleau. She filled the Hermitage at Versailles with fresh flowers every day. She had the architect Lassurance design a house called Bellevue near Sèvres (which had scented china flowers from Vincennes), and Les Réservoirs at Versailles. Her Parisian house, the Hôtel d'Evreux, is now known as the Elysée Palace, a legacy that has had incalculable esoteric influence on the taste of French presidents.

Madame de Pompadour was the ancien régime version of the 'born to shop' phenomenon. Her pursuit of material acquisitions was on the sinister side of neurotic. They included Dresden, Meissen, pot-pourris from Chantilly, sculptures, carvings and ornaments by Pigalle, Verberckt and Falconet, pictures by Chardin, Van Loo and, of course, François Boucher. There were also storehouses filled with other pictures, porcelain (2,000 pieces of Sèvres), tapestries, linen, tools, carriages, wine and autograph furniture (including an escritoire by J.-F. Oeben, now in the Jack and Belle Linsky Collection of the Metropolitan Museum of Art. At the Rothschilds' Waddesdon Manor in Buckinghamshire there is a gold and porcelain snuffbox with portraits of her dogs, Inès and Mimi, painted on the lid – another example of how the Pompadour *arriviste* taste crosses generations.

Although, according to Jules Beaujoint, 'the Marquise was not a blue-stocking', she left a library of 3,826 books covering such subjects as commerce, finance, industry, philosophy, theology and history. Pompadour – whom Beaujoint describes as a woman of 'severe taste' – was artistic dictator of France in the years before the Revolution: she had Jacques-Ange Gabriel design the Petit Trianon, the perfect proportions of which were later to inspire Le Corbusier in his belief that all fine architecture is the product of an invisible grid, or *traces régulateurs*. She also created the Cabinets du Roi at Versailles, and, with her intuitive flair for dealing with craftsmen and designers, arranged the Gobelin tapestries, the damasks, the secretaires, the bibelots and the pictures. Perhaps as a consequence of her

preferred diet of vanilla, truffles and celery, Pompadour, France's first arbiter of taste, died at the age of forty-two.

The story of Madame de Pompadour, with its engaging details, is not of mere anecdotal interest. Her extraordinary position as artist of the state gave her huge power and influence to indulge her aesthetic preferences. Her canvas was not stapled to a stretcher, but covered all of modern material France. Her achievements created the role of 'tastemaker', whose ghost exists today, but her understanding of marginal utility and the role of desire in design led to the '*objet du goût*' which has passed … from mistresses of kings to owners of chain stores.

In Britain less elevated bourgeois taste at the time of Pompadour was represented by furniture, ceramics and the idea of the *souvenir*. Popular design was already in the market-place in the late eighteenth century. Neo-classicism expressed this taste sometimes uncertainly. Josiah Wedgwood and his artist John Flaxman extended trade far beyond Joshua Reynolds's conception of the world, converting a peasant craft into an industrial business supported by the ancestor of the modern skill of marketing. He gave class to the primitive kilns of Staffordshire and became a major influence on the development of taste.

Wedgwood's creamware service was inspired by the chaste simplicity, noted also by Winckelmann, of antique art (although in fact antecedents of Wedgwood were doing much the same thing in Rome). However, this was not just an aesthetic preference; from the mass-producer's point of view there were practical and economic imperatives for this desired simplicity in that simple designs were easier to make than the more elaborate rococo ones.

In furniture there was a desire to achieve certain standards of dignity and order. The Preface to George Hepplewhite's *The Cabinet-Maker and Upholsterer's Guide* (1794), a compilation of designs for jobbing craftsmen to copy and for the gentleman pleasurably to survey, declares, 'To unite elegance and utility, and blend the useful with the agreeable, has ever been considered a difficult, but an honourable task.'

Hepplewhite's designs were described as 'good and proper', an interesting phrase that hints at the relevance of manners and appropriateness to English taste. The *Guide*, besides being a hymn to gentility, reveals itself as a confident arbiter of taste: 'Mahogany chairs have seats of horse hair, plain, striped, chequered &c. at pleasure ... Japanned chairs should always have linen or cotton cushions.' Hepplewhite's designs were so adaptable and so durable and successful that they have been continuously reproduced, but it was not until the mid-nineteenth century that a technical revolution in furniture manufacture radicalized taste.

Innovations in ceramics came sooner. Interestingly, improvements in the processes of making ceramics, in the brave Wedgwood tradition, coincided with an emerging neo-classical taste – the artificial stone produced at Coade's factory in Lambeth helped to make the neo-classical version of the antique popularly accessible. Since the collection of classical statues at Fontainebleau had become famous, they had served as marks of modernity, as Montesquieu explained in his *Voyage d'Italie*: 'These statues cannot be sufficiently looked at, for it is from them that the Moderns have built up their systems of proportions.' There was an element of élitism, even snobbery of the intellectual sort, in possessing such a canon.

By about 1700, foreign craftsmen in Rome were preparing lead reproductions of ancient statues for commercial manufacture, for those who could afford neither original antiques nor the more costly bronze copies. While Wedgwood was not above making heads of ancient worthies as souvenirs, the real popularization of antique imagery and ideals came from Mrs Coade and from John Cheere's sculpture yards at Hyde Park Corner, illustrated as the frontispiece of William Hogarth's *Analysis of Beauty* (1756), itself an exemplar of modern taste in the arts. With Josiah Wedgwood, John Cheere (1709-87) was the first Englishman to realize the potential market for tokens of taste. By collecting Cheere's mass-produced souvenirs, anyone could have a collection of marbles as ennobling as François I's.

By the mid-nineteenth century, such didacticism was institutionalized. In Paris a Musée des Copies was established by Thiers and in London in 1864 Brucciani opened a 2,500-ft gallery of plaster casts in Russell Street, Covent Garden, portentously called a 'Galleria delle Belle Arti'. Brucciani's statues were not only educative (in that they prepared visitors for their trips to Florence, Naples and Rome); they also found their way into all the provincial art schools of Britain, as required since 1859 by the Lords of the Committee of Education of the Privy Council. In a prototype gesture of suburban disdain for Italy, the *Art Journal* reasoned that the success of Brucciani's collection lay in the fact that Covent Garden provided an environment 'much purer' and therefore more conducive to contemplation than Italy. At the same time, when certain casts found their way into private hands, status was conferred on the owner. This form of intellectual property was highly valued. Contemporary garden statuary is a mongrel descendant of these copies.

The development of taste as an idea and as an aesthetic prescription parallels the rise in popular expectations which grew with the increase in spending power. Taste and money are inseparable in nineteenth-century culture. Honoré de Balzac was obsessive about money (even while he romantically despised the monied classes); his descriptions of interiors created by financiers and industrialists betray the dependence this generation of consumers had on the antique in forming and projecting their taste.

The term 'consumer' had come into use as a description of bourgeois economic activity in the eighteenth century. In the new markets of the rapidly industrializing nations, making and using became known as producing and consuming. It is interesting to chart the relative decline of the old-fashioned, more genteel word 'customer' against the rise of the more abstract, aggressive 'consumer'. Semantically, 'customer' suggests familiarity and regularity and a one-to-one relationship with a retailer or a manufacturer, while the remote 'consumer' is a more relevant, impersonal tag in global markets giddy with excess. 'Consume' almost always has an unfavourable, even hostile, connotation, as in 'consumed by fire'. Tuberculosis was known as consumption during the whole period when it was a killer disease, and Vance Packard's *The Hidden Persuaders* (1956) makes great play with the derogatory term 'consumer society'.

The history of the word 'consumer' reveals the development of the Western economy. Mass production and all that it entails – investment, long lead-times, low unit costs and ready availability – replaced a system where simple makers could articulate and satisfy needs; the new distant customers alienated from the production process became consumers. Deconstructing meanings in this way helps explain how taste operates in the modern world. Just as the modern idea of money involves credit (from the Latin *credo*, I believe, or I trust), the concept of taste came to fill the vacuum created by the possibility of limitless consumption brought about by the possibility of limitless credit. The etymology of credit makes it clear that money, like taste, is very much an act of faith.

The Frankfurt School social scientists Walter Benjamin and Theodor Adorno noted the extraordinary paradox that under capitalism taste is not autonomous – as one might expect in a system which promotes competitive individualism – but tends to be collective. Market researchers know what are the most effective contemporary symbols of privilege and instruments of status.

The status symbol is as significant today as it was in Madame de Pompadour's time, but it takes different forms and serves different purposes. It is not surprising that in the eighteenth century tokens of taste were classical statuary and in the nineteenth moral values. In a century still cowed by the machine, consumer durables have become touchstones of value, and none is so numinous as the wrist-watch. Its very familiarity and availability has, by a Darwinian process, forced special and intricate patterns of discrimination on consumers. What Antinous was to Cardinal Albani, the expensive wrist-watch is to the taste-makers of the late

twentieth century. Giovanni Agnelli of Fiat has a personal foible: he wears his on the outside of his cuff.

Although not the most expensive, the most exceptional watch as status symbol is the Swiss Rolex, since its reputation is based on technical merit (a patent for its remarkable watertight stem was granted in 1926). This gave rise to an aura of professionalism and expertise which has since proved especially attractive. Ever since Mercedes Gleitze wore a Rolex Oyster for a heavily publicized cross-Channel swim in 1927, Rolex has been more than merely a watch.

Before the First World War wrist-watches, as compared to fob-watches, were considered effeminate, but when artillerymen needed the convenience of a wrist-watch (as bicyclists had just before them), they became important symbols. Ever since, the basic architecture of the wrist-watch has depended on innovations made for the trenches. The number of press advertisements for new bracelets coming on to the market between 1914 and 1918 attests to its growing popularity, even though conservative spokesmen for the watch industry thought it was an idiotic fashion to expose so sensitive a mechanism on the most restless part of the body.

Because of the stigma of effeminacy, the wrist-watch has always been marketed in a pointedly masculine way. Cartier's most famous wrist-watches are the 'Tank' (made for the US Army Tank Corps, another innovation of the First World War) and the 'Santos' named after the swashbuckling pioneer aviator Santos Du Mont), while all Rolex models make some sort of persuasive appeal to professionalism – that of the diver, the aviator, the racing-car driver or the opera singer.

Ever since the 1920s Rolex has concerned itself with developing its customers as much as its watches, and for fifteen years the simple theme has been 'famous people wear Rolexes'. These people include Yehudi Menuhin, Kiri Te Kanawa and Reinhold Messner. An article in *Campaign* (November 1987) explored reactions to 'the timeless timepiece'. Dave Trott, socialist Buddhist partner in the advertising agency Gold Greenless Trott, commented: 'I wouldn't be seen dead in one. What it says is that you have no originality and you need to wear an accepted badge to say you have made money. It's like people used to wear clothes and shoes with the YSL label on the outside, or buy a Porsche 911 and never drive outside Soho. It's a cliché.' But rival ad agency boss John Hegarty more shrewdly retorted: 'It says I've made it. I've achieved that, done it, sorted that area out. It is about two things: awareness and achievement. It is also obvious with a Rolex that you have money because they cost so much.'

The same was once said of the Apollo Belvedere. But unlike Apollo, Montres Rolex SA know that sales go up when they increase the price: as Andre Heiniger explained, 'We are in the luxury business. We are selling taste, selling fashion, selling status. If you have a Rolex you are a member of a select international club.' Franco Zeffirelli considers a Rolex 'above fashion. It is standard... in my own work I never try to be fashionable. Never. And the same could be said for the watch I have chosen to wear.'

It is significant that Rolex users are so self-conscious about their choice of wrist-watch and that to many of them its value lies either in its overt expression of professionalism or in its reticent expression of neutrality. The proper maintenance of the middle classes' self-regard depends on their values being necessarily good, superior to those of the upper as well as the lower classes. This is why snobbery is essentially a distinction of the middle classes and why the Rolex is an essentially middle-class watch.

Brixton and Vienna

Between 1850 and 1910 the population of Britain grew from 27 to 45 million. The growth was in the urban classes. When this huge, new and (by some standards) ignorant class emerged, supply and demand was no longer controlled by the *cognoscenti*, but by the principles of market economics. This produced such a fundamental revolution in behaviour that it soon become clear that Reynolds was wrong: there was more than one taste

and a great many decent people apparently did not share his.

The new middle class neither knew nor cared about Reynolds's polite strictures, but preferred to clutter themselves with meretricious junk, mass-produced by cynical manipulators of the means of production in Birmingham, Sheffield and Glasgow. A bookcase got up to look like the west front of Lincoln cathedral was typical. For the nineteenth-century consumer, the rules of taste were replaced by market forces; philosophical musings were replaced by homely tracts admonishing avaricious and fashion-crazed housewives for their want of judgement and their excess of competitive acquisitiveness.

Charles Eastlake in his *Hints on Household Taste* (1868) described with the unfluctuating certainty of someone comfortable with his prejudices the proper application of the principle of taste to all the minutiae of domestic life. He argued that the artistic chaos of most homes resulted from no one being trained to make aesthetic judgements (and in saying this he echoed the rationalism of the eighteenth century). He believed that guidance in the matter of what he called 'right taste' should form a necessary part of every genteel woman's education. His use of the absolute 'right', as opposed to the somewhat less certain 'good', reveals most clearly his conviction that one taste alone is correct. Nor is he innocent of the charge of puritanism, revealed in his abhorrence of consumerism and its appetite for novelty:

When did people first adopt the monstrous notion that the 'last pattern out' must be the best? Is good taste so rapidly progressive that every mug which leaves the potter's hands surpasses in shape the last which he moulded? But it is feared that, instead of progressing, we have, for some ages at least, gone hopelessly backward in the art of manufacture.

This charge of shoddy workmanship levelled at the workshop of the world was a powerful weapon in the aesthetician's armoury. It is true that applied ornament was often used to camouflage manufacturing faults, but in his criticism of popular decoration Eastlake became confused about taste and design:

This commonplace taste...compels us to rest on chairs and to sit at tables which are designed in accordance with the worst principles of construction and invested with shapes confessedly unpicturesque. It sends us metalwork from Birmingham which is as vulgar in form as it is flimsy in execution. It decorates the finest modern porcelain with the most objectionable character of ornament.

In his strictures Eastlake may have been influenced by Augustus Pugin, visionary architect of the Gothic Revival, who made the same point, more forcibly, in his *Apology for the Revival of Christian Architecture* (1843):

It is impossible to enumerate half the absurdities of modern metalworkers; but all these proceed from the false notion of disguising instead of beautifying articles of utility. How many objects of ordinary use are rendered monstrous and ridiculous, simply because the artist, instead of seeking the most convenient form and then decorating it, has embodied some extravagance to conceal the real purpose for which the article has been made!

The rich brew of art and morality, the roseate view of history, caught the mood of the time, and – setting a disastrous precedent for British culture – suggesed that the solution to the immediate artistic, moral and social problems of England existed at the end of a long journey back to the Middle Ages. Here Pugin imagined a world of God-driven beauty and harmony, of innocent men, of organs booming basso profundo solid, spiritual goodness. There was no smog and no proletariat, only placid, satisfied peasants. Viewed from one of Gustave Doré's railway arches, it was a persuasive vision.

But beneath the apparent certainties of Victorian England lay paradoxes which are still unresolved today. There is more snobbery in one copy of the nineteenth-century middle-class journal *Punch* than in an entire run of the patrician eighteenth-century *Gentleman's Magazine*. Pride in Britain's industrial eminence was moderated by disquiet at the quality, purpose and appearance of most of what was produced. While paternalism suggests a positivist belief in progress and improvement, the aesthetic zealots sought their inspiration in distant history. The concern for the moral welfare of the working classes, though real, was also pragmatic, in that the country was more troubled by fears of public disorder and urban insurrection than popular views of the Victorian age allow. Above all, the interests of a ruling minority were contrived to appear to coincide with the good of the many.

The idea of taste has a peculiar force which nineteenth-century philanthropists were quick to exploit. Visions of depraved and enlightened taste were the invisible illustrations in self-help tracts, designed to help demoralized consumers. The paternalistic cultures of the nineteenth century set up museums to guide popular taste to more elevated (which was to say formal, antique) levels by exhibiting objects held to be of the highest artistic perfection. A necessary extension of this idea of presenting exemplars for imitation was, at least to the paternalist, the provision of equal and opposite exemplars for avoidance.

Nowhere was such philanthropy and opportunism, public purpose and self-interest, combined with more genuine enthusiasm for popularizing art than in the person and career of Sir Henry Cole (1808-82). From an unpromising training as a civil servant in the Public Record Office, Cole created a curriculum vitae to rival any; he was chillingly described as 'over active' by one of Queen Victoria's aides, and at mid-career he played a leading role in the conception and execution of one of the century's most significant cultural events: the Great Exhibition of the Industry of All Nations held in London's Hyde Park in 1851.

Cole's most influential accomplice was Prince Albert, whose interest in manufacturing ranged from export performance to the viciousness of superfluous decoration (although he did himself specify tartan linoleum for Balmoral). While the aims of the exhibition organizers had been didactic, the mood of the public was celebratory. Promoted as an exercise in national pride, the underlying purpose of the Great Exhibition was to educate through exposure to the best and the worst, allowing visitors to draw their own conclusions. The intended lesson in taste may have been lost on many of the revellers, but the popular success of the enterprise encouraged Cole and his supporters to renew their educational efforts yet more energetically by other means. The profits from the Great Exhibition were used to buy some of the exhibits so as to form a permanent study collection of contemporary industrial art for public edification and enlightenment.

Cole bought 2,075 items of foreign manufacture, 1,500 goods from the East India Company and 890 from British manufacturers. In descending proportion these comprised metalwork, fabrics, enamels, furniture and ceramics. According to the Catalogue of the Great Exhibition, 'Each specimen has been selected for its merits in exemplifying some right principle of construction or ornament ... to which it appeared that the attention of our Students and Manufacturers should be directed.'

There were some crucial distinctions, betraying many a prejudice. Eastern products were generally illustrative of 'correct principles of ornament', but suffered from 'rude' workmanship. European specimens show 'superior skill' but are 'defective in the principles of their design'. When European products attempt direct imitation of nature, the results are 'very inferior ... to the ruder scarfs of Tunis'. This bizarre study collection – 'illustrating the Correct principles of Taste' – was opened to the public at the Department of Practical Art's Marlborough House premises.

The gallery displaying 'The False Principles of Design' soon became known as Cole's Chamber of Horrors, a sort of industrial freak show. With true paternalistic zeal, Cole produced a catalogue which listed the false principles, so visitors could be forewarned against later forays in the market-place, as opposed to the museum. These false principles included: lack of symmetry, disregard of structure, formless confusion and superficial decoration. Alas, Cole's skill with public relations did not match his flair for didactic entertainment and the Chamber of Horrors was short-lived; complaints and withdrawals by the pilloried and vilified manufacturers best versed in false principles soon made the business of organizing loans impossible rather than merely difficult.

During its short career the Chamber of Horrors

attracted both public ridicule and healthy scepticism; officials found it risible, yet unsettling, but Cole had touched a nerve. His museum had to revert to the traditional idea of solemn, unquestioning contemplation of works of applied art. An astonishing experiment in setting up a public clinic where the maladies of manufacturing industry could be inspected by consumers failed, but provided a model for imitation.

Similar objections from the trades curtailed another experiment in creating a museum of bad taste in Prague. Here Gustav Pazaurek had considered showing visitors to the Northern Bohemian Museum gross and horrible things for the home, an ambition he had to forgo until he reached the more liberal province of Württemberg, where, as Director of the Industrial Museum in Stuttgart, he created his Museum of Art Indiscretions. In this he included a modern suit of armour, intended for a parvenu castle; tin boxes coloured to imitate faience; wood looking like granite; iron faked to look like Wedgwood; and 'presumptuous' metals: tin looking like silver, zinc looking like bronze. He also did not like chocolate busts of the Kaiser, proving a popular line in certain tasteless Konditoreien. Like Henry Cole, Pazaurek's aesthetic outrage was sustained by moral force: Cole damned the false, while Pazaurek condemned anything intended to deceive the ignorant. Although one might detect the germ of modern movement ideology in the insistence of truth to materials, Pazaurek was as quick to damn the errors of undue simplicity as of undue excess.

But faults of construction were as repugnant to the Museum of Art Indiscretions as preciosities of materials. Here we find an element of functionalism creeping in: unstable vases, thermally inappropriate materials for containers, eccentric ornaments (empty shell cases and imitation helmets), thermometers fashioned like riding whips and uncomfortable chairs made out of stag's antlers were presented for obloquy. Souvenir trash, patriotic trash, religious trash and advertising trash were also included.

These were popular concerns. Henry Morley (1822-94) became a close associate of Charles Dickens, who had become acquainted with his work on reading a series called 'How to Make a Home Unhealthy' in the *Journal of Public Health*. Morley soon followed the Zeitgeist and switched from public health to popular taste, from the inner to the outer man. His clever parody, 'A House Full of Horrors', was published in 1852 in *Household Words*, a journal established by Dickens to monitor the growing cult of the middle-class home in the middle of the century. It was the social equivalent of the self-improving, democratic pamphlets which circulated at the same time among the new industrial workers. Morley describes the nightmares suffered by one innocent visitor to the Museum of Practical Art, a certain Mr Crumpet, as he finds himself surrounded on his return home to the new suburb of Brixton by the very objects he has been didactified into abhorring:

> The matter is this: I have acquired some Correct Principles of Taste. Five week ago I went to the Department of Practical Art in Marlborough House to look over the museum of ornamental art. I had heard of a Chamber of Horrors there established, and I found it, and went through it with my catalogue. It was a gloomy chamber, hung round with frightful objects in curtains, carpets, clothes, lamps and what not. In each case the catalogue told me why such and such a thing wasn't endurable.

In particular:

> That tray with a bit of Landseer's pictures on it, you will find to correspond with the seventy-ninth item in the Catalogue of Horrors, at which you will find these following observations. It is 'An example of popular but vulgar taste, of a low character, presenting numerous features which the student should carefully avoid: First, the centre is the piracy of the picture; Second, the picture on which most labour has been bestowed is thrown away ... It is wrong to hide a picture by putting a teapot on it.

Mr Crumpet becomes dismayed to discover that he is actually wearing some of the unendurable clothing on show. From then on his newly acquired sensitivity in matters of taste has alarming consequences:

> After hanging up my hat in the hall, I had great trouble in straightening my hair as I went into the ladies, it would stand upright at the horror of my friend's hall-paper. I had seen it in the Chamber of Horrors — perspective representations of a railway station frequently repeated. Why is

it that people who do not understand what I have understood quite well for the last five weeks; that pictures of any kind, and above all, perspectives, are unusually out of place repeated around a wall ... When a picture is repeated up and down and round about the place, the result is a nightmare.

Morley gently concludes that while Cole's medicine was worth taking, a smaller dose might have been advisable. Mildly ridiculous even in its own day, Cole's prescriptions would be unthinkable now. With the passing of extrovert paternalism went behaviour so lacking in irony or in the supposed objectivity of intellectual reasoning. It was an exercise only possible in an age whose executives were backed by mighty moral certainties.

Henry Cole has provided prototypes for many things, from the professional civil servant to the Victoria and Albert Museum, but perhaps most significant of all is his role model for the embattled middle-class aesthete, outraged by the impropriety and pretension of lesser folk, dismayed by the obdurate philistinism of those of higher rank. Good taste was what made Henry Cole feel good and less threatened. Bad taste was the other thing.

Cole's use of the museum as an active medium (rather than a passive collection) was not unique. In the United States Mellon, Frick and other *nouveaux riches* were establishing, at the last historical moment when such a thing was possible, their own private collections rivalling in splendour and swagger the national collections of Europe. Their presence, both physical and spiritual, gave the public certain expectations of art – and still does. What animus drove the collectors? The answer is this: an art collection validates the status and confirms the arrival of the parvenu. The Firestone heiress said her compulsion to collect eighteenth-century furniture was similar to the effect peanuts had on her: have one and you want the whole lot.

Museums buttressed self-made egos and gave to emergent nations the sanction of the past. They stabilized art, but art needs to be volatile, so to redress the stability of the marble halls, the concept of the avant-garde emerged. The avant-garde (which, at least semantically, has military and then political origins) is fundamental to an understanding of modern taste. Somewhere out there is a huge graveyard of French expressions, memorials to past conceits and fancies which died when France ceased to dominate global culture. Avant-garde belongs alongside *thé dansant* and *noblesse oblige*; it comes from a period when culture was a battlefield, when creativity could be quantified by capitalizing the offence, hence the appropriateness of a *nom de guerre*.

Pugin and Eastlake could not be said to be avant-garde. With the middle classes entrenched in their comfortable philistinism and their false principles, artists since, say, 1880 have operated on the fringes. With the concept of the avant-garde the idea of novelty became, at least for the time being, inseparable from progress in art. The idea that art has leaders and followers has imposed a structure on our imaginations which has been difficult to shift. Baudelaire presented a paradox which captures the contradiction inherent in the ceaseless quest for novelty: 'The chief task of genius is precisely to invent a stereotype.'

The avant-garde was a reflection of society's image of itself, but seen in a distorting mirror: decadent poets, wacky artistic types throwing paint in the public's face, slaves to the senses and brutes to their lovers, were convenient inventions which in fact emasculated art by stringing a *cordon sanitaire* around artists, defining their territory as out of bounds. The dangerous Bohemian in hat and cloak with a fevered imagination behind a smouldering brow made glossy by absinthe and pale by late nights and later mornings had a trembling lower lip. Only the eyes were fixed with the singular purpose: *épater les bourgeois*! This was exactly what Albert Jarry did when he shocked the audience at the first performance of his play, *Ubu Roi*, with the opening line: '*Merde.*' It is a measure of the durability of the avant-garde that nowadays this is almost all that is remembered of Jarry's script.

And later, when familiarity had dulled the shock value of the sleaze, the avant-garde found expression in another strange bird, but one of a rather different feather – the technocrat. Here again, in a rapidly industrializing world, there was an image

both to lionize and to demonize. From just after the First World War avant-garde artists abandoned their fedoras, cheroots and dirty habits and became missionaries from another territory equally alien to the stay-at-home bourgeois: the laboratory and the factory. Whereas if you had been researching a television programme on the avant-garde in 1880 you would have had to go to Paris and sip wormwood liquor with oddball painters and poets while dancing girls demonstrated the contemporary deficiencies of laundering, by 1920 your producer would have had to send you to Germany to meet Hungarian *émigrés* in boiler suits teaching metalwork, photography and callisthenics to wide-eyed, flaxen-haired, firm-thighed delegates of the master race. Nowadays to discover the avant-garde, you have to look in history books.

In the nineteenth century art became a commodity, and the avant-garde was a reaction to this. Restless neophilia, supported by Baudelaire's romantic interpretation of the artist's purpose, is as much a product of consumer culture as kitsch, its mirror image. The two extremes help define the middle ground of consumer values. The feverish quest of the artist is to capture the beauty which Ezra Pound characterized as that evanescent gasp 'between one cliché and another'. The avant-garde rejects convention and taste is not so much disregarded as deliberately confronted. A certain sort of thin-lipped joyless overstuffed, polished taste existed in every Victorian Parlour, even Freud's, and especially in those redolent with morality. The existence of the avant-garde had a curiously stabilizing effect on already conservative middle-class taste: if taste is a matter of choice and discrimination, what choice can there be when only the radically new is acceptable?

Henry Cole's century was as obsessed with the past as ours is with the new. Eclecticism in architectural style had put all of history into the market-place – to Mr Crumpet's distress. Henry Cole's false principles are one example of a search for meaning in a clutter of senselessly reproduced stylistic motifs. Adolf Loos (1870-1903), Viennese architect, polemicist and *fin-de-siècle* man-about-the-Ringstrasse, was one of those keen to reject the eclectic delusions of the nineteenth century which had so dismayed Crumpet. Loos wrote: 'Ever since humanity discerned the stature of classical antiquity, one single thought has united all the great architects. They think: I am building the way the ancient Romans would have done. We know that they are wrong. Time, place, purpose, climate and setting all make this impossible.'

Loos saw the history of civilization in terms of mankind's progressive emancipation from ornament (a conceit more workable, perhaps, in Brixton than Vienna). He equated decoration with degeneration, pointing out criminals' liking for tattoos. It is not too fanciful to suggest a similarity between Loos's rejection of artifice and ornament and Freud's exposure of the devices and delusions which disguise the essential primitivism of the psyche. The extraordinary climate of Vienna about 1900 was, for a nation largely unaffected by the industrial revolution that brought us Mr Crumpet, the product of a crisis in classical reason.

This crisis, which we can see in what Freud thought, what Klimt and Schiele painted, what Schoenberg composed and what Loos built, produced extraordinary fertility in art and social science. It is perhaps worth cautioning that this splendid flowering coincided precisely with Austria's political and economic decline, and may, indeed, have contributed to it. No longer able, or even much inclined, to influence external events, artists became introspective and somewhat desperate. Freud excavated the soul, Klimt and Schiele made a sensuous and lascivious sort of eroticism into fashionable high art, and Loos tried to make architecture systematic. Arthur Schnitzler, the most successful playwright of the day, whom Freud described as his alter ego, filled the theatres with his plays on sex, death and the soul. His best-known novel was called, characteristically, *Sterben* (To Die).

Meanwhile, adrift from any particular social group or class, avant-garde artists justified their elected alienation as a necessary tension-builder in the process of creation. As a consequence alienation became a test for high art, rather as drowning in witch trials was proof of purity. Simultaneously,

a fashionable lack of content in abstract art (*c.* 1906– 66), forced artists to develop exquisitely high standards of self-consciousness, self-reference and self-veneration. In painting, the generalized quest was for reduced form, a goal pursued at the expense of meaning and communication and in the teeth of public censure. Some painters, including Brice Marden, achieved total meaninglessness. Soon, public censure gave way to public apathy and indifference – and, for instance, to the founding of the Saatchi Collection, where avant-garde art was apotheosized in the service of social mountaineering.

Avant-garde is an extreme perversion of taste. Sometimes it is in dramatic confrontation with nostrums of good taste; at others, to take an absurd example in the work of a sculptor like Richard Serra, it is a triple distillation of refined good taste and therefore comes very near to being something else entirely. Under the despotism of the avant-garde, art was reduced to serial fads. In the age of post-modernism, which actually *depends* on copying and on restless neophilia, both the avant-garde and kitsch have become emasculated – or become the same thing, depending on your point of view.

Although a diligent researcher would quickly find an early-nineteenth-century reference to the radical avant-garde, the concept makes most sense when politics and art bifurcated, and that happened most convincingly in Vienna. The Viennese avant-garde, perhaps more so than any since, was both the product and the scourge of the bourgeois society that gave rise to it.

There have been many Whig interpretations of art history which draw facile connections between the artistic revolution of Vienna in 1900 and the social engineering which the modern movement attempted after 1920. The two are very different, but they share avant-garde characteristics in their pointed rejection of safe bourgeois taste. Heath-Robinson in *How to Live in a Flat* (1936) satirized the fashion for modernism:

> Whereas formerly the best furniture was made by carpenters ... the trade is almost entirely in the hands of plumbers, riveters, blow-pipers, and metal-workers of all sorts. As a result, the ultra-modern living room resembles

a cross between an operating-theatre, a dipsomaniac's nightmare, and a new kind of knitting. The advantages of steel furniture, of course, are that it does not harbour worms, requires only an occasional touch of metal-polish, and can be bent into all manner of laughable designs … It is quite possible … to construct a chromium-steel dining-room suite in one continuous piece – that is, without lifting the pen from the paper. This can be moved bodily from room to room – and even set up on the roof, in the event of anybody wishing to dine there – in about one third of the time needed to shift an old-fashioned mahogany suite. Moreover, when the conversation at the dinner-table flags and all present are wondering what the dickens to say next, the host can create a diversion by inviting his guests to guess where the suite begins and ends, and awarding a small prize, such as a book of stamps or an unopened tin of peaches to the winner.

The modern movement was an attempt to make the avant-garde *popular*, its leaders – unwittingly – imposing their own exclusive tastes upon reluctant populations. The vegetarian lady novelist sitting in a tubular steel chair reading Schnitzler in front of a rug with an abstract pattern was an easy target for conservative architect and moralist Sir Reginald Blomfield. In *Modernismus* (1934) he attacked the idea of novelty: 'What impresses us most in these struggles for something new, is not their originality, but their immodesty, the folly of thinking that it is worthwhile to abandon the beaten track and stand on one's head in the ditch in order to attract attention.' Blomfield deplored the fact that 'The Modernists blandly ask us to exterminate any aesthetic preferences and instincts we now possess, and offer ourselves as passive victims.'

Every page of Blomfield's coarsely argued text proves that he did not know of, say, Le Corbusier's romantic early work at La Chaux-de-Fonds (which the architect himself in fact suppressed). Those who did knew that Le Corbusier was engaged on a mission of continuous refinement, development and discovery. *Modernismus* is too simplistic a book to accommodate a more sophisticated analysis of the flawed ambitions of modernism, but Blomfield was right in questioning the exact standards by which the modernists declared their taste to be perfection: 'What we complain of in the propaganda of Modernism is its confusion of thought, its persistent habit of begging the question, and of laying down as

accepted principles what are, in fact, merely dogmatic assertions.'

What the modern movement got wrong, in all its heroic special pleading, was its confusion of idealism with purpose, its mistaking paternalism for the commonwealth, and, as Baillie-Scott remarked, its impudent claim to having a monopoly of practical efficiency. If you were that vegetarian lady novelist in Cambridge *c.* 1930, you might well enjoy your tubular steel, your Schnitzler, and your non-representational rug, but that would be a matter of taste, not of scientific certainty. The assumption that the technical solutions to furniture and building design of 1929 were permanent was, as Blomfield said, based on mistaken sociology and arbitrary psychology. The icons of the modern movement were as historically specific as the nineteenth-century obsession with modesty, which led the Victorians to dress table legs in little pantaloons. Just as they felt it necessary to disguise household apparatus and buildings, so the modern movement demanded the clear articulation of an internal mechanism through external form.

But then Blomfield's objections to the modern movement were also a matter of taste – and his particular taste was influenced by snobbery: as a patrician grandee, he disliked the foreignness of modernism (hence the sly title of his book which he puts into the German form), and he disliked its Jewishness even more: 'I detest and despise cosmopolitanism.' Blomfield warned that the modernists' taste for order would not win friends and in its place he offered evolutionary traditionalism. Today it is axiomatic that the modern movement's absolute belief in the idea of progress was a weakness: sadly, new forms have not stimulated a revolution in the human spirit. Osbert Lancaster spoke for the majority when he wrote in *Here of All Places* (1958):

This apparent failure of the reformers in the realm of domestic architecture is, one fancies, one of psychology. The open-plan, the mass-produced steel and plywood furniture, the uncompromising display of structural elements, are all in theory perfectly logical, but in the home logic has always been at a discount.

The modern movement was the most extraordinary

international exercise of the avant-garde will. The fabled unwillingness of architects and designers to accommodate the tastes of the public was hardly calculated to ingratiate themselves with the toiling masses on whose behalf they made such extravagant claims. This version of the avant-garde failed, despite some powerful rhetoric and some magnificent monuments, to provide a widely acceptable unifying symbolic order. If the modernists had known Mr Crumpet better, they would have been aware that the explosion of mass-consumption meant the eternal loss of even the idea of a homogeneous society, and hence of a single value system.

The avant-garde only ever captivated the high culture of an intellectual élite (which has been aped by the social élite from Peggy Guggenheim to Doris Saatchi). But, as the art critic Clement Greenberg pointed out in an influential essay, *Kitsch and the Avant-Garde* (1939), 'Where there is an avant-garde, generally we also find a rearguard.'

Greenberg popularized the term, which until then had been almost exclusively the province of obscure German philosophers and aestheticians, such as Fritz Karpfen, whose book *Der Kitsch* (1925) was among the first on the subject. Kitsch – which comes from the German word meaning to cheapen – and the avant-garde look very different, but are correlative in substance: they are the equal and opposite manifestations of that unique historical awareness (Blomfield called it 'hysteria') which produced the concept of modernity. They are the fruits of bourgeois capitalist society in what Marxists call its decline and the rest are glad to see as its evolution. Just as the avant-garde places novelty and originality above all else, so banality and vulgarity are lionized in kitsch. Both violate everyday conceptions of good taste.

Kitsch is unthinkable without industrialization and feeds off it. Something kitsch almost invariably involves an adaptation from one medium to another, from appropriate to inappropriate, transformations made possible by advances in technology. It is all very well to have tongue-and-groove wood panelling, if that is what you fancy, because that is a matter of taste. Wallpaper looking like tongue-and-

groove is, however, kitsch. Similarly, kitsch almost always diminishes size and scale. On sale in Japan, for instance, is a lavatory paper dispenser in the shape of Mount Fuji. Witless adaptation, diminution and relentless cheapening categorize kitsch.

In a funny way the achievement of nearly universal literacy in industrialized countries turned cultures that were once homogeneous into segregated classes. The virtuosi were a privileged élite with easy access to art, music and literature, and among this minority it was not difficult to settle on standards and expectations for art. By about 1900 reading and writing had become everyday skills. Literacy, according to Clement Greenberg, 'no longer served to distinguish an individual's cultural inclinations, since it was no longer the exclusive concomitant of refined tastes.'

Unable or unwilling to transfer peasant culture to the city, the new urban proletariat and petty bourgeoisie were equally ill-equipped to participate in the traditional high culture of one of Sir Joshua Reynolds's salons. Kitsch was, to use another German word of uncertain provenance but perpetual value, an ersatz version of high culture called into existence by a new form of demand. Greenberg, a left-wing champion of modernism, scathingly describes the trash sold to those he considers insensible to 'genuine' culture: 'Kitsch, using for raw materials the debased and academicized simulacra of genuine culture, welcomes and cultivates this insensibility. Kitsch is mechanical and operates by formulas. Kitsch is vicarious experience and faked sensations. Kitsch is the epitome of all that is spurious in the life of our times.'

Kitsch has the external characteristics of art, but is actually a falsification of it. The modernist view was that kitsch was unreflective enjoyment. At worst, kitsch was seen as a pernicious influence against which 'genuine' culture must be constantly vigilant. Not only is kitsch an inevitable consequence of industrialized society; it is dependent on mechanical and electrical reproduction for its existence and transmission. Kitsch is made in factories and consumed in bulk, growing the while; it blurs the distinction between art and life and supplies information in place of meaning. The hunting-scene formica place-mat is one example. A gilt chandelier is another.

There are different types of kitsch, but they all share an element of *inappropriateness*. A carpet woven in the pattern of an ornamented ceiling complete with beams and mouldings (shown at the Museum of Practical Art, London, 1852), an ashtray made of postage stamps (Museum of Art Indiscretions, Stuttgart, 1909), 1960s 'colonial' kitchen (Gillo Dorfles, *Kitsch*, 1969), Ronald Reagan's bedroom (1983) or the new Department of Health and Social Security Offices in Whitehall (1987) – what each example has in common is bad faith: each strives for an effect which is at odds with the true and proper purpose.

An instantly recognizable form of kitsch, as common today in Japanese restaurants serving sushi on wood-effect, plastic platters as it was a hundred years ago when a bar of chocolate was made to look like the Kaiser, is the transfer of a work of art to an inappropriate medium. Before post-modern architecture, this sort of nonsense was the definitive kitsch object, because it so manifestly undermined one of the highest forms of genuine culture – the original work of art. Mass reproduction of unique works is in itself a violation of one of the most precious tenets of Western art, and reproductions applied to mundane merchandise heighten the violation of traditional values. The destruction of what aesthetes call 'the privileged moment' when a viewer communes with a unique work of art is caused by a debasing familiarity with reproductions. This applies to music as well as to painting (and to a lesser extent to architecture and literature – think of the mythical tourist who left a production of *Hamlet* because it was made up of old quotes).

The regular abuse of fragments of classical music in advertising sets up banal associations when the piece is played in full: for the time being at least, Bach's Air on a G String is inescapably associated with cheap cigars, the chorus from the last act of *Turandot* with an Italian airline. Recently, the post-modern architect Michael Graves has taken abuse of classical values further by endorsing cheap shoes in US press advertisements.

If the avant-garde is consciously individualistic and self-referential, then the expression of communal values is, by definition, anti-art, which is to say, kitsch. This is just one of the ways in which the avant-garde expresses its modernity when compared with the art of the past (whose highest aim was to articulate contemporary spiritual, philosophical or political ideals). It also explains why the political art of the twentieth century – one thinks of firm-thighed Nazi athletes, Soviet tractor drivers – is of necessity kitsch. Milan Kundera develops this idea in his novel *The Unbearable Lightness of Being* (trans. 1984): 'The feeling induced by Kitsch must be a kind the multitude can share. Kitsch may not, therefore, depend on an unusual situation; it must derive from the basic images people have engraved in their memories: the ungrateful daughter, the neglected father, children running on the grass, the motherland betrayed, first love.'

To the Victorians, as well as to the modernists, who in some curious ways resemble them, kitsch was irredeemable, but our less certain age is not so dogmatic. Kitsch can be rehabilitated by context, or at least by intention. In his book *Kitsch* (1969), Gillo Dorfles discusses the Manhattan skyline, which comprises many individual monstrosities, yet the overall effect is stupendous. But the extent to which a sophisticated environment can transform the meaning of the objects it contains prompts Dorfles to caution, 'This is why we will never be altogether sure that fake marble columns, papier-mâché statues, wood imitation wallpapers, glass animals from Murano and even mother-of-pearl shells and Brazilian hardstone in the shape of ashtrays, although themselves undoubtedly Kitsch, are beyond recovery.'

The deliberate cultivation of outrageous bad taste has long been a favourite device of the avant-garde. A sly, knowing sophistication at odds with safe bourgeois values suggests that an excess of good taste is just as lamentable as evidence of bad. Taste which is too good is a tell-tale of conformity and insecurity, what George Bernard Shaw called moral cowardice. In this exquisitely balanced equation the amount of admissible bad taste is subject to fine measurement by social scrutineers. Artistic, aristocratic and wealthy élites set their own rules, but ordinary citizens have to be more cautious. There is a parallel in the well-rehearsed cycles of fashion: a suitable amount of time must have passed for a revival to be acceptable, but there is a fine line between being at the forefront of a revival and simply being out of date.

As soon as it loses its original offensive impact, avant-garde hyper-kitsch is soon subsumed into the mainstream as another 'school' for art historians to ponder and catalogue. In the early 1980s the most radical Milanese designers, including Alessandro Mendini and Ettore Sottsass, were producing furniture for Studio Alchymia and for Memphis, whose designs were calculated to offend. Andrea Branzi used patterns derived from Mondrian and Kandinsky paintings on his *poltrona falsa* because they were 'good and cheap'; Mendini spoke boastfully of his *galleria del copismo*. By the time these gaudy, banal bastardizations of 1950s suburbanism, artfully contrived to oppose every assumption of the modern movement, had been included in more than 200 international glossy magazines and had appeared in Karl Lagerfeld's Paris apartment, they had become just another style of rich man's chic. Now used everywhere, from Victoria bus station to department stores and food packaging, the Milanese movement, which started as an ironic gesture by Sottsass, soon became, quite appropriately, the most celebrated cliché of recent years.

Memphis was a reminder that contemporary eclecticism differs from nineteenth-century historicism in this regard: today everything quickly becomes a cliché and therefore potentially kitsch. Like postmodern architecture, of which it is a poor relation, Memphis refuted positivist faith in progress, and, defined negatively in opposition to modernism, signalled only an ironic awareness of the end of all movements. Its media success was fuelled by the notion that popular culture is at odds with the high or genuine stuff. Before the assumptions of modernism were regularly called into question, the self-appointed guardians of the avant-garde derided popular taste. Thus Virginia Woolf snobbishly stigmatizes the hapless middle classes: 'The true battle lies not between the highbrows and the lowbrows joined together in blood brotherhood but against the bloodless and pernicious pest who comes between... Highbrows and lowbrows must band together to exterminate a pest which is the bane of all thinking and living.'

Highbrows believe that they alone can appreciate culture. Good taste in their interpretation is constantly under insidious attack from the philistine lowbrows with their coarse pretensions (which continuously threaten the exclusivity of highbrow culture). Clement Greenberg was a highbrow. Until very recently highbrows could write without irony this sort of condescending gobbledygook in the pages of *The Partisan Review*: 'Middlebrow culture attacks distinctions as such and insinuates itself everywhere... Insidiousness is of its essence, and in recent years its avenues of penetration have become infinitely more difficult to detect and block.'

Meanwhile, the highbrows (defined by A. P. Herbert as the sort of people who look at a sausage and think of Picasso) are happy to patronize the lowbrows, listening to their jazz and taking an interest in their 'vernacular' art or their cooking. The lowbrows do not threaten because they are uninterested in highbrow values.

What is most interesting in this discussion of the self-evident is the precise mechanism by which the dominant classes impose their own distinctions between high and low, or 'good' and 'bad'. To Baudelaire, bad taste was 'intoxicating' because it offered the aristocratic pleasure of not pleasing, thus confirming that whenever taste is discussed, notions of class cannot be too far away. Snobbery is one of the most effective mechanisms by which this dominance is maintained. The manifestations of snobbery, or turning class into performance art, are also often taken to be 'good' taste. Listen to Harold Nicolson in *Some People* (1927): 'Sir Sidney Poole had asked me to dinner: Mrs Lintot had called me by my Christian name: and the Grand Duke Boris had said, quite distinctly, '*Monsieur, j'ai connu votre père* ... Lady Dury had bought a Tang horse.'

Had Lady Dury just bought a Thermos flask, Nicolson would not have thought it worth mentioning. Snobbery is a remarkable and profound prison system and certainly as characteristic as the age that created it. It can be attributed to Thackeray and dated quite precisely to the years when the laws of consumer culture were being established; *The Book of Snobs* was published in 1848. Snob was undergraduate slang for low-bred and – in a device later adopted by Nancy Mitford – Thackeray made it plain that it is snobbish to worry about snobbery.

Critics transferred this social game to the world of material things, where it became known as 'good' taste. Deadly competition burst out about what objects mean. It is remarkable how very charmless things regarded highly in 1850 appear today. When Owen Jones dreamt about interior design in *The Grammar of Ornament* (1856), 'There are no carpets worked with flowers whereon the feet would fear to tread, no furniture the hand would fear to grasp, no superfluous and useless ornament which a caprice has added and which an accident might remove,' his ideas sound astonishingly prescient, but the quickest glance at what Owen Jones himself designed shows that the words themselves flatter modern ears only to deceive contemporary eyes – his designs look as hideous as much of the stuff he reviled. While he praised those things in which 'nothing could be removed and leave the design equally good or better', the passage of time demonstrates that a good deal remained to be removed from designs of his own making.

The terms good taste and bad taste do not represent absolutes, but their usage is distinctive and telling, since it reveals the preferences and prejudices of particular social groups. They are crude ways of assigning value to things, but their validity derives only from the power and prestige of the social group that uses them. Most often, the value is not inherent in the object itself, but in the intention of its consumer. If good taste means anything, it is pleasing your peers; bad taste is offending them. But cultivated bad taste, or kitsch, can achieve either result.

Taste is more to do with manners than appearances. Taste is both myth and reality; it is not a style.

Taste, 1991

ON THE URBAN PLIGHT OF THE SWIRLY NUMBERPLATE (AND THE THREE-SPOKE ALLOYS)

'The less sophisticated the public, the greater the appeal of decoration,' at least according to the distinguished Marxist historian, Eric Hobsbawm. This area, where style crosses into manners, is a favourite territory of mine and I'm strongly inclined to agree with the professor.

Our Royal Family, for instance, has triumphantly resisted the snares and delusions of cosmopolitan aestheticism, and the results are there for all to see. Take the deplorable Queen Mother Gates in Hyde Park, a 'design' by a third-rate sculptor called David Wynn. Factor in Prince Charles's ludicrous architectural tastes for turrets and gables and Quality Street details and you'll agree that never in the history of human conflict has such a generous provision of visual nastiness been imposed on the public by so stingy a dynasty.

Back down on earth, there is no more certain sign of imbecility than the choice of non-standard numberplates, the ones where the alpha-numeric data have been prostituted into whoops and swirls creating a typographic effect suggestive of a Balinese cattery. For all its other absurdities, the Department of Transport has managed to create and legislate typographic standards for vehicle licence plates which are a model of clarity. The traditional big, square-cut characters are both legible and dignified. To want to change them into some bastard copperplate is irrefutable evidence of depravity or, at least, of a pitiably counterproductive initiative to be 'different'.

I recently saw a late-model Turbo Porsche cruising past those very same Queen Mother Gates. Painted in that distinctive metallic burgundy, here was a car that said, 'Rich and on the prowl,' as unambiguously as the case required. Yet the owner had replaced the standard-issue plates with something that looked as though it had come from the options list of a Chinese takeaway.

In this iconography of depravity there is one other

contemporary motif that is irrefutable evidence of low intelligence. This is the 'alloy' wheel with three spokes, which has become an important bit of heraldry in certain unsophisticated urban territories, especially the sort where you find Hoppa buses and doner kebab bars and grannies with body perforations. What offends here is the ignorance, even more than the crude urge to decorate. Just as the expressionist numberplate is a travesty of design since it departs from the very standards of clarity and uniformity vehicle numbering was intended to impose, so the three-spoke wheel is functionally and symbolically farcical.

All alloy wheels owe their credibility to the ghost of an idea that connects them to a superior world of competition, where lightweight components of a high specification are commonplace. Of course, no one believes that the split-rim 17-inch BBS alloys on a Saab cabrio auto turn it into a car capable of winning Le Mans, but the romantic association endures. Problem with the three-spokes is that no wheel with a mere trinity of supports has ever been seen on a successful competition car. With near tragic irony, the very same individuals who wish to lay claim to a culture of specialized componentry and put three-spokes on their 1991 Corsas merely demonstrate, in their melancholy taste for decoration, the profound depths of their very low brows.

These are all questions of taste. In this vexatious area there are few singular truths, but one is that nothing is more commonplace than the desire to be exceptional. Mass production demands standards and standards lead to perfection. The Queen Mother Gates, custom numberplates and three-spoke alloys all have their place in history: the dustbin of history. How much cooler it is to be ordinary and excellent than to wish to stand out.

Car Magazine, 1996

THE CHAMELEON OF FASHION

In 1967 you could, if so inclined, buy a Porsche 911 in a shade of toffee. This is a startling thing to write, but remember, if you were a bit of a follower-of-fashion, you'd be driving your caramel Carrera down the King's Road in damson-coloured crushed velvet flared loons with a lavender tank-top underneath a Fair Isle cardigan. You'd have aviator-style mirror shades, shoulder-length hair and quite possibly be wearing Danish clogs. 'Tuners' had not been invented – still less cassettes or CDs – so you'd be listening out on the radio to catch a whiff of the sensational 'Sergeant Pepper' in between what was then still the Light Programme's preference for Cliff Richard and Val Doonican … so misleading to call it 'easy' listening.

Ten years on, views about colour have changed, although gastronomic metaphors remain the most persuasive way of describing the Zeitgeistlich oddities of the contemporary Porsche palette. Toffee has been replaced by tangerine and lime. 'You can, sir,' I hear the salesmen saying, 'have it any colour you like so long as it's retina-searing orange or wince-inducing green.' Designers, being sensitive to these things, are more accurate barometers of taste than, say, plumbers or accountants, and it's noteworthy that they have often favoured the 911 on account of the purity of its design, if not – it has to be said – always on account of the purity of its colours. Lurid lime green 911s lured two of Britain's most influential designers during the mid-1970s.

Wally Olins, founder of Britain's pioneering corporate identity consultancy, Wolff Olins, the one which did for BT and the Pru, chose a 911 the colour of an irradiated frog during the period when he sported an intellectual-Afro. This car was eventually passed down to his successor, Brian Boylan, who, as the managing director of Wolff Olins in 1997, still drives it around Chelsea on Saturday mornings. Terence Conran – now in a current black 911 – once also had a bright green 911 and enjoyed the retinal rush so much he used it as a colour swatch for the Habitat warehouse. If you don't believe me, check out Wallingford now.

Few things are more eloquent of the spirit of the age than colour and, as in all matters of taste, it's not a question of absolutes, but of chaotic variables influenced by any number of indefinable, but nonetheless potent, factors. In architecture, it was always assumed that the ancient Greek temples were an austere, bleached, marmoreal whit ... at least until Jakob-Ignaz Hittorff (the architect of Paris's Gare du Nord) demonstrated via archaeological research that they were in fact vividly polychromatic.

In matters of fashion, the same variables apply both in culture and in time. Diana Vreeland once wittily remarked that 'pink is the navy blue of India' and while today few women would argue that you can have a cocktail dress in any colour so long as it's black, at the beginning of the last century an opera dress might have been in chamois-coloured Gaze de Smyrne, a ball dress in rose-coloured gauze over a fine gros de Naples and a walking-out dress in *gris lavande*.

The experimentation among Porsche owners which led from toffee via purple to tangerine and lime was an expression of a culture that was slowly coming to terms with the profligate variety of choice in modern consumer society. At just the moment when Terence Conran was stuck in traffic thinking about his *Bed and Bath Book*, a similar new liberality in colour choice was affecting the home as well as the Porsche showroom.

There are few terms more likely to stigmatize - note even 'patio', not even 'car port' - than 'avocado suite' another gastro-hue, this time the 1970s builders' equivalent of the psychedelic Porsche. A spokesman for the swanky estate agents Chesterton's, when asked for a reaction to receiving instructions on a house whose bathroom contained an 'avocado suite', said: 'I'd vomit.' Today bathrooms are certainly as white as 911s are ... well, we'll come to that later.

Like the tangerine and lime Porsche, the avocado suite was an expression of liberation from historic constraints. Each emerged from the primal soup of the automobile and sanitary ware industry's imagination during a period of bold chromatic experimentation. Visitors to early Habitats will recall bright red Polish enamel coffee pots. Circa 1970 the most popular colour for everyday cars was Positano Yellow. The geographical references suggested new cultural horizons as surely as the eclectic gastronomic ones: the avocado pear was, like its contemporary the courgette, a symbol of newly won middle-class refinement and adventure.

By the 1980s the avocado suite had disappeared and so too had the camel and tangerine and lime green Porsches. Instead, in this most over-confident of decades, new influences came to bear on colour choice. When someone comes to write the definitive study of consumer psychology, there will be a long chapter on the Porsche phenomenon of the 1980s. Here were cars which, long admired by fastidious individuals who took a serious interest in vehicle engineering, suddenly fell into the hands of over-paid striped shirts who might know the overnight yen-dollar exchange rate or the price of 1999 Spanish Fly, but couldn't define brake mean efficiency pressure or illustrate the Otto Cycle to save their world-beating collection of yellow silk ties or Church's shoes.

To these cuff-shooting individuals who stepped almost straight from BSM to bhp, the 911 became an element of personal heraldry, a statement about self more eloquent than even their braces or bonuses. And what colour did they specify for their Porsches? Not caramel, tangerine or lime (although Porsche's bespoke paint service could have provided anything not actually in the catalogue, including polenta yellow, tiramisu brown, Cajun black or Veuve-Clicquot orange). Instead, fully 27 per cent of mid-1980s' 911 customers chose Guards Red. This strong, elemental – even feral – colour seems in retrospect to be the psychological signature of the age. Red stands for danger, aggression and confidence. Those who found red too assertive chose white (19.2 per cent) or black (10.3 per cent). Interesting thing is there were no popular metallics: the 1980s was not a historical period much given to subtlety or refinement.

You could write a design history of the second half of the twentieth century simply by looking at the 911 and colours it was painted. It's an astonishing testament to the staying-power of the car that when the first 911 appeared (at exactly the time of The Beatles' first LP and just after the discovery of sexual intercourse) it was an engineering concept in recognizable descent from Dr Porsche's original Volkswagen. Since then The Beatles have come and gone and come again and gone again and a version of the 911 is still with us, although no longer in quite such obvious descent from the Volkswagen. The extraordinary mutation of the 911 has taken place against a kaleidoscopic background of changing colour preferences.

Perhaps in puritanical reaction to the excesses of the 1980s, Guards Red is now shunned by 911 customers. In 1995, less than one per cent were ordered in this colour and while this figure rose to less than two per cent in 1996, the trend towards fustian subtlety is clear. Today's 911 drivers don't wear double-breasted suits and shirts with square mile stripes and don't know what cuff-links are. Today's 911 driver is wearing a black moleskin jacket with a T-shirt or grey polo underneath. And his car is very dark blue or silver. In 1995 variations on dark blue and silver accounted for more than 70 per cent of 911 sales, dipping to 68 per cent in 1996. Look around in 1997 and you'll be able to confirm the trend.

Germans have a concept of Zeitlose Kunst, or 'timeless art'. The 911 shape qualifies here: it seems to be beyond the depredations of fashion. In the next millennium a Porsche whose body is clearly in descent from Ferdinand-Alexander's original drawing of 1963 will still be in production, a record for longevity exceeded only by the Mini.

It's this aesthetic resilience that makes the 911 such an accurate tell-tale of fashion. Rather as the great gourmet Brillat-Savarin said that chicken was to the chef what an empty canvas was to the painter, so is the 911 to colour. Line up best-sellers from the 1960s to today and you'd have a perfect record of contemporary taste. And here you have the rub.

The one thing certain about taste is that it changes. I wonder where all those toffee-coloured 911s are now … and when they're coming back.

The Marque, August 1997

FROG GREEN: The colour that was the cultural temperature of the 1970s: assertive, brash, an offence against good taste and deliberately so. But this shade of iridescent pond-life was also interestingly compromised, being a 'natural' colour but – in fact – barely so. Just wacky enough to be in touch with the 1960s acid rock peace-and-love, but also in its chemical intensity as suggestive of high-tech as it was of low-life. There was no great music from the 1970s, but there was a lot of great architecture. Before post-modernism made experimentation ridiculous, sassy 1970s industrial buildings in nursery paint-pot colours tested the limits of acceptability. So did Porsche's Frog Green.

GUARDS RED: For the me-first decade, Porsche's red provided the poetic chromatic expression. In both nature and culture, red is the colour of danger and aggression, of blood and fire. The 1980s was an aggressive, acquisitive, energetic decade and Guards Red articulated the Zeitgeist. Masters of the universe did not wear grey braces. To savour the depths of relevance just imagine a successful bond trader of 1985: making millions overnight, fuelled on vintage champagne and numbed by first-class air travel, rigid with adrenal rush. His car? Obviously a thrumming 911, the universal symbol of masculine success. Now what colour is it? Powder blue? Eau-de-Nil? Never! Money doesn't talk, it lies, and its fibs are solid red.

DARK BLUE: Two different shades of dark blue dominate late 1990s Porsche colour choices. For a period when conspicuous consumption is gauche and tactless, dark blue is the colour of discretion and good taste. Those who favour it are confident, assured and have no need of crude display plumage. The latest paint technology allows dark blues to generate lustres of special depth, appropriate to a generation of laid-back individuals who want to suggest that their success is fundamental, not superficial. Dark blue says, 'serious, intense, but very, very smart.' See the depth of my sheen? Read the fascination of my soul. I may be rich, but I appreciate quality.

SILVER: Silver, the racing colour of Germany in those quaint days when national identity meant more than the loyalties of football riots, is the one colour that is a historically consistent choice among Porsche buyers. Silver is the colour of technology. It is clean, bright, optimistic, but without frivolity. Black was too compromised by 1980s fashion to claim timelessness, but a silver Porsche approaches the absolute. It isn't a colour, it's a finish. It's not faddish, but beyond fashion. It's cold, hard and emotionally neutral. Unless, that is, you are the sort of person who gets carried away by the curvature of an alloy panel or the texture of a precious casting.

TASTE SENSATIONS UNFIT FOR HUMAN CONSUMPTION

In the jungle of values that represents our metaphoric confusion over taste, there are two clearings. One is appropriateness and the other is authenticity. In matters of aesthetics there are few certainties, but it is inescapably the case that things which give us consistent pleasure are appropriate and authentic rather than incongruous or bogus. That is why an electric kettle with a transfer 'design' of an ear of corn is so grotesque, and why anyone who would make, sell or own one is an irresponsible moron. Not that decoration in itself is wrong: it is simply that that sort of decoration is cynical, joyless and fraudulent. It is inappropriate and inauthentic.

There is something in the architecture of the brain that eventually makes us all long for the genuine and reject the fake. These are values which Brian Sewell, the art critic, would not flinch from supporting when writing about Goya or Rembrandt and their forgers, yet for as long as I have known him he has demonstrated a strong preference for being shod in running shoes, sometimes even with a suit. This, when his event is the vernissage on parquet floor and a little chilled Chardonnay, not the 400m. Sewell compounds the error by preferring running shoes in a spectrum of tan suede. This doubles the inappropriateness factor, although it does flatter his colouring.

Can there be anything less appropriate, anything less authentic, than someone who is not – or who is not about to be – engaged in athletic activity wearing running shoes and a track suit? Of all the possible solecisms, vulgarisms and errors of taste which consumer civilization provides, there is none so profound or unsettling as athletic shoes on the potbellied. The taste for pseudo-sporting garb is not restricted to art critics: shuffling grannies at Gatwick airport sport footwear which a generation ago would have attracted admiring glances in a White City locker room and conferred higher performance on the most accomplished sprinter. American tourists, in conditions of physical derelic-

tion and oedemic inflation so profound that they would risk rupturing vital organs if they did anything as energetic as mop their sweating brows, slump through Fortnum & Mason wearing track suits.

But maybe I should not be so prompt and severe in condemning a foible that is becoming universal: the taste for inappropriate use of trainers and sweats is as common in stylish Italy as it is in technocratic Germany and built-for-comfort Britain. The new Europrole has found his folk costume, and it is made of nylon and covered with speed flashes.

But fashion has consistently been invigorated by motifs lifted from the artisanal or the vernacular: the Edwardian gentleman's jacket was inspired by sailing costume; the classic tailored and waisted Savile Row suit coat derives from the cut of the huntsman's pink; jeans, Levi-Strauss's functional wear for miners in the Californian gold rush, became popular after wealthy Eastcoasters holidayed in desert bed and breakfasts in the Depression. This now universally accepted garment was originally the tough working trouser of Genoese sailors, hence 'jeans' from Genes, the French name for the Ligurian city.

Most famously, Coco Chanel was inspired by artisanal dress and sailor suits, creating designs of timeless elegance. I can go on. The slip-on loafer derives from the aboriginal American running moccasin, much favoured as a hunting and gathering accessory; it would be tautological to explain the polo shirt's origins, but it is another example of sports clothing finding its way out of the kitbag and into the wardrobe.

There is a wide range of precedent when it comes to the assumption of sporting, working or sailing motifs into mainstream fashion. Can we therefore assume that the evolution of the wardrobe will eventually entail absorption of trainers, sweatpants and jockstraps into the established repertoire? Will the next generation of Wildsmith shoes make deferential gestures towards the garish iconography of Adidas? Are the tailors at Anderson & Sheppard studying shell suits? Are the grannies of Gatwick fashion pioneers? I think not.

The difference between Coco Chanel's inspiration and Mr and Mrs Vauxhall-Nova wearing garish, high-specification polymer warm-up suits on shopping trips to Kwiksave is that one is artful, the other artless. The squeamish do not like to think in this way, but it has to be said that trainers and track suits are an overwhelmingly proletarian vice: John Major wore running shoes with what he probably calls 'slacks' at his last Washington press conference. Maybe he thought this was classless when, of course, it was quite the opposite: someone so sensitive to the nuances of social slighting should be aware of the aesthetic horror of what he did. At least George Bush actually runs.

In Gateshead's Metro Centre, slack-bottomed people-who-eat-sweets-and-smoke are at ease with themselves, gaily caparisoned in comfy sweats with drawstring waists and elasticated cuffs at the ankle, while ten years ago they would have been in Major slacks and sandals. Meanwhile at a recent party, where guests with names to drop included Bunter Soames, Alistair McAlpine and Mark Birley, there was not an Adidas, Puma, Nike, Reebok, Hi-Tec, LA Gear, Champion or Russell Athletic logo in sight. Yet one of the frontliners in the class war chooses to dress as though he is in training for Barcelona. What is going on?

There are two reasons for this dreadful eruption of trainers and sweats in places where trainers and sweats were not designed to be. The first is comfort. Ingeniously, the prole in the jogging suit has discovered by chance one of the chief attractions of fine quality single-needle tailoring: a sense of relaxation that confers gentlemanly languor on Soames, McAlpine and Birley, even as it corrupts still further the already simian posture of the man on the charter flight to the Costas.

The perfect fit of a Savile Row suit is one of its greatest and least understood attractions: the reason the English gentleman acquired his reputation for being easy-going is that his suit does not pull around the armholes or constrict his breathing. His handmade shoes do not cause blisters. Inappropriate it may be, but cladding in sports kit achieves these same ergonomic advantages for strangers to Jermyn Street, but at some cost to beauty.

The other reason is imagery. Because of exceptional advertising, sports clothes achieved outstanding visibility during the past decade. Possession of branded trainers offered a frisson of the 1980s' pay-and-display experience. This led to, and was supported by, considerable growth in leisure activity and, later, what you might call leisure inactivity.

It started in California in 1983, when an agency called Chiat/Day began a noteworthy series of gigantic billboard advertisements for Nike, featuring Carl Lewis and other celebrity athletes. Creatively, these broke moulds. There is a basic distinction in the world of advertising that says ads are either 'image' or 'claim'. Chiat/Day's ads for Nike made no claims, but were dense with image power. Daringly, one Lewis billboard had him jumping off the edge, breaking through the frame as well as the mould. The ads caused more jams on the freeways and helped Nike to achieve iconic status. In retrospect, the stylish, aggressive solipsism of these ads, their celebration of effort and achievement, make them articulate, evocative period pieces.

More than any other company, Nike is responsible for the transition of sports kit from athletic necessity to lowbrow cladding. Nike is a phenomenal success, its phenomenal success a cameo of the Zeitgeist. Founded in 1956 by Bill Bowerman and Phil Knight, students at the University of Oregon (one of America's great athletic schools), Nike began by importing Onitsuka Tiger running shoes from Japan.

At the time, German manufacturers such as Adidas dominated the athletic shoe business. Nike was small, studious and, until the 1970s, modest. A tradition of diligent research developed lightweight nylon uppers in 1966; hitherto, athletic shoes had been leather. At first the preference was to sign up athletes rather than advertising agencies: Ilie Nastase was the first to wear them (for a retainer of $2,500).

An amazing fusion of logo and celebrity was followed in 1979, after the detailed study of some 5,000 feet, by 'Air' technology. This pneumatic form of cushioning created a new standard of comfort. Soon Connors, Coe, Ovett, Decker, Cram, Botham and McEnroe were wearing and endorsing Nike; later Jordan, Krabbe and Agassi. Their popularity, the global explosion of television sports and supremely effective advertising combined to create an international image bank of sweaty heroes whose projected character also seemed to be the character of the age. In an aggressive decade, celebrity athletes were convenient shorthand symbols for prowess and achievement. Possession of same-brand foot and outerwear was the consumer's introduction to sympathetic magic.

The annus mirabilis of sports kit was 1987, when Nike introduced the concept of the 'crosstrainer'. There was a moment when austere technical considerations gave way to more smutty marketing ones. Future fashion historians will consider the crosstrainer the start of a dubious season in fashion. In strict athletic terms it is a functional nonsense: serious athletes need shoes dedicated to a sport. In fact, Nike's crosstrainer was a comfortable, durable shoe for people who did not take any sporting discipline very seriously.

From it developed the notorious ghetto heraldry of the hightop, chief item in a solemn underclass liturgy with elaborate shades of meaning: status can depend on the precise length of the tongue and your attitude to doing up your laces. A kind of international uniform was being created, one which makes an obscure, misguided – but very strong – appeal to notions of international glamour.

It was a small step from the crosstrainer, an athletic shoe for people who do not do athletics, to the sweats and shell suits for people who could not tell a block from a hurdle and have heart-lung functions to prove it. Is it just Olympian snobbery to deplore the vogue for inappropriate sports clothing? No, because it debases a powerful symbolic language. Symbols can only retain meaning if there is a ghost of substance behind their use: the track suit and the trainer will cease to mean anything if candidates for

EMT (emergency medical treatment) continue to wear them in supermarkets and theme parks during their QLT (quality leisure time).

But wait a minute. Maybe what seems to be barbaric degeneration is assuming an evolutionary pattern, a Darwinian dynamic, of its own. The trainers and track suits of the shuffling classes are now so distinct from their source in real athletic kit that they constitute a new category of dress, but do not even think about it if you stigmatize easily: ridiculousness is too high a price to pay for comfort. On the other hand, appropriateness and authenticity are never out of fashion. Wear a track suit and trainers for any activity not bound to increase your pulse to 130-plus and you are lost in the jungle.

The Times Saturday Review, 11 July 1992

LUXURY – A DATED CONCEPT IN THE 1990s

Luxury, at least as defined by many of the goods people accumulate, is vulgar and venal. Luxury, in my observation is not necessarily about pleasure, but more likely about excess.

Other than a meretricious and crass display of wealth, there is no good reason, for example, why taps should be gold. In a sense, luxury is the opposite of design. Industrial civilization has the potential to provide the best goods and services to the entire population at a modest cost and, miserable as we may be in this fin-de-siècle, it is a fact that for many Western citizens this paradise has been achieved.

That is what all the early Modernist Bauhaus theory was concerned with. Now stigmatized by those who would often wilfully aim to misunderstand them, Modernist architects and designers were not trying to impose an austere machine aesthetic on the glum and downtrodden people of Europe. Rather, the metal furniture and concrete houses were just making the best of materials available, making the most of contemporary possibilities. The classics of modern design made a popular form of luxury commonplace in that for the first time in history, efficient, safe and beautiful furniture and appliances became universal. That the word 'luxury' now connotes something more vulgar and expensive than a Breuer chair or a Citroën 2cv is both a repudiation of the Modernist adventure and a reaction to it.

The rot set into the meaning of 'luxury' in Britain when, some time in the 1950s, a hotshot marketeer working for Ford, the motor company, decided that a premium-priced model of the Ford Anglia might be ennobled with the name 'de luxe'. In the poetics of car specifications, de luxe meant the addition of external chrome strips, elaborated mouldings around the rear light clusters and two-tone upholstery. It was hard for words to recover from such debasement.

In America, where the achievement of status has long been measured in terms of accumulated possessions, the idea of luxury has acquired a fetishistic quality. It can be defined by a powerful and evocative list of artefacts. In her autobiography, Ali McGraw, the actress, describes her astonishment on arrival in Hollywood. The house was mock Georgian on a huge plot, with an artificially fed 300-year-old sycamore. There were scented candles (a sure definition of luxury at work) and in the linen cabinets hundreds of bars of Guerlain soap. She cannot have been under anything other than a very clear impression that this was a luxury dwelling.

Although Flaubert, in his sardonic *Dictionnaire des idées réçus* posed as the *homme sérieux* and defined luxury as 'the ruin of nations,' the French are more confidant with their tastes and sense than the English or the Americans.

There is something marvellous about French culture which allows intellectual rigour to go hand-in-hand with intense sensual delight. The best French cooking or wine is a challenge to the intellect as much as to the palate; and while the German Modernists of the 1920s were doggedly making severe and honourable metal furniture out of discarded industrial components, Le Corbusier's 'Grand Confort' armchair kept the Modernist faith, but was also a supremely elegant, comfortable and luxurious artefact.

The tradition continues: Andrée Putman is perhaps the leading European interior designer. She is rigidly modernist, but sensible of her clients' and their customers' needs. She says: 'To God and to artists all materials are the same.' This is a sophisticated belief that unites the purist ethics of modern design with the sensitivity of a mondaine sensualist. No gold taps here.

But, if in general, luxury and modern design are at variance, then in the past decade they have been at war. London and Paris have long established tradesmen-craftsmen houses specializing in luxury goods, whether Lobb shoes, Purdey shotguns, Swaine Adeney & Brigg saddlery, Cartier watches, Christofle silver or Baccarat glass.

So influential are these makers of exclusive premium-priced personal-ware that entire personalities are defined by them. In France, a certain type of woman is known by the deadly accurate acronym 'FHCP': Foulard Hermès, Collier de Perles. In this way, luxury goods define their customers in a process which anthropologists would recognize.

In France the luxury goods business is taken seriously. With typical French panache for bureaucracy, 71 luxury goods makers (including Louis Vuitton, Hermès, Cartier, Dior and Chanel) have formed the portentously titled Comité Colbert, as if to suggest *mallettiers*, *vignerons* and *joailliers* are providing the continuity of French artistic culture. Despite the recession, the Comité Colbert reports rising sales.

One explanation of this may be psychological. A Paris psychiatrist called Michel Lejoyeux says he has identified a form of obsessive-compulsive disorder which seeks gratification from buying things, as if the act of purchasing (irrespective of eventual use) establishes power and authority over a harrowing world.

But the real explanation of the continued demand for luxury goods is social and aesthetic rather than psychological. The twentieth century has made the major Western economies rich in that most own, or have access to, a range of machines from the car through the video to the cellphone to the occasional use of a Boeing 747. Marinetti's dream of motorways and aircraft is part of our daily routine. As soon as those things – which by their familiarity and accessibility are a triumph of our civilisation – become everyday, the insecure or the greedy will seek specialist treatment. This is where the taste for gold taps comes from.

It is why Donald Trump sends out morocco-bound invitations to his latest pleasure palace. It explains the astonishing demand for the S-class Mercedes-Benz, a car of boastfulness and arrogance three times more expensive than other cars in its class.

The greedy and insecure take refuge in this limited definition of luxury. They can find another version of it in the immature, brackish splendour of, say, London's new Lanesborough Hotel. But in truth is there not something inadequate about definitions of luxury which entail exclusiveness, expense and rarity? Are not luxury goods consumers living in a costly fantasy world? Of course, but maybe that is the source of the pleasure.

In times of excess, real pleasure is defined by experience rather than merchandise. Only the most curmudgeonly would deny that lunch in Paris's Crillon Hotel is a life-enhancing experience.

But then I look around and feel glad I do not have gold taps. In a crowded world the great challenge is to make life more simple and less complicated. Real luxury is the ability to choose how to spend your time and arrange your space.

'Luxury' goods may be of supreme quality and may confer a certain cachet in the village long-hut of the international rich, but the concept is dated and limited.

Sixty years ago, in *The Price of Things*, Elinor Glyn had a character say: 'If one consciously and deliberately desires happiness ... one must have sufficient strength of will to banish all thought.' Writing today,

she would banish luxury.

Financial Times, 21-22 November 1992

A DISPUTATION ABOUT TASTE

Taste is an outrageous subject. Among a generation habituated to detailed and po-faced discussions of minutely sophisticated sexual preferences, of overdrafts, mass murder and treachery, the mere suggestion that there might be objectifiable standards by which we can judge quality in the man-made world provokes a response most familiar from the black magic novels of Dennis Wheatley where, if you sprinkle holy water over the embodiment of the Anti-Christ you get an effect which includes the rolling of eyeballs, the tongue clamped between teeth munching it in a spastic staccato, and a general purpling of the countenance.

The Visitors' Book at the recent *Taste* exhibition I arranged in the Victoria & Albert Museum's Boilerhouse provoked on its first day this entry from a commentator identifying himself as 'Sloane Basher':

> 'Ga! Burn it all! Back to Hampstead and Henley with y'all. Yeurgh. Who is this man?'

Everybody feels proprietorial about taste. The Romans were sure that there was no good to be had by disputing about it, but a crisis of values, brought about in part by the perceived failure of the Modern movement in architecture to redress all the social evils its heroic pioneers set up as their targets, has left people suspicious of order and of rules. The attitudes which define the limits of that crisis can be found in the pages of the same Visitors' Book: what was 'unobtrusively intelligent' to one signatory was 'bollocks' to another.

So there is some disputing about taste, although this was not always the case. To the literati of the eighteenth century it was an absolute, not susceptible to change or modification. Sir Joshua Reynolds said that any 'reasonable' man could achieve it. But Reynolds was speaking for only one social class, in his case the ruling one, although the very fact that he needed to speak about it at all suggests that he saw the approaching crevasse into which his academic ideals were going to tumble. The industrial revolution called mass consumption into being and almost every citizen became a consumer, with a chance to exercise his taste. From that moment taste was no longer a synonym for idealistic quality in the visual or the literary arts, but it became a means of tribal identification.

We are the inheritors of that movement, which first of all identified taste with morals and ideology and then, later, identified it with social class. It was Henry Cole and John Ruskin, those most influential of nineteenth-century engineers of the soul, who persuaded their public that certain forms of decoration and certain means of production were necessarily appropriate for their age. It was at this moment that taste surreptitiously acquired its familiar qualitative adjectives, 'good' and 'bad.'

The coupling of taste with morality also for the first time locked the business of making judgements about the design of the material world into the Western dissident tradition. Just as Weber had seen in the structure of Luther's Reformation anticipation of the capitalist work ethic, and just as later commentators have seen in Marx's concept of deferred gratification the ghost of the Christian heaven, so the nineteenth century's reforms in taste and design brought another form of materialism into line with another form of morals. It was this very assumption of rectitude which lent so much force to the Modern movement in the twentieth century: with the Calvinist intolerance of Le Corbusier and the Prussian dogmatism of Walter Gropius a particular 'taste' for minimal decoration, combined with the machine aesthetic, became identified with what was 'good' in design.

But it was in America – where Russell Lynes established the terms highbrow, middlebrow and lowbrow – that taste, or, at least, a preference for a particular style of architectural decoration, became identified with social class. Here, Elsie de Wolfe's

House in Good Taste (1915) was the key work. While there had been earlier books on household management (typified in 1869 by Catherine Beecher and Harriet Beecher Stowe's *The American Woman's Home*) which included tips on decoration and interior design, it was Elsie de Wolfe who first perceived taste as a marketable commodity.

Her book began as a series of articles commissioned by Theodore Dreiser for a middle-class journal, *The Delineator*. De Wolfe, who scaled several vertiginous peaks as a social climber, performed the remarkable feat of introducing new American money to old French furniture. Although she ushered into American homes a form of brightness with her motto 'plenty of optimism and white paint,' and replaced the brooding dark stains and damasks of colonial Victoriana with an anticipation of Modernism, her devotion to French antiques introduced an almost irrevocable inertia into upper-class taste. In terms of the prospects for modern furniture design, Russell Lynes called it 'defeatism in high places.'

The same reaction to novelty in interior design as been a prominent characteristic of upper-class taste in Britain. In *Noblesse Oblige* (1956), the *locus classicus* of English snobbery, Alan Ross observed that, like Gaul, the class system was divided into three parts and that while social progress meant that ' ... a member of the upper class is ... not necessarily better educated, cleaner or richer than someone not of this class...' the upper class was distinguished almost solely by tribal signs, symbols and attitudes. Ross observed a preference for games such as real tennis and picquet, together with a dislike for technical innovations, including the telephone, cinema and (as it was then known) wireless. This last loftily proclaimed disdain was a reminiscence in the 1950s of the 'fatal newness' which Ruskin had noticed and condemned in modern machine-made furniture a century before.

The three parts of Ross's English class system translate neatly into the three journalistic clichés of taste in modern Britain: the flying-ducks caste (a preference in interior decoration which survives only in the imaginations of certain feature writers);

Habitat modern (a dim generalization: Habitat does not sell one style, but many) and the Sloane caste. Ann Barr and Peter York's trademark-laden 1980s' version of Nancy Mitford's U and non-U. Each class has its preference in taste, but each is becoming more aware that, at least as perceived by your peers, you are what you own and, by extension, you can become what you can acquire.

Or can you?

In some eyes, huge changes in the international nature of consumption and production will shortly bring local tribal variations to an end.

A notable article by Theodore Levitt was published in the *Harvard Business Review* (May-June, 1983). Called 'The Globalization of Markets,' it spoke of Iranian mullahs in new man trousers, dwellers in Bahian bidonvilles watching Sony and driving Volkswagens, Biafran soldiers consuming Coca-Cola and McDonalds on the Champs Elysées. It even claimed that the rare and intrepid Western travellers who reach the Siberian city of Krasnoyarsk are often importuned for digital watches and solid-state calculators. Levitt addressed himself to the major manufacturing corporations and told them that they '... must learn to operate as if the world were one large market – ignoring superficial regional and national differences ... ' and defiantly announced that '... the world's needs and desires have been irrevocably homogenized ...'.

Beguiling as the dream must be to global corporations (and apparently to Levitt) that national tastes will disappear under a mountainous wave of homogeneous products, the argument did not acknowledge the existence of a taste for variety and symbolism – a taste which, if accepted only as a general level in Isfahan, Bahia and Biafra, is developed to great states of sophistication within these shores. Moreover, Levitt's view of the performance and deportment of some great multinationals charitably attributed omniscience to them, an opinion that scrutiny of Coca-Cola's and Sony's recent balance sheets could not support. More critically still, Levitt's article dismissed the possibility that changing means of production, brought about by new

technology, might alter consumer appetites and enhance manufacturers' capacity to satisfy them.

Perhaps Theodore Levitt does not know that nowhere else in the world are markets so stratified as in Britain. Despite the prophecies of journalists who rely on the stripped-pine cliché as their sole source of figurative language, Habitat will not overwhelm the entire face of Britain because the people who plan where the stores go are sure that there is a finite number of locations where they can operate profitably and they are already now approaching that number. In another, more literal, matter of taste, Britain has uniquely strong culinary preferences tied to its regions: there is little hope or fear of a certain style of cooking, presently fashionable in the capital and those starred haunts in the west country, ever catching on in, say, the west midlands: a pink rack of lamb and *al dente* beans that would earn a breathless hush elsewhere would be rejected as raw in Kidderminster. Similarly in fashion: Paul Smith makes subtle, traditional men's suits and he clothes regiments of board-level 'creative people' in all of Covent Garden. He is their darling, but Smith (who comes from Nottingham) readily acknowledges that his clothes cannot be sold outside London: beyond the capital the well-to-do market demands clothing that speaks more vividly of affluence than Smith's hard-won, soft-spoken style.

These strong variations are a potential basis for a revival of British consumer-good manufacturing. While the old smokestack industries decline and Dunlop sells out its tyre-making facilities to Sumitomo, the British are meanwhile unobtrusively building a national information structure which will be the railway of the future. With its per capita population of video recorders and computers at present the highest in the world, Britain has an information network that will not eradicate traditional distinctions, but will help to maintain them. The factory of the future will not be a single manufacturing plant turning out sinks or castings fifty thousand dozen a day, with long lead times and low unit costs only if absolutely everybody buys the same one. The factory of the future will use flexible manufacturing so that one day the supervisory computer will teach the production line robots to do one kind of onerous task, the next day another. These factories will not necessarily be owned by a single concern, but will be used from time-to-time by different entrepreneurs and designers to make products which are momentarily responsive to popular taste.

The prospect of the future is not Theodore Levitt's, with its Chamber of Commerce vision of a Levi for every rump, but one of greater variety in matters of taste and consumption.

To extract the most flavour from the future every consumer will have to define more thoroughly what he and she wants and expects from the products which stock the material world: the customer will have to know himself better than he does today. He might even have to discover that delicious sort of solipsism which has been central to every influential taste-maker of the past. Choice will become real when, one day, the ordinary consumer can eye a product and say, as Elsie de Wolfe did of the Parthenon: 'It's beige! *My* colour!'

New Society, 22-29 December 1983

OUTING THE CLOSET

I once attended a very smart party in Milan, in one of the magnificently gloomy apartment blocks that surround the centre of this most urbane of cities. The host was an architect, savouring the afterglow of a double-headed *succès de curiosité*: a lavish book and an even more lavish shop design.

Women with Titian hair and men in fastidiously rumpled wild silk suits chatted solemnly. The vista was enormous. There was low-voltage lighting with complex little bulbs giving starbursts of hard white light; there were lush, low-slung banquettes and tinted glass and marble. Marble? Well, yes, this *was* Italy, but it took me half an hour to realize that the party was being held in a bathroom.

The progress of the bathroom from being a closet for intimate ablutions to a showpiece – occasionally

for entertaining – has been slow. Yet there is no doubt that the provision of hygiene has always been a mark of civilization; the bathroom a cradle of harmonious, civilized life. It also has a political character. A Bolshevik once remarked that there could not be any revolution in America as the citizens were too clean, 'You can't feel revolutionary in a bathroom,' he concluded. But you can feel a lot of other things, embarrassment being the most familiar.

The set of verbal evasions we use to refer to a bathroom is evidence of its symbolic importance in our lives. In American English, 'bathroom' is a euphemism for lavatory. A tourist at London Zoo, witnessing an elephant evacuate with spectacular and steaming effect, explained to her child: 'Look, darling, he's going to the bathroom.'

Anxiety about bodily functions goes deep in Western culture. It is not simply a trait of sexually repressed Anglo-Saxons. Even priapic Greeks vaguely referred to the lavatory as *to menos* or 'the place'. The oldest term in English is 'privy', suggestive of seclusion and intimacy, just like (water) closet.

The design of the bathroom evolved out of the design of the bedroom. Around 1900, at least in grand country houses, they were aesthetically indistinct. Clearly, a part of the house in which so much of the semantics of seclusion have been invested is not the most obvious place to make assertive style statements. But over the past generation, the bathroom has attracted more attention from designers.

Strange, then, that in the glossary of shorthand terms that stigmatizes any house style there is none, not even 'patio', not even 'car port', so evocative of a type-to-be-avoided than 'avocado suite'. When I phoned Chesterton's, the estate agents, and asked their reaction to receiving instructions on a house with a bathroom containing an 'avocado suite', a spokeswoman said: 'I'd vomit.'

Hampton's agreed that pure white was what was expected in central London, especially when Far Eastern clients were involved (although

Chesterton's did say, rather mysteriously, that the Middle Eastern community around Marble Arch was more tolerant of avocado suites than other easily identifiable groups). Another factor influencing the acceptance of coloured bathroom suites among houseowners who are not drop-dead smart is that the softer water in the suburbs made rainbow and greenhouse shades more scum-tolerant, a rare and wonderful conjunction of chemistry and taste.

How did the avocado suite so ingloriously break the established tyranny of white in the bathroom? The late 1960s, when it first emerged from the primal soup of the sanitaryware industry's imagination, was a period of bold chromatic experimentation, as visitors to early Habitats will recall. They may even have their bright red Polish enamel coffee-pots to jog the memory. At about the same time, the avocado 'pear', like the courgette, emerged as a symbol of newly won lower-middle-class refinement. Enter the avocado suite: to the modishness of the exotic avocado was added the cloying francophonic 'suite'.

It was introduced by Armitage Ware (now Armitage Shanks) in September 1969, and for the next ten years was their best-selling colour. Why exactly it became an industry standard remains a mystery. There is a story, probably apocryphal, that someone over-ordered a consignment by a factor of ten, so they were pushed out to builders' merchants at knock-down rates. The result was that any bodge-artist turning a depressing Cricklewood semi into even more depressing self-contained flats could buy one on the cheap.

The question of colour is fundamental. 'Plenty of optimism and white paint' was Elsie de Wolfe's stirring motto for the interior design profession, which she virtually created. The symbolism of hygiene enforced the preference for white in the bathroom, but then industrialization took over. There is an unwritten (but universally acknowledged) law that man's ability to manufacture things runs a step ahead of his ability to use them with taste.

In fact, avocado was *never* considered highly fashionable. Manufacturers of bathroom fittings collaborate on their choice of colours to ensure that, for example, a plastic bath and a ceramic bidet match. They put avocado – with 'Pampas' and 'Sun King' and 'Honeysuckle'– in a more sophisticated category than white, turquoise, pink, primrose or sky blue, but less sophisticated than dark red, dark blue or brown.

As avocado suites are weeded out, houseowners are increasingly seeing the bathroom as a status symbol. A tentative language of approved design is emerging. Statistics suggest that priorities for home improvement are first kitchen, then bathroom, then central heating.

Indeed, the only room other than the kitchen that is fitted is the bathroom. It has not yet reached that zenith of systematized design represented by the modern German kitchen manufacturers, for it is still a much more private area than a kitchen, with a level of expenditure proportionately smaller (although the evidence shows that this figure is increasing).

Germans dominate the supply of bathroom hardware, at least at the top of the market: Villeroy & Boch in pottery items, Hansgrohe in shower fittings and Bette or Duker with baths.

The language of bathroom design remains altogether more flexible than that of the kitchen, so how it will evolve as it assumes a greater prominence in the home is unclear. Predictions of the late 1970s about future patterns are now risible. The idea that the 1990 bathroom would take its style cues from *A Clockwork Orange*, Nasa mission control, Montessori schools and exercise bikes – in dark green – did not gain common assent, even in the age of the avocado suite.

The bathroom will not become a public place until we lose the last of our inhibitions. This gives us a long time to take pleasure from the conceits and pretensions, the laudable triumphs and the laughable failures of designers and ambitious individuals as they struggle against generations of neglect to make the bathroom an interesting place. Strange to say, the avocado suite was a step in the right direction.

The Times Magazine, 16 July 1994

The styles:

LUTYENS – No other name summarizes so completely that boiling stew of nostalgia and longing represented by the English country house. Its bathroom is a phrasebook for travellers in an imaginary past: note free-standing roll-rim bath, stuffed birds or other treasured possessions, battered leather club chair and (possibly) piles of Sotheby's sales catalogues. The lavatory seat will be made of mahogany, and while sitting upon it you can savour the smell of kedgeree coming up the stairs.

PAWSON – John Pawson has established a richly evocative minimalist style. But it is minimal in name only, since the dramatically reduced contents of one of his bathroom designs disguise a whole catalogue of references from Japanese wash-houses to medieval charterhouses. Pawson is a designer of genius whose radically simple spaces and forms – flush-fitting doors with hidden ironmongery, monoliths of granite – are dramatic proof of how richly satisfying simplicity can be.

PUTMAN – Andrée Putman has been described as the Simone de Beauvoir of French interior design. She has made a stylized and gussied-up version of Parisian art deco her signature. A Putman bathroom is dazzlingly tiled in monochrome ceramic with unforgiving angles. Accessories are made of chrome or stainless steel.

RAMADA RENAISSANCE – The well-travelled, middle-ranking executive likes to replicate his hotel bathroom in Camberley. Note the 'marbled' basin top, light grey tiles, stainless steel finishings, pot plant, white terry robes and little baskets of complimentary soap. This fatigued version of modernism is now a Euro-norm.

The details:

BASKET OF LOO ROLLS – A nicely utilitarian expression of prosperity and generosity.

BATH MAT – Unless matched to the towels, evidence of depravity.

BIDET – Still a token of polish and refinement, especially if used to store literary novels.

CARPET – A misbegotten and short-lived luxury. Cork tiles, woodblock or terrazzo are better floor coverings.

DECORATED TILES – Ethnic imports are allowable (but only just); domestic versions with keylines evoke a world of cheap laminates, plastic knobs and self-tapping screws.

FREE-STANDING ROLL-RIM BATH – The ultimate in bathroom prestige.

PLANTS – No, not under any circumstances, not even pot-pourri.

GOLD TAPS – An aesthetic solecism so profound that even ironic use is unacceptable.

SALT AND OILS – Here there is clear evolution and a distinct hierarchy. Bath salts were replaced by Badedas, now displaced by expensive oils in handsome glass jars. Penhaligon's is the best, followed by Czech & Speake and Floris.

SOAP-ON-A-ROPE – Rhymes with dope.

SUNKEN TUB – In all civilizations there is no surer sign of decadence.

THE CABINET ROOM

There is something cruelly revealing about the kitchen, for it is a laboratory of taste. Here people experiment with style, and ambitions and credentials are stripped bare for inspection. It is the modern equivalent of the games or trophy room, a mixture of utility and comfort, a place where passions are on display.

Kitchen style suggests aspiration, and details form a rich symbolic language. Few things betray an individual's sophistication or slovenliness more accurately than the state of the kitchen. The sight of a well-scrubbed and pleasingly worn chopping board is a marvellous character reference.

The preparation of good food is a moral matter as notions of nutrition, function and well-being are closely allied. So it follows that the place where food is prepared has a special role in culture. To know the correct saucepan is just as important as choosing the correct ingredients. Someone who thinks they can 'make do' is not to be trusted.

For many, the kitchen is the most romantic room in any house. Certainly, it is increasingly the one people head for. Harassed commuters, bruised metropolitan souls take refuge there. A generation or two ago, you threw off your coat and had a gin and tonic in the library or drawing room. Today you go to the fridge and unplug a bottle of sauvignon blanc and stare at the cereal packets while you wonder where the day went. A whole culture of design has grown up to fulfil our expectations about the kitchen environment. But is there such a thing as an 'ideal' kitchen?

A great deal of romance is involved in any definition. When the American food writer M. F. K. Fisher acquired her own kitchen in Dijon in 1929 she said it was: 'Perhaps 5ft long, and certainly not more than 3ft wide. Its floor of uneven baked tiles was scoured to a mellow pinkness. There were two weak shelves, slanting towards the floor. A two-burner gas plate on a tottering table was the stove. To stand at it I had to keep the door open into the other room, but that was all right. The door had been stuck open for several decades.'

That description represents a starting point. In the subsequent history of its design the kitchen reveals our changing – sometimes uneasy – relationship with machines as well as our increasingly sophisticated attitude to leisure and to style. In architectural terms, the kitchen has evolved in exact parallel with advanced consumer tastes.

The kitchen emerged from below-stairs to become an all-purpose middle-class entertainment suite in the 1930s when pioneer modernists – the machine romantics Walter Gropius, Le Corbusier and their followers – tentatively sketched the sculptural possibilities of explicitly mechanical plant in their kitchen designs. Photographs of Le Corbusier's luxury villas show kitchens looking like sewage plants. Soon this uncompromising rhetoric was civilized and socialized by the Americans, who gave us the streamlined fitted kitchen of the 1950s and 1960s. Frigidaires, styled to look like Flash Gordon's flight-deck, were designed by the same man who styled the Chevrolet Bel Air.

American equipment, in all its over-engineered, massively proportioned indestructibility, is still the ultimate, but the British were as uneasy with the streamlined kitchen as they were incapable of realizing it effectively. While the scale and budget of an American home allowed kitchen equipment designers to create technophile fantasies on a cinematic scale, British domestic attempts at the modern kitchen were depressingly half-hearted, not least because there was another ideal always nagging at the native imagination.

It's a commonplace that the British were captivated by Elizabeth David (who said that, in the bleak post-war context in which she worked, just to mention 'lemon' or 'garlic' was pornography). The link between appetites and interior design was made law by Terence Conran. It was a short step from making, say, *chou farci* to wanting a kitchen which provided an appropriate working environment to do so. The original Habitat idea and its subsequent developments have left Britain with a generation which knows, through terracotta and wood and simple kitchen tools, how to unlock the romance hinted at by M. F. K. Fisher and has left Conran himself with the most frequently photographed kitchen in Britain.

Since Conran made the ineffable link of 'terracotta = Provence', a rich kitchen semiotics has developed, illustrated in the lush photographs of the manufacturers' catalogues. Certain styles are always propped with certain comestibles, to strengthen and reinforce their meaning and their appeal to the market. There is infinite variety here, but to offer an example of the codes:
- limed oak: a bottle of *vinaigre de l'estragon* (slightly sophisticated)
- stainless: an intimidatingly massive hunk of provolone (very sophisticated)
- old pine: Schwartz dried spices (unsophisticated), washed pine – loose brown eggs, antique cider crocks (innocent)
- 'Provence': terracotta, capsicums, a garlic clove, half a lemon, an uncooked chicken spattered with dried herbs (aspirational)
- brightly coloured: racily shaped champagne flutes (filthy rich)
- 'traditional': dried flowers, copper pans, Windsor chairs (credulous)

But this cosy kitchen of the imagination has been invaded by industrial forces. In 1958, in *French Provincial Cooking*, Elizabeth David could write with conviction that French was the language of the kitchen. Twenty years later, thanks to the influence of Conran, it was still the same. But now the kitchen is increasingly German. Not that factory-fresh Bratwurst has replaced the great set pieces of *estouffade de bœuf cassoulet* or *coq au vin*, but it } is German manufacturers which dominate the industry of fitted kitchens, especially the overtly technical ones with those hectares of medicinal whiteness and uncompromising stainless steel. There seems to be something about the manufacture of kitchen furniture that suits the German love of systematic processes.

Bulthaup, perhaps the most accomplished of all the Germans, produces a range of more than 600,000 separate elements: handles, doors, baskets, rails and bins in an astonishing variety. You could assemble more kitchens from the Bulthaup catalogue than there are atoms in the universe.

The great influence on Bulthaup design was the late Otl Aicher, an austere German designer of the uncompromising Ulm school. Aicher has also been responsible for the beautifully clear graphics on BMW instrument panels, but he was never known for his gayness and frivolity. When it was once suggested that an exhibition he designed might be a tad clearer if he used tiny coloured dots to articulate distinctions between dazzlingly similar white panels, he turned on a look of apoplectic rage and shrieked: 'Vot! You want to make a pop artist?'

Whether you want to pretend you are working in the executive kitchen of Deutsche Bank or preparing a simple little *plein* air lunch for twelve friends in your *masse* at St Rémy is a simple aesthetic preference. The real determinants of kitchen design are functional ones. Strip the glossy laminate off a German unit or peel back layers of Wiltshire limed and fretted oak and you'll see that the underlying structure is identical.

The influential gourmet 'Curnonsky' had the best definition of good cooking: when 'ingredients taste of what they are'. The same can be said of kitchen design: the functional imperative is paramount; the rest is cladding. There is profound truth in Auguste Escoffier's remark that Elizabeth David made her own. 'Faites simple!' If it works, it's good.

The Times Magazine, 26 March 1994

STYLE 1 – WILTSHIRE: This represents a vigorous rustic rearguard action against the stern German technical style. One of the leading makers is Smallbone of Devizes, whose sonorous name evokes Thomas Hardy and suggests the romance and drama of choosing and using a kitchen. Surfaces are wood, often limed or stained. Splashback tiles have cute floral motifs. There are dressers for teapots, fussy panelwork and complicated handles often in 'antique' metal. Food here is often prepared by Marks & Spencer and delivered to the table by Range-Rover, so there is rarely adequate provision of preparation space.

STYLE 2 – GERMAN: The German kitchen industry – disciplined, orderly, ruthless – becomes ever more fanciful in its efforts to win customers. Once the modern German kitchen was chaste. But this is tending to give way to an unruly quest for expressive Baroque excess. Germans handle flamboyance badly and a new wave of kitchen designers strives to achieve ever more gaudy effects with a vast toybox of wacky industrial finishes. It is not unusual to see mirror-finish aubergine and black units atop computer flooring: elegant technical austerity surrenders to a style that looks like a München Gladbach disco designed by St Laurent.

STYLE 3 – CONRAN: Terence Conran was inspired by visits to France, by reading Elizabeth David and by the famous kitchen equipment shop run by Mme Cadec in Greek Street, Soho, once full of simple white porcelain and robust tools. It was Conran who made the epochal connection between the style of food and the style of the kitchen, even of interior design as a whole. Here you have massive refectory tables, well-used butcher's blocks, generous bull-nosed details, over-sized pots, pans and huge celery glasses. The Conran style – influenced by idealized notions of Frenchness – is an artful evocation of the luxury of simplicity.

Those other looks:

TUSCAN: The Provence of the 1990s. What was discovered in St Tropez is now to be found in Radicofani. The Tuscan kitchen is an artful Anglo conceit. Nothing like it is actually known to the natives, who prefer strip lighting and wood laminate-finish chest-freezers. Tell-tale signs are stone floors, painted wooden furniture, a marble sink and colour-washed plaster in two tones, separated at dado height.

ARTISTIC CLUTTER: A degenerate version of the Conran style, affected by people who collect milk jugs in the shape of cows and layer upon layer of 'amusing' postcards to distract visitors from inhuman and witless chaos.

ARCHITECTURAL: In 1979 Joan Kron's and Suzanne Slesin's *High Tech* had gullible New Yorkers fitting kitchens with galvanized panels, hospital trolleys, sample jars and sinister steel bowls. Successful modernist architects often develop this language in an imaginative way: in his eviscerated Chelsea house, Sir Richard Rogers has designed an ingenious stand-alone steel unit where all the functions of a traditional kitchen can be performed at a metal shrine.

THE MODERN DILEMMA

We live in an age with no style. This will astonish newsagents and consumers, bewildered by the multiplying decorating magazines that tell you how to have your Victorian bath re-enamelled or where to find experts in distressing freshly minted pine or laying medieval oak floors. Style, it sometimes seems, has replaced sex and success in the competition for middle-class attention. But our style is borrowed. Not from exotic places distant in space, but from fanciful places distant in time. We live in that other country, the past – or rather, a contemporary version of it.

For the first time in history no one actually knows what a modern house should look like. There is no consensus about authentic modernity. To give you an absurd but revealing example of this crisis in taste, compare the work of two of Britain's best-known architects, Sir Richard Rogers and Quinlan Terry. Rogers is a cosmopolitan hedonist-technocrat with a real claim to being a figure of genuine historical importance: his Centre Pompidou in Paris and his Lloyd's headquarters in the City of London are among the most astonishing buildings ever designed, and we are talking Parthenon and Taj Mahal.

Yet Rogers has not designed a house since he did a modest little chalet for his parents-in-law in Cornwall nearly thirty years ago. If Rogers did design a house, no one except the man himself and a handful of his sophisticated chums would want to live in it. Given a blank sheet of paper, a Rogers house would be made out of stainless steel and aluminium, have exposed air-conditioning units, open-work metal stairs and microprocessor-controlled, louvred, solar glass vanes. It would hum and purr like a nuclear submarine. While Miranda Knit-Brain of Parsons Green would supply you with horsehair skeins to tie back your rough linen curtains, Sir Richard Rogers would suggest you achieve the same functional purpose with a titanium aerospace unit.

If he had curtains, which he wouldn't. A house may be, as Le Corbusier had it, a machine for living in –

but only for those who think of the soul as a DNA computer.

On the other hand, consider a house by Quinlan Terry, the pasticheur whose clients include Michael Heseltine. Terry is Britain's leading exponent of what his supporters are pleased to call the Classical Revival. Certainly, Terry has a facile way of aping Classical details, but his is a bogus antiquarianism. He lacks the taste in matters of materials and proportion that was commonplace even among the most inept jobbing Georgian builder. And as for his ability to conceive and plan architectural spaces, he is laughably maladroit, as anyone who has looked at his Richmond Riverside development knows. Here, internal floors transect sash windows. Terry provides for those who prefer repro furniture to originals. A house designed by him would have an embittered and charmless pedantry about it, something conceived as a flat pattern, not a living space.

Britain is, of course famously in love with its past and suspicious of its future. When Ruskin wanted to condemn the morals of the Lothario depicted in William Holman Hunt's magnificent Pre-Raphaelite painting *The Awakening Conscience* (1856, the Tate Gallery), he said you knew the man was a cad because of the 'fatal newness' of his furniture: glossy, machine-made, shop-bought. More recently, Robin Leigh-Pemberton, one-time governor of the Bank of England, commissioned a fake Queen Anne house in Kent. The moral guardian of sterling, a man empowered in all sorts of metaphorical ways to put himself above counterfeiting, elected to live in a counterfeit house.

Never mind that three-quarters of British traditions were inventions of the nineteenth century; we are in love with sanitized versions of our history. There are national and international reasons for this. The national reason is that anybody born since 1945 has lived through a period of continuous economic and moral decline. The perspective has been remorselessly grim. We have all been inured to a perception of steadily decreasing standards of living, of universal deterioration: no other options appear to exist. It is a downward-only progress. Small wonder, then, that in the slow and inexorable slide towards bankruptcy, those of us with any economic flexure have a reach which does not exceed our grasp, but settles comfortably for a house style that speaks of a more comfortable and confident age. Which is to say long ago.

After the storm of modernism, a stifling calm filled the vacuum of taste. For all its practical flaws, the modern doctrine was like its distant cousin communism, immensely satisfying because it offered a prospect of progress. Yes, maybe today more people think that prospect was a delusion, but nevertheless modernism was something to believe in. It presented firm standards by which architecture and design may be judged: in many senses the high modernism of Gropius, Le Corbusier and Mies van der Rohe may, in fact, be compared with academic classicism in its insistence on order, correct proportion and rules.

And who can say just where it went wrong? Was it when the award-winning American Pruitt-Igoe development was dynamited as a social disaster? Was it when Ronan Point collapsed? Or was it simply that the most intelligent architects began to realize, circa 1970, that authentic modernism was an attitude rather than a style? Rectilinear concrete blocks and exposed industrial finishes were too literal an interpretation of the philosophy. And besides, while modernism made a creed out of 'functionalism', people eventually realized that, when it comes to sitting down, an overstuffed sofa is much more functional than a chair made out of gas pipe and rivets. Moreover, while the other modernist doctrine of 'truth to materials' worked with elemental stuff such as iron, stone and glass, the arrival of more complicated materials did for its validity. Teflon does not beg to express any particular truth. It is a whorish material. So is laminate. No wonder, then, that the public was confused, and while corporate architects expressed their new sense of freedom and designed windy, overbearing, post-modern headquarters for clients who knew no better and were not embarassed to have eggcups on the roof or pseudo-Egyptian lotus capitals in the lobby, the public took refuge in history. For every grimy image of a point-block in the Gorbals that was published in *The Guardian*'s Society pages, an eager appetite for a Lutyens bench was excited.

In Japan, things are different. Anyone born in those happy islands since 1945 has enjoyed the invigorating prospect of continuous economic growth, of expanding consumer choice and of a power fuelled by economic strength. Of course, the Japanese do not repudiate their history and traditions, but they use them as a basis on which to build, not a shelter to protect them from a harsh modern world. Given the choice, the modern Japanese does not want to live in a fake *riyokan*, but in something like a Lexus LS400, with a life of three years and replaced after two.

But there are international reasons, too, for this retreat into the past. Now that we live in a global flux of international capital movements, chirruping cellphones, chundering faxes and a microwave environment so intense that you could barbecue a chicken in the airspace between most computers, information has replaced merchandise as the chief material of exchange. Everywhere in the West, from Connecticut to Clapham, people cling to the stability of the past.

At dinner the other night in the house of a well-known manufacturer and retailer of wallpapers and coverings, the host said: 'Come and look at the new chair I've just bought.' I promise, he did say 'new', but he meant old. We were invited to inspect and admire not a ravishing novelty from the workshops and studios of the National Institute for Ergonomics and Pleasure (alas, no such agency exists), but a weary piece by a very minor Arts and Crafts figure, a distant relation of William Morris's bootblack. The curious fact is that, in furniture design, we seem to have reached the end of history. Odd to say, but no decent new furniture has been designed since the mid-1950s, when Charles Eames worked for Herman Miller. Of course, since then, Shiro Kuramata has proposed a sofa made of glass, and Ron Arad can even find customers for sofas made of bent metal, but in terms of serious functional design, the chair's development stopped forty years ago.

It is remarkable to be sitting here at the end of history. It must be rather like what the people who settled California a hundred years ago must have felt – with everything behind us we are on the edge. Anything goes.

Lord Gowrie has a nice story about going to parties 30 years ago and people saying: 'You must meet so-and-so, he's a senator/publisher/novelist.' Now they say: 'You must meet Philippe [it *would* be Philippe]; he makes curtains.'

The rise and rise of the decorator coincides with the descent and descent of the architect, now ranked in professional prestige below the traffic warden. But the decorator himself has not always enjoyed great prestige. In 1868, writing in his *Hints on Household Taste*, Charles Eastlake said of them: 'I have never met a class of men so hopelessly confirmed in artistic error.' You can chart the change by close analysis of comparable magazines. Pick up a copy of *The Architectural Review* of 1955 and you will see confident articles about the Ministry of Pensions in Helsinki, bright new typography from Switzerland and optimistic reports of new buildings in Copenhagen or air terminals in Virginia. Pick up a decorating magazine of 1995 and you will find art-directed colour photography of broken-down Fens farmhouses or hunting lodges outside Ghent. Ideologically, the scene has moved from a studio loft in Copenhagen to a *brocante* in lle-sur-la-Sorgue.

Of course, the rise of these decorating cults reflects a popular frustration with the architectural profession, myopic when it is not blustering. Since people do not feel it likely that they will ever be in a position to commission an architect to design their home, they do not – somewhat naturally – take a great interest in what the architect does. But interiors represent vacuums of taste which amateur and professional decorators abhor. In they rush. And in the process, the expertise and erudition acquired is astonishing. While no Chelsea or Wilmslow wife would have the least idea what you would do with, say, a bush-hammer or an Acrow-prop, she can talk knowledgeably about Germolene-coloured National Trust paint or the thermal characteristics of antique French wood-burning stoves.

In a sense, there is nothing new about the veneration of the past. There is one version of the history of architecture which looks on it as a continuous succession of Classical revivals with only the odd unpredictable eruption of the Gothic or the modern to break the continuous flow of orders and pediments. Certainly, educated Romans prized Greek antiques, just as Merovingian kings collected Roman treasures. The Renaissance was just the most remarkable example of a Classical revival. But at all these moments, veneration for past achievements was set in a context where there was genuine conviction about creating new, relevant buildings.

There is only one worthwhile definition of quality in architecture and design, and that is 'making the most of contemporary possibilities'. There are too many cooks in the kitchen of history spoiling a minestrone of half-understood pastiche. We don't have a style because we have too many of them. In this *fin de siècle*, we are living an illiterate anthology of warmed-up architectural reference, an expression in building of the sampling phenomenon that also typifies post-modern literature and film, characterized by sly borrowings, brazen plagiarism and doggedly un-academic quotation. Interior design is Pulp Fact. Even robust modern has been assumed into a mainstream of the available styles, although it is true that we have yet to experience Gothic Revival II.

Viewed charitably, the present condition is a hiatus, a liberal interest in excellence, whatever its provenance, pending a welcome return to order in the new century. Viewed more realistically, it is humiliating and dismaying to be a part of a culture where value can only be seen in a parade of historical regurgitations. Meanwhile, we have to live with the single most telling witness to our moral and aesthetic poverty: the fake gas fire. Sixty years ago the great modernist zealot Nikolaus Pevsner could think of nothing baser than a fake coal-effect electric fire. He tirelessly used the example of these cynical devices to demonize and stigmatize popular taste and cynical manufacturers. It was evidence of depravity and exploitation. Now, technology marches on, and you can get *real flame* gas fires. They have spread like Level 4 virus. Even some hard-nosed modernist architects find it's difficult to do without them. In our bleak little island with only the

past lying before us, a 'living' hearth is a symbol of the comforts of the past.

What's wrong with national health? Fatal oldness.

House Style, 15 April 1995

PART TWO – CULT OBJECTS, STATUS SYMBOLS AND TRIBAL HABITS

WHAT TURNS AN OBJECT INTO A CULT?

Just as the Christian church threw up various sects which found their homes in the catacombs, so cult objects have emerged from the uniformity of mass-production. With the idea of producing consumer products in multiples came the notion of democratic objects, able to be shared by everyone, but it was inevitable that at the same time certain objects would stand out from the uniform field of mass-production as having a special value or meaning.

A large part of the history of modern design has been involved with individuals who made more or less sophisticated attempts to define what was inevitable and, it was assumed, therefore permanent in matters of making things. As soon as it was realized, however, that even modern ideas were subject to revision and change, the first modern cult objects appeared, thrown up by the tide of change. Thus early tubular steel chairs, juke boxes and Bakelite radios, once reckoned by their manufacturers to be the material currency of the modern age, became highly collectable and cults in a limited sense.

But the cult object has a finer definition than mere nostalgia for a lost age of popular industry. It exercises appeal by other means than history: in its true form it has an esoteric chic which is shared and respected by a privileged clique. 'Cult' is a distinction within the concept of catholicity and it means a form of religious worship distinguished from the main body of a religious system by a special concentration on the external rites. If we take the entire business of mass-production as a metaphor of the religious system, then how do we define the cult object today?

The cult object is a mass-produced artefact which has become a focus of reverence for a certain class of consumer who is anxious to be distinguished from the catholic mass. Sometimes it is remarkable for its mere expense and consequential rarity, but more often there is a subtler appeal to the effect. Exclusivity is, by definition, a part of its character, but that does not define it completely. All cult objects are united by claiming for their owners access to a sophisticated way of life, a tangible separateness and a certain view of quality, but most specially they lay claim to a mystic connection with some sort of expertise, perhaps military, technical, sporting or professional, beyond what may be expected from an everyday consumer.

Thus the cult object is a powerful totem which, trading on appearance, acquires for its owner an appearance of specialized taste. It is this particular ingredient which defines the cult object and sustains its appeal in advertising.

Sony Walkman: Users of the Sony portable stereo are elevated above the throng by the very privacy of the entertainment they enjoy. In providing first for the chairman's in-fight entertainment, then for roller-skaters everywhere, it defined the myopic, self-referential attitudes of an age and soon became a cult object.

The personal stereo isolated its users into a privileged minority with funk or fugue for only one or two in an age of mass information and stench in the ears, while the machine itself achieved the status of a minor item of jewellery, adorning those with access to the rites of private entertainment.

Zippo lighter: Designed by George Blaisdell, whose concern was to build a better mousetrap when it came to igniting cigarettes, the Zippo has a flame-guard like the muzzle of a tank to defy the wind. It was included as standard issue to GIs during the Second World War and, along with the Bic pen and the Honda 50, has become one of the most successful and imitated of all mass-produced artefacts. Of the three, only the Zippo is a cult object: its price militates against crude exclusivity, but its nostalgic charm, to say nothing of its nostalgic petroleum stink, set it apart from a sea of disposable LPG [liquefied petroleum gas] dispensers and over-engineered electronic playthings. At the same time, its rainy mackintosh looks and its military associations evoke a rugged cult.

Burberry: Like other outstanding cult objects, the Burberry mackintosh maintains its status not only because price makes it exclusive, but because its character launches its wearer into the penumbra of two different types of probably alien expertise: the trenches of Flanders and the point-to-point.

At the same time, the design of the Burberry has, by a principle yet undefined, achieved the quality of timelessness; the trenchcoat is unalterable, unimprovable and widely imitated. The effect is achieved in a large part by complexity. Its construction and details once had a basis in function but are now, like a French butcher's diagram, a composite abstract pattern which confers on those it adorns the mystique of accomplished in the field.

Volkswagen Golf GTi: There are two special cult cars - the Citroën 2CV and the Golf GTi. The Citroën was taken up by those who, abandoning their scooters with dependent squirrel tails, adopted a taste for sandals, wholefood and a dislike of nuclear warfare, while the GTi provides a leg-up to brief tinsel stardom on Knightsbridge for boutique owners, estate agents and coiffure artistes who are unable to restructure their borrowing for a Porsche. The GTi is a car immediately identifiable with a group, as though the product planners had been in direct contact with the Architect of the Universe when it came to structuring society and its tastes. Ferdinand Porsche intended the original Volkswagen Beetle to replace the motorbike in the 1930s; the GTi is for today's motorbiker with social gloss.

Ray-Ban: These sunglasses make you feel like you just slung a fur-booted flying foot down the airstair of your shot-up B29 on a sunny morning in Suffolk forty years ago. The primordial archetype for all subsequent tear-drop shades, the Ray-Ban aviator glasses bring the romance of the Wichita flyboy to the Sunningdale 18-holer. Bausch and Lomb, Ray-

Ban's specialist optical manufacturers, lay claim also to another expert taste. By larding its advertisements with technical data, it compliments by the suggestion of technical numeracy the Ray-Ban consumer already seduced by the romance of the air.

Rolex: Although the Cartier watches retain the qualities which make beads attractive to jungle-dwellers, and the garish golden-screwed Audemars-Piguet probably requires exactly that from its recipients, the Rolex Oyster Perpetual is unquestionably the one cult watch that transcends fashion. The Rolex is an ideal, and its owners are united in a belief that quality and function are more attractive than looks or technology. The Rolex enhances its formidable expense by offering specialist models designed to appeal to land-bound divers, earth-bound airmen and mundane astronauts.

Mont Blanc: Certain pens are very popular: the Parker 51 brought science fiction to the everyday breast pocket and kept it there for 40 years. But it is the Mont Blanc, with a fuselage to take dry cells, a nib like a panache and a facility for laying a trail of ink down your arm as readily as on your A4 pad, which identifies graphic designers, architects and intelligent television producers as people who care as much about the form and means of what they write as they do about the content.

Tizio: The lamp by the German-Milanese architect Richard Sapper for one of the city of design's leading manufacturers, Artemide, achieves cult status by virtue of its expensive exclusivity and its subtlety and quality. In concept a high technology Anglepoise, the Tizio is owned by almost every single designer and design journalist in the world. Like all the outstanding examples of current Italian design it eschews utilitarianism and in form it is highly articulate and suggestive while in function it is deliberately complex: a transformer in the base converts mains current to a low voltage which travels directly along the arms, denying fussy cables. The elegance is assertive and economically available only to a few.

Epilogue: The cult object may be defined as what taste requires of mass-production. The fallacy of utopian functionalism was that only the rudest human material requirements could be met by merely utilitarian production of democratic artefacts. Mass-production, the evidence shows, is required to produce exclusivity as well as accessibility in products. The phenomenon of the cult object is not an episode in fashion but a reflection of a profound human need to identify emotionally with abstract products. Its lesson is that manufacturers must continue to acknowledge the ineradicable taste for symbolism.

Design and Art, 30 July 1982

WHY IT'S TIME TO BAN THE DREADED BASEBALL CAP

No doubt JFK Jnr will be receiving letters of sympathy from around the world. After all, he has just been caught with a mystery blonde and Daryl Hannah has dumped him. She'll be getting consolation too, at narrowly missing her chance to join the nearest thing America has to an aristocracy.

But looking at pictures of the couple in happier times, their problems were obviously more than merely romantic. He is one of the richest young men in the US and she is a highly-paid film star, yet they felt the need to express their affection by wearing children's clothes and baseball caps, in his case turned back to front.

If Jackie had really cared about her son, instead of warning him off Daryl, she'd have paid for him to attend her therapist. By wearing that cap he was clearly signalling his inability to sustain adult relationships of any kind.

It is an item of clothing that has no function except to say: 'Shucks, I may be nearly 40, but I'm still a little fella at heart.'

Yet poor JFK Jnr would seem to be in good company. For, stuck in the same strange time warp, thirty-something playmates Princess Diana, Bruce Willis and even otherwise stylish Tim and Helen Windsor persist in wearing these ridiculous caps.

Wherever ageing rock stars, Hollywood hunks and unemployed royalty are to be found – in showy burger bars, Alpine resorts and Massachusetts .compounds – the baseball cap rivals expensive orthodonty and an all-terrain vehicle as a token of me-too right-on cool. But teeth and jeeps have some practical uses while the baseball cap has none. What is going on?

Why does a princess wear a cap which suggests she is a crew-member of a US Navy aircraft carrier? Why should a zillionaire movie star want to look like a Brooklyn welder? Why do scions of the Windsors or Kennedys display allegiance to the Minnesota Vikings? This small mystery of contemporary life must be explained.

The answer is that the baseball cap is a successor to blue jeans as a facile token of solidarity with the working classes, a talisman of mild rebellion. Its incongruity is a short-cut to the nirvana of hip, for those that can't find the way themselves.

But there is a big difference: jeans were functionally perfect and soon became classless, a genuine staple of fashion. But the baseball cap was never a very useful garment, nor will it ever become a wardrobe classic.

Classic designs are rooted in elegance and utility. The baseball cap has neither. Unlike jeans, it has no thermal or protective function. It is superfluous and, like the people who wear it, superficial. It's sole purpose is to advertise allegiance to a caste, or a dodgy aspiration to one.

Carrying advertisements on their heads, the wearers are like megalomaniac sandwich boards, even when they are on rollerblades.

The Beatles never wore them. Rather, the workaday baseball cap was first translated to the rarefied regions of cool in the late 1970s when entertainers such as Billy Joel wore one to emphasize his Real Man credentials. But it was the last decade that saw this graceless item established in the fashion repertoire by two wonderfully incongruous soul brothers: Jean-Paul Gaultier and Ronald Reagan.

Reagan, who closed the gap between play-acting and the rude pride of the high prole, was a model taken-up for ironic deconstruction by Gaultier and the followers of his brattish fashion.

Together with his weakness for brown suits, Reagan's chosen head-gear made a defiant gesture of working-class pride. Here was a mass of symbolism ready to be plundered by sly socialites.

Somehow, the Americans have always had a marvellous knack with vernacular clothing, the ability to make workwear – jeans, chinos and T-shirts – or sportswear – baseball caps and letter jackets – into international democratic clothing.

To savour the achievement; while it is just about possible to imagine the late President Kennedy wearing a Boston Celtics cap while shrimping off Hyannis, it is quite inconceivable to summon up an image of his elegant contemporary, Sir Alec Douglas-Home, wearing, say, a Sheffield Wednesday supporters' scarf while shooting grouse on the North Yorkshire moors.

In one sense the new interpretation of the baseball cap, with its lumpen logos, is a clever satire on that consumerist vogue which had couturiers' signatures on the outside of handbags, scarves and suitcases.

Detroit Diesel and Pittsburgh Plate Glass make a refreshing change from Louis Vuitton and Yves Saint Laurent, but this is a game that you have to be very sure-footed to win.

In Diana's case, of course, it is all part of her populist appeal, her love for white knuckle rides, and burgers, attendance at public gyms, and holding hands with pensioners.

She is desperate to be loved by someone, even if it is only Joe Public, and like film stars of old, she has discovered that the fleeting love of an audience can almost make up for the lack of contented domestic life. For her, the cap is a badge of solidarity with us, the thronging, admiring crowds.

But ultimately, the implied humility of the baseball cap is bogus. It acquires its fashion force from absurdity. It is bad taste.

Of course, Diana doesn't work aboard the USS Coral Sea. Rich kids of any age in baseball caps mock the very people with whom they so contemptuously suggest an association. As Golda Meir once said: 'Don't be humble, you're not that great.' Anyway, there is justice in all of this. Rich kids in baseball caps look very stupid indeed.

Daily Mail, 23 November 1993

REQUIEM FOR THE TRAINER

Let me tell you what tennis star Ilie Nastase has in common with your plumber, the man in the Montego in pursuit of 'quality leisure time', and the toughest kids on the block: *Trainers*.

In 1967 a small Oregon sports-shoe company called Nike gave its account to a small advertising agency called Chiat/Day. Nike was so short of money that mainstream global advertising was out of the question; so it decided to go in for sponsorship. It paid Nastase $2,500 to wear and endorse Nike tennis shoes – and all the rest is sociology. But now, with the news that sales of trainers are in sharp decline, an era is at an end.

An explosion of interest in sports – supported by a proliferation of television coverage – made Nike into a celebrity as Nastase sweated and swore his way across the tennis courts of the world.

Before too long, Sebastian Coe, Steve Ovett, Steve Cram, Boris Becker and John McEnroe joined the trademark footwear roster. Later came basketball's Michael Jordan, sprinter Katrin Krabbe and Andre Agassi who, Nike now being rich, also began to appear in the advertisements. Later still they were joined by the plumber. The man who comes in the Astramax van to clear your drains is routinely dressed in jeans and running shoes.

During the competitive 1980s, acquisition of footwear favoured by leading athletes seemed a token of success. For the man-in-the-mall, wearing trainers while doing the weekly shop for high-fat groceries seemed an appeal to sympathetic magic. Wear Coe's shoes and, though you might be losing life's race and forced to shop in a supermarket, at least your feet were in contact with the essence. Louis Vuitton, Hermes and Gucci might be out of reach, but Nike, Reebok and Hi-Tec were easily acquired.

Can there have been a stranger decade than the 1980s when the curious fashion of wearing athletic shoes for non-athletic activities became tribal? Never can a decade and its cast of disenfranchised millionaires have fallen so rapidly from grace.

Something about the 1980s seemed to encourage a weird sort of dissimulation. People who had trouble reversing off the drive of their semi bought Porsches. Other people who were fretful about cross-Channel ferries started wearing Rolex sub-mariner watches, water-tight to 600 metres.

People with unhealthy habits began to concern themselves, not very energetically, with keeping fit. This last vanity closed the loop between famous sportsmen's footwear and the liturgy of brand names that characterized the decade.

Sport has always influenced fashion. The classic, waisted Savile Row suit has its cut modelled on hunting pinks and button-down collars were first used by polo players distracted by flapping.

The slip-on moccasin is based on a North American Indian hunting shoe. Coco Chanel popularized the sailor suit. Twenty years ago, it looked fine to wear tennis shoes around town.

Fashion has developed by this sort of assimilation … and that is why the trainer is so absurd. The reason we find trainers so risible and people who wear

them so daft is that, deep down, we all realize they are bogus, witnesses to a confused mass delusion about style and status.

The manufacturers understood this magnificently and, in accordance with the spirit of the age, rapidly developed a powerful vocabulary of visual detail which richly semanticized the consumer's affair with his feet.

Nastase's shoes were simple, white leather things with the trademark flash, but soon more details were added to justify upwardly mobile prices. Substances known best to rocket scientists were used for soles. There was massive competition to find the perfect cushioning substance, based on artful sophistry about the relative advantages of gel or captive air. Fluorescent colours were introduced.

In profile, a modern running shoe looks like a poly-technic lecture in ergonomics. An amazingly sophisticated language of form evolved to satisfy every consumer desire. As if to confirm the complete separation of the high-street running shoe from any genuine athletic activity, Nike introduced the 'cross-trainer' in 1987, a shoe which by definition was not particularly well-suited to anything more energetic than a desk job.

Women office workers in Manhattan started to wear them incongruously with their business suits. A metre below every Dagenham cleavage you now find athletic shoes. Pensioners on coach holidays sport similar footwear to Carl Lewis.

That man in the Montego buying barbecue briquettes from the 24-hour service station convenience store is dressed, at least from the ankles down, for the 400 metres.

Of course, it would be churlish to deny these credulous victims of athlete's foot the one sensible advantage which trainers bring … comfort. But the failure to address notions like elegance and appropriateness mocks their spirit, even as the shoes cushion the balls of the feet. And now they have rumbled it.

It is rather elegiac to think of Nike as the goddess of victory and her demise as a story not of a fallen idol but of fallen arches in a glummer decade.

Daily Mail, 9 November 1992

FOUNTAIN PENS MAKE A BIG COMEBACK WITH THE SMART SET

The fountain pen has never been so popular. For manufacturers, designers, buyers, consumers and sociologists brought up with a belief in technical progress, this is a daunting reversal.

There is no good reason why leaky, expensive, fragile and unreliable fountain pens, temperamental ghosts from the past, should be in demand today.

Except that people demand them. They are a sure and relatively affordable status symbol. The choice and use of a fountain pen speaks volumes not only for discretionary spending, but about your respect for writing.

While ten or fifteen years ago you would have had to look hard in dusty specialist stationers to satisfy a perverse whim to buy a fountain pen, nowadays they are one of the fixed currencies in the language of luxury goods.

In airport duty-free shops, in full-page advertisements in glossy magazines, big names such as Parker, Sheaffer, Waterman and Mont Blanc take space and demand attention.

Ever more expensive, ever more luxurious pens regularly appear. Manufacturers in the US, Germany, France and Britain are trawling the archives to find yet more obscure prototypes to revive. It is as if a telecommunications expert was wanting to restore Marconi's telegraph. History is in reverse, but why is it happening?

Memories of awful, scratchy things, delivering too much – or too little – ink, haunt the imaginations of anyone born before 1960. For the fountain pen, familiarity bred neglect. Those born later have never known the miseries of a rapid disgorgement of permanent blue all the way across their homework, and subsequently over the cuff and up the forearm.

Instead, the current generation has become flabby in its discriminations, numbed to the niceties of handwriting and blotting paper by the mass availability of cheap ballpoints and felt-tip pens, often technically excellent. We tend to believe that progress and technology lead to perfection. Maybe, but the evidence is that technical perfection bores consumers.

The technical problem with creating a pen is (a) storage of the ink and (b) delivery of the ink and (c) the ink itself.

Broadly speaking this means: (a) external dip or internal reservoir; (b) whether you get no ink at all, or all the ink at once and (c) does the ink have density and dry immediately, but rot the nib, or is it thin stuff with long-term wetness which rots the paper?

The answers to these questions involved rubber sacs, ancient valves, pistons or levers and some of the patents which define the history of technology in its most hucksterish phase.

Their appearance was not rapid: it was, for instance, quite a long time after the discovery of rubber that someone developed the rubber sac.

Lewis E. Waterman's technical achievement was to develop a simple capillary valve (comprising three extremely thin slits at the end of the barrel interior) which allowed air to enter the reservoir as the ink escaped, obviating rushing blobs, scratches, and facilitating easy handwriting.

Waterman, of New York, was followed as a pioneer of the popular fountain pen by George S. Parker of Janesville, Wisconsin, whose Duofold of 1921 was a breakthrough in product design.

In 1937 Parker introduced the '51' to celebrate the

company's 51st birthday. Technically, it evolved from the Parker Company's experiments with fast-drying inks. Eventually, the '51', a masterpiece of stream-lined styling, became a totem of the industrial design movement. The popular appeal of the '51' brought production into the millions every year but, just as the fountain pen appeared to reach its apotheosis, it was sabotaged by two fundamental developments in the proletarianization of the pen – the ball-point and the felt-tip.

In 1943 a Hungarian called Lasso Biro, working in Argentina, patented a design for a ball-point pen with quick drying ink which did not blot. By 1945 it was being manufactured in Europe. Crucially, by 1953, a Frenchman called Marcel Bich made it disposable.

When he dropped his 'h' Bic became synonymous with ball-point. In a similar mood of post-war endeavour in 1946, a Japanese called Yokio Horie founded a company called Pentel (a Japanese-English word combining the sense of pencil and pastel). Pentel's innovation was to adapt traditional Japanese practice to industrial production. Using the principles of bamboo-based techniques (where the fibrous core soaked up and delivered the ink to a chiselled point by osmotic pressure), Pentel intro-duced the felt-tip marker in 1960. In 1963 came the sign pen and in 1970 came the famous green-barrelled R50 roller ball. And all the rest was graffiti.

Of all new technology, mass-produced, inexpensive pens, the R50 Ball Pentel has been outstanding. It replaced the Bic as the universal, global writing instrument. It seemed another example of Japanese ingenuity taking advantage of Western complacency.

At about the same time as the bright green Pentel (about 50p) was becoming ubiquitous, the fat, shiny expensive Mont Blanc Meisterstück (two or three hundred times more expensive) was becoming famil-iar in well-heeled pockets.

The massive, reactionary, archaic, intensely desir-able Mont Blanc is the paradigm of the pen, not as a functional tool, but as luxury product.

Luxury is the opposite of function, which is not to say it lacks utility. It is a marvellous testament to our civilization that a functionally perfect pen can be bought for a matter of pence. But that is the prob-lem. The consumer is capricious. As soon as his basic needs are satisfied, he seeks more obscure appetites to gratify.

Bored with sterile perfection, he wants the unpre-dictable. An individual's pen has always been an expression of self-esteem because the act of writing is so intensely personal. Our own word 'style' derives from the Latin stylus. Lewis E. Waterman recognized this: his great commercial innovation was to sit in a New York shop window demonstrat-ing his pens to a sceptical public. Consumers are once again enjoying the same sense of showmanship.

The massive interest in fountain pens is not simply a taste for nostalgia, although for the time being this may be the expression favoured by most manu-facturers with their evocative lacquers, finishes and names.

It is also an expression of a growing interest in the process of owning and using everyday things, of tak-ing serious pleasure in small details. People who want to own a decent fountain pen want to do it right, whichever way you spell it.

Financial Times, 21-22 November 1992

SLOPING OFF

I think about skiing much as Dr Johnson thought about the Giant's Causeway in Ulster: worth seeing, but not worth going to see. Substitute 'ski' for 'see' and there you have it.

I enjoy exercise, fresh air and drinking immoderate-ly in strong sunshine. Equally, Alpine culture excites all manner of smugly satisfying associations for anyone with even the most cursory interest in Romanticism: you can get a heady dose of mountain mysticism within thirty minutes of Geneva's

Cointrin airport (which is something you couldn't say about Gatwick).

Earthy peasant food appeals strongly too: raclette and rösti potatoes in combination with unusual amounts of clean air and rough wine tend towards very refreshing earthy peasant sleep. So there are pleasures to be had skiing. But there are pains too.

It's not just the après-ski I detest, but the avant-ski too. Harold Acton reviled skiing as 'communism deluxe'. It's the collectivization of the brightly-coloured suburban middle-classes in cute fret-worked and barge-boarded Valais vernacular that's just one part of the aesthetic horror. The same middle classes want their tribal habits – queuing and braying included – translated to the Alps.

I sometimes think that skiing only really appeals to individuals whose lives at home lack almost in entirety any element of competition. This leads to a harrowing environment where there is the continuous threat of distressing, but not life-threatening, injury – the jostling in the lift queues; the morons in the ski shop; ski-poles in the ear; the timid accountant from Barnes who – as soon as he ascends beyond the treeline – becomes a reckless, untamed black run beast; the snow-yobs in four-wheel drives; the gruelling conversation in the cable cars – and so it goes on. Memories of Ruskin and Viollet-le-Duc aside, a ski holiday is not a place to take a fastidious aesthete.

But still, even in this catalogue of horrors, there are favourite resorts. Courmayeur for its odd mixture of France and Italy. Gstaad for its swank. Saas-Fee for memories of those earthy peasants in leather snow-shoes and Courchevel for glamorous creatures in mink coats with moonboots. Cortina because it was my first car.

But for the best ski experience you have, naturally, to go to the United States. Harold Acton would have cared for Snowmass, Colorado, even less than he did for St Moritz.

But if it's the snow, the air, the sun and the exercise which appeal more than competitive tittle-tattle in the bubble and the promise of world-class hot choco-late, you have to get to Denver's Stapleton airport and then ask for Aspen.

The Guardian, 13 November 1997

WHITE SPACE

What does white say? White says you don't care about the cleaning bills … Milan is Italy's most slick, cosmopolitan city and the garish tomato is all but unknown in its cooking. Milanese cuisine disdains polychromy: the classic dishes are veal and risotto, their whiteness suggesting a patrician respect for restraint. But white has other meanings too.

There is no colour so evocative. It is a symbol of purification: in Biblical times, the Jewish custom of whiting sepulchres (so that form was in contrast to rotting content) has furnished us with the best image of the hypocrite. In Western religious art white lilies are symbols of the Virgin. In Western tradition, white is associated with weddings, christenings etc. To the Chinese in their oriental contrariness, it is the colour of mourning. It was once Mayfair folklore that a woman, alone except for a white dog, in a white car was available for hire.

Depending on where you look, white is busy denoting availability, purity, simplicity, candour, innocence, truth, death and hope. Recently added to this rich repertoire of meanings is … *luxury*. Once, pattern and ornament signified wealth and opulence, but since they became cheaper to produce, plain colours became important tokens of taste and, as white is about the plainest colour you can get, it also appears the most luxurious.

In decoration, white has acquired its potency because it is luxurious, but not ostentatious. Having things white means you can afford to have them cleaned or have them replaced: an all-white room gives off an impression of military grade confidence. The fact advertised is that you are not one to tolerate soiling or squalor. It is exactly the same as those most exquisite of materials, silk and linen. They wear much less well than acrylics and require constant maintenance. Besides the actual pleasure of wearing them, there is the demonstration that it's no bother to you to have your rumpled linen suits valeted twice a day because the implication is that you have many more to replace them ... and the servants on hand to do the manual work.

Is it the same with these white cars you see around? These are not just cars which happen to have been sprayed white, they're *all white* – bumpers, screen-wipers, wing mirrors and the entire area of the wheel hub, whether appointed with the ubiquitous near flush 'cap' or with purposeful spoke effect. I asked the painter Martin Fuller what he thought:

'White cars are like white sofas, a conspicuous display of the impractical.'

He added, as one used to clandestine operations and equally unfamiliar with car washes,

'The colour one *should* have is of the local mud. . .'.

But how come Ford, Volkswagen and Fiat are promoting all-white cars in the middle of winter? I asked John Meszaros, the charming, understated, soft-spoken, but insistent Hungarian-born marketing manager of Audi-Volkswagen. Why, I wanted to know, did the people who gave us the chilling Vorsprung durch Technik and Arbeit macht frei also give us the 'All White' Golf GTi convertible?

He told me that since the days of the old Beetle cabriolet, Volkswagen has traditionally sold convertibles at Christmas. It may be that soft-tops have something of the indulgent toy-like quality you expect in a gift, something genuinely unnecessary, but nevertheless intensely pleasurable. Children enjoy playing with things which have doors, lids and flaps and it may well be that the convertible's folding lid provokes an unconscious reminiscence of this childhood pleasure. It's rather reminiscent of Peter Behrens' ancient dictat about the role of fantasy in design that 'a motor *should* be like a Christmas present'. Meszaros confirmed that these white cars were usually bought as gifts in what the marketing

idiom describes as 'the discretionary part of the market'. He said it's not a Cortina 1.6L world. They are bought by young fashion-conscious people who don't drive much. He didn't add that they want to be seen, but he should have done.

Once colours were used on racing cars, just like heraldry. It was green for Britain, red for Italy, blue for France and silver for Germany, but the present vogue taps a deeper source of meaning. White has such a potent symbolic force that the effect of an all-white car is very different to the effect of an all-black one: in all-white the fashion conscious wear trademark sun-glasses, in all-black the fascist-conscious can pretend they're in the Wehrmacht. Just as a white room accentuates its contents, giving every little bitty detail a centre-stage prominence, so a white car accentuates you. Black cars are like sculpture, made to be admired from afar by their owners and others. A white car is like an empty canvas and you, the owner, are going to be the daub.

This business about colour is only the latest novelty in the vocabulary of car styling. It was chromium in the 1950s: scallops and frills and fins gave form to the space-age optimism of an innocent, expansionist age. By the time the R5 and Alpine appeared in the early 1970s with grey plastic bumpers ... the language of chromium was virtually dead and the way was open for car designers to produce a monochrome car.

A change had occurred in the pattern of manufacturing which encouraged this development. By the 1980s when Europe's major manufacturers had been shaken down to a handful of giants, all producing technologically respectable but often dull cars, there was an inevitable appetite for more variety, for more style. The modern car is a perfect product, but buy one and you pay the price for the economies of scale won by mass-production: your Golf works like a Swiss watch, but so do five million others. It's a case, in terms of customer satisfaction where semantics is concerned, of more is less.

People with a personality they wanted to wear on the street looked for a solution to this problem of the perfect product. They found it in *customizing*, that tribal enhancement of machinery that was once the province alone of America's West Coast and London east of the Dartford tunnel. For customizing to become culturally available was rather like an artist receiving new critical praise after a thin career patch. Interestingly, customizing began in Germany, Europe's most conservative market, where Mercedes-Benz was the last manufacturer actually to use chrome. It didn't take a moment for after-market wizards to realize that dechroming a car now raised its profile. Rather as once you could judge someone's funkiness by the length of his side whiskers and you now do so by their shortness, by 1981 it became the same with chrome on cars. The richer you were, the less you had.

Soon the manufacturers started doing it themselves, taking the high margin business away from Hamburg garages and putting it into urban and suburban showrooms. This is the context of all white cars, but they surely mean something else larger besides.

Transport is a relatively insignificant function of the private car: the real purpose and meaning of owning a vehicle reach far deeper into human needs than the mundane requirement of getting to the shops. Promoting their (discretionary) 'Highline' range in the United States, BMW say:

> 'Your life isn't all grey, so why should your car be?'

We have been here before. In an ironic, but highly memorable, trope Roland Barthes declared that 'cars today are our cathedrals'. I wonder if he knew about Le Corbusier's essay '*Quand les cathédrales etaient blanches*' in which the architect writes:

> The cathedrals of our time have not yet been built... Everything is blackened by soot and eaten away by wear and tear: institutions, education, cities, farms, our lives, our hearts, our thoughts. Nevertheless, everything is potentially new, fresh, in the process of birth. Eyes which are turned away from dead things already are looking forward...

Barthes had meant that cars are like cathedrals in that, while they are the most familiar symbols of their respective civilizations, they are at the same time the most mysterious and moving. All those people driving whited Golfs, Escorts and Pandas are demonstrating, as Battleship Britain drifts aimlessly into the late evening of its industrial decline, that, for those folk lucky enough to be able to make discretionary statements about luxury, it will be all white on the night.

Tatler, 1985

WHERE THERE'S MUCK THERE'S BRASS

When someone wants to study the social history of Britain in the last quarter of the twentieth century, they will be better off looking at the Range Rover than poring through the mountains of data produced by the Central Statistical Office. Henry Ford it was who said, 'History is more or less bunk,' but he also said that you can read any object like a book, provided you know how. And the Range Rover is a text rich in meaning and nuance, one that is extraordinarily eloquent of social conditions in post-modern Britain.

No one who wasn't there could know exactly what went on at Rover when the Range Rover was being developed. But let's guess. Remember that Rover in those days was a small, independent company, still working in the tradition of the two brothers who founded it. Their product line was based on upper-medium saloons of better than average quality, of greater than average prestige, of a conservative caste, but often with well-considered design and engineering details. Indeed, the Rover 2000 of 1963 can claim to be the best-designed all-British car ever made. And then, of course, there was the Land Rover.

Looking back, you can see how the Range Rover combined both traditions. Following Einstein's description of the process of genius, it ignored an axiom. No one had believed there was a market for a four-wheel-drive off-road vehicle that had civilized behaviour on road. That was axiomatic. But the basis of creativity is the ability to make unusual connections. Rover had some very creative people amply able to connect in very unusual ways. The result was a unique synthesis: a car that could cross bogs hub-deep in primeval glop and also carry four adult passengers and loads of kit in civilized comfort at surprisingly high speed.

In a world numbed by exaggeration and superlatives, the Range Rover was a sensation. Quite genuinely, no one had ever seen or experienced anything like it before. Perhaps the first few thousand were actually bought by farmers trading up from Land Rovers. Perhaps. But then something very odd happened. People whose only experience of Land Rovers had been when one belonging to the AA came to tow their overheated Vauxhall Cresta away began to buy Range Rovers.

To understand why, you have to appreciate the symbolic allure of the Range Rover. The British have a unique attitude to the countryside. In this country, farmers have status. While Americans have 'station wagons' because cars like that are used for picking up people from train stations, we have 'estate cars' because we like to think we belong in the country. Because Britain industrialized so long ago, the peasant class has long since been deposited into cities where they were tragically drawn by the prospect (or rather the illusion) of work. The only people left in the British countryside are either prosperous farmers or the non-professional land-owning titled classes.

Compare this with the position abroad and you will see the contrast. While the word 'farmer' connotes prosperity to the British, the Dutch word *boer* (German *bauer*) gave us our word 'boor'. In Italy, a *contadino* is not a ruddy-faced fellow in tweeds and brogues having a pink gin at The Game Fair, but a crushed Etruscan throwback living in a pigsty, with dirty fingernails, given to practising incest and bestiality (where they are not the same thing) and driving an unwashed and faded 12-year-old Fiorino van. It's the same in France. When Citroen had to make a car for the French farmers, it made the 2CV. Even in the United States (where the old Ford Bronco and GMC Blazer were faint premonitions of

the Range Rover formula), 'farmer' means a terrible fat person in dungarees and flannel shirt with a factory-fit red-neck, given to driving pick-ups and hanging out all day at diners, issuing sexist and racist grunts.

So it was a new class that was attracted to the social and cultural symbolism of the Range Rover and its suggestions of life on the farm. This class consisted of prosperous, rootless, middle-class, British citizens, the ones with money to spend but nowhere to go, and the Range Rover provided them with powerful automotive heraldry. This class detests the city because it is full of the descendants of peasants, but at the same time craves the style and convenience of urban society. This same class admires the countryside because it suggests to them everything to do with status and privilege, but on the other hand the Nigel or Caroline you find in a Range Rover would wet their cavalry twill jodhpurs if they had to wring the neck of a bantam, deliver a lamb, get up at 3.30am or do any of the other things real country people do. The Range Rover allowed this class to dissimulate, wherever it was. On Fulham Road, you think they are on the way to Cirencester. In Gloucestershire, you imagine they are going back 'up' to town.

In its progressive refinements of the Range Rover – from two to four doors, from four to five speeds and then automatic, from vinyl to club leather – its maker seems to have acknowledged this. The car remains as effective off-road as ever, but by far the greater part of the evolutionary effort has gone into developing comfort and tarmac performance rather than cross-country ability.

But while the affectations of many Range Rover users are politely laughable, I wonder whether there is a yet more fundamental explanation of this exceptional car which shows its owners in a more favourable light. Although it is perhaps not a thing of ravishing or sensuous beauty, the Range Rover is a masterpiece of dignified design. Forget the fripperies of wood and wool and leather; in the really important matters of proportion and stance the Range Rover is virtually flawless. It is all but unimprovable, which is why the same shape remains in production after a quarter of a century and why the new-generation car is an evolution of it and not a revolution against it.

Remember that in 1970 you could still buy a Vauxhall VX4/90. For those too young to know, or who have suppressed the memory, this was a car designed ruthlessly to test the proposition that the consumer is a complete mug, a car where a tacked-on tachometer signified 'performance' and whose general appearance and demeanour was a chilling rebuke to all ideas of good taste. Other manufacturers were at it, too: when the Range Rover went on sale, there were GXLs and de luxes and Supers all over the place. You could still buy whitewall tyres. Into this maelstrom of overblown under-engineered kitsch, Range Rover introduced a design that was quietly dignified and stable. It is true that the panel gaps were big enough to put your fist in, but in terms of aesthetics that doesn't matter if the cut-lines are in the right place in the first place. And they were. The original handles were a delight. To those tired of being had by cheap accessories, the Range Rover offered an aesthetic absolute: utility was made chic. The manufacturer's confidence in the car's correctness was further demonstrated by offering only one specification.

There are social explanations for the Range Rover's success, but I think those arguments would not be valid with a vehicle that was less than complete aesthetically. The very best designs are the ones with integrity, where substance and appearance are as one. Get that right and you have a timeless design. There are precedents for this. Seventy years ago, Coco Chanel looked at matelot outfits and from them created a wardrobe of timeless elegance which has since been refined rather than changed. A Chanel suit is a joy for ever. Although some social presumption plays a part in any decision to buy a Range Rover, what gives the car its real substance is more substantial. History is not bunk. History shows that, come what may, the market appreciates good design.

Car Magazine, November 1994

PART THREE – COMMERCE AND CULTURE

WATTEAU, ART AND TRADE

As the twentieth century ends, commerce and culture are coming closer together. The distinction between life and art has been eroded by fifty years of enhanced communications, ever-improving reproduction technologies and increasing wealth. This has changed patterns of behaviour, as well as the character of institutions. Shopping has been described as one of the legitimate cultural pursuits of the 1980s, while at the same time, traditional museums are realising the hidden value of their collections, treating them not merely as cabinets of curios, nor even as a scholarly resource, but ever more frequently as assets which can be reproduced, merchandised and marketed. Knowledge is valuable and both shops and museums are realising it. Shops by adding quality of experience to the banal exchange of goods for money; museums by selling information and maybe, one day, even selling objects too ...

This new synthesis blurs the edges of our value system, outraging both the critical left (which interprets the process of elision as the Muses whoring in the market-place) and the conservative right (which condemns the same process as vulgar populism). But no one denies the change is taking place. Withal, it is possible to speculate that maybe in future museums and shops will become the same institution, huge repositories of objects, images and information – in anticipation, they have been christened 'knowledge centres' – with everything available for inspection, comparison and for sale.

The appetite for knowledge is both a symptom and a cause of this potentially huge change. The public is becoming better educated and consequently more discriminating, demanding superior merchandise and better environments from shops and at the same time expecting museums and galleries to provide a service which is not simply scholarly *de haut en bas*, but treats them more as clients in the information and entertainment business.

A similar process is at work in publishing and television: in certain magazines it is actually difficult to distinguish editorial content from paid advertising insertions. Occasionally, this is deliberate, as in the case of the 'magalogs' published by leading stores, including Harrods in Britain and Bloomingdale's in the United States. When the chain store Next published its Directory in 1988, suddenly a mail-order catalogue began to look somewhat like an international design guide. On television, the advertisements are often 'the best things on tv' with larger budgets than the programmes they punctuate as commercial breaks: thirty seconds of Coke or Colgate often has superior production values to thirty minutes of Hollywood fizz or soap.

This historical moment is one of very specific character, but does it mean – with shops becoming more educational and museums becoming more sensitive to the market-place – that civilisation is under threat, that the values so carefully nurtured by a discriminating élite are menaced by the barbarous populism, born of politically inspired consumerism?

The jeopardy is only real if you accept the Romantic model of the world, an idea crafted during the early years of the nineteenth century, in defence against industrial production and mass-consumption which looked about to undermine the tastes of a powerful élite. Artists took refuge in styles of behaviour and expression which validated their work by its distance from the public and consumerism.

But art was not always as remote from the everyday as the Romantic artist longed for it to be, nor was it as inaccessible as it was in the traditional museum. In fact, it is a curious paradox that, while not immediately obvious, it was the first museums which contributed to the banalisation of art. As André Malraux observed, art galleries 'turned gods into statues'. While once, a Greek votive sculpture, a Romanesque crucifix or a Renaissance Madonna were magical, mystical, religious images, by the time they were assembled into public museums, as the voracious Western appetite for consumption demanded, they were demoted from deities to mere statues and pictures. The museum arose out of the same social, cultural, historical conditions of the nineteenth century as the department store and other institutions such as hospitals and prisons. Each has imposed on the spectator a wholly new attitude to the appreciation of artefacts ... whether works of art or consumer durables. Civilisation is not really under threat from these changes. On the contrary, the synthesis of commerce and culture is a unifying process, bringing together the two appetites for consumption of knowledge and of goods which were once artificially separated.

Perhaps the most perfect example of art and its relation to trade is Antoine Watteau's exquisite painting, *L'Enseigne de Gersaint*. Watteau (1684–1721) was a painter of languor and grandeur, of poetic scenes from the *commedia dell'arte*; his are pictures which offer vignettes of a theatre of courtly conversations. On election to the Academie Française he was described as a *'peintre de fêtes galantes'*, a category all his own. But throughout his brief career, he became increasingly sensitive to the commercial opportunities of a new age, particularly after a visit to England in 1719, where, according to the Goncourts:

> Watteau began to acquire a taste for money of which he had hitherto made light, despising it to the point of indifference.

On his return to Paris he lodged with the dealer, Edmé Gersaint, who kept a shop called Au Grand Monarque on the Pont Notre-Dame. Gersaint recalled that

> Watteau ... asked me if I would allow him, in order to keep his fingers supple ... to paint a sign to be exhibited outside his shop. I was not in favour of the idea because I would have preferred him to work on something more substantial; but seeing that it would give him pleasure, I consented ... This was the only work in which he ever took the slightest pride.

It is sobering for those who believe that great pictures belong only in museums to learn that one of the most celebrated eighteenth-century works of art, painted by one of the great poets of the century, was, in fact, created as a fascia board for a Paris shop ... even if it did remain there for only fourteen days before another enterprising dealer snapped it up.

For the Romantics, the tragic, itinerant Watteau was a prototype hero. This passed through to some of the fashion magazines of the nineteenth century which encouraged their readers to affect Watteau gestures both in their clothes and their interiors. This outraged the Goncourts, who, in order to salvage art from the depredations of middle-class use, turned Watteau into a genius, just as history turned his fascia board into a work of art.

Commerce and Culture is concerned with middle-class use, about how consumer choice can effectively be made against a background of fast changing social, technical and artistic values. The inversion of standards so clearly illustrated by *L'Enseigne de Gersaint*, where a fine artist willingly put himself in the service of 'trade' are as familiar in our own century, but no better understood.

The Victoria and Albert Museum now has a subsidiary called V. & A. Enterprises. One recent venture has been a collaboration with the Habitat home furnishings stores. Habitat is using the Museum's textile collections, including designs by C. H. Townsend and C. F. A. Voysey, as source material for a new consumer range called the Habitat/V. & A. Collection.

In turn, Habitat sponsored an exhibition called *The Textiles of the Arts and Crafts Movement*. Previously the chain store Laura Ashley launched its Bloomsbury Collection, using designs by Vanessa Bell and Duncan Grant first seen at the Sussex farmhouse, Charleston. Similarly, perhaps the single most exciting thing to happen in the torpid world of British furniture during 1988 was the decision by the Lutyens family to begin reproducing designs made by Sir Edwin for the Viceroy's Palace in New Delhi (1920–31).

Appropriately, it was exhibitions which inspired Laura Ashley's decision to recreate the arts and crafts of the rural Bloomsbury set for their customers of the late eighties. It was seeing the Arts Council's exhibition *The Thirties* (1979) and the Crafts Council's *Omega Workshop* (1984) show which gave the company's design director, Nick Ashley, the idea. Interestingly, Duncan Grant himself would probably have approved. In his own lifetime he had designs for dinner and tea services put into production by Wilkinson and Brain, but the market potential was never realised since distribution and communication during the thirties were considerably more primitive than they are today. Grant explained his own predicament:

> If there existed today some form of liaison between art and industry, some centre to which artists could offer their work and on which manufactures could draw for ideas, the cost to industry would be no higher than that of the individual employment of working 'designers' … Indeed, as things are, the idea that an independent artist demands a prohibitive fee is quite unfounded.

While Habitat and Laura Ashley are offering their customers the stuff that was once in museums, even supermarkets want to add the allure of culture to their perishable merchandise. A press advertisement for Sainsbury's shows Gainsborough's painting *Mr and Mrs Joseph Andrews* (c.1750) made out of cooking chocolate, while other ads in the same series use extraordinary copy-writing whose purpose is surely more subtle and complex than merely trying to stimulate sales of comestibles. Once all that was required to sell sherry was a luscious packshot of the bottle; nowadays Sainsbury's sell it with an authoritative, even educational text, somewhere in style between the oenology of Hugh Johnson and the travelogue of Norman Lewis. Here is copywriter Richard Foster on the humble manzanilla:

> About 20km north-west of Jerez lies the small fishing village of Sanlucar de Barraneda … Sanlucar's coastal position gives it a cooler, more humid climate than that of Jerez … Ideal conditions … for the development of 'Flor', a film of yeast that forms naturally on the surface of sherry in the cask.

That ads for sherry nowadays read like text books, that Panasonic use Cubist pictures to sell office machines and Mercedes-Benz is pleased to compare itself to the eighteenth-century visionary architect, Claude-Nicolas Ledoux, are symptoms of an age demanding value and meaning, even in very ordinary, everyday things. In product design, functional excellence is now the baseline and to be successful consumer goods have to offer something more culturally seductive than mere efficiency. Customers demand what the advertisers call shared values: when Renault introduced a new model to the American market in 1988, they used the actor George C. Scott to present the car, since market research had shown that Scott, best known for his role as General Patton, represented strength, dependability and honesty. These were exactly the values Renault wanted to share. To a social theorist of the left, such as W. F. Haug, these charades demonstrate the vapidity of high-consumption capitalism. Design appears as just another way of stimulating sales, no different in substance from hiring an actor to hype your new car.

But if design and art are becoming subsidiary to sales, the consumer is bright enough to realise it. Decades of emphasis on surface and packaging have taught that mere possession of goods is not enough, especially when the Japanese have proven that anything can be made ever more efficiently at ever reduced cost, thus making any notion of intrinsic value in hardware mere sentiment. The make-up of the new consumer, hardened by functional perfection in the goods he buys, changes the purpose of shopping and of museums. An executive at the advertising agency, Ogilvy & Mather, defined the new consumer:

> In the 1960s and 1970s, possession alone were sufficient. But nowadays the concept of ideal homes stuffed with material goods doesn't work. Now that most people have a full pantry of electronic wonders, people are looking for meaning beyond the fact of possessions. Possessing is not enough.

In commercial response, advertising no longer merely offers merchandise, but suggests experience. The most successful television ads of recent years have been Bartle Bogle Hegarty's beautifully crafted campaigns for Levi's jeans and Audi's cars. These do not make an offer for sale, but rather seek to provide ambience and layers of imagery for the consumer to decode. In them, texture is at least as important as message. Buy me and become me, they seem to be saying.

If the cultural response is presently more difficult to define, there is evidence everywhere, easy to detect. In the early sixties Andy Warhol, who was an advertising art director, began his career as a painter with his ironic canvases depicting deadpans and Day-Glo tins of Campbell's soups. By 1985, with endorsements for Pontiac, Diet Coke and Vidal Sassoon already in his portfolio, and a print or canvas in every Modern Art museum, Warhol's avant-gardism had been comfortably accommodated into the mainstream of both commerce and culture. In that year Campbell's commissioned Warhol to paint its latest product, a dried soup. Unveiled at New York's Whitney Museum, this event served also as the product launch as well as a *vernissage*.

Between Watteau on the Pont Notre-Dame and Warhol on Madison Avenue there are two hundred and fifty years where commerce and culture have been involved and then separated and then involved again. Out of this anthology of conflicts and liaisons emerge the special circumstances of the late twentieth century. To some, the disturbance of the existing order and the promiscuous adaptation of art in the service of business is only evidence of a corruption in standards and a decadence characteristic of the *fin-de-siècle*. But what the future holds is not a narrowing of choice in a market full of lowest common denominators, but an expansion of it in pursuit of highest common factors. Watteau is no less an artist for having painted a fascia board while Sainsbury's is no less effective a business for producing advertisements which entertain and educate instead of condescending and exploiting.

For the consumer, whether in a shop or in a museum, commerce and culture, being more than the simple sum of their parts, offer an enriching experience.

Commerce and Culture, Fourth Estate 1989

REPRODUCTIONS AND ORIGINALS

Why do we still, almost instinctively, confer greater value on original works of art than on reproductions? What does this distinction tell us in an age of mass production of everything where image, form and sound can be instantly captured, recorded and reproduced, when everything is potentially available, ephemeral and almost free? Two parts of the answers are clear: technologies or reproduction bring into question the value of tradition and the special status of art. In industrial societies, the very notion of design is dependent on the potential to reproduce ideas, images and objects.

There is nothing new about the idea of reproducing works of art. The celebrated Apollo Belvedere, considered by Winckelmann to be 'the highest ideal of art' and thereby becoming the touchstone of eighteenth-century values, is itself a reproduction. Here we have a work of art, understood for more than two hundred years to be the maximum expression of nobility attainable in sculpture, which is not even in its true medium: the statue now in the Vatican is no more than a Roman marble copy of an original Greek bronze. What is more, the copy was made some five hundred years later. The history of its reproduction is as absurd as if a cast-iron Victorian copy of a medieval sculpture had had a decisive, even formative, influence on the development of modern art.

Yet copying works of art was not alien to the nineteenth century. In painting, the process was formalised by the French Academy in Rome where Colbert insisted that the students copy 'everything beautiful', thus creating a seventeenth-century manufactory for works of art. Two hundred years later thousands of copies of greater and minor pictures had been commissioned to furnish the bureaux of all ranks of the French Administration from Djibouti to Calais.

In the ateliers of the Academy, copying was considered a valuable stimulus to the creative imagination, not a substitute for it. Since it was thought a copyist could possibly improve on the original, copying became the second most important discipline after drawing from life models, where all the students were expected to do was improve on nature. Major copies were housed in the Musée des Études for the instruction of students, the Academy putting a high price on diligence. Eventually in 1874 an actual Musée des Copies was established, housing one hundred and fifty-six copies of masterpieces. This venture was the less curious if it is emphasised that an educational system which values diligent study as much as 'creativity', just as it prefers technique to interpretation, was able to consider the contents of the Musée des Copies as works of art in their own right.

This notion of copying appealed to the bureaucratic French mind, which also graded painters and supported them with commissions. The French Academy's formal institution of copying was characteristic of a nation's preoccupation with cultural bureaucracy. At the same time in London, a similar museum of copies was established which was equally characteristic of its host nation's preoccupation with commerce.

Domenico Brucciani ran a successful plaster-cast business in Russell Street, Covent Garden. In a sense, one of the descendants of the itinerant, jobbing *stuccatori* so familiar with the British building trade in the eighteenth century, Brucciani busily adapted his craft from artisan decoration of houses (already industrialised by the nineteenth century) to purposes better suited to the demands of their age. Since 1841 the government schools of design had been collecting casts of statuary and even had a 'keeper'; Brucciani made his business the supply of casts to the burgeoning system of British art schools, a trade which flourished well into 1950s.

In 1864 Brucciani opened a unique institution, part shop, part museum … his 'Galleria dell Bell Arti' which contained copies of the finest statuary in existence, at least according to contemporary taste. Widely reported in all the art journals, Brucciani's 'Galleria' was both a showroom for the sale of merchandise as well as an educational experience for its inquisitive visitors.

It was Brucciani who cast the Portico de la Gloria at Santiago de Compostela in 1866, still one of the most technically remarkable and physically impressive of specimens in the Victoria and Albert Museum's Cast Courts. […] The painter, Ingres, for instance, had had doubts about the system of copying employed by the French Academy since he believed, rather like Owen Jones, that the mysterious essence of a masterpiece did not lie in mere details. But for the new middle classes, ignorant of the theory of art, negligent in connoisseurship, cast courts were a special attraction. In New York, the Metropolitan Museum had a Hall of Casts which, hubristically, included the Parthenon and the hypostyle hall from Karnak.

Certain fine artists may have felt threatened by the prospect of art being licensed, copied and distributed in the form of reproductions, but the practice had eloquent champions, including George Wallis, the keeper of the art collection in the South Kensington Museum. Wallis had noticed that the expansion of museums would mean that eventually the demand for art would outpace the supply. He explained:

> As personal wealth increases, and taste for collecting extends, the private buyer comes into the market … as museums increase, they also become competitors, chiefly with each other.

Wallis's rationale for using reproductions was that the study of them would improve popular taste at modest cost, but this canny commercial observation was not his only conviction, since he was intellectually committed to the idea of using copies in education. He scorned the connoisseur, with his fetishistic, precious demand for the unique and wrote a stirring defence of the very modern notion that quality in art is quite independent of uniqueness:

> Nothing to the true lover of art can appear more absurd than the worship of intrinsic value, and the neglect of that extrinsic value which comes from the beauty of form, proportion and adaptation to use.

While it is tempting to interpret Wallis's arguments as a prophetic defence of industrial design as a genuinely popular art, to do so would be an error in historical method. What Wallis's interpretation of the role of the Cast Courts does represent is an early expression of an idea which was to gain currency in the twentieth century: new technologies, in John Berger's words, make art 'ephemeral, ubiquitous, insubstantial, available, valueless, free'.

This liberation of art from 'value' was a fundamental part of the ideologies of the various modern movements, most of which attacked both the bogus respect for pictures and their preciousness in the market-place. This stigmatisation of painting allowed design to flourish as a major – perhaps the major – creative discipline. Bogus respect and market value, they said, were mere replacements for that magical quality which painting lost as soon as photography was invented.

The most eloquent spokesman for the persuasive idea that photography, the most efficient and universal of the new reproduction technologies, had robbed traditional art of meaning and value was Walter Benjamin, a social critic belonging to the Frankfurt School. Benjamin was obsessed by the parallel development of photography and socialism and felt that each fed off one another. Enthused by the evocative stills of Eugène Atget and the heroic movies of Abel Gance, Benjamin wrote an influential essay called 'The Work of Art in the Age of Mechanical Reproduction'. Here he argued that the emergence of photography and film suddenly robbed images of any 'cult' value and, instead, promoted secular, insubstantial, images for popular scrutiny. It is not so much that photography and film (and he might also have added, industrial design) are necessarily arts in their own right, but that their invention changed the entire nature of art.

Benjamin took his own life at the beginning of the Second World War, so did not live to witness an extraordinary phenomenon which both validated his conviction about the universal appeal of photographic images, but also supplied powerful evidence on the contrariness of human nature which, even against powerful rational arguments, finds comfort and delight in the bogus. The story of the most famous photographic image of the war proves that it is only a short distance from reproduction to fake. The 28th Marines of the 5th Division were ordered to take Mt. Suribachi, an extinct volcano on Iwo Jima. After a bloody exchange, resolved in favour of the Americans, a lieutenant was given a small flag and a length of pipe to act as a flagpole. The makeshift assemblage was erected as the victory celebration and that would have been that, cult value and all, until a photographer of the Associated Press news agency, one Joe Rosenthal, decided a picture opportunity was being wasted, so he came up the slope with a larger flag and another team. They had some difficulty erecting the now huge flag, so the original detail joined in and, there you had it, a stage-managed image, a styled photograph, which became a symbol of the United States' Pacific war effort. The same picture was used for the 7th War Loans fund-raising drive and served as the model for the largest bronze statue in the world, the Marine Corps Memorial in Arlington, Virginia. The Mt. Suribachi anecdotes closed the gap between reproductions and fakes, providing wry proof of Benjamin's theory that the invention of photography changed the nature of art.

There was a moment in the nineteenth century, somewhere about the time when the great museums and the great department stores were being opened, when the poster ceased to be a straightforward broadsheet of printed information, and became a mixed-media advertisement, using illustration and copy to create an effect which was more than merely workaday. Henri de Toulouse-Lautrec and Jules Cheret are familiar as creators of the 'art poster' and the tradition they established has continued through the century. The value of the reproducible image, as opposed to the value of an 'authentic' original is articulately defended by Milton Glaser, when he says

Why don't we discard the word 'art' and replace it with the word 'work'?

The concept of 'fake' tests many of the rooted prejudices we have of culture. The very idea makes assumptions about authenticity, which are undermined by developments in twentieth-century technology and design. Mass-produced design, whether of a poster or a product, makes a nonsense of the prejudice against fakes.

The concept of authenticity has moved on, no longer is it inherent in a unique original, for when Ford produces hundreds of thousands of Escorts every year it is clearly nonsensical to talk in terms of reproduction or original. Instead, today we have piracy. No one has yet made a counterfeit Ford Escort (not least because the initial investment in tooling would render the project financially inefficient, given Ford's own commitment to selling global products), but counterfeits of more technically simple products are abundant. That there is demand for fake watches, fake luggage and fake furniture is evidence of human bondage to tradition, although in this case tradition of a novel sort. It is also evidence that our contemporaries value the authority of brand names: as the cost of hardware tumbles, the aura of famous names, including Cartier, Rolex, Vuitton and Hermès, begins to acquire value, hence unscrupulous piracy and counterfeiting.

It is a beguiling paradox that companies such as IBM, whose growth has depended on the vitality of mass-production businesses, now spends £30m every year to protect its secrets. Similarly, the furniture manufacturer, Cassina, which owns the rights to manufacture Le Corbusier's design, says that his designs were never intended for 'commercial reproduction', a declaration that seems to run entirely contrary to the architect's own beliefs about the role of design and products in the modern world.

So, there are two forces in conflict, or, at least, in tension. One is the universality of design in the modern world, the other is the need of the manufacturers to protect their property, even when that property is an idea or an image rather than, say, real estate. It was the simultaneous development of the department store and the museum in the middle of the nineteenth century which gave rise to them.

Commerce and Culture, Fourth Estate, 1989

GOODBYE TO THE AVANT-GARDE

Somewhere out there is a huge graveyard of French expressions. In it the headstones are memorials to past conceits and fancies which died when France ceased to dominate global culture. *Serviette. Noblesse oblige. Thé dansant. Entente cordiale.* But it was not only manners and politics that were Frenchified, it was also art. What would happen if some cultural necrologist were to exhume the avant-garde?

It is a beguiling paradox that nowadays there are few things more *passé* than the avant-garde. An expression once used to give cachet to the expeditionary forces of art, the avant-garde belongs to that period when culture was a battlefield. When artists were busy throwing pots of paint in the public's face, creativity could be quantified by capitalising offence, hence the appropriateness of a *nom-de-guerre* for the shock troops.

The practice and technique of rape, loot and pillage briefly were applied to art. When outrage was a measure of freshness, a talent to distress was confused with the ability to enlighten. Nowadays we get our outrage and our distress elsewhere, in newsagents, traffic and on the street. Life is pretty shocking. We are all in the avant-garde now.

Yet, redundant and bereft of meaning, we are still living with the consequences of the creation of the avant-garde: the idea that art has leaders and followers imposed a structure on our imaginations which has been difficult to shift. During the nineteenth century, the growth of mass-consumption undermined the notion that art was meant to cause delight. Culture was not a consensus, but instead actually represented opposition to the tastes of the booming market-place. Stripped of their public, artists did not know whether they were meant to be leaders or outsiders, creators or conformists. This conflict has still not been resolved: today, nobody can really decide whether creative people are meant to be inventive or synthetic.

Charles Percier expressed the conservative view:

'The true perfection of every art consists less in the discovery of unknown things than in the judicious use of those elements already sanctioned by custom and taste'.

But Charles Baudelaire thought quite differently, declaring that 'The chief task of genius is precisely to invent a stereotype.'

The avant-garde was a reflection of society's image of itself, but seen in a distorting mirror: the wacky artistic type, bent on outrage, was an invention which in fact sanitised art by stringing a *cordon sanitaire* around the artist, defining his territory as out of bounds. To the comfortable and prudish bourgeois of late nineteenth-century Paris, the avant-garde artist was a poet or painter, a slave to his senses and a brute to his mistresses. This dangerous Bohemian in a hat had a fevered imagination smouldering behind a furrowed brow made glossy by absinthe and pale by late nights; on a bearded face the lower lip trembled. Only the eyes were fixed with a singular purpose: *épater le bourgeois*. This was exactly what Albert Jarry did when he shocked the audience at the first performance of his play 'Ubu Roi' with the opening line: '*Merde!*' It is a measure of the durability of the avant-garde that nowadays this is all that is remembered of Jarry's script.

And later, when familiarity had dulled the shock value of the sleazy Bohemian, the avant-garde found expression in another strange bird, but one of a rather different feather ... the technocrat. Here again, in a rapidly industrialising world, there was an image both to lionise and to demonise. From just after the First World War the avant-garde artist – speaking generally – abandoned his fedora, his cheroot and his dirty habits, and became a missionary from another territory equally alien to the stay-at-home bourgeois: the laboratory and the factory.

Thus, if you had been researching a television programme on the avant-garde in 1880 you would have had to go to Paris and sip wormwood liquor with oddball painters and poets while dancing girls demonstrated the contemporary deficiencies of laundering; by 1920 your producer would have had to send you to Germany to meet Hungarian émigrés teaching metalwork and photography in ambitious art schools to the wide-eyed, flaxen-haired delegates of the master race.

For a while it was all so very interesting and attractive. The imaginary model of human endeavour which casts artists as leaders was persuasive. Both Romanticism and modernism depended on it for their continuing success. But while the Romantics suggested a utopia of the imagination, the modernists offered a utopia of material things. The idea that life and art can be continually refined in pursuit of tangible – if distant – goals was at once the strength and weakness of modernism. For so long as the goals were unrealised, Modernism was seductive, a style to express the positivist certainties of industrialised capitalism.

Chief among the tribe of claims made by the modernists was that new forms and new ways of life were in reach and should therefore be grasped. Indeed, the pursuit of them – whether in painting or architecture – became a test of credentials, or articles of faith. The claim to originality was perhaps the most enduring of the modernist myths and perhaps the most damaging, an avant-garde inheritance from Baudelaire which could not satisfy the scrutiny of a market more interested in comfort and security than in shocking revelation.

During the progress of the twentieth-century drama, the bourgeoisie has been recast as 'the consumer'. Just as the failure of modernism to redress the injustices of the modern world became apparent, so a multitude of choice became available. Since 1968 everything has been possible in politics and society; and since about 1981 everything has been possible in design. It was in this year that Italian furniture designers, in a destructive, ironic final spasm of avant-garde creativity, made all of history, past and present, available for Day-Glo laminate artists to make chairs out of.

It is perhaps fitting that the avant-garde delivered itself of the final *coup de grâce*, with its most outrageous gesture: offering domestic furniture intended to shock, dismay and amuse by its artful banality. Pushed to the brink of the chasm named 'anything goes', popular taste recoiled and regrouped around the 'classics'. It is significant that the most interesting recent developments in furniture and interior design have been Habitat's licensing of the Victoria & Albert Museum's Arts and Crafts textiles, Laura Ashley's Bloomsbury collection of fabrics by Duncan Grant, and the Lutyens family's decision to start reproducing Sir Edwin's colonial furniture.

The avant-garde once offered the prospect of continuous refinement through a process of restless innovation, as if human destiny could be reduced to a business plan. But since post-modernism generalised both copying and neophilia, both the avant-garde and its mirror, kitsch, have become worthless through familiarity. Like the airlines, history has been deregulated and the avant-garde is a casualty (rather like the schedules). With the entirety of human endeavour available for regurgitation, attention is removed from novelty and concentrated on understanding what is already available.

There was a recent newspaper picture of a morose Italian conceptualist artist, squatting on a stool in the Royal Academy, burdened by a serious moustache, set before a collection of neon tubes he was pleased to foregather in the name of art ... and it provoked neither acclaim nor outrage. Looking for all the world like a modern version of Dürer's *Melancolia*, this prototype of gloom showed that approbation is no more valid a test for art than disgust is a proof of it.

At the moment there is a malaise of history characteristic of the fin *de siècle*. The consumer takes refuge in polite reproductions and refuses to be provoked by tiresome demonstrations of novelty such as chairs made out of broken glass. Curiously enough, it was conditions similar to these which once gave rise to the avant-garde. But now we are too conscious of the past to fulfil Santayana's prediction that 'those who are ignorant of history are condemned to repeat it'.
– *GQ*, April-May 1989

Writing to his wife one day late in the summer of 1926 after a walk near the Bauhaus where he taught, Lyonel Feininger broke off from a lyrical passage about the lakeside landscape to describe the subtle beauties of the wing construction of a Junkers flying boat tied-up in the harbour.

From the Dadaist Francis Picabia (who used illustrations of carburettors to suggest metaphors for sex), to the painter Fernand Léger (who filmed a Bugatti engine for his semi-abstract film *Le Ballet Mécanique*) to architect Le Corbusier (who thought that the steely perfection of aeroplanes and cars taught an irrefutable lesson that the house should be a 'machine for living in'), it was the great modern artists who were first to notice the beauty of industrial design. And in all industrial design, few things were more self-consciously beautiful than the car.

The great adventure of the twentieth century, the one sensed by these pioneer modernists, is the extraordinary leverage which industry gave to creativity. Mass-production and mass-media made the idea of a lonely artist, struggling and starving, a quaintly romantic conceit. Mass-production and mass-media offered the real artists of the twentieth century a canvas huger than even the most megalomaniac academic painter or sculptor could imagine. If you can draw something that has direct emotional appeal to the entire population of the planet, then for a real artist that is something more seductive than painting a picture, or casting a bronze to be enjoyed in solitary contemplation.

At one moment in this century, 'design' became the most truly democratic and therefore the most powerful art. Beauty must be convulsive, according to the surrealist, André Breton. But to industrial designers, beauty must also be everyday. Industrial design, of which car styling is the most influential and persuasive form, has usurped art. Popular aesthetics are determined by motor industry designers, not what happens in a Soho loft. Today a writer would rather do a movie script than a thin, sensitive novel; artists would rather do a car than a bronze of St John the Baptist; and sheep picklers such as Damien Hirst are stuntmen clinging to an outmoded and irrelevant interpretation of art.

The disciplines of industry stimulate creativity while the licence of 'art' mocks it. The great American designer Walter Dorwin Teague wrote in 1940: 'The automobile manufacturers have made, in the past few years, a greater contribution to the art of comfortable seating than chair manufacturers had made in all history'. And, of course, it is a more impressive achievement to design and manufacture a million seats at a bafflingly inexpensive real dollar cost than it is to hand-make a wantonly extravagant bird's-eye maple and ocelot *fauteuil* for a railroad billionaire.

It was in America that this aestheticization of the mass-produced object first began to take on the dynamics of creativity. It was in the late 1920s that the first generation of industrial designers, including Teague and Raymond Loewy, sensed the spirit of the age and became possessed of the (then novel) idea that making utilitarian objects attractive would enhance their pleasure (and their sales). The mood soon spread to the auto industry where, circa 1927, Harley Earl established GM's [General Motors'] Art and Color section. This evolved into Styling and became, by the 1950s, the most astonishing source of visual ideas – at once strange, crass and amazing – ever seen.

The annual new model change put auto industry designers under enormous pressure to innovate and if, in the puritanical view, it was a conspiracy, then it was a conspiracy in which the public gladly participated. Prim Germans called the excesses of US car styling 'Detroit Machiavellismus', but as one of Harley Earl's colleagues noted: 'We have not depreciated these cars, we have appreciated your mind'. If you need a visual interpretation of American culture of, say, 1957, then a Chevrolet Bel Air is at least as eloquent as a Franz Kline or a Barnet Newman painting. That's at least a partial definition of 'art'.

In Italy, the transition to industrial culture was so late that a great many old traditions remained. Besides, Italy had had no fine artist of international repute since Tiepolo, hence neither reputations nor vested interests were at stake when cars became art. Instead, the great *carrozzieri* were run like the studios of Renaissance painters: masterpiece following masterpiece, executed by a succession of studio assistants who eventually rose to prominence in their own right.

Bertone was typical. The first master he employed was Franco Scaglione (b.1917) who, from 1951 to 1959, was Bertone's original design director. Under Scaglione, Bertone produced, for instance, the sensational series of BAT (Berlina Aerodinamica Tecnica) cars based on Alfa Romeo running gear. The BAT cars were completely uninhibited visual narratives on the possibilities of car styling, more imaginative than anything else ever seen at the time: complex, sweeping curves betraying an exciting, emotional response to what a car might be. They were ideas on wheels and, in contrast, make Italian gallery art of the 1950s look insipid, pallid and irrelevant.

Scaglione was followed as *capo stilista* of Bertone by Giorgio Giugiaro (b.1938). From 1960 to 1968 he laid the basis for his own reputation as, what an American critic described as, a talent to handle 'plastic volumes better than any Italian since Michelangelo'. For Bertone, Giugiaro drew the Alfa Romeo GTV, the Fiat Spider 850 of 1964 and the epochal Lamborghini Miura of 1966: no car designer has ever understood better the expressive possibilities of pressed metal, nor handled them with more lascivious refinement.

Continuing the studio metaphor, Giugiaro left Bertone when he reached his maturity and was followed by the last great master, Marcello 'Lello' Gandini (b.1938). Gandini's style was extreme: an aggressive, razor-edged style, occasionally lurching into near parody. The 1973 Fiat X1/9, a neat mid-engined economy sports car, and the rally-championship-winning 1974 Lancia Stratos were typical and so too was the Lamborghini Countach, still – and perhaps indefinitely – the last word in supercar semantics.

All cars are, as Roland Barthes memorably put it when writing about the 'New Citroën' in his 1957 book *Mythologies*, 'our cathedrals' – everyday objects conceived by often anonymous artisans which retain a sense of magic and exert a compulsive appeal over the population. Their status as folk art was given authoritative approval when Arthur Drexler, curator of architecture and design at New York's Museum of Modern Art (MOMA), opened his 'Ten Automobiles' exhibition in September 1953. On display were not only bespoke masterpieces by Bertone, Pininfarina and Vignale, but also more mundane vehicles including the Aston Martin DB2, the Porsche Super and Raymond Loewy's Studebaker Starliner. Just last year MOMA closed the loop by acquiring a Jaguar XKE. It made studio sculpture of the 1960s look ham-fisted.

Cars not only dominate the Western economy, but also define expectations of Western culture. Once this might have been a daring assertion, but the cars-as-art thesis is now approaching the mainstream. Thus, about twenty years ago, C. Edson Armi, the professor of art history at the University of North Carolina at Chapel Hill, wrote an award-winning but ineffably obscure book called *Romanesque Burgundy: the new aesthetic of Cluny III* – but his next book was *The Art of American Car Styling*, prominent on the lists of Pennsylvania State University Press in 1988.

Bruno Sacco, chief designer of Mercedes-Benz, recently wrote about something that was, 'A work of art through and through'. What did he have in mind? Joseph Beuys or Pauline Rego? No. Raymond Loewy's Studebaker Avanti.
– *Goodwood: Festival of Speed*, 1998

3.5 The myth of progress

Before his actual visit to Lenin's Soviet Union in 1919, Lincoln Steffens had been rehearsing the remark that made him famous: 'I have been over to the future, and it works'. Subsequently he refined and polished his nugget until it became the shiny, familiar, long-term *Dictionary of Quotations* resident it is today. And there you have the pathology of futurology: fabrication, myth, wishful thinking, all cocktailed into a lethal mixture with premium-branded capacities for self-promotion. From Nostradamus to John Diebold, via Lincoln Steffens, the folly of predicting the future has attracted those vain enough to imagine they have a place in it.

Perhaps the single most significant element uniting industry with culture during our century has been the idea – almost a religious belief – of forward motion, of movement towards a goal. Machines embody this; we remember our history by its artefacts. We are obsessed with clairvoyance because the entire structure of our culture supports the idea that tomorrow should, if at all possible, be better than today. In this charming fiction, the designer has always had a role.

In the great days of Detroit in the fifties, Harley Earl told his General Motors' designers, 'Go all the way you can and then come back some'. They visited the future in their minds and reverse-engineered it so as not to frighten visitors to the local Buick showroom. Harley Earl's creation of the annual model change – which his critics called planned obsolescence, but he termed 'the dynamic econo-my' – let the public into the theatre of futuristic design. For this privilege they paid freely and handsomely. Throughout the fifties, Harley Earl was the impresa-rio of General Motors' amazing Futuramas which presented the American consumer with the giddy fantasies of his studios. Even today, motor-industry designers think in the future. When the Sierra was launched in 1982, Ford's product planners had already determined the features list of its replacement, the

CDW27, soon to appear in the showrooms. By the time that car is on sale, it will
be old hat to its designers.

There is something elegiac about this, something touching about the hubristic vanity of prediction. There is something even more elegiac and touching if you realize that it is not car designers who are ten years ahead, but the here-and-now which is ten years behind. Of course, it is incredible that a small band of professionals in Basildon, Russelsheim, Ingolstadt or Worthing have privileged access to the future and, in concert with the marketing department, offer it to the public as a hand-me-down. Incredible, unless you believe in parallel universes with the public down here and the motor industry over there.

The truth is elsewhere. As product life cycles fall, the gap between the designed future and the present moment of consumption shrinks. Yet as this happens, design is tending to become more conservative. It is noteworthy that progressive refinements of process technology have actually slowed down innovation in design. Do people actually talk about innovation any more? Not where I go, they don't.

In terms of aesthetics, automotive design has reached a virtual stasis, with successive generations of vehicles bearing remarkable family resemblances to their ancestors. It will take an as yet unanticipated technological revolution to bring about a fundamental change in car design. In architecture, now that the excesses of post-modernism can be seen in the dull glow of the property crash, and the most strident modernists acknowledge their own quaintness, we can sense what a thrill it would be to have the chimera of progress removed from the galaxy of human expectations.

Creating effects of spectacular progress is relatively easy, but now there is less and less demand for it. Teachers and practitioners of design will be required to abandon the facile quick fix of change and concentrate instead on the subtleties of refinement. From what I can see, this will present some difficulties.

But it is folly to predict such things. If there is one thing to be learned from attempts to read the future it is to ignore them. Marx was wrong and so was Lincoln Steffens and so was John Diebold. So was George Orwell: 'If you want a picture of the future, imagine a boot stamping on a human face – for ever'. What rubbish! It isn't a boot, it's a tassel loafer.

The entire structure of our culture supports the idea that tomorrow should, if at all possible, be better than today.
–Design, December 1990

4.1 The sad downfall of the world's oldest workshop

One of the leaders of Matsushita of Japan, the world's largest manufacturer of consumer electronics, recently said: 'America will provide the world with food, Japan will provide the world with industrial products and Europe will be their playground'.

As far as Britain is concerned, the process of decline from the dignity of manufacturing to the shaming barbarism of consumption is well advanced.

Alas, there is no racket of industry coming from the old workshop of the world; we no longer make our own cameras and optical instruments, typewriters, televisions, hi-fi, clocks, watches, pens, machine tools, tyres, and we are nearing the end of the period when we make cars, trucks and buses. The only reason the Japanese don't yet dominate our white-goods market is that, for the time being at least, they can't be bothered to ship metal boxes of air from one side of the globe to the other. The time will come.

The noisiest signs of wealth production are the subdued, sophisticated whines of the fans cooling the disk-drives of the American, Italian and Japanese computers which run the most effective parts of our economy. Without this imported hardware, the celebrated City would become paralysed and dumb and the men with the yellow ties would have to decamp. Without German presses, Fleet Street, Wapping and *Today*, wherever it is, would be mute. If it weren't for Ikegami, Sony and Nagra our broadcasters might as well spend the entire day in their wine bars.

To remark on this is not crude xenophobia or quaint patriotism but an expression of anxiety about the state of a country which is no longer willing (if still able) to manufacture the hardware it needs to maintain its civilization.

Politicians and economists are unconcerned: scratch one and you'll find a lobbyist for the service industries. There's a dangerously misleading idea that manufacturing has no place in a mature economy. If any odd Taiwanese Joe can make a microwave, if Johnny from Nagoya turns out reliable motors, cameras, hi-fi, bikes, clothes, felt-tip pens, televisions, computers and word processors, why should we make them? In sophisticated Britain, their argument goes, we can sell cashmere, run hotels and bus tourists around clogged London in Swedish coaches. We have been a trading nation for longer than we have been a manufacturing nation, they say.

Sir Edwin Nixon, chairman and chief executive of IBM UK, doesn't see it that way, as he said in a speech last year: *Let us begin with the harsh facts of our economic decline. Firstly, take the traditional bedrock of our economy: our manufacturing industry. The scale of decline here is disastrous. A trade surplus in manufactured goods of over £5,000 million in 1980 has turned to a trade deficit of some £3,700 million in 1984. What is most worrying about this trend is that we have not yet really begun to feel its effects, as our oil trade surplus has masked the deficit. Yet all agree that by the*

early decades of the 21st century we will not only have lost our oil surplus position, but
we will need to import oil as we did before the seventies.

The problem is that the service sector is showing signs of being just as sluggish as manufacturing used to be. And right now, even though the service industries' share of GNP has grown, in terms of output per hour, they are much less effective than manufacturing. There is the other question (and in the phrasing it's hard to avoid emotive words like shame and dignity) of whether the descendants of Brunel, Telford, Watt and Stephenson want to grow up to be merchant bankers, short-order chefs, hoteliers and dry cleaners.

In Britain manufacturing – which is to say making things – is now less than 20 per cent of the economy and that proportion is falling. Everybody is aware that we no longer make cameras, typewriters, motorbikes and just recently Britain's last remaining television manufacturer, the beleaguered Thorn-EMI, gave up the struggle and contracted to make Japan Victor Company sets under licence. This is what Americans call a 'hollow corporation', a company that parodies the industrial process by trading, advertising, scooping up profits and doing everything except actually making things.

With very few exceptions, high-technology consumer products are no longer made in Britain: if you don't believe me, just look at the mark of origin on a familiar branded product and don't be misled by recent changes in legislation which allow Japanese manufacturers to assemble components in factories built with Welsh Development Agency grants and declare them 'Made in Great Britain'.

The very few native high-technology consumer products, including some mobile radios, are manufactured by multinationals, including Philips, who are heavily represented here. All those car phones you see are American, Japanese, Finnish or Swedish.

Broadly speaking there is still activity in low technology, long lifecycle products requiring modest investments, but even in an area as fundamental as furniture, Britain has a £400 million balance of trade deficit. In luggage, imports account for 80 per cent of the market. We can still make cigarettes, bricks, biscuits and shoes, but companies specializing in these areas, including Hanson Trust, produce their sensational figures and become darlings of the City through a harrowing sequence of voracious acquisitions and speedy disposals.

There is really very little money in low technology. What used to be called asset stripping is now dignified as 'disposal of surplus facilities' which Hanson Trust tends to do as soon as it acquires another company. In the case of its recent acquisition of Ever-Ready, the vital research department was closed down.

Yet, still there are people who will tell you that the British are pretty bloody terrific when they have their backs to the wall. A comforting myth of sub-cutaneous excellence has disguised every British manufacturing failure. The Spitfire, a fine structural and aerodynamic achievement, was expensive and difficult to manufacture, requiring three times the factory man-hours of the enemy's Messerschmitts. The Mini, one of the world's most influential car designs, was so expensive to make that Ford ran a mile and made the Cortina, leaving BMC [British Motor Corporation] to make a loss for the first 17 years of the Mini's life.

Even the recent sentimental debate about Land Rover obscured the sad facts. For the decades when Solihull was either incapable or unwilling to produce the vehicles in the numbers the world demanded, the Japanese moved in with inferior products which were, at least, available. By the time the Third World had got used to Toyota Land Cruisers, a market had been lost and once markets are lost they are almost impossible to regain.

Now, the Japanese can make very effective cross-country vehicles out of standard car components and they lose very little to the Land Rover, lumbering on in its minute numbers and custom-made components, a sort of metal monarch of the glen, proud, but doomed (and as depressing, in its way, as the Landseer painting).

The wretched state of the British manufacturing industry is in part an inheritance from a culture whose social and educational systems disdain the market-place and hold trade in contempt. Even in the most innocent environments, anti-industrial sentiment smoulders with menace: *The Wind in the Willows* is not what it appears. Kenneth Grahame believed in an ideal England, perhaps somewhat similar to William Morris's mythic utopia or Robert Blatchford's *Merrie England*. Toad's world is not a fantasy for children but a powerful expression of the English longing for a country without industry and without a proletariat, a county ignorant of socialistic progress. Yet you see scarlet Majors in the country in their BMWs and I'll bet they wouldn't be without them. Fifty miles away from the Oxfordshire church where I found German cars double parked, there are car plants virtually idle because years of neglect have left Britain's motor industry bereft of the values necessary to make products desirable to consumers.

The anti-industrial sentiment and technophobia exist not only in children's books but also in the media, and especially in the City. When pressure from financial institutions forced the resignation of Standard Telephone Company's Sir Kenneth Corfield, after a brave and visionary (if somewhat on the foolhardy side of audacious) series of acquisitions, the journalists were quick to sneer. Corfield had a vision of turning STC into a world-class information technology company, manufacturing semiconductors, telecommunications and computers. Of course it was going to be expensive: the *Financial Times* explained that STC had irritated the City because of its long-term strategy and its grandiose vision, meanwhile encouraging its readers to invest in contract-cleaning companies puffed in the pages carrying ads for Japanese equities. The long-term view – say ten years – necessary in the manufacturing industry to carry a complex product through research, development, prototyping, manufacturing and marketing is beyond the vision of bankers (whose arms, of course, are always proverbially too short to reach even their pockets).

No one knows whether manufacturing is going to survive in Britain, but the signs are not promising. Vauxhall (in any case American-owned) sells cars made out of steel supplied by Welsh mills but pressed in Germany. The engines come from Australia. Bedford light vans are, in fact, made by Suzuki. Amstrad is a rare example of a 'manufacturer' apparently doing well. From an office in Essex, it orders up components from Asian parts bins. Good for them, but it's not going to keep 60 million people fed and warm on a damp island at the northern extremities of the playground of the world.

Very soon, any discussion of manufacturing in Britain becomes not so much a question of design as one of political economy. Besides our onerous cultural, social and educational inheritance which discourages technical education and commercial activity, there has been the inheritance from the war. Our factories were never reconstructed and remained nineteenth-century until they were run out of business; their managers for the forty years after 1945 when the competition got hot were not concerned with product or performance but were more actively engaged in booting the backsides of recalcitrant workers.

For four decades key men in the manufacturing industry simply were not aware of the available innovations in technology, design and process engineering that would lead to better products. And then it suddenly became too late.

Civilizations are remembered by their artefacts, not by their bank rates, yet in modern Britain there are very few things which are authentically British. We haven't got any beads and mirrors to offer gullible natives. The competition is too smart and if that competition decides to stop visiting us in its Swedish coaches at the same time as the oil runs out, we will simply be bankrupt. The politicians wittering on about the service economy won't be around to look at redundant deep-fat fryers, a depopulated Alton Towers and the empty hotels. I hope there aren't any politicians who think that once you lose the capacity to make cars or televisions you can get it back. At this late stage of industrial capitalism, you can't.

Design is not going to solve any of this ... but if we actually had some integrated manufacturing industry dedicated to consumer products it could, at least, help. But design cannot exist in a vacuum: without industry, design is merely styling.

Yet we hear politicians telling us that design will make things better. The poor old Austin Rover company has recently been making a bit of a splash with 'concept' cars quaintly called MG and Rover, shown at the Frankfurt and Turin motor shows. Elegant enough they certainly are, but they are only models and could not be made in England without the help of Japanese collaborators who will supply the engines, transmissions and the other complicated bits we find it difficult to manufacture ourselves.

Manufacturing is fundamentally important not only because it is good for the economy to be able to sell things, but also because it is satisfying for people to be involved with making things. After all, who but a Swede could love a Scania? But more important still, both for the economy and for culture, manufacturing is vital because of its knock-on effect. To manufacture successfully you have to maintain in good order all the educational research, development and design facilities which precede the industrial process, as well as the marketing and commercial functions which follow it. In fact: all the apparatus of civilization.

Unless every political, economical and cultural effort is put into British manufacturing, this island, like so many of the companies who call it home, will become a hollow corporation. I can't get John Ruskin's resounding Biblical cadences out of my head: 'Life without industry is guilt, and industry without art is brutality; and for the words "good" and "wicked", used of men, you may almost substitute "Makers" or "Destroyers".

I can scarcely bear to think what Ruskin would have felt about Britain in the late eighties.
– *Campaign*, 16 May 1986

4.2 Stiffen the sinews – this is war

The Japanese dominate world banking, world trade and world industry. They are richer, more powerful, more influential and less responsible than us – and yet we continue to indulge ourselves with a sense of genteel protectiveness in their favour. We are disinclined to offend the Japanese not because we are afraid of their power but because we are elegantly reluctant to embarrass them with the pain of confrontation. They take full advantage of our good manners.

Ever so slowly, however, people are beginning to realize the threat that Japan presents to the West. A remarkable and disturbing new novel by Michael Crichton articulates a profound American fear that was dormant when the Japanese were simply cute orientals who made transistor radios. Crichton's book is called *Rising Sun*; it could have been called *Yellow Peril*, a term coined in Germany this time last century to describe the scare that Japan would expand and take over the West.

To be scared of the people who provide us with the conveniences and pleasures of modern life – reliable cars, neat computers, amazing CDs, felt-tips that don't leak – may seem neurotically alarmist. It is not. The Japanese have ritualized industry: preoccupations with consensus, miniaturization and quality in a protect-ed economic environment that favours long-term strategies and encourages steady improvement of products bring consumers fine machines, but bring men-ace too. Japan is not only a culture of rituals, but also inflexible beliefs. One of them is: business is war.

Our culture encourages individuals, eccentrics, personal romance: competitive individualism is instilled in us throughout our social and professional lives. Unfortunately for us, competitive individualism is not best suited to industrial production. The Japanese system, which encourages collective action, works bet-ter. No matter that the Japanese pay a terrible cost in human terms for their domination of the planet's manufacturing industries, no matter that a new gener-ation is getting restive: Japanese companies possess knowledge about manufacturing which is beyond the reach of any Western competitor.

This knowledge breeds arrogance and impunity. When, in 1987, Toshiba was found to have supplied essential components to Soviet submarines, Americans were fearful of being too censorious lest Toshiba be tempted into reprisals such as denying the US computer industry its bulk microchips. When you own the playing field the goalposts are yours to move.

Are we right, then, to regard the Japanese as a menace? Is there a Yellow Peril? There are many interesting things about contemporary Japanese business. Here are three of them:

1 – The Japanese are profoundly opposed to sharing, except amongst themselves.
2 – Toyota, to choose just one example, has such a huge cash mountain that its treasury activities alone can service its wage bill, its tax and social obligations. This makes mere manufacturing of motor vehicles a discretionary activity which the company can address with an attention to detail which boggles even the most advanced Europeans – three thousand engineers were dedicated to Toyota's Lexus luxury car project. At the company's test track in northern Japan there is a strip of road which is perfectly flat … except for a slight bowing of a few centimetres at its midpoint to compensate for the curvature of the earth.
3 – There is a new wave of literature from America that is hostile to Japan, just as a new wave of literature from Japan is prepared to criticize Western manners and institutions where hitherto they had been respected and emulated.

In a restaurant in The Netherlands I had a conversation with a young English engineer who was terribly proud of his position in a Japanese company. And rightly so: without the help of this young engineer, his company would have been years behind in establishing the European presence they so urgently demanded. It was clear to him that I was impressed by the influence he said he had on the evolution of new product, yet there were understated reservations of disturbing dimensions. He said he felt excluded from decisions. Some to which he should have been party were made without consultation. He was treated as a talented inferior.

The fax, currently chief symbol of Japanese dominance of world trade, played a crucial part in his isolation and humiliation. Typically, the technology is not so very new, deriving from the wire-telegraphy of photographs which the big US news agencies had established by the 1930s, but its refinement is of the moment and characteristically Japanese. If soldiers believe that time spent in reconnaissance is never wasted, then Japanese businessmen have the same attitude to faxing.

When Ayrton Senna's Honda engine misses a beat, the telemetry records it and the blips on the graph are faxed straight back to Tokyo for immediate technical analysis. My engineer friend had enough authority to have sight of faxes, even if he could only read the odd Roman abbreviation in a sea of spidergraphics. Crucial Roman abbreviations included CA = cautious; NG = no good; OK = OK. You see why he felt excluded. His opinion was not sought.

Crichton's *Rising Sun* has been a runaway best-seller in US hardback fiction this year. Crichton, author of earlier sophisticated techno-thrillers *The Andromeda Strain* and *Jurassic Park*, fears that the big threat to world order is not cloned dinosaurs, but the fact that Japanese interests own the majority of the world's capital and therefore the majority of the world's politicians.

His plot revolves around the sale of an American high-technology company to a huge Japanese conglomerate. At one point a Senator expresses to a detective his anxiety about selling out to the Japanese: *MicroCon's advanced technology was developed in part with American taxpayer money. I'm outraged that our taxpayers should pay for research that is being sold to the Japanese – who will then use it to compete against our own companies. I feel strongly we should be protecting our intellectual resources. I feel we should be limiting foreign investment in our corporations and our universities. But*

I seem to be alone in this. I can't find support in the Senate or in industry. Commerce won't help me. The trade rep's worried it'll upset the rice negotiations. Rice...

The Japanese are not above a little protectionism of their own, and there are a thousand stories about the cavalier changing of statutory details of a rear lens specification to frustrate vehicle importers. They have a way of doing business that still mystifies us. The concept of *nemawashi* means approximately 'root binding', which is to say that everybody makes up their mind about what they want to achieve and have agreed on it before any discussions begin. In fact, the Japanese tend to regard it as sloppy and wasteful for work actually to be done in meetings. Rather, they prefer to have a lot of pre-argument (usually in their own language) and get it sorted out beforehand. Indeed, any hint of contradiction or contrariness is taken as evidence of the undisciplined, even barbarian, nature of the Western psyche: the Japanese have a loathing for confrontation.

Knopf rushed publication of *Rising Sun* earlier this year to take advantage of publicity from President Bush's embarrassing trade delegation to Japan. America's mood, so brilliantly captured by Crichton, is not a momentary refocusing of national paranoia after the Soviet Union ceased to be a conveniently diabolical adversary to demonize. Here with America and Japan there is a basis for conflict at least as real as the cold war. It is fertile ground: Crichton powerfully revives the American loathing of Japan, a loathing which was disguised after 1945 when the vanquished Japanese were allowed to get out of their Pearl Harbor uniforms and assume the less threatening role of being docile, short-sighted, industrious imitators. But Japan fought back with Sony, Honda, Toyota and Canon.

Some in the West want retaliation. Lester C. Thurow, Dean of the Sloan School of Management at Massachusetts Institute of Technology, has recently published *Head to Head: Coming Economic Battles among Japan, Europe and America*. Thurow predicts a future pattern of trade which will be increasingly *adversarial* as Western manufacturers struggle to retain expertise while Japanese walk it with global market share. In the key industries which dominate the world economy confrontation is going to be necessary for survival.

Maybe the last advantage left to us is a taste for the confrontation that the Japanese so loathe; but politicians, greedy for the short-term benefits of cash investment, do not understand the issue: in the war of business the Japanese own all the weapons ... and so do you and I. The green rollerball pen is a symbol of defeat. Yes, there *is* something menacing about it.
– *Life & Times*, 9 July 1992

4.3 Did BL [British Leyland] throw a vital tool away?

Roland Barthes, the French savant whose essays on steak and chips and Marilyn Monroe gave intellectual gloss to both the material and spiritual aspects of modern meat and, thereby, made popular material culture a respectable subject for academic discussion, also wrote an essay about cars. It was, in his characteristically sarcastic style, an exercise in irony, but one which nevertheless defined some of the tastes and aspirations of the age.

He was writing about the new Citroën car, the one which was unveiled at the 1955 Turin salon as a piece of sculpture: mounted on a pylon, its wheels removed so as not to compromise the public's perception of it as pure form, the new Citroën DS became a cult vehicle. Barthes said that, in his opinion, cars today are our cathedrals. He meant that while in the Middle Ages the technology and the art of whole nations were poured into buildings, which represented the aspirations of whole civilizations, in the late twentieth century the technology and the art of whole industries are poured into cars. They are the tokens by which our phase of Western civilization will be remembered.

Cars, of course, are more than mere transportation in the same way that cathedrals are more than mere buildings. A Japanese critic once wrote that cars betray your sexual fears and the successful car manufacturer must have a complete understanding of consumer psychology in creating and marketing his product.

BL, even its friends would say, has only been patchily efficient in producing and marketing successful products, but now that there is limited evidence that it has turned the corner (with Jaguar sales in the US up and Metro sales in the UK down), it's an appropriate moment to survey the condition of Britain's only volume car manufacturer. BL's problem has always been design.

Design is a complex subject, incorporating technology, finance, commerce, technique, art, production engineering and marketing. A cheapskate sceptic would say that design is only the application of fashion to industry, but this would be to do violence to the customer: design concerns not only the initial conception and subsequent creation of mass-produced products, but also the control of every aspect of the public's response to them and underlying all these statements is the assumption that design is fundamental to economic success. Design is not just the matter of doing dramatic magic-marker renderings to art-up a nasty product at the last moment. It is, more simply, a matter of thinking – a matter of not holding the public in contempt.

In BL's case this could be directed to the question of why the switch panel in the Rover SDI is invisible at night and why the Allegro was assembled out of obsolete bits gathered from Longbridge parts bins while all the time Honda was busily developing a range of cars engineered down to the last original thou.

Indeed, now that parts of BL seem to have abnegated their, in any case, delinquent attitude to design to the Japanese, a remark recently made by the astonishing Soichiro Honda deserves special attention. Honda said, in effect, that Alec Issignonis taught him everything he wanted to know about cars. He was polite enough to make no comment about BL ... and thus from Tokyo was the state of British industry neatly described: manufacturers are, in general, incapable of taking advantage of native talent.

There are, however, some extremely positive aspects of BL's past, but in each case a great opportunity to capitalize on an outstanding product has been lost because of weak compromise, indecision and lack (until lately) of clear corporate strategy. While some comfort may be taken from the fact that the recent decline of the domestic US auto industry will make BL's troubles look like a house of cards in an avalanche (changing the course of GM [General Motors], a critic recently said, is rather like attempting to change the course of France), BL's problems have been dut to its sheer size.

Yet it is hard not to admire a corporation which can produce the Austin 7 (which formed the basis of car manufacturing for both Datsun and BMW); the Morris Minor which, with even an accountant's minimum development and promotion could and should have blown the Volkswagen Beetle into the weeds; the Jaguars, whose value to European and American customers can now be seen in colossal prices as collectors' cars but were systematically abused by BL managements interested only in narrow-minded cost-cutting and crude short-term accounting benefits; the Mini, a product so radical in engineering and marketing terms that the lessons it taught are only now being learned by other European and oriental manufacturers, but a car which scarcely made any profit for its manufacturer and which still today, given some development and serious attention to detail, could be a European market leader; and the Rover SD1, an astonishingly daring design by David Bache, inspired by the look of the Ferrari Daytona, but which was too expensive to compete in America and became a curate's egg in its home market because of the traditional problems of quality and image.

BL's character as an innovator in products can be summarized by saying that it seems to get its products right at about the third go (all the time contemptuously testing under-designed and under-developed products on a public which eventually goes over to Datsuns). With the Maxi, Allegro and Princess, BL launched cars on the market about five years before their development was complete. And the sales show it.

This business of under-development is exacerbated by a failure to capitalize on products which are potentially successful. With the TR7, which could have become the most popular sports car of modern times, BL refused to incorporate adequate powerplant and adequate development.

Almost against fate, BL has managed to produce some excellent products, the envy of the world. Under the engineer Spencer Kind and the designer David Bache, the Range-Rover became a product inimitable elsewhere. Even the Metro, compromised by management's decision to introduce a designer only at the last stages and by a disastrous advertising campaign in Europe that left the product looking about as sophisticated as liquorice allsorts, is still among the best cars in its class.

What is so depressing is that it could have been so much better. Short-term accounting, lack of strategy and lack of integrated design policy have left BL in an exposed position. David Bache has now left the company and the best young British-trained car designers go to work in Germany. The truck and bus division still employs the outstanding talent of Tom Karen, an independent consultant, to create its heavy goods vehicles and they are the best of their type in Europe. The problem is that now that BL has a good product, the truck market is in recession.

BL's heritage of uncoordinated management, of unsophisticated marketing and of poor quality control has left it with a serious public relations problem. While someone in BL was wondering what type of cheap and nasty badges to put on

the face-lifted 18/20 Princess and Ambassador, Daimler-Benz was developing
mass-production cars for the twenty-first century. Almost ten years before,
when the first generation of special class Mercedes cars was introduced, the
British Leyland dealerships in places like Antwerp were selling Allegros side-by-
side with flyblown Czech Rotavators.

There is talent and energy within BL and the British design community as a whole
has the most sophisticated consultancy services to offer whatever extra expertise the corporation needs. Too often, however, the ghosts of the past re-
emerge. It is very late for BL to save itself by design ... but it is not quite too late.
– Campaign, Design and Art Direction supplement, 1982

4.4 Vision that was blurred by big business

Anybody working for Habitat during its great years had a sense of mission. It was
always more than a shop, not much less than a crusade.

There was a sense of religious purpose enhanced by Terence Conran's genius for
myth-making.

Habitat was one man's vision but many, many people's work. The man with
the vision was Conran, memorably described by one of his colleagues as a
'superb editor of merchandise'. Certainly, Conran had been a designer of textiles, crockery, furniture, but his great skill was not as an inventor or a maker,
but as someone who had a perfect pitch when it came to interpreting the tenor
of the times.

Conran always believed that excellence in design was an identifiable, numinous
quality, often difficult to define, but under his tutelage easy to detect; simple,
clean forms, sometimes with an element of wit.

Over the years he had acquired and lost money and his friends in equal measure,
but even his severest critics would never deny his conviction about the role of
design in everyday life, the importance of making houses beautiful for everyone.

Habitat opened in London in 1964 when the mood was confident, optimistic,
experimental.

As a struggling furniture designer in the 1950s, Conran had found it difficult to
persuade the big multiple stores to stock his unfussy – ironically, it now seems,
Scandinavian – modern furniture. He was always eloquent about the depressing
oceans of brown moquette you found in early 1960s furniture departments.
Continuous rebuttals at the hands of boorish buyers convinced Conran to set up
on his own.

This one inspiration was a stroke of genius that has been a huge influence on
British domestic taste.

As well as an outlet for his own furniture designs, the first Habitat also stocked an encyclopaedia of goods which had caught Conran's eye: electricals by Braun, ethnic basketware and French kitchenware. Suddenly, in a British shop (of all places) you could buy things that had hitherto been known only in illustrations from American and Continental architectural magazines.

But Habitat also had a catalogue. As the chain of shops expanded, so did the catalogue. From being a folded piece of coarse paper in 1964, ten years later it had become a handsome portfolio of contemporary opportunities to improve your life with honest design.

At its best, Habitat was like a museum, an eclectic exhibition of good design. But critics, including Vico Magistretti, the Italian furniture designer, accused Conran of plagiarism.

Certainly, Conran was reluctant to give credit where it was due (and it was due in a great many places: both the design of the stores and of the graphics were by other hands) but an accusation of plagiarism was to misunderstand the messianic nature of this crusade.

Maybe Habitat's most successful chair was a knock-off of a Marcel Breuer design; maybe a lot of the textiles were 'influenced' by Marimekko, maybe even the shop itself borrowed ideas from Design Research in Boston, but individual bylines play no part in a crusade.

Conran's sense of mission was so profound, his infectious sense of changing Britain's taste was so strong that to mutter about authorship and acknowledgement seemed churlish.

And then things began to go wrong, although at the time it looked as though they were going more and more right.

The 1981 flotation made Conran very rich but it also introduced this Dr Faust of furniture to Mephistopheles in the form of merchant banker Roger Seelig.

Year after year until Seelig's resignation from Morgan Grenfell in 1987, the two men grew the business into the calamitous Storehouse. Suddenly, the Conran who had been pleased to be photographed in Chelsea wearing a butcher's apron was translated into the less convincing Conran who was chairman of what was briefly a £2 billion business.

With Conran's eye elsewhere, Habitat – which had always been neglected in terms of investment capital and starved of proper advertising and PR – now became a pitiable parody of itself. At the same time, Storehouse began to founder, and Conran became irrevocably separated from his darling brainchild.

A New Yorker called Barbara Deichman was brought in as design director. She introduced attractive vernacular merchandise, but the purity of the original idea had been lost. The truth is that despite the ambitions of the 1980s, without massive educational initiatives (which I spent ten happy years helping Conran organize), without a massive shift in popular taste towards the enlightened liberal aestheticism of Conran and his class, Habitat was always going to be a minority exercise.

I remember the look of horror when somebody explained that a majority of customers actually *preferred* easy-care nylon sheets: Terence Conran, always believed that absolutely everyone should want and should have fresh river-washed linen.

But crusaders are inevitably about persuasion. It is very sad that this one failed.
– *Daily Telegraph*, 27 October 1992

4.5 Zagato's family business

The traffic in Milan is so bad that drivers are inclined to take the *tangenziale*, or ring road, no matter how short or apparently direct their journey. It is rather as if in London you used the M25 to connect Chelsea with Westminster. Milan has now banned private cars from its historic centre; but with an irony characteristic of the Italian condition, this seems to have made congestion worse. There are few more fumy, frustrating and generally bloody-minded places to attempt to drive than in Italy's industrial and commercial capital. There is nowhere better in which to ponder the paradox that the motor car, created as instrument of democratic expression, a tool of freedom, has become tiresomely oppressive.

Yet, Milan is the scriptural home of some of the most beautiful and wonderful cars that have ever been made, machines whose optimism, joy, tangible plastic beauty and innocent aggressiveness defy the dull imperatives of rational consumer choice and utterly transcend the sum of their simple mechanical parts.

Milan is the home of Alfa Romeo, one of the great manufacturers (whose badge is the city's coat-of-arms). It is also the home of Zagato, one of the great traditional *carrozzeria*, or coachbuilders, the artisan designers who create car bodies which clothe the machine, ravish the eye and stop the heart.

When you arrive in an English town, the first sign you see is usually the one that says 'Car Park and Toilets'. In France, you are more likely to see a sign pointing to the historic centre. In Milan, as you cruise the *tangenziale*, the messages you see are acronymic and ugly – SMEG, SNAM, MAMM, Wacker Siliconi – rather than revealing. But they are signs of flourishing industrial activity. Perhaps supported by the immanent spirit of workshop traditions that go back to the Etruscans, Italy has managed to preserve a nationwide network of small, semi-industrialized family workshops, which can build and sell competitively anything from a fitted kitchen to an extravagant motor car. The reason why it has so many furniture, lighting, fashion and car design companies is not just that it has brilliant designers, but that it has so many small, highly skilled manufacturers capable of realizing their designs in short series. Zagato is one of those manufacturers.

The Zagato factory is at Terrazzano di Rho, a nondescript Milan suburb hard by the roaring *autostrada* which leads from the lugubrious city to the light and air of Como and the lakes. The administrative building is a bravura piece of Italian style, a terrazzo block of concrete cantilevers and canopies with the proud name in free-standing letters on the roof. You pass through drawing offices with huge parallel-action boards attended by solemn draughtsmen in white coats, into an area where men are using hand-tools and bending and burnishing metal, rather than making marks on paper. At 30,000 square metres, the Zagato factory is impressively large, but it is not impressively modern. This is not like aerospace, this is more like Aston Martin: manufacturing by a process that would be quaint were it not so heroic. Chassis sit on dollies awaiting the paint sprayer or the trim line. There is an air of benign and pregnant lethargy. The sense of tradition is tangible, the confidence real.

Ugo Zagato was a poor boy, but apparently a self-possessed one, whose experience as a metalworker in Germany won him a job first at Cesare Belli's old carrozzeria (where he was among the very first Italians ever to work on car body design) and later, in 1915, at Officina Pomilio, an aircraft manufacturer in Turin. When Gabriele d'Annunzio made his bravura 1918 leaflet-drop over vanquished Vienna in a heavily modified biplane, it was Ugo Zagato's handiwork – in gaining extra range with heavier tanks at no weight penalty – that helped make the poet's remarkable 1,000km flight possible.

In 1919, when Zagato set up his own workshop in Milan, politics and poetics were in a glorious *imbroglio*, and the design of any transport system was an affirmation of a belief in progress. There was less distinction between cars, aeroplanes and boats than there is today: they were all Newtonian mechanisms which needed shrouding from liquids or gases during their passage through them. What Zagato had learned about light structures and functionally inspired elegance in building aeroplanes he was soon to apply to sports cars in his own distinctive and sometimes idiosyncratic style.

The catalyst in the Zagato story was Aldo Finzi, a wartime acquaintance, who in 1924 introduced Ugo to the newly founded Alfa Romeo factory. In Italy, perhaps more so than elsewhere, racing was a part of the evolution of the car; and Alfa Romeo made some of the best racing cars. Initially a privileged and boastful aristocratic pastime whose founders included the original Giovanni Agnelli, father of the Fiat empire, racing eventually became popular, even proletarian.

In those days, long before he built his own cars, Enzo Ferrari, a wily and opportunistic but inspired peasant mechanic, was a racing driver. It was for Ferrari that Ugo Zagato, with engineer Vittorio Jano, worked on the original Alfa Romeo 1500 6C. A development of that car won a race at Modena in 1927 with Ferrari himself at the wheel – and, in the two subsequent years, won the Mille Miglia in the hands of Campari and Ramponi.

Racing has been the continuous inspiration for the Zagato aesthetic: to the elegant and potent simplicity of the Alfa Romeo chassis, Zagato added bodywork of uncompromised efficiency but outstanding elegance, which helped establish an architecture of the sports car that was not to change for twenty years. What Zagato had once contributed to d'Annunzio he now contributed to Enzo Ferrari. The Mille Miglia was their stage.

But by the Second World War technological change in aerospace had marginalized *carrozzerie* and it was no longer possible for artisan craftsmen, no matter how inspired, to contribute meaningfully to the design of aeroplanes. Instead, Zagato built trucks. But this was only a brief diversion: soon after 1945, Italy began to enjoy one of the periodic renaissances which distinguish its history, and one expression of this era was motor racing. Ferrari started making cars under his own name (adapting, typically, a First World War pilot's prancing horse motif for his own badge).

In the same period, the Zagato workshop (now in the hands of Ugo's son, Elio, a distinguished racing driver in his own right) began to refine its expedient vocabulary into a new language of form which still today limits and projects our expectations of the sports car. To the Zagato studio, one of the first to experiment with plexiglass and aerodynamics, we owe the development of features such as faired-in headlamps, assertive embrasures around ventilation orifices, all enveloping bodies and cut-off tails. While there was a great deal of aesthetic preference in these designs, there was also a good measure of intuitive science, suggesting a sensible relationship between the demands of the sport and the taste for functionalism.

It is rare for a *carrozzeria* to be run by a racing driver; and Zagato has always designed from assumptions other than elegance – in the art-for-art's sake sense. All Zagato cars have been conceived from inside out, but an aesthetic rationale emerged because not only the racing cars but the entire business was driven by a racing driver. *Grintosa sportivita* (the power of sport) defines the style, as well as the business ethic. Sometimes this has created cars of rare and exceptional beauty, such as the Lancia Appia GTE, the Fiat-Abarth, or the Aston Martin DB4GTZ, sometimes cars whose appearance seems wilfully odd or gratuitously perverse. Always it has led to designs of real presence and profound integrity.

For Zagato, the 1960s were perhaps the period of greatest creativity. The increasing professionalization of motor racing again marginalized semi-industrial artisans, but one influence was now replaced by another, this time that of the designer Ercole Spada. Although the Zagato family, in correct workshop tradition, is reluctant to attribute authorship of any design to any individual, it was from 1960 to 1969 while Spada was at Zagato that many of Zagato's most creative designs appeared: the Lancia Flavia Sport (1963), the Alfa Romeo Giulia TZ1/2 (1963-5) and the Lancia Fulvia Sport (1965). Glass became a part of the designer's language and with some of the extraordinary four-seat configurations of the Lancia coupés the idea of sport – or, at least, *turismo veloce* – became an experience available for all four passengers.

Even though Ercole Spada is now on the staff of IDEA, currently the busiest and most creative Italian automotive design consultancy, it would be misleading to credit the bad patch of the 1970s to his departure from Terrazzano di Rho. The 1970s were the period of the oil shock and, especially in Italy, of urban terrorism: 'A period', according to Andrea Zagato, Elio's son, 'when the coupé was not quite up to date'. A period, too, when Aldo Moro was found dead in the boot of an Alfa Romeo. So with artisanal guile, Zagato started making armoured cars, and is still the market leader in this field of discretion. Cash flow at the time was helped by the contract to build the convertible Beta Spiders for Lancia.

Visiting Zagato today is a moving experience, not just because here, in one of the oldest surviving *carrozzerie*, there are the ghosts of so many wonderful cars, but also because Zagato has recently rediscovered its true spirit. Elio Zagato sits in the light dust and sunshine of his office supervising a business that has developed without having changed. In conversation he repeatedly explains that the Zagato philosophy is, in a word, "*sportivita*". Whatever the question you ask Elio, his brother Gianni or Andrea Zagato, the answer is always something to do with motor sport. Andrea says: 'The great designs don't come from wanting to do a good shape; they come from something else. From racing. Making cars faster and more intelligent'.

Zagato now does about £2.5-million-worth of work for Maserati each year, building two or three Spyder bodies a day. It does a similar amount of business with Autech, a Nissan subsidiary in awe of Abarth's old relationship with Fiat, for whom Zagato has designed and will build 200 of the curiosities called the Stelvio, a car of real character, not all of it good. A mere 50 Aston Martin Zagatos are being made. There is even a Zagato watch, but this is an amiable promotion rather than serious diversification – although there are now 13 staff in a separate division called Zagato Design prepared to do more watches and steering wheels as the airport shop and aftermarket demands. But there are 119 people in Zagato Car. They are proud of their contribution to Maserati, Aston Martin and Autech. But most of all they are proud of the new car they helped to design and are now building for Alfa Romeo. With the wonderful SZ, Zagato has rediscovered its soul.

The Alfa Romeo SZ is both shockingly brutal and arrestingly subtle. It has short overhangs, an ostentatious pout and bizarre details executed with utter conviction. In the tradition of all the great Alfa Romeo racers Zagato has built, it is wicked but seductive, a piece of rough trade in an Armani suit. It reminds you that although Ugo Zagato was an artisan his contemporaries called him a *gagà* – a dandy.

Just as the sale last February of a Zagato-bodied Aston Martin for £1.4m confirmed, in one sense at least, that cars have become negotiable commodities like works of art, so the fact that the Alfa Romeo SZ even exists is evidence of one great manufacturer's fascination with the car as a work of art and one great *carrozzeria*'s ability to turn sheet steel and moulded globs of ICI's Modar composite material into astonishing sculpture.

Of course, there are other great *carrozzerie* in Italy. But none is quite the same as Zagato. Pininfarina worships at the altar of elegance and designs for mass-production. ItalDesign is highly diversified and entrepreneurial, with considerable resources in research and development. Bertone orchestrates the odd *coup de théâtre* at motor shows. Zagato, even while it has recently reorganized itself into divisions concerned with cars and with industrial design, will always remain committed to specialist cars.

Nowadays, distinctions in the motor industry are made by brand managers. The big car manufacturers all have very sophisticated design departments of their own. It seems unlikely that in future the traditional *carrozzerie* will have much influence over the design of everyday motor vehicles: the bored hush around Bertone's stand at this year's Geneva Motor Show was significant of a new age.

But look through the old books and you'll realize what makes Zagato distinctive is not simply the very particular house style, but the commitment to making small batches of cars. By supplying the chassis and mechanical components of the

SZ, Alfa Romeo has helped Zagato discover the future in its past. In March 1965, an *Autocar* journalist wrote: 'By including in their standard catalogue ranges a few individualistic creations by the specialist coachbuilders, the major car manufacturers of Italy broaden their own commercial scope while lending support to local industry'.

At motor shows nowadays it is not unusual to find more people looking at Japanese sports cars than Ferraris. It is not too fanciful to see in Zagato's Alfa Romeo SZ a hint of the future for car building in Europe. Because Zagato offers integrated design and construction, ideas can quickly be realized for limited production at premium prices. By the time production stops at the end of 1991, only 1,000 Alfa Romeo SZs will have been built, but at a considerable profit and with considerable benefit to the industrial culture of Alfa Romeo, Italy and Europe.

Maybe average speeds on the *tangenziale* are approaching those of the nightly stroll in the piazza, but Zagato is able to recapture – for a fortunate few – the elementary thrill of owning a motor vehicle. Even in a traffic jam.
The Sunday Times, 1991

4.6 Zen and the cycle of motor art

In Manhattan or the Middle East, besides American detergents and soft drinks, the most nearly universal commodity is the Japanese car. Yet less than a decade ago, an acquaintance (the owner of a stately British Bristol and a growling German Porsche) said to me: 'I long to buy a Nissan ... but I'm not self-confident enough'. Now the seven leading Japanese car manufacturers (Toyota, Nissan, Honda, Mazda, Mitsubishi, Subaru and Suzuki) supply vehicles to satisfy every customer preference between wanton cupidity and utilitarian need.

In 1964 the response to the very first Japanese car (a Daihatsu Compagno Berlina) to be imported into Britain was one of patrician derision. From behind the wheels of their Humber Super Snipes and Austin Westminsters, the clubbable old buffers who ran the British motor industry (into the ground) tittered at the oriental impertinence. So what happened?

In 1958 Datsun (now Nissan) sold 83 cars in the entire United States. That lonely Asiatic tribe was represented by a car whose design was described as 'melancholy' in the contemporary press. There were reasons to laugh: Datsun used to produce a model called the Cedric, based on faulty market research which reported that this was a popular name in Australia, another pioneer export market.

Now the Honda Accord is the year-in, year-out best-selling car in the US and Toyota's Lexus luxury brand sold more than 90,000 cars there last year. To offer a chastening comparison, in the same period about 4,000 Americans drove home in new Jaguars.

Cars are the precious metal of industrial culture. Demand for them is an indicator of economic well-being; the ability to manufacture them at a profit is the surest sign of technological competence; the quality of their design is cruelly revealing evidence of the intellectual fitness of a nation. Japanese cars have never been in greater demand and sales in Europe are held back only by quotas.

In a declining market for new cars, Japanese manufacturers are alone in predicting growth. The quota system, which Europeans imposed in a spasm of decadent protectionism, has not achieved its purpose; rather, it has given the Japanese a rationale for attacking the very heart of European expertise – the luxury car.

If you tell a Japanese manufacturer he may only import, say, 10,000 cars a year, his reaction will be that those cars will be premium-priced products with the highest profit margin. The fixed costs of making a car are similar whatever its size. Without quotas, chances are the Japanese would still be supplying banal mass-market run-abouts. But with the stimulus of the quota system, they have been given an irresistible incentive to confront the Europeans on what they thought was their own patch. If you had said ten years ago that Toyota was building a car to rival, even humiliate, Mercedes-Benz, people would have laughed in your face. But today you can buy a Lexus.

In most respects, the design of Japanese cars now leads the world, yet Japan had no serious car industry before the 1960s. Toyota started out making looms. Nissan was only established as an automaker with technical assistance from a (now defunct) American company. Soichiro Honda was an uneducated, artisan experimenter, occasionally given to hitting his apprentices over the head with a hammer to emphasize a point. His dearest ambition was to manufacture piston rings, but history cheated him: by 1960 he had destroyed the British motorcycle industry, before moving on to cars.

Honda used the stern discipline of motorcycle racing to train his engineers. More recently, the company has been competing successfully in Grand Prix motor racing as part of its research and development programme. Young engineers, designers and materials scientists were exposed to the Darwinian processes of racing in which components have to be designed to operate to extraordinary tolerances. The pits of the circuit were laboratories.

Just as his contemporary, Akio Morita of Sony, was inspired by the pursuit of miniaturization and innovation, Honda sought mechanical efficiency. Quests of this sort develop their own dynamic, with one small innovation here leading to an unanticipated improvement there, but best of all was what racing did for the personnel. Back in the factory, full of hard-won racing experience, the engineers transferred their expertise to road cars.

Today Honda ensures that all its workers understand the entire process of designing and making a car: materials scientists get rotated to the marketing department, marketeers get sent to work on the production line. The result is cars with a lapidary depth of quality.

Despite the rapidly rising number of patents filed in Tokyo (the surest measure of industrial creativity), the great achievement of Japan has been essentially pragmatic, based on ritualized refinement and an attention to detail which have their roots in traditional culture.

The Japanese have a saying: 'The nail that stands up is hammered down'. They
seem to have a horror of being exceptional, preferring collective effort to idio-
syncrasy. While we cultivate our personalities with rites of competitive
individualism, they nurture a curious hybrid of capital-intense collectivism. The
disciplines of Zen proved surprisingly helpful in the mass production of cars.

In the 1950s just when Morita was learning about the transistor from Western
Electric, Taiichi Ohno of Toyota toured American car factories. His observations
of the American method of mass production led him to return to Toyota City
with a new manufacturing concept: lean production. Ohno was horrified to see
that if a car proceeding down a production line in an American factory was
observed to have a fault, it would remain uncorrected until it had reached the
end of the line.

This slapdash method suited the unsophisticated linear certainties of American
mass markets, in which high demand and low expectations went hand-in-hand,
but the Japanese recoiled from such a clumsy industrial aesthetic. Ohno helped
to develop a production method that fixed faults as they occurred. The process
is now so advanced that Toyota's Lexus has been designed in a way that means
faults are virtually eliminated at the conceptual stage. It is almost impossible for
errors to be made in its assembly.

While it is true that austere engineering disciplines and a keen sense of economy
have influenced Japanese manufacturing methods, the contribution of cultural and
religious values to the quality of cars cannot be exaggerated.

Patience, attention to detail, discipline and subordination of personality all have
their roots in Zen. There is even a word for it – *muda* describes the waste and
inefficiency found in Western factories. And Americans are slow to learn: in
1987 the purchasing department of General Motors had 6,000 staff; Toyota
made better cars with only 337.

Geographical circumstances also forced efficiency. Because transport is difficult
in mountainous Japan, suppliers based themselves close to factories. This was the
origin of the famous *kanban* (just-in-time) system of component supply, which
allowed Japanese manufacturers to make dramatic savings in inventory costs.
Then there was the blessing of government intervention: the Ministry of
International Trade and Industry helped manufacturers to establish specifications
and insisted that they pool research.

One consequence was that manufacturers did not waste time and money on
duplication of effort. Everywhere in Japanese culture, this emphasis on avoiding
waste recurs. Equally, during those decades when complacent Westerners derided the Japanese for 'copying' Chevrolets or Fiats, they misunderstood. The
Japanese were copying only in a limited sense.

What they were doing was avoiding the wasteful business of developing their
own product. Why design your own Chevrolet or Fiat when Americans or
Italians have gone to all the trouble of doing it for you? Instead, they concentrated on creating new industrial processes and found ways to make Chevrolets and
Fiats far better than they could in Detroit and Turin.

It is this revolution in process that has led to the superiority of Japanese cars. Their engineers have no special knowledge unavailable to their European or American counterparts. It is just that they have learned to apply it better.

Japanese cars at first won grudging acceptance on grounds of economy and reliability. Even conservative Americans saw the virtues of small, cheap cars that worked. The Japanese seemed to be offering European scale and convenience with comfortingly familiar styling (then as now, some of the best Japanese cars were designed by Americans) *and* American standards of reliability. The cars inspired loyalty rather than passion, but then the Japanese pulled off their really great trick, the one that still baffles industry experts.

Their *coup* was to make incremental changes in successive new models of an order far exceeding all prudent and reasonable projections. Within the past ten years, the Japanese have made an institution out of astonishing design. The lean-production method seems actually to stimulate creativity. Product life cycles are a measure of industrial efficiency: some Japanese manufacturers can now renew models every twenty-four months, while struggling Volkswagen, once Europe's most efficient manufacturer, takes eight years.

Lean production also increases consumer choice: the dramatic pace of evolution in the 1980s allowed Japanese manufacturers to double the number of cars they offered the public. Now all that patient nurturing has produced a magic formula of which Japan Inc appears to be the sole proprietor. New models of Japanese cars exceed the ability of our imaginations to guess what is coming next. Forget a new badge, a new grille, a new range of colours. All those years of slow improvement have turned out to be just the prologue. Now we are in the main feature and it's amazing.

Take three recent examples: the Nissan Micra, the Toyota Space-Cruiser and the Lexus. The old Micra was one of the least interesting cars ever made, sought by unadventurous pensioners; its replacement is the best in its class, a no-apologies gem. The old Toyota Space-Cruiser was an ugly van with Dan Dare styling; the Previa is a brilliant new category of vehicle with curvaceous styling creating Astrodome quantities of interior space and an engine buried beneath the centre of the car to give extraordinarily good handling. The old Toyota Crown was a sloppy motorized *pachinko* parlour with antimacassars; the Lexus is the most refined car in the world, bettering Mercedes-Benz in most respects at half the price.

The Japanese design and manufacture cars so that quality is inevitable. Just as in electronics the pursuit of miniaturization generates its own dynamic of technical progress, so in manufacturing the quest for efficient production pushes car makers higher and higher up a creative helix. So far up, some would say, that they are now beyond the reach of European and American imitators.

Of course, the Japanese do get some things wrong. Names are still a bit of a problem: on its home market Mazda sells something called the Bongo Brawny and Daihatsu until recently had a charming Fellow Max on its lists. And the styling of some of the cars is on the maladroit side of quirky. But then you consider the opposition: us. Take a long look at the meticulous shape of a current Japanese car, with its paper-thin gaps between panels, its mirror-finish, its

careful details, sensible textures and its overall desirability. Now you know who
won the war.
— *The Times Magazine*, 9 October 1993

4.7 Robots take over the Boilerhouse

For two hundred years, the history of design has been a list of styles and ideologies, one succeeding the other and each moderated by fashion. But now this is going to change. A new technology is beginning which is so universal in its scope and potential that nice discussions about *style* will soon become apparent for what they always were: polite banter about taste, exchanges of views about what pleases us and what does not. The modern movement arose out of the first age of industrialization when circumstances were produced which changed the ground rules of design. As soon as machine production underlined the traditional notions of ornament and craftsmanship, then thinkers proposed a set of rules about design which altered the appearance of the contemporary world. The second age of industrialization promises changes that will be just as profound.

Robots are the machines at the core of this new technology. They promise to alter our attitudes to the organization of work and to patterns of consumption. Robots will change design and they will change many other things besides.

All the mass-produced things around us have been made by men and machines… yet for years analysis of the manufacturing process has been confined to production engineers and ergonomists. Only recently, under the influence of the apocalyptic changes promised by the new technology, have designers and economists renewed their interest in the mechanization of work. Superb consumer products from Japan have forced managers to become aware of the benefits of automating the production process.

To understand the implications of the robot we must first dispel the mythology of the past. There has been a thin, but consistent, tradition of men fashioning their own image in the form of machines. Cabalistic times and pioneering studies of surgery employed metaphors of machines and buildings in attempting to explain the composition of man.

There is a story that the great French rationalist philosopher and mathematician René Descartes made a mechanical woman, called Francine, who travelled with him in his hand baggage. Francine was designed on mathematical principles to demonstrate the existence of order in the universe, but although 'she' was thrown overboard when a superstitious sea captain feared the influence of black magic, Descartes's faith in the rational character of man was unshaken.

A century after Descartes and somewhat because of his influence, man began to replace God as the chief subject for speculative intellectual inquiry. During the eighteenth century a series of rational thinkers made the blasphemous proposition that man could be best understood by analogy with machines. Julien La Mettrie published a book called *L'Homme Machine* (Man as Machine, 1784) in which he offered the extreme proposition that man was entirely comparable with clockwork mechanisms, that there was no need for intuition or emotions and not even any need for death. La Mettrie proved himself wrong by dying of gluttony, but his thought was very influential on intellectual development in France during the second half of the eighteenth century.

Mary Shelley's book *Frankenstein* was published at the same time as the Luddite riots. It was the first literary expression of man's fear of the machine. For a hundred years that book provided the most memorable image of 'artificial intelligence'. Then in 1920 a Czech playwright called Karel Capek, described by *The Sketch* as 'the H G Wells of Czechoslovakia', gave us the word robot (which is Czech for 'serf'). Capek's play RUR (*Rossum's Universal Robots*, performed in New York in 1922, in London the following year at St Martin's Theatre) was a fantasy where android workers in Dr Rossum's remote island factory developed minds of their own and became rebellious.

Capek set his play in the 1950s, anticipating by twenty years the dilemma we are facing with our own very different type of robot civilization. Rossum's factory uses a secret process to manufacture 'artificial people', properly known as 'biological androids'. From a microbiological soup of his own devising, Rossum produced hearts and livers, bones and flesh, but due to either a technical or conceptual lapse, crucial to the dramatic development of Capek's play, was not able to manufacture souls. Rossum's robots had enough intellect to obey orders, but lacked both emotions and the capacity to feel pain. Under the influence of Helena Glory, a visitor to Rossum's island factory, the robots become humanized. The robot leader is called Radius; he is the first to develop a sense of discontent and under his leadership, like Frankenstein's monster, the robots turn against their makers. Like Frankenstein, Rossum offended natural laws by making a scientific substitute for God.

In Japan the robot of the movies became a cult. The Japanese have a curious obsession with robots. First of all given form in powerful feature films such as Inoshira Honda's *The Mysterians* (1957), the fabrication of home-made automata became a minor cottage industry. Then, with Japan's industrial renaissance under way, native toy manufacturers began to turn out tin-plate and plastic robots in immense numbers. At first these toys only imitated the stereotypes of Hollywood, but the market soon became sufficiently sophisticated to encourage the creation of a unique robot vocabulary that is characteristically Japanese and which replaced Hollywood as a major international source of robot symbology.

Just as the Japanese monopolized world production of toy robots so they now monopolize world production of industrial robots.

The 'robot' in literature, theatre and film has either been an experiment in body-snatching and cell manipulation, or a science-fiction automaton with space-age materials got up to look and perform like the human frame. Not since the end of the Age of Reason have robots (or replicants, or automata) been presented as optimistic creations... until George Lucas's epic film *Star Wars* (1977), itself a product of California's computer industry, presented the spectacle of R2D2 and C3P0 as 'user friendly'.

Modern industrial robots owe very little to the imagery of the past, but still have a mythology all of their own. Karel Capek's melodramatic robot reached a very fundamental layer of human awareness … and stayed there. Although *RUR* now reads as ham-fisted and naive, Capek's story carries subtexts which in the coded language of the theatre summarize our fear of the machine. The speculation in the press about how industrial robots threaten man and will alter the world recalls both that tradition of literature which began with *Frankenstein* and that more material fear of the machine which once found expression in the Luddite riots when textile workers in the North of England destroyed their new machinery, blaming it for their distress. Together these two strains of thought provide a considerable obstacle to an acceptance of the new technology which industrial robots represent.

In fact robots are intelligent machines consisting of hands and arms controlled by supervisory computers. According to Mike Skidmore, European Manager of Cincinnati Milacron, a robot has to have four special qualities: the capacity to learn a characteristic behaviour; facilities for perceiving the environment; data analysis faculties; the capacity to modify their characteristic behaviour.

Already the capabilities of industrial robots are astonishing: an IBM robot's arm can move to the same spot on a printed circuit board within one two-thousandths of an inch *every* time; Cincinnati Milacrons move at two hundred inches per second; some Unimation robots can 'recognize' up to nine different assemblies with up to twelve separate components, while the small PUMA (Programmable Universal Machine Assembly) robots expect to work for 120,000 hours, or sixty man-years; an experimental General Electric robot can learn to recognize any alpha-numeric code you can teach it … and will read it back to you in its own synthesized 'voice'. The qualitative distinction between an ordinary machine tool and a robot is the intelligence factor. A robot begins to become intelligent when it has senses. The most usual sensors are activated by touch, but photo-electric cells, or television cameras, are now adding 'sight' to the machine's capabilities, although what the robot's 'brain' sees is only a stark computer-digestible image, as binary in its composition as its computer brain is in operation.

Interpreting this sensory input allows a robot the machine to make judgements which influence its action. It is 'judgement' which is crucial to working in industry. A recent West German survey showed that while simple robots can only do about two per cent of existing human jobs, as soon as they have 'eyes' that figure rises to 35 per cent.

There are five basic types of working robot presently in use in factories around the world:

Cartesian. A Cartesian robot is the most simple sort, one which only operates along the basic Cartesian axes, the x, y and z of simple geometry. Cartesian robots are usually the limited sequence 'pick-and-place' machines used to transfer parts between work stations.

Cylindrical. To the basic functions of a Cartesian robot the cylindrical machine adds the capacity of waist movement so that it can handle jobs within a given radius of its base.

Spherical/Polar. This is a more sophisticated type of robot which uses a jointed elbow so that its 'work envelope', or all the points in space which can be touched by the end of its arm, is a sphere.

Articulated Arm. The articulated-arm robot is the one that appears most anthropomorphic because its dual-jointed wrist and elbow functions offer a convincing replication of human movement. Articulated arm robots are the ones which appear most often in television-news scare stories which exploit the 'robots are coming...' theme.

Scara. Scara is an acronym for Selective Compliance Automatic Robot Arm. It is the most recent development in the mechanical articulation of the robot idea. Scara robots, developed by Hiroshi Makino of Japan's Yamanashi University, are similar in capability to the articulated-arm robot, but (like the Japanese domestic screen which was their inspiration) their joints are all in the horizontal plane.

Scara-type robots are beginning to dominate factories (such as Sanyo, Yamaha, NEC and Pentel) where speed and flexibility in simple tasks such as screw driving and bolt running are more important than pure dexterity.

With all these types of robot the real technological problem lies in the three-dimensional mathematics of telling the hand where to go in space. Nature provides an exemplary, but technically daunting, example for imitation. The human hand has twenty-two separate degrees of freedom (sometimes known as 'control axes'), while even the most sophisticated present robots only have six.

While any human can unconsciously direct his or her hand to go to any point in a continuous path ... the machine language required to perform this simple task with accuracy needs the power of advanced computers. What a human being can do unconsciously almost defies computer power: the three-dimensional geometry of moving through space is immensely complicated because while a human can see where his hand is going and can feed back information to change its course, the present robots can only achieve this by referring the first predetermined coordinates to the next and so on until the coordinate mathematics backs up to a degree that threatens to cripple movement.

The great quest in robotics is to develop real electronic brains clever enough to think. At the moment it is a laborious chore to teach robots how to move, but as the cost of electronic memory comes down the erratic Cartesian thrusts and jerks of the first generation machines are already being replaced by smooth movements in a continuous path. It is increasing computer power which generates the movements of industrial robots allowing smooth progress through space, regardless of the number of translational and rotational axes that may change during the hand's short journey.

First-generation robots were blind, deaf and dumb. Today's second-generation are sensitive to their environment through touch and 'sight'. Third-generation robots could be sensitive to every different type of sensory input. These machines will respond to voices and will be able to infer logically with a degree of subtlety and flexibility approaching that of the human brain. In the past twenty years the cost of transistors has fallen by a factor of 1,000 and it seems likely that a similar change will occur with the pricing of the computers which drive robots:

more cheap powerful computers will mean that robots become both more intelligent and less expensive.
– *Blueprint*, July/August

The seven myths of robotics:

Robots are like human beings. Today's industrial robots can weld, spray paint or imitate any form of mechanical work. But real artificial intelligence is some years off.

Robots are new. Robots are simply another sort of machine tool. They are driven by electricity and by hydraulics, a traditional industrial means of transmitting power. The mechanical features of the robot use technology that has not changed in its fundamentals for two hundred years.

The latest robots are merely more intelligent than traditional machines. The new thing about them is the flexibility of their intelligence.

The gear ratios on a bicycle are a crude form of 'intelligence': the different number of teeth on the crank and on the final drive mediate between effort entered and force delivered. But electronics allows robots to process information more flexibly and therefore more efficiently than cogs and sprockets used to.

Robots will raise productivity. Robots can raise output per man hour: at a factory in California, Apple uses robots to make a Macintosh every 27 seconds and the cost of labour is less than one per cent of the cost of the product. But, just as important, robots can reduce inventories and work-in-progress and thus reduce costs. Robots are also predictable, precise, reliable and untiring; they can improve quality and help make savings on materials and energy. There are economic and practical problems which will have to be solved before there is likely to be widespread utilization of robots in factories, but it seems inevitable that these machines will play a fundamental part in it. Itsuo Sukemune, the manager of Matsushita's television plant at Ibaraki in Japan, says: 'We will increase the amount of automation in the future, but it is to improve quality as well as productivity. We don't do it to reduce the number of workers'. Joseph Engleberger, the entrepreneur/engineer who created modern industrial robotics, adds: 'Any country that does not increase its production will not continue to manufacture goods. Its people will end up being in servicing, they will not be manufacturers'.

Robots could turn nasty. Not yet. This most ineradicable of myths is true only in the sense that powerful machines can cause accidents. This happened two years ago when a human worker in the Kawasaki Heavy Industries shipyard in Japan was killed by a robot that did not 'notice' the intrusion into its working cell. But robots are not yet intelligent enough to make a purposeful swipe sideways ... yet one day super-intelligent machines could develop the guile to defy and outwit their masters.

Robots will build other robots, so we can all retire ... Machines have long been used to build other machines, and robots are already assembling other robots. But the image of a single robot reproducing itself, or even evolving, is a bogus one ... at least for the moment. The deepening software dimension of robotics suggests that the 'human factor' will remain critical to it for some time to come.

Robots will cause huge redundancies. Robots are expensive and it can cost as much to program and install them as it can to buy them. Given today's low profitability and the downward pressure in wages brought about by unemployment, the cost of robots promises to make their diffusion a slow one. Moreover, since most of the world's robot population is already in car plants, the big scope for redundancies lies no longer in metal bashing, but in factories where the more subtle tasks of assembly and inspection are vital.

Nevertheless, it is futile to deny that industrial robots are going to fill jobs once held by human workers. A survey in 1981 showed that paint-spraying robots installed in General Motors' car plants produced redundancies in a ratio of 12:1; a study by Commerzbank suggests that by 1990 half of West Germany's 1.2m assembly jobs will be threatened by robots.

The Japanese say that by the year 2000 the manual worker will have disappeared and they will only employ people in 'knowledge jobs'.

Robots will create jobs and make work easier. Although the robot industry is growing, it is very capital intensive. Jobs created in it will not match those it removes.

The humans who actually remain in the factories of the future may find their shifts longer and more arduous; because robots are expensive there will be pressure to get a lot of use out of them. In highly automated Japanese factories, human beings are often required to work overtime to avoid valuable plant being under-utilized.

Robots will inevitably change the patterns of work for remaining human factory workers: already the West German trade union, IG Metall, has declared that there should be no job with a cycle time of less than 90 seconds given to a human being. Robots can very easily handle the repetitive tasks with short-cycle times, leaving human workers free to perform more complex and satisfying work. – *Boilerhouse,* 1984

4.8 God is in the fast lane

When I was a child, I used to read architecture magazines because I was fascinated by modern interiors. At school in a magnificently depressing Gothic pile with dark wood and stained glass windows, *Architectural Review* or *House and Garden* presented me with visions of clean, rational alternatives. They provoked an intense longing. Certainly, there was a lot of emotional energy swirling around my adolescent reading.

So, when I was flicking through features illustrating Helsinki apartments or exhibitions in Milan or a new airport in Texas, the atmosphere was highly charged. I was receptive, my imagination a suction pump. It was in the same journals that I first came across the people responsible for these interiors of desire, the designers. I don't mean the well-intentioned, homespun, Cotswold artisan craftsmen, but colourful exotics with far more appeal to a boy with wandering eye and mind. There used to be features showing sleek, pomaded, moustachioed creatures like Raymond Loewy. I first saw him circa 1962, dressed in a white suit, extravagant foulard and spats, posing by the new Studebaker Avanti whose striking body he had just designed. Or Charles Eames, handsome, square-jawed, tough, but sensitive, drop-dead cool. He was in a wash'n'wear plaid shirt, sitting in the artistically cluttered studio of his Venice, California, house. This habitation he made from industrial components. Then take Eliot Noyes, the very picture of New England refinement with his crew cut, his button-downs and his Beechcraft. Noyes was the Harvard architect who redesigned the entire appearance of IBM, telling the chairman in a memorably pithy memorandum 'You would prefer neatness'. In the American magazines, Noyes was frequently photographed with his wife, Molly, near their beautiful Connecticut house. They always used to have matching cars: this year Thunderbirds, then Porsche 356s, even Land-Rovers.

And all of this was marvellous, giving a clear impression that design was all about shaping appearance, about changing the look of things. And so in a way it still is, but it has become other things as well, and because of that the look of things has moved somewhere else in the system of values where we judge the quality and character of things. Nowadays, design is not simply about appearance, but is increasingly concerned with ... experience.

The most important experience of the twentieth century is speed. Indeed, as Aldous Huxley once remarked, speed is in fact the only entirely novel sensation of our age. Flight, after all, was known in the eighteenth, if only to the Montgolfier brothers and whoever shared their pillow talk. And speed is exciting: in his 1905 essay on infant sexuality Freud explained that children, especially boys, get particular excitation from sensations of movement, hence the historically specific engine-driver fantasy.

Certainly, specialists in sports medicine understand the effects which velocity and, more important, rapid changes in velocity can have. Severe acceleration leads to a complete lack of vision (black-out), or restricted vision (grey-out). On the way to black or grey, heart-rate always increases under the effect of positive g loadings and researchers have found that racing drivers' pulses are often in the 160+ range. The normal rate is nearer 70. In acceleration, as blood pools in the legs, less is delivered to the heart and, what with one thing or another, you feel high.

Such is the fascination of speed that marketing men – and not just in the automobile industry – have made it their business to equate speed with success, thereby creating as a by-product one of the most enduring and least endearing myths of the century: the contribution of owning a fast car to personal aggregates of sexual activity. One interpretation of the sexual character of fast cars is that you are having intercourse with a machine. Karl Ludvigsen, in his book, *At Speed*, observed: *For one who enjoys motor-racing there is no satisfaction that surpasses that of a perfect sweep through a difficult turn... the strain in the neck muscles against hard acceleration. These are joys that the racing driver shares with no one because he cannot. They can only be experienced.*

There may be endocrinological aspects of this solitary sensation but there are all too obviously onanistic ones as well. The organ which speed is going to work on in future is located not beneath the belt, but above the collar. The sexiness of speed in terms of nought-to-sixty is only a very primitive response to this most twentieth century of experiences. Our attitudes to speed are now becoming rather more sophisticated.

Speed compresses time and space. You can have a lot of fun compressing time and space in a Ferrari, but, quite frankly, it is from the infantile stages of industrial production and doesn't have all that much to do with the future development of Western material culture. Speed in a more metaphorical context most certainly does.

This thought came to me a few months ago when I was hanging around the edges of a conversation between some big names in the motor industry. Eavesdropping ten years ago would have been all about design: the industry men would have been muttering knowingly about its importance, its contribution to the bottom line and all that. Nowadays they know it's important and confer on it that greatest of compliments, of being taken for granted: they would be no more likely to have a heated exchange of views about design than they would about any other accepted fact of industrialized production in the First World, such as discounted cash flow or inventory control.

Instead, the know-all mutterings today are about distribution. Now that functional and aesthetic excellence are the baseline for any company that expects to survive beyond the end of the week, the real competitive advantage comes from mastery of time and space. You speak to Fiat or Toyota or Benetton and you will find this is what concerns them most.

In its Castrette warehouse, Benetton owns the most sophisticated distribution centre in the world, serving the globe from one building. Benetton does not manufacture a single garment until it is ordered and just as soon as the order is processed your woolly is documented and tracked through the entire manufacturing process all the way into the 280,000 cubic metre warehouse. Here Comau robots store it and its sibling woollies in a random-access system not dissimilar in its complexity and efficiency to a computer's memory.

To the human visitor the system looks bewildering, with boxes for Chelmsford hugger-mugger with boxes for Tokyo, but the computer knows where everything is, sees it onto conveyors, into trucks and speedily to market. Benetton says the whole process takes no more than seventeen days, of which a rigid seven are accounted for by distribution irrespective of destination. This system keeps Benetton in constant, direct contact with its stores and turns on their head all the old assumptions about design for industry because now the possibility exists, within that amazingly short seventeen-day cycle, for designer and manufacturer to be directly responsive to changing taste. Soon they might start responding, rather than imposing.

But other applications of speed will have a crucial influence on design. For about three decades after 1945, the Japanese devoted most of their considerable ingenuity and organizational energy to process efficiency rather than innovation. This characteristically long-term view has now endowed them with an investment of factories so bewilderingly efficient that creativity actually comes out of the shop-floor. It is like calculus: the Japanese have some brilliant designs not simply because they have brilliant designers, but because they can manufacture anything imaginable in their factories.

In Europe even the most advanced manufacturing companies, Volkswagen for instance, have product life cycles of about eight years. The Japanese motor industry is approaching twenty-four months and electronic products are, in some cases, down to a matter of weeks. When you learn that Hitachi manufactures video recorders in ninety seconds, you realize that the example of Loewy, Eames, and Noyes are as remote from contemporary issues as Hepplewhite and Grinling Gibbons.

Some Western manufacturers are catching up: Motorola now makes its pagers in two hours when before it used to take three weeks. Hewlett-Packard too has learned the lesson of the Japanese. Chief executive John Young, says: 'Doing it fast forces you to do it right first time'.

With this new emphasis on distribution, time, space and the innovation cycle, aesthetics seem as quaint as *ars longa vita brevis* did to General Motors in the fifties...or is this going too far too fast?

The old focused transfer lines and the principle of linear production established by Henry Ford produced a very particular aesthetic: designers reacted to the disciplines of mass-production by developing a visual language whose vocabulary included things like cut-lines, proportions, radii, mouldings. But the new industrial divinity is not manufacturing, but speed. Eventually, when the awareness of this reshuffle seeps into culture, the divinity will have idols made in its image. God used to be in the details, but now he's in the fast lane. When he pulls in for a breather, the Loewy, Eames and Noyes of the next generation are going to be waiting for him.

–*GQ*, June/July 1989

5.1 The Coca-Cola bottle: the shape of the century

Since 1916, the Coca-Cola Company has manufactured more than 840 billion contour bottles.

In 1948, Columbia introduced the first long-playing record, as significant an indicator of the beginning of the modern world as any. Recorded music was no longer scratchy and snatchy: recorded music could become an album of related ideas capable of artistic development and commercial packaging. But other things happened too. It was the year Gandhi was murdered. Israel and the National Health Service were born. There was the Berlin airlift. Chuck Yeager flew the Bell X-1 rocket plane at a record altitude of 67,000 feet. T. S. Eliot won the Nobel Prize and a young Scottish artist of Italian descent made a collage.

Eduardo – now Sir Eduardo – Paolozzi was born in Leith in 1924. Soon after the war he studied at Edinburgh College of Art and travelled to Paris to meet the sculptor, Alberto Giacommetti, and to learn about the lofty absurdities of Dada and Surrealism at first hand, rather than in the college library. Paolozzi's restless curiosity about modern imagery was the equivalent in art to Elizabeth David's passion for exotic ingredients, another product of the time. The poet, Kenneth Rexroth, described eating out in England fifty years ago:

How can they write or paint
In a country where it
Would be nicer to be
Fed intravenously

Of course, this complaint concerned more than just eating out. This was all about an exhausted and demoralized culture. Mrs David's reaction to this civilization of rissoles and beige soup was to mouth the words lemon, garlic and oil as if they were pornography and to start on her heroic series of cookbooks which let the sun shine into a damp and dreary Britain.

Paolozzi's reaction to a world as starved visually as gastronomically was, circa 1947 after his first one-man show at The Mayor Gallery, to make his first contacts with what was to become The Independent Group. Here Roland Penrose, confidant of Picasso, and Herbert Read, the persuasive champion of modern art, together with the young Paolozzi, laid the basis at the new Institute of Contemporary Arts for what would later become known as pop art. Paolozzi had a voracious appetite for US imagery and, while ironic collages had been familiar since Kurt Schwitters and Max Ernst, he assembled his own iconographic pastiches in an entirely original style, anticipating by more than ten years the later profusion of pop in New York. Using US magazines, comic books and mail-order catalogues, Paolozzi began to make arresting visual compilations, with as many layers of meaning as they had layers of paper. Seven years before Britain had seen television advertising, Eduardo Paolozzi had predicted its style.

These collages Paolozzi was later to use in his landmark 1952 lecture at the ICA.
In heavy ironic reference to Henry Ford's view of history, *Bunk* was illustrated
with his inspirational collages of girls, cars, appliances and straplines. *Refreshing
and delicious* was one and *You can't beat the real thing* was another. The earliest of
these is now preserved in the Tate Gallery. One element is a picture of the classic 61 ounce Coca-Cola contour bottle, the first time this innocent piece of
vernacular American design had been assumed into high art. But not, as we shall
see, the last.

The postwar landscape in Britain might have been glum with only the odd relief
provided by dazzling peaks like Elizabeth David and Eduardo Paolozzi, but
America in the late 1940s was enjoying an altogether different mood. If in Britain
the events of 1945 had meant an uncomfortable refocusing and downgrading of
national expectations, the end of the war confirmed for Americans the rightness
of their system. If Britain felt wounded and defensive, America felt confident and
imaginative. The great age of US international economic expansion was about to
begin and in the vanguard of the commercial armies was the generation of industrial designers which, having set up studios in the late 1920s and astonished the
world with fanciful confections of streamlined trains and wastepaper baskets,
was now ready to apply these glossy visions to manufacturing industry.

Foremost in a generation that included Walter Dorwin Teague (later remembered for Boeing interiors) and Henry Dreyfuss (author of the classic Bell
telephone) was Raymond Loewy, a pomaded, sun-tanned and co-respondent-
shoed huckster genius of positively cinematic style and glamour. Loewy
employed a publicist to keep his name before an avid American public. His brief
to her had been to get a cover of *Life* magazine and this was achieved by 1950.
Loewy presented himself to journalist, John Kobler, as a universal impresario
genius of American capitalism, a claim which, if extreme, was not entirely to be
discounted. Adopting a patrician tone which came easily, Loewy surveyed the
vast range of US consumer goods and posed as *arbiter elegantiae* of all he saw.
What Kobler himself saw on Loewy's studio shelf was a classic 61-ounce Coca-
Cola bottle. When he asked the designer to explain the presence of this
humdrum artefact in an ocean of chrome and enamel, of streamlined locomotives, speedboats and sportscars, Loewy delivered of himself one of the most
quoted and misquoted of all remarks in the history of design.

He described the Coke bottle as 'perfectly honed' and admitted that he spent a
good deal of time 'brooding' on its shape (which he memorably described as 'cal-
lipygian', a scholarly reference to Aphrodite's voluptuous anterior curves). To
Loewy, the Coke bottle was an absolute exemplar of excellence in industrial
design: the ordinary thing done extraordinarily well. He acknowledged that the
bottle might well have been in retreat from the streamlined metaphors he had
made famous, but was happy to concede that some things simply defined themselves and created their own standards of excellence. The Coke bottle was such
a one. Again, he referred to the sexual symbolism and said the bottle's shape was
'aggressively female' adding that this was a 'quality that, in merchandise as in life,
sometimes transcends functionalism'.

Through countless *rédactions* this elegant quote has sometimes been misinterpreted to mean that Loewy claimed authorship of the famous bottle ...
something which the designer, as cautious as he was flamboyant, never intended

(although it is significant that on the many occasions when the design of the contour bottle was attributed to Raymond Loewy, his normally energetic and resourceful legal advisers never bothered to refute it). Still, for whatever reasons, Loewy's assumption of the Coca-Cola bottle into his œuvre, even if only by happy association, gave it immediate classic status. Just as Eduardo Paolozzi had recognized the symbolic power of this remarkable package and absorbed it into modern art, Loewy's perception of the same qualities elevated a glass bottle into the Pantheon of contemporary design. How exactly did this process of ennoblement happen to a simple bottle of soda? How did the Coca-Cola bottle become the shape of the century?

Commercial sale of carbonated drinks began in the United States in the very first years of the nineteenth century. Among the first recognizable individuals in the primitive beginnings of what was later to become one of the defining activities of industrialized capitalism were Benjamin Silliman of New Haven and Joseph Hawkins of Philadelphia. At the time, 'Belfast' and 'Dublin' ginger ales were popular imports and a colonial favourite was 'switchel', a brew of molasses, ginger and vinegar. One entrepreneur, a certain Charles E. Hires, exhibited a do-it-yourself package of root-beer herbs at the Philadelphia Centennial of 1876. Contemporary domestic products also in demand included sparkling phosphade, lime-juice champagne, French currant cuisinnier, strawberry punch, grape milk, Checkerberry and the alarming sounding Vigorine. A busy, thirsty and restless population demanded more and more refreshment. By the 1890s, stimulated by consistent national advertising of the new brands which had begun in journals such as *Harper's Weekly* the decade before, the United States had about 1,400 soft-drink bottling plants, a figure that was to double by 1900 when it was estimated that the soft drinks industry was worth $25m annually.

This was the context of Coca-Cola, whose very first retail sale was at Dr Joseph Jacobs's Drug Store at Atlanta's Five Points intersection in May, 1886. The barman who first mixed a shot of Dr John Pemberton's syrup with soda water was Willis Venable. Pemberton was an itinerant pharmacist whose earlier adventures into branded healthcare products included Triplex Liver Pills and French Wine of Coca. Not a quack, but not a Harvard professor either. First-year sales were inauspicious, Willis Venable managing only – perhaps because of stiff competition from Vigorine and switchel – to dilute a mere 25 gallons into 3,200 individually carbonated servings. Pemberton could not afford a commercial artist to design his trademark, so in a benign insight of world-historical proportions, he asked his book-keeper, Frank M. Robinson, to do it for him. Today's Coca-Cola logogram is the direct descendent of a laborious clerk's copperplate so unselfconsciously transcribed in an Atlanta drugstore 111 years ago.

Slow sales and declining health dispirited Pemberton and he sold the rights to his concoction to Asa G. Candler who incorporated the Coca-Cola Company in 1892. The conception of 'Coca-Cola' was not at this time the quintessential consumer good, adroitly packaged, efficiently distributed, economically priced, cleverly advertised and universally available. That was to come later. In its first years Coca-Cola was sold only as a syrup; a capital commodity rather than an end product for a consumer. The evolution of this most famous brand from an Atlanta pharmacist's wholesale goo to nearly total global recognition was down to the singular inspiration of a 28-year-old candy entrepreneur from Vicksburg, Mississippi. This was Joseph August Biedenharn, whose sarsaparilla and strawberry drinks had already made him rich. In 1894 he had the happy inspiration of bottling Coca-Cola as a premixed drink. Using a green-glass, generic 'Hutchinson' bottle, the type with a ceramic stopper retained by a wire contraption whose over-centre physics created a seal, this was the beginning of the popular phenomenon that led to the shape of the century. Speaking in 1944 on the fiftieth anniversary of his first bottling, a now extremely rich Joseph Biedenharn recalled: *I just went to work and started bottling Coca-Cola. I did not say anything to Mr Candler about it, but I did ship him the first two dozen cases of Coca-Cola I bottled. Mr Candler immediately wrote back that it was fine.*

It has to be appreciated that while Robert Woodruff was later to describe the Coke commercial machine as 'the essence of capitalism' at this time, bottling was an extremely precarious business. Yet other entrepreneurs took note of Biedenharn's fine innovation and soon the first official Coca-Cola bottlers were established, the beginnings of a world-wide network of soft-drinks manufacturers which is still the basis of the Coca-Cola Company's present fortune. Among these first bottlers were two Chattanooga lawyers, Benjamin F. Thomas and Joseph Brown Whitehead. It was Thomas who was the first to recognize the need for a distinctive package for what was fast becoming a popular phenomenon. From the cumbersome Hutchinson flask, bottlers had moved on to straight-sided vessels and a familiar crown seal, but there was no uniformity of presentation. These second-generation Coke bottles came in clean, brown and amber glass. Graphics were inconsistent and, while they did not have a term for it in those days, 'brand values' were being eroded. It was Benjamin F. Thomas who created the informal brief for what was to become the most successful package design of all time.

He wrote: *We need a Coca-Cola bottle which a person will recognize as a Coca-Cola bottle even if he feels it in the dark. The Coca-Cola bottle should be so shaped that, even if broken, a person could tell at a glance what it was.*

With the support of Harold Hirsch, general counsel to the Coca-Cola Bottlers Association, a brief was sent to interested parties and one copy arrived at the Root Glass Company of Terre Haute, Indiana, the workplace of Alex Samuelson.

Alexander Samuelson had been born in Surte in rural Sweden in 1882, the son of a blacksmith who spelled the family name with two esses. He learnt about traditional glassmaking in Germany and in 1882 emigrated, via Britain, to the United States, abbreviating his Christian name and dropping an 's' from his family name on the way. He first found work as a wagon-maker in Iowa, then joined the glass industry in Steeler, Illinois, moving to American Glass in Newark, then to the brewers Anheuser-Busch, and ultimately to Root Glass. Samuelson, an artisan inventor of genius, had acquired a reputation as an innovator: in 1894 he had patented his Continuous Glass Melting Furnace which eased the way for mass (rather than batch) production of bottles.

When the Coca-Cola brief came in, Samuelson sent Root Glass's cost accountant, T. Clyde Edwards, and a factory machinist, Earl R. Dean, down to Terre Haute's Emily Fairbanks Library in Chapman S. Root's own chauffeur-driven Peerless limousine. He had had the inspiration that a unique shape for the Coca-Cola bottle might arise from some scrutiny of the natural history of certain ingredients of the beverage, beginning with the eponymous coca leaf and the kola nut. Edwards and Dean diligently studied the best reference book they could find in provincial Indiana: the 11th edition of the *Encyclopaedia Britannica*. Neither coca nor kola provided much useful inspiration, but a few pages on they found an illustration of the cocoa bean which far better suited their purposes. Thus did the unsuspecting cocoa bean become the source of the Coca-Cola bottle design.

In a letter of 1971 Earl R. Dean described the picture of the cocoa bean he saw in the *Britannica*: *It had a very short neck at the stem end and the body had four different diameters and vertical ribs which I incorporated in my first drawing.*

In those innocent days before ferocious copyright legislation, Dean patiently copied the encyclopaedia's illustration and for his drawing was offered a choice of $500 bonus or a job for life at Root Glass, an offer which endured until 1932 when the Owens-Illinois conglomerate took over.

It was Alex Samuelson who turned Earl R. Dean's swattish *Britannica* crib into first, a wider model and then into a bulbous pre-production prototype, much slimmed down (into what is virtually today's shape) for the assembly line. It was in the furnace of the Terre Haute glassworks that a picture from an encyclopaedia was, through the medium of an inspired artisan glassmaker, finessed into the famous Coca-Cola bottle. The eventual design was given US Patent No.48160 on 16 November 1915 and went into production the following year. The patent was renewed Christmas Day, 1923 and, with some slight modifications, again on 3 November 1937, two years after the death of Samuelson. When this last patent expired on 2 August 1951, the bottle became protected under common law rights as a 'badge of identification' of the Coca-Cola Company. In 1960, US courts recognized the contour bottle, a registered trademark thereby protecting it in perpetuity (a distinction enjoyed at that time by only one other branded product: Haig whisky and its distinctive 'pinch' bottle). British law took thirty-five years to catch up. A sarsaparilla entrepreneur and a trip to the local library in Terre Haute had, through the inspiration of an untutored genius of an immigrant Swedish glassmaker, created the world's most identifiable package, a mythopoeic combination of entrepreneurial vision and artisan genius in the service of mass production.

Coca-Cola was sold in bottles in Britain from 1935, in France from 1920, in Germany in 1929, in Italy in 1927 and in Spain in 1928. Australia and South Africa followed in 1938. It usually first appeared in new territories in the distinctive 'Georgia Green' blue-green tinged glass, only later reverting to clear. As late as the 1960s when bottled Coke first went on sale in Japan, the contour bottle was first sold in Georgia Green, a cast of colour which adds an almost jewel-like quality to the bottle. These were straightforward commercial conquests, but the universal acceptance of Coke as a symbol of delight and excellence – exactly the pop credibility that Paolozzi and Loewy were picking up on – was a direct consequence of the Second World War.

From the moment that the United States entered the war, bottles of Coke followed GIs. It's often said that Coke is the first 'global product'. Maybe, but its global credentials were established by a global war. It is said that between Pearl Harbor and VJ Day, American servicemen drank 106 billion bottles of Coke, more than a third of them overseas. After landing in North Africa, General Eisenhower promptly sent a cable requesting 'eight Coca-Cola plants immediately'. Eventually, the commercial ambitions of Atlanta's Coca-Cola Company were amply satisfied – possibly even extended – by the American soldier's appetite for the American way of doing things. During the War, sixty-four exported bottling plants helped to satisfy the needs of both military victualling and personal motivation: at once propaganda and psychology. These laid the basis for the international presence of Coca-Cola when the Company consolidated in peace time the territorial gains made during the war. There's a story about a German prisoner of war arriving at an Atlantic port who, on seeing the familiar logo, said 'Ach! So you have Coca-Cola here too'. In 1945 there were six portable Coca-Cola bottling plants bobbing on the ocean off the coast of occupied Japan. Soon, Coke men dressed in military uniform would land as 'technical observers'.

It was after 1945 that Coca-Cola in the United States began to create its own utterly seductive iconography of consumerized well-being, in the magnificent advertising art of Bob Peak and Haddon Sundblom. During the 1930s Sundblom had developed a painterly technique of hallucinatory realism, giving Coke 'owner-ship' of Santa Claus, who in the memory of a generation of mid-century Americans is as inseparable from the 61-ounce contour bottle as he is from his red-nosed quadruped, sleigh-towing friend. Postwar, Sundblom's Christmas iconography was complemented by Bob Peak's more contemporary style of advertising art. This was much closer to fashion illustration than to Sundblom's Norman Rockwell vernacular genre and in a powerfully seductive series of advertising illustrations, Peak acquired for the Coca-Cola Company the entire culture of American recreation: barbecues, speedboats and tourism, all made more enjoyable – all validated, even – by the presence of a Coke bottle. If it was a good time, it was a good time to have a Coke. There is no accepted formula which allows us to calculate how images affect us, but serial repetition of these striking pictures helped to achieve for Coca-Cola an unassailably robust deposit of well-being.

It was exactly this confident, even boastful, demonstration of affluent hedonism that had attracted Eduardo Paolozzi and Raymond Loewy. But the same mixture had a different effect on American artists. British pop art was enthusiastic, voyeuristic and good-naturedly derivative. American pop was darker and more irreverent. The line between art and advertising had been crossed as soon as Marlon Brando, to cite just one of the most visible examples, was photographed in a Schott leather jacket in an epochal film role with a bottle of Coke. When mainstream popular culture upstaged art in its ability to provide effecting and moving symbols to America's consumers, then art had to explore new, some-times more sinister, territories. With Robert Rauschenberg and Andy Warhol, American pop took a sideways look at its native culture.

While Paolozzi's assumption of the Coca-Cola bottle into his late 1940s collages was a sign of cheerful, aspirational associations, Robert Rauschenberg's *Coca-Cola Plan* of 1958 (now in the Museum of Contemporary Art, Los Angeles) was more morose. This was the first time the famous bottle had been used in first-rate US gallery art. In 1963 Rauschenberg explained:

My fascination with images open 24hrs is based on the complex interlocking of disparate visual facts heated pool that have no respect for grammar [sic].

Rauschenberg's dark irony was the other side of the cheerful product promotion that found Coca-Cola appearing in the hands of actors, musicians and sportsmen. He engages no less actively in the rhetoric of product promotion than the illustrator of a Coke ad, but the same language is turned on its head.

Andy Warhol's treatment of the Coca-Cola bottle was different again to Rauschenberg's. As an art director in an advertising agency, Warhol knew very well how muzzy were the distinctions between gallerified fine art and paid-for communications. Warhol enjoyed the power of mass-market imagery, which his mature style exploited for all – maybe even more than – it was worth. His *210 Coca-Cola Bottles* was sold at auction in May, 1993 for $2.1m. The mantra-like repetitions of Warhol's mature style, whether Liz Taylor or Marilyn portraits, Brillo cartons or Coke bottles are to some wordy commentators the artist's critique of the numbing sameness of industrial culture, but not I think to Warhol himself. His repetitions are an act of love or, at least, serial acts of passionate recognition and admiration. If you love images you must be utterly besotted by the most powerful image of all: the 61 ounce Coca-Cola contour bottle. Warhol did and was. In 1959 *The New Yorker* wrote that: *Coca-Cola is a fluid that, like gasoline, is indispensable to, and symbolic of, the American way of life.*

Warhol agreed. In *The Philosophy of Andy Warhol* (1975) he explained: *You can be watching TV and see Coca-Cola and you can know that the President drinks Coke, Liz Taylor drinks Coke, and just think, you can drink Coke too. A coke is a Coke and no amount of money can get you a better Coke than the one the bum on the corner is drinking … Liz Taylor knows it, the President knows it, the bum knows it and you know it.*

The assumption of the Coke bottle into gallery art is fascinating territory for art-historical exploration, but the real groundbreaking was happening elsewhere. No territory provides a richer account of the adoption and assumption of significant imagery than car styling. Here in the 1960s, the Coca-Cola bottle began to influence an industry as pervasive as its own. The agent of that influence was, again, Raymond Loewy and this time the 'vehicle' Studebaker.

These were people who knew about images. In 1961 the Studebaker Corporation of South Bend, Indiana, was also the local distributor for Mercedes-Benz. They had hired the industrial designer, Brooks Stevens (the man who first put an observation window into a washing machine and had made Harley-Davidsons glittery) as a consultant. In a commercial version of sympathetic magic, Stevens had given the Studebaker Hawk and Lark Mercedes-like radiator grilles, but that hadn't worked too well, so Studebaker's President, Sherwood Egbert, hired Raymond Loewy (who had last worked for the company in 1956).

Loewy's commission was to relaunch the brand with a remarkable car. With characteristic melodrama, Loewy took his designers, John Ebstein, Robert Andrews and Tom Kellogg, off to a secret rented house in Palm Springs. Here, using established Studebaker components, they sketched one of the most remarkable car shapes ever. Deriving some of its remarkable architecture from the Lancia-based Loraymo concept car Loewy had shown at the 1960 Paris Salon de l'Automobile, the 1962 fibreglass Studebaker had a brilliant repertoire of styling innovations: phallic proportions, a unique bluff nose with an air intake hidden below the bumpers, razor-edged wings, a huge wraparound rear glass (soon to be copied on the Plymouth Barracuda), individual bucket seats, an internal air-craft-style console and astonishing kicked-up rear haunches that were explicitly influenced by ... the Coca-Cola bottle.

The Studebaker Avanti was the first American car to use disc brakes and announced the 'Coke bottle look', soon to appear on John Najjar's 1964 Ford Mustang and Bill Mitchell's 1967 Chevrolet Camaro. With Andy Granatelli driving, in late 1962 an Avanti broke twenty-nine Bonneville speed records, creating an enormous international celebrity for the car with the 'Coke bottle curve', but production problems delayed its launch and a virtually bankrupt Studebaker managed to make a mere 4,600 examples before production stopped in late 1963. Still, the Avanti has become a fixed part of the history of car styling, so much so that, writing in 1990, Bruno Sacco, head of design for Mercedes-Benz, described the car inspired by a Coke bottle as a 'work of art through and through'.

And so in its way is Alex Samuelson's bottle. After the name and the logogram, the shape of the Coca-Cola bottle is the most valuable asset of the mighty Coca-Cola Company. Once described as the 'sublimated essence of all that America stands for', this simple, but subtle shape remains a paradigm of successful design. More than amply fulfilling the original brief, the Coca-Cola bottle was inspired artisan genius, refined through the processes of law and popularized by an intoxicating album of imagery of the shapers of the century, many of them shown here, who recognized in the Coca-Cola bottle even more than the most successful packaging exercise of all time. They recognized a compact and potent symbol. The famous contour bottle is more than just a package, it's a genuine modern icon: an image of faith for a global civilization committed to pleasurable consumption not just of delicious drinks, but of favourable imagery too.

The history of branded goods may be the social history of the twentieth century. Sometimes this affects observers rather mordantly, as in Alan Bennett's droll little ditty:

Here I sit, alone and sixty.
Bald and fat and full of sin,
Cold the seat and loud the cistern
As I read the Harpic tin.

The Coca-Cola bottle has a reliably more uplifting effect, thanks to the global catalogue of favourable imagery recorded here. In 1969 Lippincott & Margulies, the corporate identity consultants, derived the 'dynamic contour curve' from the bottle and used it as a two-dimensional graphic device which has served Atlanta well. But while other packaging technologies have competed for attention, it seems the wonderful contour bottle will never go away. In March 1994, the Chairman of the Coca-Cola Company, Roberto C. Goizueta, pledged that by the year 2000 all versions of Coke would be available in contour-shaped containers, whether single servings or two-litre bottles.

The following year the Coca-Cola Company became the most successful American business ever, achieving in 1995 a record of nearly $61bn market value added. It was not all down to the callipygian bottle, but no one's planning to replace it in the hierarchy of all-time wealth creators.

What is Coke? According to William Allen White, a decent thing honestly made, universally distributed, conscientiously improved. And recognized everywhere … thanks to a wonderful bottle that can reasonably claim to be the most successful packaging project ever.
– *The Coca-Cola Bottle,* Design Museum, 1997

5.2 Top marques

What is the difference between a trademark and a logo? There's not much really, except that a logo is a trademark that went to art school. To get a sense of the distinction, dwell on the different semantic aromas coming off the terms 'commercial artist' and 'designer', the one a rather quaint thing of the past, the other very much of the here and now.

The modern logo is more knowing than the humble trademark. If the trademark belongs to the early history of modern business, the logo comes from a more highly evolved phase. Once exclusively art school and agency jargon, the word has now entered the popular vocabulary, but usage often confers a meaning suggestive of the 'quick fix', with the implication that design is a superficial remedy, not a fundamental of business. Sales are down, costs are up, investor confidence has gone for a walk: what we need is a new logo and some Day-Glo flashes.

Some of the world's greatest trademarks evolved by accident. Harley Procter, founder of Procter & Gamble, acquired the idea for Ivory Soap one quiet evening in 1879 while reading Psalm 45. Coca-Cola is the book-keeper's signature. The sublime Chanel identity was devised not by a sophisticated consultant but by a jobbing printer. The famous Ferrari prancing horse was lifted by Enzo Ferrari from the coat-of-arms adorning the fuselage of the plane flown by Francesco Baracca, a First World War fighter ace who had purloined the motif from the Piedmontese Cavalry Regiment.

Strictly speaking there are two types of logo: the logo*type* and the logo*gram*. The first is a trademark relying exclusively on typography. The second employs imaginative devices, with or without typography. The logo emerged – as did the consultant design profession – out of American advertising.

By the mid-1920s, the American consumer's basic needs had been satisfied. Cars, phones, fridges were universal. Markets were stagnant, and it was at this moment that one of the genuinely epochal creative events that have defined our century occurred. A handful of commercial artists – mostly working in ad agencies, but some as window-dressers and stage designers – realized that you could add appeal to products as banal as waste bins and pencil sharpeners by *styling* them.

These commercial artists, who included Norman Bel Geddes, Walter Dorwin Teague, Henry Dreyfuss and Raymond Loewy, were the first professional designers. So pervasive was their work that by the 1950s it was quite possible for an American citizen to spend an entire day in the company of products and packages which were the fruit of, say, Loewy's vivid, not to say vulgar, imagination. Pepsodent, Rexona soap and Schick razors in the bathroom, Nabisco cereals at breakfast, a Studebaker or a Greyhound bus on the way to work, a Carling beer and a Lucky Strike cigarette at lunch, and so on throughout the stylized day.

At the same time, advertising was evolving from the primitive task of making claims ('cheap', 'new', 'effective') to the manipulative fabrication of images ('use our product to appear successful and attractive'). Say what you like about the beauty and usefulness of the results, but from this end of the twentieth century, it is clear that the great visual symbols of our age have come not from fine art but from the images and symbols devised as the heraldry of modern brands.

There are, of course, absurdities about the modern logo. The more puffed-up contemporary design consultancies would disdain the commission to create a humble trademark. Something so straightforward is more the province of the commercial artist, not the armies of men in Hugo Boss suits in their panzer divisions of BMWs. Rather, they will insist on instigating a 'corporate identity programme'.

This will involve serial presentations with flip charts, the generation of fanciful 'research' from focus groups and profound heart-searching. The result will be a trademark spread over everything, the trucks as well as the letterhead. No aspect of a client's business will escape refreshment. If the benefits to both the client and the customers are questionable, the exercise is seen as a humane sacrifice on the altar of professionalism. The full-blown corporate identity programme is a magnificently impressive way of separating marketing directors from their budgets and helps to turn £500 of expenses into £100,000 of fees.

At its best, corporate identity is a finely executed liaison between art and management, between creative intuition and business strategy, something which creates memorable and meaningful symbols. At its worst, it is pretentious, expensive and ridiculous. Good or bad, the logo is central to its success. It is a small work of art, a lapidary reduction of motif and data into a universally recognisable sign.

The rules for the design of logos are straightforward:
– they must be legible;
– they must have a style appropriate to the client's 'culture';
– they should be evocative but understated;
– they must be practical and versatile;
– they should eschew fashion.

A survey of some of the world's logos reveals an essential truth about design as a whole: to be effective, it must be authentic.

The worst:
BT. British Telecom has the worst logo of any company of comparable size, designed in 1991 at fabulous cost by Wolff Olins (estimated fees were £250,000 and the implementation costs 800 times as much). As creaky BT shuffled towards modernization, a gauche and inappropriate piper was proposed. Nauseating colours were simultaneously selected for a parallel corporate identity programme. BT was then further humiliated when it was suggested that Olins's piper may have been inspired by a logo created for Royal Insurance's arts sponsorship by Dolores Fairman, a freelance illustrator who had been paid £1,000.

British Leyland. Now defunct, but the memory lives on. Never has anything so vile as Lord Stokes's motif been so commonplace. Leyland was a lacklustre group of under-capitalized manufacturers. At least the logo, crudely suggestive of mechanics, was a fair expression of the company's value.

Prince. Having made a career out of explicit lyrics, Prince recently decided to take refuge in a fabulously obscure logo. To safeguard sales he has had to withdraw it, to be saved for 'future projects'.

Prudential. Another Wolff Olins clanger, from 1986. This conservative institution, in pursuit of a 'new look', was given a badly drawn and frivolous image of Prudence set atop tricksy typography. The conjoined 'U' and 'D' are intended to evoke solidarity. The loose brush style added bogus sophistication.

The Conservative party. At the launch of the new Conservative logo in 1989, Kenneth Baker said that the design, by Michael Peters, 'captures the values of the Conservative party'. The torch motif, in use since 1981, is suggestive of a guiding light, but the execution is commonplace and coarse.

miu miu. miu miu is the diffusion line of the grand Milanese dress shop Prada. Miuccia Prada designed the logo herself. While the original Prada mark is an icon of dignified clarity, miu is simply unreadable, perhaps appropriate for a name that is unpronounceable.
– *The Times Magazine,* 19 February 1994

5.3 Brand new ideas

No one bothers to ask what's in a name anymore – because they all know that the answer is a great deal of money.

Akio Morita is the founder of Sony. Once dubbed 'Mr Transistor' by Vincent Hanna, Morita's achievement was not solely to realize the hidden value in a device whose unwordly inventors at Western Electric considered to have no commercial potential. Morita also had a way with words. On the same early 1950s American trip on which he and his partner purchased the transistor patents, he also discovered something just as lucrative: the power of a name. Noting that Oldsmobile (which in Japanese comes out as 'Oh Roads Mow Beer Ah') was more difficult to pronounce than Ford, on his return home he decided to change the name of his business from Tokyo Tsushin Kogyo Kabushika Kaika (which in English comes out as though you're talking with a mouthful of toothpaste) to Sony. Neatly, the first machine to make the miniature transistor useful was also the first to bear one of the greatest – and smallest – of all brand names.

The revolution which began with using transistors in pocket radios has led directly to all the other innovations in solid-state electronics – giving us global, electronic, information-based businesses which Marshall McLuhan could scarcely have imagined and wouldn't have believed if he could. One consequence of the increasing population of intelligent machines in factories is that hardware, whether the metal of a motor car or the plastic and silicon of a CD player, is falling in value, or rather cost, because of new and astonishing efficiencies. With this decline in value of *things* there has been a consequent increase in the value of ideas.

The recognition of the value of ideas was almost as important in the progress of industrial civilization as mass production. The declining value of hardware is acknowledged by law: patents only protect an invention for 50 years; *design* is legally defined as superficial – the precise wording is 'outward form' – and is only protected for 15 years. However, the law recognises that trademarks have an indefinite life.

It is already becoming clear to many shrewd companies that their intellectual property may, in the long term, be the most valuable thing which they possess. For instance, if you subtract the value of its assets from the worth of the Coca-Cola Company, you find that the formula for the syrup and the brand name are worth about thirteen billion – watch my lips, that's thirteen billion – on their own. Similarly, a former chairman of Quaker Oats recently said: 'If this business were to be split up, I would be glad to take the brands, trademarks and goodwill and you could have all the bricks and mortar – and I would fare better than you'.

The valuation of brands is the gigabucks equivalent of the megabucks 'designer' phenomenon. Just as 'designer' adds a sort of specious value to merchandise, consumers assert their identity through their choice of brands, creating what Daniel Boorstin, author of *The Image – a Guide to Pseudo-Events in America*, called 'consumption communities'. After all, the success of Coca-Cola depends not so much on the drink itself, whatever you may think of it, as on its imagery. Buy Coke and you participate in an international fantasy about the American Dream.

Nowadays, the contribution which design makes to manufacturing industry is not so much in the shape of the products as in the imagery of the business. As graphics are fundamental to the perception of a brand, this form of design has recently assumed immense significance in the post-industrial economy: brand evaluation, a species of refinement by London consultancy Interbrand, is a technique of quantifying the unquantifiable, of measuring the value of ideas and images.

In terms of the brutish persuasiveness of statistics, if the significance of design can be measured in terms of economic activity, then the corporate identity consultants, graphic designers, packaging experts, and all those other turbo-charged, blow-dried types responsible for the appearance of Hob-Nobs and Kit-Kat, are at least as important as the industrial designers of yore and the food engineers of the here and now. Mr Jacobs, the bruised loser in the Rowntrees take-over battle, said it was never really factories he wanted: 'anyone can make a chocolate bar'. What *he* wanted was the consumer loyalty established over the years by Kit-Kat. When in late 1988 the food-processing company Rank Hovis McDougall valued its brands, it was able to add nearly £700m to its balance sheet. What, in the days when accountancy was what you did if you had spots and couldn't do anything else, was once called 'goodwill' had, by voodoo, been translated into 'brand valuation'. This meant that a portfolio of well-known and successful names is worth a fortune: when Grand Met bought American drinks concern Heublein in 1987 it paid £880m for a company whose tangible assets were valued at £200m. News International recently bought *Car* magazine, which has no assets other than its high speed staff, but a reputation for quality journalism and good design, for an estimated £15–£20m. No wonder that while the accountants are hostile, questioning the prudence of investments in imagery, the graphic designers and corporate identity consultants have been delighted to have their work so highly valued.

The meaning of this is profoundly relevant to post-industrial man entering the *fin de siècle*. We are at the beginning of an extraordinary drama the meaning of which undermines all traditional assumptions about value: *ideas and images are now worth more than artefacts*. A gentle shift from hardware to software can be seen everywhere, even in Japan. While Japanese mastery of industrial processes gets to its fifth dan, the most successful companies are responding to the new emphasis on software as conventional markets for cars, hi-fi and cameras become sated.

Characteristically, Sony was among the first to lead into the post-industrial age, just as it led into the electronic one in the 1950s and dominated consumer markets in the 1960s and 1970s with its expertise in product design and marketing. While a good deal of the argument in favour of Sony's 1987 acquisition of CBS was that, with its huge video library, it could, in a future standards war, force its own – perhaps idiosyncratic – choice of format onto the market, the underlying argument was more dramatic: nowadays, when anyone with the Fujitsu microchip catalogue and access to a jobbing injection moulder can make hi-fi or video, ideas and images themselves are achieving economic supremacy. Maybe one day Sony will get into production of movies and music and abandon manufacturing goods altogether. Olivetti, another company with an established reputation for design and hardware, is ready to abandon making things and concentrate on software and computer services. But Sony and Olivetti only got into these positions because their names were once applied to fabulous hardware alone.

It takes time to establish a brand. Oh yes, and a lot of money as well: the method of establishing the value of a brand follows standard accounting practices for asset valuation. You take average earnings over three years and multiply them by a factor which reflects the extent of advertising support and then you get a very big number.

But is *all* post-industrial economic activity now to be directed towards inventing names for products manufactured by coolies in South-East Asia, South America and the United Kingdom? This would be sinister were the processes not so fallible. The consumer, as David Ogilvy once said, is not a moron, she is your wife. Thus neither 'Knacker' bread nor 'Krapp' lavatory paper did well in Britain, and they have not bothered to export a Scandinavian anti-freeze called 'Super Piss'. The Japanese enjoy drinking 'Pocari Sweat', but you or I would not and, famously, that neat little Toyota never had a chance in France because 'MR2' sounds much too much like the French word for shitty.
– Previously unpublished, 1994

Depending on your methodology – of whether you consider, say, Rover a separate entity to BMW – there are about 18 major passenger-vehicle manufacturers on the planet. Between them they have about 50 brands or what, in more innocent days, used to be called marques. But adspeak is overwhelming us and while we used to talk about a marque's traditions over foaming pints, we now sit in dichroically lit meeting rooms discussing *brand values*, styrofoam cups in hand.

In fact, you won't find motor industry leaders talking about much else nowadays. It's strange that in the autumn of the private car, its manufacturers are turning to mysticism. For many individuals, the car has ceased to be a viable means of transport: legislation and congestion mock the spirit of democratic mobility which inspired the first makers of automobiles. At the same time, technical distinctions are thinning and today there are very few positively bad cars on sale. No wonder then that competitive activity is focusing on what cars mean rather than what they say. Increasingly, manufacturers are not trying to tickle your right foot, but gain access to far more sophisticated and sensitive parts of your body, above your neck rather than below your belt.

Brand values means all those things which can't be quantified in Newton/metres, ecus or rate of change of velocity. Thinking about it subjectively, you'd have to agree that Rolls-Royce has the most: like Coca-Cola, it's a name that unambiguously summons up a whole set of clear ideas and images.

BMW has a lot too: never has a single machine so succinctly said success, sex, speed and status. There's a whole hierarchy here. Jaguar? Right up there with Rolls. Range Rover? Step this way. Citroën? Doing fine. Skoda? Yes, lots. Ford has plenty and so does Nissan, even if in the later case they're not ones you'd specially want. But Vauxhall? Here's an interesting case. Does Vauxhall have any brand values at all?

Vauxhall is a complete mystery since, in this context, it represents an almost fathomless black hole. It's hard to understand exactly why Vauxhall is so bereft of those precious brand values because the cars themselves are, if not intoxicatingly delicious, then at least honest and drinkable. Modest *appellation contrôlée* rather than magnificent *grand cru*, but that's all right: there's material to work on here. Yet somehow, in the matter of elusive imagery, Vauxhall's (black) whole is much, much less than the sum of the respectable parts. If you were Vauxhall, you'd be concerned: it would be like people don't talk to you at parties, waiters ignore you in restaurants, no one wants to buy your house, no one fancies your wife, no one covets your ass. This is depressing and Vauxhall knows it.

Maybe I can help. It should be easy to calculate. I'd say the equation looked like:
$BV = w\,(csh)/np$, where
BV = brand values
w = weight of advertising
c = celebrity endorsement
s = success in competition
h = heritage factors
n = numbers found in suburbs
p = whether used by police.

Interestingly, Vauxhall scores admirably in some crucial areas of this calculation. Recent advertising has been striking and effective and there's been lots of it around. Celebrity endorsement has been less obvious, although success in competition has been outstanding. Heritage factors are a bit of a problem for Vauxhall for so long as people can recall the pre-Cavalier period, but the BV figure's really dragged down by the surviving cars which find their way to auction and by the alarming preference which the police exercise for Vauxhall products (the equivalent, in automotive status terms, of being a close relative of Frederick West).

Clearly, Vauxhall could radically improve its BV figure by buying in and scrapping used cars before they transgress to an undead state diminishing BV the minute they are converted into mini-cabs. Refusing to supply the police would be another clear option. There are dirty tricks Vauxhall marketeers might consider as well: it would be cheap and impressive to have a fleet of AA-liveried Montereys towing apparently broken-down N-registered BMW's around Knightsbridge for 12 hours a day every day for a year.

But these are only adjustments. Vauxhall's image problem is not that it has a poor one, but that it does not have one at all. Happily, the product is getting better and better. So much so that an Omega can be compared to a BMW and not found wanting in any measurable way. Try that a generation ago with a 2002 against a VX4/90 and people would have nudged and winked as you went by. But the curious alchemy which makes a favourable image has to do with art not science; this is an imaginative business, not a technical one. It's a truism that image lags years behind reality (how else to explain Rolls-Royce's enduring prestige?) and there's no doubt that if Vauxhall's products continue to improve then, eventually, popular acceptance of Vauxhall brand values will improve too.

But maybe we can't wait that long. The source of the problem is not the integrity of the product, but the integrity of the idea. No one really believes that Vauxhall designs those cars. Big buildings in the centre of Luton notwithstanding, the existence of Vauxhall is a polite fiction. Why preserve something which means so little? If you put the customer into deep hypnosis you'd find that he retains only the most fragile belief in a Vauxhall ethic, a Vauxhall style, a Vauxhall engineering credo.

The slow fix to Vauxhall's image problem would be to establish autonomous research and design activities for the company so that cars wearing Vauxhall badges were a genuine expression of a corporate idea. As it is, we all know they are designed in Germany. The quick fix would be to acknowledge reality and call them Opels. There's a point where brand values touch on that ancient tradition: badge engineering.

—*Car Magazine*, January 1996.

There can be no trade – although its members rather grandly like to think it a profession, despite the fact that the Estate Agents' Act (1979) cannot manage a definition – which better deserves the opprobrium the public heaps upon it. If you are selling, whenever you are selling, the market is soft. If you are buying in the same area on the very same day, the market suddenly becomes hard. Tumescence and detumescence, at whim, are part of the estate agent's portfolio of accomplishments. If you are buying 'ahead of the market', as they like to say and to encourage, you are buying into an urban slum or a rural wilderness. If you are buying 'behind the market', you will be overpaying.

The vanity of estate agents is laughable. The grander ones publish catalogues which they are pleased to call 'magazines', although if there were a Trade Descriptions Act with a relevant clause operating here they would be denied use of the word, since the editorial content is close to zero. These lacquered lists of properties for sale are customarily divided into regions, affording the opportunity for regional directors to pose in themed costumes: tweeds and gun-dog if representing the Highlands; cuffs and many-textured stripes for London and the South-East; smartish light suits for the South-West. They stand like an insane army of generals let into a yuppie dressing-up box, surveying new territories to conquer with their terrible weapons of hyperbole and blather.

They warn buyers that not many properties are coming on to the market. They warn sellers that too many properties are coming on to the market. They tell you that top-grade properties are selling at a premium, but average properties at a discount. This, they feel, is an impressively professional way of sounding like merchant bankers (whose example they try to emulate), but to the rest of us it seems like a nancyfied way of describing a commercial principle which says that attractive things command a higher price than unattractive ones.

It is this principle which moderates all communications from estate agents. Withal, estate agents *are* communicators. The essence of their business is the same as advertising: they are engaged in the alchemical process of turning a not necessarily attractive commodity into something the prospective purchaser must regard as essential. But while advertising agencies have layer upon layer of over-paid professionals to execute their deceptions, the poor, dim Justins and Ruperts have to be account executive, creative director and copywriter all in one.

This is why estate agents do so much damage to our language and to our view of property. They are perpetually involved, although ill-equipped to engage, in a process of heightening our perceptions through the creative use of words. A generation ago, when the possession of two telephones was considered a definition of luxury, estate agents could communicate effectively with a mixture of algorithms, abbreviations, mnemonics and acronyms. 'Croydon, semi-d, mod-cons, c-h, dbl-gl, £75k.' Now we are more sophisticated. The consumer is better educated and demands more.

To meet this demand, estate agents have evolved a fabulous language of decep-tion, both literary and visual. They work in a world where only hyperbole and positive associations are allowed. It must be like trying to write in one of those ancient Aramaic languages which have no device to express a negative concept.

Every expression or description has to be affirmative, driving the copywriters into a lunatic helical Babel of exaggeration and deceit.

This fabulous vocabulary of dissimulation would not be complete unless it worked in tandem with an equally misleading visual repertoire. This is an artful semantic code designed to conform to the principles of affirmation which govern all estate agents' communications. Those photographs you see in the glossy magazines have been contrived with bad art and low cunning to create the best possible effect. Never mind if there is a large stubborn stain on the seagrass floor covering (differential focus will see to that) and – who knows? – the Kuwaiti Hilton chandelier might impress the credulous. If the description does not *say* it's south-facing, it won't be. Photography can compensate.

The view you are looking at has been, well, optimized. This picture was the very best it was possible to achieve. One step further back and the photographer would have been in the dog basket or on the street. If the room looks compact in the photograph it will be claustrophobic in reality. If the kitchen looks a little tacky in the picture, it will be a health hazard. Remember, too, that the photographer has probably used a wide-angle lens (tell-tale sign: bent orthogonals at the edge of the frame) to create a favourable impression of the room's proportions.

Reality will not be like this – but in the phantasmagoric world of estate agents' communications, reality is at a premium to the market.
– *The Times Magazine*, 24 September 1994

5.6 The new British Airways

On June 10, British Airways unveils its new corporate image. It is one of the most massive rebranding exercises in corporate history; the company's entire fleet of aircraft, ground vehicles, stationery, catering, the uniforms of all its customer contact staff, everything from the towelettes upwards will get a fresh and dynamic new look. This is not a mere change of graphics; it is nothing less than a change of culture for the airline. The new look is inextricably linked with a newly defined philosophy, one designed to build on British Airways' unrivalled reputation for customer service and take it into a new and more globally minded future. Over the next three years, the airline will unveil new products, new technology, new services, new schedules, new network partners and a renewed commitment to remain the world's favourite airline. The airline is introducing new training programmes to extend its expertise in management and customer service. Indeed, chief executive Robert Ayling has set a not unambitious target: to make British Airways the best managed company in Europe and the world by the year 2000. How did the new vision get from the sketch book to the skies?

Be absolutely frank. Just what do you expect from a refreshing towelette? An astringent rush of saccharine citron wipe-me-down, ideal for removing fragments of in-flight salmon just before landing. Pretty straightforward, really. It can't possibly excite or satisfy the same expectations as, shall we say, a Boeing 747-400, an aircraft containing six million separate components and 60 miles of wiring, not to mention more than 300 passengers.

The one is ephemeral, disposable and cheap. The other costs hundreds of millions of dollars and will happily fly more than 12 hours a day every day of the year for a quarter of a century. Different things really, but that's the problem facing the design teams working for an airline. How do you create a corporate identity that's suitable both for simple toiletries and complicated airframes, not to mention humble Transit vans somewhere in between? Difficult; so that's why British Airways has completely rethought its whole corporate imagery.

But good design is never superficial: it has to be the external expression of basic values, to have genuine integrity. And a great corporate identity is much more than skin deep. It's in the soul, not on the surface. British Airways has certainly acquired a new look, but it's much more than a paint job. You can get paint jobs in spray shops. An organization of the complexity and stature of British Airways needs more sophisticated techniques to change its character. This is not a makeover or a disguise. It's an entirely new way of thinking about how an airline serves its customers and manages its people. The eye-catching graphics are the beginning of the process, not the end. You see: you don't finish a corporate identity programme, you start it.

A modern airline is an immensely complicated entity. When sheepskin-clad pioneers first spun props at Northolt or Croydon, sending juddering stringbag Vickers or Handley-Pages scrambling into the air on their way to Paris or Cairo, an airline was simply a conduit for rather chilly and bewildered fee-paying passengers. Today's airline is rather different: part engineer, part hotelier, part travel agent, part caterer, part restaurateur, part entertainer, part ambassador, part financier and entirely dedicated to customer convenience and shareholder value. Its complexity is a metaphor of modern international business.

What connects this diverse portfolio of interests is the growing awareness that, more than being an engineer, a hotelier or a travel agent, British Airways is something even more significant. It's a brand. We are now in the third great era of modern business. In the first era wealth was produced by the people who owned (or discovered) resources and processes, whether coal mines or production lines. In the second era, recently past, wealth was produced by the manipulation of obscure financial instruments. Now in the age when knowledge is power, wealth belongs to those who possess image.

But images are only worth having if they mean something. British Airways owns something much more precious than the mere cash value of its fleet of 308 planes. It owns shedloads of image capital, that mixture of recollection, association and expectation shared by all successful businesses. After more than a decade of successful and insistent advertising designed to reinforce a continuously improving service, British Airways now owns the idea that it is 'The World's Favourite Airline'. Kurt Vonnegut once remarked that the key to success was to appreciate that you soon become what you intend to be. This is what has happened to the descendants of the prop swingers at Northolt.

British Airways' image capital is unique and can't be copied. Anyone who can afford it (and get the slots) can buy a 747 and sell seats, but what they cannot acquire, at any price, is image. Image can't be manufactured any more than a family tree can be invented. It depends on substance and depth, not on a superficial change of typography or colour. So when British Airways decided in April 1995 to brief leading design consultants on creating a new identity it was well understood that what was required wasn't simply a new lick of paint, a cheery new letterhead and a few self-adhesive stickers, but a complete and thoroughly insightful reappraisal about what it meant to be the major international airline.

Airline graphics have an interesting history. In Europe, airlines were originally colonial instruments, means of getting safari-suited administrators out to suppress insurrections or deliver new and urgently required supplies of Earl Grey. The names reflected this. The ancestor of the plc flying you today was Imperial Airways. Still today in Europe, rather quaintly in defiance of emerging trends toward privately owned multinationalism, airlines tend to be construed as national 'flag carriers'.

Consider Air France and Lufthansa. Air France's livery was designed by the Compagnie de l'Esthétique Industrielle (founded by pioneer industrial designer, Raymond Loewy) and Lufthansa by the austere typographer, Otl Aicher. Each is a distinguished exercise in professional design – however much they may reflect, in some eyes, the graphic traditions of state-ownership and corporatism.

In the United States, where the business history of the airline industry was from the start entrepreneurial, the more adventurous and less slavishly respectful graphics reflected a tradition of expressive freedom. West Coast designers, including the late Saul Bass and the late Walter Landor, created bright, positive, confident imagery for their clients, none more so than textile and interior designer Alexander Girard, whose work for the now defunct Texan airline, Braniff, was a benchmark in commercial creativity. Girard was among the first to recognize that an aircraft was an advertisement, or at least a highly visible calling card. He commissioned artists, including Alexander Calder, to paint DC8s as they would a blank canvas, and when Braniff flew a 747 between Dallas and Gatwick it was... the Big Orange.

British Airways' current identity dates back to 1984. It was the work of Landor Associates, also responsible for Alitalia, and at the time caused a deal of righteous indignation among the sometimes hermetic British design business, insulted that such a major job should be given to a business in California, not Camden town. Landor replaced the old British Airways livery (designed by Dick Negus of Canonbury) with a completely different interpretation of what British Airways was meant to be.

The old Trident-era imperialist red, white and blue were scrapped in favour of a radical scheme using a sober navy-blue belly and light-grey upper fuselage. The logotype was all in roman capitals and the reference to a Union Jack on the vertical stabilizer reduced to an almost oriental ideogram. Critics sneered that Landor's new work for British Airways looked like a cigarette packet. What it in fact looked like was an extremely professional repackaging: the airline was made to look not like a pensioner of the State, but a free-standing international business.

The Landor identity was ideally suited to a newly privatized company and worked well at establishing a universally recognized identity, a brilliant piece of repositioning that was so successful that it's even established a stereotype: recent new liveries for United Airlines and Canadian are very evidently school-of-British Airways. Still, after ten years it was time to think of a change.

134

Initially, British Airways issued a brief to fifty designers in April 1995. This long shortlist was narrowed down to four consultancies. The winner was Newell and Sorrell, a firm of corporate identity consultants with offices in London and Amsterdam. By August 1996 the redesign had been given board approval and, following the introduction of interim livery at the beginning of this year, the full scheme is being implemented now. It will take three years to complete.

Newell and Sorrell co-chairman John Sorrell is used to interrogating his clients and firmly believes that for a modern designer, 'drawing' actually comes last. There's a popular misconception that designers are not far removed from the Romantic idea of the artist: idiosyncratic, talented individuals, quick-on-the-draw with inspiration and a bravura flourish of the pencil or (these days) the computer mouse. In fact, the contemporary corporate identity consultant is more at home in a business school than a Bohemian atelier. What you have to do first is cross-examine the subject and disentangle the rational and emotional components of his personality. Only after this process can you begin to resolve all the conflicting ideas in a winning design.

Sorrell was aware that the airline culture of the mid-1990s was very different to what it was a decade before. While business use of airlines is certainly not diminishing, leisure flying is expanding rapidly. Research was beginning to show that, despite its wearing well, some problems were emerging with the current identity. It was no longer possible to think of a singular type of British Airways customer, or, for that matter, shareholder. With 60 per cent of its business originating overseas and with more than a hundred different logos, the old identity was being stretched to the point of being strained.

The great mark of a truly successful design is that it is capable of sustained development and can be valid for different applications. As much as they admired the dignified Landor repositioning, many were beginning to feel that it was rapidly becoming too inflexible and introspective, no longer appropriate to a fast-evolving global carrier with many different faces to its personality.

It was John Sorrell who started wondering about whether a towelette really needed to carry the same graphic personality as a high-bypass turbofan-powered aircraft. It was, he argued, a delusory 'logic' that necessarily had packets of peanuts and ticket wallets and bathrooms looking the same as Boeings. Carriers these days are more relaxed about presenting a human face to what had always been assumed to be the desiccated technical necessities of running an airline. After exhaustive customer research, it was decided that British Airways was global and caring and this is what the new livery should say.

But before anything could be designed, some more interrogation was necessary. What does 'global and caring' mean? In rude practical terms it means that British Airways is not only the planet's biggest international carrier, it is also one of the world airline industry's biggest employers. And while British Airways' staff, from Bogota to Bangkok, may feel intense loyalty to the airline itself, being Colombians or Thais, they do not necessarily feel a similarly intense loyalty to any narrow definition of British nationhood.

In any case, British Airways is a freely traded stock with international ownership, not a civil service department dabbling in air transport. So, a subtle redefinition took place. Instead of being a British airline with global operations, British Airways has become a world airline whose headquarters happen to be in Britain. A world brand, in fact.

Newell and Sorrell decided to retain some key elements of the 1984 identity, one of which, the 'speedwing' itself, originated from Imperial Airways visual archaeology and the earlier 'speedbird'. Now Newell and Sorrell suggested a new 'speedmarque', an energetic flourish that suggests movement and freedom with echoes of the Union flag, but not slavishly so. Main body colours were adjusted rather than changed: the underbelly blue is a little lighter (black for Deutsche BA) and the old grey becomes a more optimistic pearl white. The typography is an evolutionary step from the hard-edged style of before, although it was redrawn with more emphasis on the curves to achieve a more approachable and friendly character. So far, so normal, but it was at this stage that a creative event occurred which allowed British Airways to vault over the species barrier and establish not just a new identity for itself, but a new type of identity.

In the 1990s, 'global and caring' does not mean post-imperialist flag-waving. It has to mean intelligently sensitive relations with customers and communities. On an aircraft, the vertical stabilizer is the flag by which carriers are identified (which is why aircraft landing at night have the tails lit-up with 'fin floods'). Out went the ghosts of the Union Jack – except on British Airways' flagship, Concorde, where, in the new 'rippling flag' design, it has taken on a dynamic new life.

For the rest of the fleet, Newell and Sorrell and British Airways' design management team decided on a unique campaign of acquiring new works of art from many of the communities which British Airways serves, and putting versions of the works onto aircraft tails: a Celtic knot, Chinese calligraphy, paintings from South Africa. There will be 15 new 'world images' at the launch; many more in the years to come. And if rosterings and routings create surreal combinations (a 757 with a tartan tail in, shall we say, Athens) then that only serves to demonstrate what a global airline means in practice. Next, taramasalata in Prestwick. The new fin designs bring a kaleidoscope of stylish and emotional benefits to British Airways people: friendly without being frivolous, international without being colonialist. This sort of variety amid uniformity is a perfect demonstration of modern management practice in a big, international business.

Better still, here is a corporate identity for British Airways that is more than a mere style, rather a communications solution with an inexhaustible range of applications. If British Airways has become a brand of world travel, it's not too fanciful to imagine this new identity one day appearing on more than fins and fuselages.

The experience of being on a plane lasts only a few hours. Yet the experience of the airline is much more profound and enduring. Very few passengers insist, at their travel agent's, on flying a 747 400 with RB211-424/E4 engines – only plane-spotters can tell the difference – but a goodly portion may insist on a particular airline. Human factors interest passengers more than technical ones and this is why an ingenious new corporate identity which genuinely expresses a sense of optimism and well-being is good both for British Airways and its customers.

The fleet will now be seen in new colours which are a creative expression of a company which, both in the letter and the spirit, regards the whole world as its customer. It's a new and refreshing philosophy which embraces every area of the airline's activity. And that includes the refreshing towelettes.
– *Highlife*, 1997

5.7 Don't phone the identity man yet

It was a slow afternoon at the new Department of Corporate Identity. Although the civil servants had voted to move from stuffy Whitehall to a site next door to Oddbins in Upper Street, Islington, many of the old guard regretted the change. It was all very well the Secretary of State for Brand Values arguing that it was essential to be near the department's high-profile consultant, Wally Pantone – they just thought it didn't feel like government in N1. And the compulsory Burberry-patterned baseball caps with Wally Pantone's Anne Hathaway mascot and the legend 'I'm backing West Mercia' made them cringe.

Suddenly, anticipated by clouds of Floris lavender scent, the Junior Minister for Emblematic Constructs rushed in, waving position statements. 'Bugger!' he screamed. 'I've just had a meeting with Wally Pantone and the Minister for Cognitive Dissonance. They've insisted on putting the new Welsh flag out to focus groups. Seventy-four per cent of A1/B1s in Carmarthen won't accept a coypu as a mascot and are insisting on reinstating the leek. And this is just ten days before Dyfed's relaunch as The Geoffrey of Monmouth Centre!'

Science provides marvellous metaphors for human frailty and foibles. Who does not know a sluggish individual whose intellectual limitations are not best described by saying he has read-only memory (Rom)? How many once-promising but fatally stalled careers are described by that chilling term from aerospace: CFIT, or controlled flight into terrain, the accident investigator's emotionally neutral term for a crash that occurred when the flight crew were, apparently, fully alert and functioning.

But best of all is that expression from particle physics which provides a metaphor for all the spiritual paradoxes and ironies of our age: the uncertainty principle. This was Heisenberg's expression for that perverse phenomenon which occurs when you attempt to investigate the precise behaviour of capricious subatomic matter. The very act of investigation itself alters the behaviour the investigator is seeking to understand. Merely *thinking* about neutrinos makes them stamp their feet, look the other way and scream, 'Shan't! Won't!' Nothing can be certain.

It's the same with the vexatious matter of national identity, a delicate and precarious mixture of shared symbols, happy accidents, evolutionary chaos, historical inheritance, genetic roulette, political interference, cultural hand-me-downs, the history of art, palaeo-anthropology, economics, the weather, geology, sun spots, Iron Age migration patterns, religion, bus routes, taste, sex, the Gulf Stream and investment decisions made in Delaware or Zurich.

The essence of nationhood and its visual expression are an unknowably complicated and subtle amalgam of fact, fiction, perception and prejudice. T.S. Eliot said culture was everything from cathedrals to a preference for boiled cabbage.

Whatever, national identity is always easier to detect than to define. The French say that the British are *cent ans de retard et dix ans d'avance*. Quite. Our own national identity is pleasingly contradictory. We maintain in fastidious order some of Europe's oldest institutions, but cultivate the most energetic, innovative and disrespectful youth culture the while. We support world-class research and development facilities in medicine, engineering and pharmaceuticals, but do not possess the means to manufacture a five-ton truck without foreign investment. Despite a reputation for being a nation of resolute philistines, we excel in all creative activities from music to advertising to art and design.

These are all part of our national identity but, as the uncertainty principle dictates, as soon as you develop a sense of self-consciousness about something so delicate, you distort it. If you try to interfere, you break it. But in an age when brand values are the chief point of difference between manufactured goods, there is a well-argued, if ill-considered, argument for creating a brand for Britain.

Coming from the world of margarine and soap powder, a brand is what accountants used to call 'goodwill' with a trademark attached. Except that when we speak brands we have to speak logos, a logo being a trademark that went to art school. Anybody can make a carbonated beverage with herbal extracts, but only one company can make Coca-Cola, the success of which is at least as much associated with its rich iconography as its 'delicious and refreshing' taste. The argument goes that New Britain needs a new brand.

Comparisons from industry do not offer much comfort for those who would rebrand Britain. While it is inevitable that at a time when information is the chief commodity of economic exchange, the intangibles of the brand become paramount; at the same time it's indisputable that the most successful brands have been those that have evolved rather than been invented.

Coca-Cola, Ford, Mercedes-Benz and Sony are examples. Coke uses its bookkeeper's copperplate signature. The Ford Story is similar. Sony was a Japanese misunderstanding of English phonetics mixed with a careless use of a classic Clarendon face. Mercedes-Benz will never, ever change its three-pointed star. The ones that have been invented are a sorry bunch of fragile neophytes.

Whenever countries have attempted to reinvent identities the results tend to be sinister. The best corporate identity scheme of all time was the one so eagerly adopted by the Wehrmacht, Luftwaffe, Kriegsmarine, Schutzstaffel and Gestapo. The Red Army did well, too, but was hindered by a comparative lack of resources.

And, of course, the countries with the strongest identities are those that are least self-conscious about it: the mere suggestion of red, white and green immediately evokes Italy. A corporate identity consultant would have charged a few hundred thousand to attain that perception. No developed nation is less fussed than Italy about the maintenance of its past or present image; none has a stronger identity.

There are some attractive parts to the new Demos pamphlet, a mite too cutely called *Britainô – Renewing Our Identity*. It certainly would be a good idea if the country had better gateways, everybody's first and last encounters with our culture. This side of a Romanian mental hospital, Heathrow Airport must be one of the nastiest places on earth. While what everybody really, really wants in an airport is absolutely clear: they want calm, beauty, convenience and a comforting atmosphere of confident expectation appropriate to the great technological adventure of flight. What BAA plc provides is altogether different.

It provides garish factory outlets over a large part of Middlesex. BAA plc thinks travellers want nothing other than to buy a litre of single malt, a pair of cashmere socks, sunglasses, a Danielle Steel, a burger, a cappuccino and a Japanese camera. To provide the sort of aerial gateway a civilized culture deserves, however, will be achieved only by government strategy: left to BAA plc, the nation's biggest gateway will remain a crass and gaudy souk.

There are some less attractive parts to the Demos pamphlet, too. At its worst, *Britainô* reads like a transcript of a 1983 dinner party where the guests included the Design Council, the identity consultant Wally Pantone, and Professor Michael Porter, at the time working on the first draft of his 1990 toe-breaking volume, *The Competitive Advantage of Nations*.

It is full of familiar, even rather tired stuff. The citation of the troubled white-goods manufacturer AEG as an exemplar does not give confidence in the author's command of his subject. Of course Dixons calls its own brand consumer electronics by a hokey Japanese name: Britain has no credentials in this area. Who would even *want* a VCR called a Parker-Bowles 1066? Besides, the wretched Matsui range is manufactured in the Orient, so what on earth do you expect? These things are fugitive, like the essence of national identity itself. The substance is far more substantial.

But more disturbing than the odd half-baked or out-of-date reference is the pervasive aroma of something so antiquated that it's decomposing: corporatism. No sooner had Mobil decided, circa 1966, that in the interests of good design management every single filling station on the planet should look exactly the same, then someone else discovered that maybe New Zealanders liked their filling stations to look somewhat different to the ones they had in Finland.

There have been very, very few successful world brands and, so far, no examples whatsoever of a successfully contrived national identity. Doubters may wish to inspect the ruins of Mussolini's ideal towns of Latina and Sabaudia, just south of Rome, to confirm this opinion.

Heathrow may be an ugly and chaotic zoo, but it's a free and vigorous one. I'm not sure I'd actually prefer it if the Secretary of State for Brand Values had called in his Ministers for Emblematic Constructs and Cognitive Dissonance and had convened focus groups and an opinion poll and drawn up guidelines for its role in the branding of Britain. I think, curiously, it's rather effective as it is. Sure, it would be great if BAA plc behaved with better taste, more consideration and discretion, but that's another issue altogether.

– *New Statesman*, 12 September 1997

6.1 Dunne roaming

Dominick Dunne is America's best novelist. Or more accurately the best novelist of America. Certainly not the most writerly, not even the most popular. In fact the literary papers retain a lofty disdain for his books which, if they are reviewed at all, are sent to that small magazine *Siberia* where the Jeffrey Archer and paper-back crime notices appear. And it's true that Dunne's style, at its worst, can be ham-fisted and prosey with Homeric repetitions and formulas. But people don't read Dominick Dunne for a literary *frisson*, they read him because no one else better understands the nuances of American class.

Americans have printed a Social Register so you can be as certain of who's in and out as you are of a McDonald's price list. The one rule here is that to be in, you must not be notorious. There can be no late arrivals. It is a marvellous game which you have to be invited to play. Dunne says that the Trumps will get in before the Kennedys. 'And *they're* not going to get in.'

The old bags read Dominick Dunne to read about themselves. They invite him round. He trashes them completely and still they invite him back. Explains Taki: 'He gets invited because he's a single man who's not going to fuck them in a taxi. He goes out with old bags and he's very nice'. Taki says Dunne is 'respected as a saint, he wouldn't pick a fight'. But on the other hand, he is scarcely a pussy. We had this exchange: 'I only write about bad people'. 'But you wrote about Phyllis McGuire [an entertainer of the 1950s].' 'Yes, but I loathe her.' This phonic literal led to recriminations. Dunne had actually said, 'Yes, but I love her.'

No one else has such access to American aristocracy and no one else so faithful-ly and dispassionately records its mannered foibles, its greed and its vicious defence of its privileges. Everything is for sale, even freedom for the guilty. What separates and distinguishes Dominick Dunne from Tom Wolfe or Paul Fussell or other satirists is that he is writing about his own people. His social life.

It is an amusing paradox that the literary establishment exercises judgements of such fastidious superiority over Dunne's books. Niceties of preferment are one of his own best-traded stocks. As Nancy Mitford knew, only common people use the word common.

He thinks that it is hilarious pretension to spell Gladyce with a 'c'. One Queen of the Luncheon Club 'never spoke directly to a waiter if she was dining with a man'. A creature's doom is predicted when it is noted, 'Even her Rigaud candles were the wrong colour'. Another has a clutch of middle-class ladies who do her place cards, in the full knowledge that they will never be invited to dinner.

Dunne created a world and its population. The novels are episodes in a serial. Favourite characters drift in and out. There is Gus Bailey, who seems to be Dunne; Basil Plant, who is certainly Truman Capote and Cora Mandell, the deco-rator (who helps overcome the arriviste anxiety of her clients by placing strips of

tape on surfaces to show exactly where the export china should be displayed).
Scenes from one book are repeated in others. It is a compelling creation with a hypnotic clarity, but if there is an aftertaste of bitterness in Dunne's account of the way we live now it is because this refined, successful, elegant and charming man has known not one, but two or three of the worst and ugliest things that can happen to a human being: vivid professional failure; the suicide of a brother; and the savage murder of his daughter.

So who is Dominick Dunne? One London fashion PR, a tough worldly lady who knows how to look after herself, warned me – when I was meeting him for lunch – that he was 'lethal'. 'He's dangerous. An alcoholic. A hard, charming, ruthless man. A psychopath. Wouldn't you be if your daughter had been murdered?' Dominick Dunne was born 67 years ago in Hartford, Connecticut, the son of a prominent surgeon of Irish extraction, and grew up on the social tightrope between privilege and discrimination. His brother John Gregory Dunne, husband of Joan –*Play It As It Lays*–Didion, said in his curious, rambling butcompulsive semi-autobiographical *Harp* (1989): 'We carried a full cargo of ethnic and religious freight as it shifted on the long passage between immigration and deracination'.

Today Dominick Dunne remains a Catholic only in so far as he has a good relationship with a good priest. He became one of America's most successful television producers, one of the first generation of educated young men who moved into the new medium (in his case, after Williams College where he met Stephen Sondheim) following the war, in the days when there were killings to be made and markets to be won. He moved from coast to coast, and from television it was a short step to Hollywood and the movies. Dunne became a successful movie producer, with Mart Crowley's *Boys in the Band and Panic in Needle Park* his major credits. And then things began to go wrong. Mainly it was drink and drugs, but it was also – one suspects – a certain cussed self-destruction. He argued and fell out with crucial king-makers and by the late 1970s he was a nowhere man.

He left Hollywood in 1979 and said he stopped in Oregon because that's where his car broke down. It was here that he received a call from his younger brother, John Gregory, to say that his other younger brother, Stephen Dunne, had gone into his garage, carefully taped the doors and windows, turned on the engine and gassed himself. Of this moment, John Gregory says: 'There are things to do when there is a sudden death, and the first thing I did, I did badly. I called Dominick who had come upon bad times of his own – an almost terminal crisis of confidence. He was living in a small cottage in a rural Oregon community, trying to piece his life back together. It took some time to reach him – he had no direct phone – and when I told him what had happened, there was a cry of such bleakness that I can remember it still. He pulled himself together and said he had been contemplating suicide himself, perhaps even at the same moment as Stephen: it was as if the nature of Stephen's death had foreclosed an option'.

It had. Dominick Dunne was going to live, but first he had to go through something even bleaker. In Oregon he was writing *The Winners*, a sequel to Joyce Haber's *The Users*. It has the content – limos, status, a fair measure of sex – characteristic of his later work, but none of the fiercely understated moral purpose. That was to come later, after his daughter was murdered and the killer let off with a heartbreakingly light sentence. He had gone to Oregon in search of epiphany and a cruel fate had delivered it back home in Los Angeles. Although it was an apprenticeship made in hell, there is no doubt that the appalling experience of the wasteful death and the flawed trial turned Dominick Dunne from a burnt-out Hollywood has-been to a great writer. It can hardly be imagined what Dunne's feeling must have been on learning of his daughter Dominique's strangulation by her boyfriend, a chef at Ma Maison ('a West Hollywood restaurant so concerned with its fashionable image that it had an unlisted telephone number'), but, at the instigation of Tina Brown, then at the beginning of her influential stint at *Vanity Fair*, the experience wrung from him a superb piece of journalism. 'When the telephone in my New York apartment woke me at five o'clock in the morning on 31 October, 1982, I sensed as I reached out for the receiver that disaster loomed. Detective Harold Johnson of the Los Angeles Homicide Bureau told me that my 22-year-old daughter, Dominique, was near death at Cedars Sinai Medical Center.'

The whole of this long article, published as 'Justice' in *Vanity Fair*, March 1984, is written in this measured, matter-of-fact style. No detail is missed, no overt judgements made. Facts are recorded meticulously. The coolness is astonishing, but it was in the frigid mechanism of this therapeutic recording that Dunne found the spirit which drives his later novels. It was not just the appalling circumstances of a girl's brutal death, but the trivialization of the courtroom that incensed Dunne. Of Judge Katz, given to wearing sunglasses in court, Dunne writes: 'His relationship with the jury bordered on the flirtatious, and they responded in kind …One Monday morning he told them he had had a great weekend in Ensenada, that he had had the top down on his car both ways, and that he wished they had been with him'.

It was Judge Katz who disallowed testimonies crucial to the prosecution case, who turned the victim Dominique into the culprit, who turned the culprit into a victim of circumstances. Although the murderer had a tradition of choking girls, Judge Katz directed the jury against a count of first-degree murder on the grounds that there had been no premeditation.

Dunne saw his daughter murdered all over again in the courtroom. He saw her slandered as an upper-class party girl who had led on an impressionable and reckless youth. He had to watch the court look at shocking autopsy photographs. He looked at the smirking judge, the lying defendant – now carrying a Bible – whose counsel presented the case not as the wicked murder of a young girl, but as a shared tragedy. The jury was out for eight days and returned a verdict of voluntary manslaughter. Just before, Judge Katz had sentenced someone who, with no recourse to violence, robbed a flower store, to five years. The murderer of Dominique Dunne got six and a half years, two and a half with good behaviour.

Fused senses of outrage, injustice and craving for a sense of purpose in a world turned upside down began to inform Dominick Dunne's fiction. In a Dominick Dunne book, it is always apparent who actually done it. Discovery is not the point, establishing guilt and creating an appetite for justice is. The effect is cumulative. Nothing has undermined my faith in American society or my faith in American justice so much as a close acquaintance with Dunne's books. Each novel concerns the guilty going free and the pain of the innocent, who always suffer to preserve the privileges of the moneyed classes.

The books are gloriously readable with strong story-lines and a seductive narrative rhythm driven by the siren of voyeurism. Each novel is only very thinly disguised. The Woodwards, the Bloomingdales, the Kennedy's are all there in disguise. His painstakingly deconstructive journalism, as apparently polite as a feature in *Hello!*, is mesmerizing. I asked if he was worried that he might offend his subjects. He said, 'I don't give a shit about Khashoggi and his vulgar house'.

Damaged people, as another popular novelist has observed, are very dangerous.

Not the least fascinating aspect of Dunne's account of his class are his frequent and often surprisingly explicit descriptions of sex, and such unsavoury details as a character's 'bad bathroom smells'. In *The Two Mrs Grenvilles* we find the gold-digger saying to the young ensign, William Grenville Jnr, whose face she later shoots off: *'And Junior?'*
'Yes?'
'When you open the door to let me in?'
'Yes?'
'Be naked.'

If ever a man could swoon, she knew, over the telephone, that William Grenville, Junior, had just swooned.'

Later:
She saw the shirt tail stand out in excitement. 'Come over here… and let me get a good look at that thing in the light.' He walked over to her, and she reached into the opening of his shorts. 'It's really lovely,' she said. As he lunged for her hungrily, she said, 'No, no, stand back. This one's on me.' She pulled his shorts down his legs and knelt on the floor in front of him. She didn't know if she should let him see how good at it she was.

In *An Inconvenient Woman*, one of a film producer's tennis-playing tarts wears a T-shirt with the legend, 'Warning. I scream when I come'. In the same book somebody asks, 'Tell me, Mrs Cliveden, what kind of fuck was Jack Kennedy?' In his last novel, *A Season in Purgatory*, the compromised hero Harrison Burns, who had once masturbated over *Playboy* with the Kennedy-politician character, is with one of the Bradley-Kennedy girls:

He reached to the bottom of her dress and pulled it up, his hand between her legs, gently grasping her, and massaging it back and forth as they continued to kiss, their tongues pressing together. 'Oh my God,' she whispered. She reached down and unzipped the fly of his trousers … dropped to her knees and took Harrison's penis in her mouth. [At this point they are disturbed by her more chaste sister.]

Like many reformed alcoholics, Dunne leads a disciplined life. He lives alone – long separated, not divorced – in an elegant apartment on East 49th Street and in a Connecticut country house bought out of recent royalties and fees earned as America's most highly paid journalist. He keeps a journal every day, full of meticulous records of lunch or drinks party conversations, and gets up at six to write it 'just to get the words coming'. Later, he finds the characters emerge in the writing. Then they live in his head.

He is very short and has bad, blotchy skin. There are gold things on dull, expensive shoes. His single-breasted charcoal suit is discreet. He wears a colourless shirt and a pink Turnbull & Asser silk tie. He looks just what he is: a patrician American. You could easily mistake him for the president of an old university … until he begins to talk. I had expected a laid-back cautious manner, with words chosen carefully and spoken with gravitas. Not at all. Dominick Dunne has a light, almost squeaky, nasal voice and he is very animated. Within the seconds he allows you to win his confidence, there's lots of winking, eye-rolling and tapping on the forearm.

The day we met he had already had an eventful morning, full of experiences which you know will find their way into future books. Queen Noor had sent him a telegram. He was ten minutes late for lunch, waiting for the Queen Mother to arrive at his hotel. I didn't need to ask, he told me: Claridge's and green chiffon.

On the way to the restaurant he'd loved the *Evening Standard* posters 'Drama as Blandford Seized' and clicked his fingers in the retelling. As Taki says, the characters in Nick's books could probably *never* be quite as odd, or as scandalous, as the ones nature provides direct. In the restaurant he waved across the room and said mockingly, 'Hi, Andrew [Lloyd-Webber]. How's the show going?' (This at a time when *Sunset Boulevard* had very public problems).

There is a consistent dark side even to his most amusing observations. On the way back in a cab he told me a long, black and hilarious tale about the three gay men who dressed the stiffening corpse of Natalie Wood, discovering the capricious nature of tights for the first time in the most macabre circumstances. Although he made the decision to 'let it go' in order to preserve some sense in his own life, his daughter's death and her murderer's trial clearly consume him. But Dunne has also seen the dark side of his own nature. His writing about alcoholism, for instance. Of Constant Bradley, the Kennedy-politician figure in *A Season in Purgatory*:

He never sips. He gulps. One night at the club, he was always tapping his glass for the waiter to bring him another. Couldn't wait. Couldn't keep focused on the conversation until he had another glass in front of him.

John Gregory Dunne suggests – notwithstanding the moral campaign inspired by Dominique's murder – that the novels are an extension of a discovery process that began earlier: 'I was the occasional recipient of long, artful letters full of character evaluation and private secrets and revisionist family history'. This correspondence, analysed at Dunne's support group, ended with a message from Dominick to John Gregory which simply said 'Fuck you'.

This makes an arresting contrast with the last, poignant words of Dunne's famous and harrowing 1984 article. Leaving Los Angeles after the trial, he asks the driver to make a final stop before the airport. With a yellow rose taken from a hall table, he went to Dominique's grave in Westwood Cemetery, knelt down and said 'Goodbye, my darling daughter'. Dunne continues to speak on behalf of Parents of Murdered Children.
– *Harpers & Queen*, January 1994

Life is just one long succession of deadlines with a very big and unmissable one at the end.

Deadlines dominate all of us. This ugly compound word contains two elements that neatly describe the urgent futility of worldly endeavour. Yes, we are irrevocably committed to a linear progress through the seven ages of man and yes, I'm afraid, the reward at the end of this purposive, deterministic adventure is not a gold watch, but an appointment with the Grim Reaper where, since he is in charge of the schedule, we have no option other than to be punctual. For many of us, the moment of our death is the only occasion we ever manage to be on time, even early.

Punctuality, like celibacy and sobriety, is so rare a condition that I'm tempted to wonder if it is natural. Of course, it isn't. Punctuality is an invention of those busy little demons that entered the European mind about 3,000 years ago. Greeks developed their water clocks and ever since, civilized man has worried about being on time. Meanwhile, uncivilized man lolled around in the sunshine, doggedly ignorant, nobly blissful, fornicating, getting up late and altogether living in a condition not so dissimilar from that which Club Med achieves for its contemporary clients. The invention of time brought with it those three curses of regret, anxiety and guilt, sources of all human sorrow. Without time we would be free of the past and of the future. Without time we wouldn't have to be punctual.

But in the world of the deadline, you cannot turn the clock back. The American designer Saul Bass who, if you're interested, gave us the United Airlines logo, always keeps his watch running ten minutes fast. This serves two purposes, to keep him in a state of continuous twitchy frenzy (also known as 'creativity') and to make some contribution to the achievement of punctuality. Creative types like Bass always fret about being 'blocked' which means they can't start work. There is no such thing, only a matter of adjusting a relationship to a deadline. It is surprising how the looming approach of a deadline spontaneously releases blockages and makes even the most obdurately feckless, punctual in the delivery of work.

But punctuality does not just concern our relationship with work, but with people as well. In the sensitive area of manners there are exquisite niceties to be observed. Some old-school types will, on being asked the time, refuse to look at their watches since this is considered a breach of etiquette suggestive of a coarse proletarian curiosity about the here and now. Instead, they will take their watch off and hand it unblinking to the inquirer for him to examine.

To be too concerned about punctuality is very Low Church. In fact, outside Swiss railways, punctuality is more a state of mind than a precise method of working. It is an attitude, not a science, susceptible to subtle modulations depending on circumstance. You are invited for dinner at eight. Only the very maladroit would turn up on the hour. Instead, the sophisticated exercise what in Germany is called the *akademisch viertel* (the academic quarter) and arrive 15 to 30 minutes after the designated time. More than 30 minutes late is a different type of social error: arrogance.

Like all forms of good manners, punctuality is a way of making other people feel comfortable. The most familiar interface most of us have with other people's ability to make us feel uncomfortable are those agonizing occasions when you have arranged to meet someone in a restaurant. Here, if you are the host, it is absolutely necessary to be early, otherwise your nervous guest may arrive before you and be left in a flummox of indecision about whether to order a drink and risk categorization as an alcoholic solo drinker. If you are a guest, you shouldn't be more than a few minutes late for the very same reasons.

Some people are quite incapable of adapting themselves to even the most relaxed interpretation of civilized behaviour. The worst case of restaurant punctuality I know occurred a few years ago when my wife, uncomfortably eight months pregnant, turned up at about one o'clock to meet an important figure in her business life. He arrived at two-thirty and cheerily said 'Hi, I just *knew* you'd wait'. Manic punctuality may be the thief of time, being late is a felon too. Insulting as well.

Attitudes to punctuality betray fundamental character traits. You'd be correct to think it uncool to arrive at a meeting twenty minutes too soon and have to walk around the block nervously checking your watch, or fidgeting in the lobby and saying to the receptionist, 'Don't say I'm here yet, I'm a bit early'. On the other hand, a message from a secretary to say, 'Rupert is running late' confirms your suspicion that Rupert is a prat. This will be immediately corroborated when Rupert arrives, beaming, and says, 'God! I'm sorry! The traffic!' As if to demonstrate that his ugly solipsism is such that he (a) has only just realized there are such things as traffic problems and (b) thinks they affect himself alone.

The sophisticated seem to find the right balance between being embarrassingly early and infuriatingly late. Punctuality is unnatural, but then so are all the refinements of civilized life. A fuzzy sort of punctuality is the best revenge against Time's cruel interference in our lives. This inscription on a seventeenth-century sundial perfectly captures the nice friction between human caprice and the inevitability of destiny:

Time wastes our bodies and our wits
But we waste time, and so we are quits.

Sorry, I've got to go now. I'm late.
–*GQ* , September 1995

6.3 Call of the riled

There is no instrument of modern life more likely to discomfort than the phone – no device better designed for dissimulation, no apparatus suited more fully to interruption and mendacity. If you believe that making people comfortable involves being honest in your intentions and solicitous in your attentions, avoid the telephone.

A phrasebook of lies has surfaced from the swamp of telecommunication hell:

'I'll get right back to you'.
(You are a frightful nuisance and I can scarcely be bothered to talk to you.)

'I'm sorry, there's something in the oven.'
(You are a bore.)

'I was trying to call you all day yesterday.'
(I have completely forgotten about you.)

'I'm sorry, but my phone's been out of order.'
(I have been avoiding you and I also think you must be stupid.)

'Let's have lunch.'
(I assume you are a heavy drinker.)

'Let's have lunch. Sometime.'
(Fuck off. I hope I never see you again.)

Decent people disdain the phone because it is so well adapted to brutish effrontery, suiting hectoring louts or busybodies who want to talk before they reflect. A phone message is always a *demand*, hardly ever an offer. Even after a century of using phones, you still find that good news only comes in letters. The telephone is used for 'your copy's late', 'your mother's dead', or for picking your brains without a fee.

What exactly is it that gives phone callers the outrageous and unjustified assumption that they take precedence? Think of the times you have spent in queues at car hire desks in remote airports, only to achieve your objective – eyeballing the clerk, getting a glimpse of the longed-for Oldsmobile Cutlass Ciera – just as the desk set goes 'parp parp' and you go on hold while We-Try-Harder satisfies the telephone intruder, rather than the bagged and lagged person in front of him.

I think it's something to do with an awe of technology (a ringing phone must be important) mixed with a fear of the unknown. There is an assumption by phone users and a glum acceptance among phone victims that the gods of telecommunications will not be mocked, nor ignored.

In American newspaper articles on shit-stirring, if the final sentence in a story is 'Mr X did not return calls' it is there to mean Mr X is as guilty as sin; it suggests that Mr X's innocent decision to ignore a call on the grounds of taste or convenience is confirmation of any charge in the story – or at least of taking a breather to consult a lawyer.

All journalists know this. Get the target on the phone and he's as good as dead. Make any charge, the more baseless the better, and you'll get a response somewhere within the range of culpability beginning 'No comment' and ending 'Lord Hanson angrily denied that he put Dijon mustard up his greyhound's backside to make it run faster'. Those of us who know both sides of the Fourth Estate treat *never let the journalist get you on the phone* as a golden rule.

Only a device which so warps morals and communication could be used in such devious and indecent and inhuman ways. Hanging-up on someone is still a profound insult and much, much easier (and, therefore, more loathsomely craven) than having to cut them in person, slap them on the face or wither them with an acerbic remark. But it is not just the psychological aspects of phone use which make the device so unpleasant; it seems actually to militate against goodsense and good manners. I was taught as a child to pick up a ringing phone and say 'Allerton four double three one'. The Germans are taught to say '*Schickelgruber hier*'.

Some sort of ID is intelligent and desirable because, like other forms of good manners, it obviates embarrassment and confusion. Think of the frolicsome callers who say either 'It's James' (rather conceitedly and stupidly suggesting that you only know one James) or the smug asses who launch into a conversation only to stop and say, 'You don't know who you are talking to, do you?' With people so crass, I invariably don't. Even with good friends, I think it sensible, prudent and just polite to say 'Hi, David, It's Stephen Bayley here', always giving my full name.

But phone sufferers are avenged by the vagaries of technology. Just this last Tuesday I was sitting on a train when a fellow passenger dug his portable out of his combination-locked briefcase. Here is his conversation in full:

'Hello.'
'Hello.'
'Can you hear me?'
'Can you hear me now?'
'Can you hear me NOW?'
'Wait a minute.'
'I'll call you back when I get to the office.' (This last line repeated five times.)

Good manners should be effortless; telephones are hard work.
– *GQ*, February 1993

6.4 The air fix. Fear of flying: the theory and the practice

I remember sitting in a BAC-111 on the stand at Jersey. I was near the front of the cabin and minding my own writhing nerves, squirming and flushing no more than usual before take-off, when up the steps leapt a frazzled mechanic in overalls with some tools as sophisticated as you'd need to service a wheelbarrow. I winced and attempted spontaneous voluntary deafness as some crude thumps, scrapes and squeaks came from the cockpit. Some minutes later I heard the mechanic say, 'It's no good, guv, I can't fix it'. A happy vision came into view of another night, this time at British Airways' expense, at Longueville Manor, but no, they shut the door and off we rattled.

Next, a DC-9 somewhere in Scandinavia. I was at the front, not just because I'm habituated to expensive seats, but because in this case the plane was virtually empty and it was free choice. They left the flight-deck door open during take-off and I took some pictures on a 135mm lens. One warning light failed to go out and I have Ektachromes to prove it: for a flight of about one hour 'Left Gear Unsafe' blinked at the pilot, co-pilot and me.

Finally, I hope, a 747 on the ground at Kennedy Airport. There had been a mother and father of electric storms that afternoon and all the flights were being cancelled, except the one I was on which was just a few hours delayed. We boarded, but the captain said, 'Don't panic. If you look outside you'll see we won't be taking off for a while yet'. About twenty seconds later he said, 'Here we go,' and there we went. Taking off into a severe thunderstorm, with every sort of dirty air, is a dangerous business. Even the stewardesses looked grim as they buckled themselves in. All unnecessary electrics were turned off to maximize power.

It's a reliable rule of thumb for all normal flights that 90 seconds after rotation you have enough height to trade it for speed so you are out of danger. That's usually when the captain turns off the 'No Smoking' sign. This time he didn't and we circled and circled without gaining height for about an hour until he saw a soft spot in the clouds and went for it. Then there was a terrific bang, the huge plane fell out of the sky and the engines raced as the captain looked for full power to ensure that aerodynamics and brute force beat the force of gravity. They just did and we just survived, but a stewardess told me it was the worst experience she had had in twenty-seven years of commercial flying.

These were all unsettling occasions. They were particularly traumatic for me as I have a fascination, now morbid, now technical, for aviation safety and I know something about the BAC-111's murderous proclivity for deep stalls, about the DC-9's questionable longitudinal stability and about the wind-shear that affected my 747.

Like other taboos, air safety obsesses people. Despite the blandishments offered by the 'triumph of technology over superstition' school, aircraft are neither as safe as they should be nor as safe as they could be. I remember hearing the architect, Norman Foster, who flies his own Cessna Citation, saying that there are two types of pilot: the ones who are surprised if nothing goes wrong and the ones who are astonished if something does. It's the first sort you want to fly with, not the transcontinental crews described at one of last year's international flight safety conferences as being, for most of their long-haul trips, in a state of subnormal torpor.

But human factors are not the only source of danger in commercial flying. There are technical and operational factors too. When the roof blew off a Hawaiian 737 (because a water-soluble resin used in construction had contributed to corrosion leading to structural failure), Boeing's assumptions about its static test procedures were brought under serious scrutiny.

Static testing means an airframe goes through continuous simulated flight cycles in a laboratory so that the manufacturer can predict failures on the ground before they occur in the air. All airframe manufacturers have planes in laboratories which are much 'older' than even the oldest craft flying. In the case of the 737, Boeing's own static test frame had gone through something like 130,000 simulated flight cycles, while the Hawaiian jet which just missed disaster had done less than 90,000. But the static test took no account of glue failures or corrosion caused by moisture and condensation. These are now being looked at, but the fear in the industry is that other failures will soon occur that tests have not predicted. As a response, Boeing has instituted a programme reviewing the airworthiness of high-time planes. This may lead to early retirement of large parts of the global fleet with the consequential effect of increased costs. Many airlines will resist this.

Safety and cost are at war, as illustrated by a current operational change which over the past two years has seen twin-engined aircraft – operated by El Al, Air Canada, American Airlines, TWA and Piedmont – flying over the Atlantic and other large expanses of water. The engine and systems manufacturers argue that improvements in reliability of turbines, avionics, radars and flight controls have been so fundamental that these extended Twin Operations are now for the first time coming within the acceptable limits of safety. Maybe, but they do not explain they are doing this for the money: twins are cheaper to operate on long, thin routes and while the increased reliability is not in question, neither is the fact that flying an aircraft with two engines, rather than three or four, over the ocean is a calculated risk which many passengers, were they aware of it, might prefer not to take.

At the moment the airlines do not advertise safety, but prefer to publicize their booze, their canapés, their sleeper seats and their travel socks. It is only a matter of time before one of them breaks ranks and makes enhanced safety a selling point. Although a controversial issue and a hostage to fortune, there is nothing more likely to attract passengers because the old slogan about the 'safest way to travel' is somewhat misleading, a product of creative statistics. Sure, if you multiply the number of passengers by the number of miles flown, then multiply by the time exposed and divide all of that by the annual fatalities, you get a very flattering picture. But a more sophisticated approach to the figures would give a more accurate picture.

Last year the authoritative *Journal Aviation Week and Space Technology* published some figures about flight profiles. The figures indicated that 48.6 per cent of accidents occur on final approach and landing, phases of flight which occupy a mere 4 per cent of total exposure time. Put that into the equation and the true picture becomes more apparent.

Overnight, airlines could become safer if they wanted to. They could reduce passenger load, reduce frequencies of flights, decrease maintenance intervals, replace flammable seats with inflammable ones, provide smokehoods.

Manufacturers could increase the number of back-up systems such as two sets of controls to the flaps. Governments could intervene in the chaos of air-traffic control.

At the moment there is no public pressure for them to do this. But as the customer becomes more aware of the issues it is inevitable that demand for greater safety will increase.

– *Television treatment,* 1990

'Je dis qu'il ne faut pas tant regarder ce qu'on mange qu'avec qui on mange.'
('I say it's not so much what one eats as the company one eats it in.')
– Montaigne, *Essays*, 1588

It is a truth not yet universally acknowledged that the success and enduring appeal of restaurants depend more on their décor and ambience than on the food they serve.

The restaurant is a product of modern, urban industrial civilizations. In his celebrated book, *La Physiologie du Goût* (1826) Brillat-Savarin makes it clear that the restaurant was created for the middle classes, who, in imitation of the aristocracy, but with fewer resources, wanted to eat like Colbert or Madame de Pompadour. In this context, it is worth pointing out that dining-room furniture does not exist before, say, the reign of Louis XIV. It was only after the rise of the middle classes after the Revolution (which also put a lot of unemployed cooks onto the Paris labour market) that this curious subset in the history of furniture design emerges. Since then, the dining room and what goes on in it has been a persistent preoccupation of the bourgeoisie, as even the most cursory examination of home-furnishings magazines reveals. At home, a well-equipped dining room confers prestige.

Of course, this is an extension of the restaurant experience, by dint of which we bourgeois codify our values. Most people's assumptions about what is and what is not sophisticated depend on their experience of eating out. The first restaurants were simply public dining rooms, custom-made arenas for that phenomenon of post-revolutionary urban culture: the consumer. In Brillat-Savarin's account of their coming, gustatory relish vies with economic expediency. The first restaurant-goers were the first people to experience a third party inventing and providing goods, services and environment to cater for their appetites and tastes. 'The restaurant,' Brillat-Savarin sighed, 'is the gourmand's Eden'.

A few generations later the splendid Edwardian Colonel Newnham-Davis gave an account in his *Dinner and Diners* (1899) which shows how hotel restaurants were providing for an itinerant and free-spending middle class, a deal of heraldry previously sported only by the aristocracy. He writes of Claridge's:

The windows are draped with deep red curtains and purple portières; the carpet carries on the scheme of quiet reds, and the chairs have morocco backs of vermilion, with the arms of the hotel stamped on them in gold. The quiet-footed waiters in evening clothes, with the arms of the hotel as a badge on the lapels of their coats, are in keeping with the room.

And not only did the new restaurants offer paying customers the vicarious experience of having servants and, say, a country house, but they also offered something else novel: competitive culinary inventiveness. Hitherto confined to the ruling classes in France (now thinned and dispersed by the guillotine's blade) new dishes were demanded by the new bourgeoisie. So much a stock-in-trade of the current media treatment of food and cooking, it takes an effort of imagination to realize that the supply and demand for new recipes are, like the restaurant itself, a product of modern bourgeois civilization.

What happened two hundred years ago in France has only occurred very recently here. As late as 1921 it was possible for Lord Edward Cecil to write: 'An Englishman will eat anything if it is served hot, there is plenty of it, and he is sure he knows what it is'.

In an article in the *Evening Standard* in 1935 Osbert Sitwell attacked the Wine and Food Society as pretentious. In a 1983 television interview the patrician Harold Macmillan exclaimed that, as least in his household, it was considered bad form to talk about food. Somewhere in between, Elizabeth David intervened to save us. Mrs David's inspiration for her first magnificent book *Mediterranean Food* (1951) was the awfulness of postwar life in Britain. Faced with gristle rissoles, flour soup and white steam-baked bread, she reminisced – somewhat pornographically – about her experiences in Egypt and Greece before 1939. In a 1963 article in the *Spectator* she said: 'Even to write words like apricot, olives and butter, rice and lemons, oil and almonds, produced assuagement'.

The series of books which followed *Mediterranean Food* were all what the marketeers in their coarse demotic would nowadays call 'aspirational'. In just the same way as during the 1950s the Council of Industrial Design urged the salvation of English taste by the importing of Scandinavian furniture, so Elizabeth David and others wanted to do it with garlic, peppers and a *bain-marie*. This opened a path which led to chromatic experimentation and variety in all parts of English life, and in particular the experience of eating out. If you think about it, the very idea of the table d'hôte speaks volumes about the social, cultural, practical and economic assumptions of our civilization. After all, eating with a host not necessarily known to you is a somewhat surprising undertaking, as surprising as eating with strangers. It was for this reason that the restaurant has established all manner of comforting and familiar rituals.

Eating in a restaurant allows more intimacy than a meeting in an office, but less than you would have in your home. Because it is a public place, codes of behaviour dominate personal performance. It is your theatre and you have the lead. You know the plot and you depend on the staff to support your role.

What are the best restaurants for this performance? They are the ones where the ambience and the décor reinforce your sense of self, or perhaps even create it, and, clearly, this is something beyond – or beneath – the type or quality of food you are served.

Zagat's New York City Restaurant Survey publishes a list of restaurants under the rubric 'Power Scenes'. Including La Cote Basque, Le Cirque, The Four Seasons, Le Bernardin and Parioli Romanissimo, this vulgar conceit is intended to provide a guide for the deracinated consumer in this filthy, lawless and overpriced city. Only those who have witnessed at first-hand a South American Indian fish hunt have a comparable model for the competitive savagery and Stone Age regard for ritual and precedence which govern the shifting fashions of smart American restaurants. Zagat says Le Cirque has 'more power and pulcritude [sic]' per square foot than any of its rivals, but – alas – this version of power and pulchritude comprises 'presidents, corporate raiders or rockers and their model mates'. Those New Yorkers who want to eat like presidents, corporate raiders and rockers have Zagat to thank for knowing where to go. And of course, you can find the same evil brew of personnel in London, but being England the

'power scene' is one or two horses short. Yet, in the Ritz, the Caprice, the Neal 152
Street Restaurant or in the Connaught Hotel at breakfast you have a fair chance
of being mistaken for a president, a corporate raider or a rocker. Different each
in style of décor and style of cooking, they have an effect which is identical,
achieved by a common confidence and discretion. While each can provide food
that is the very best of its sort, each would serve you a jam sandwich if that was
what you asked for.

Restaurant-goers, at least in central London, are very rarely concerned with the
food. Their business is not the *quenelles*, the *brochettes* or the *timbales*; rather,
what they want to consume is the magic of the place which a particular restaurant imparts. 'I can spell Vita Sackville-West and know a *fauteuil* when I see one;
Nigel Broackes does deals here' (the Ritz); 'Jeffrey Archer has the corner table,
Eva Jiricna is the most talented interior designer of her generation, you can eat
here and stay slim' (the Caprice); 'I have a Hockney sketch and Antonio knows
more about funghi than the rest of Britain put together. Covent Garden is my
patch … Terence and I are very close' (Neal Street Restaurant); 'It's the best
place for talking seriously to serious people' (the Connaught).

Brillat-Savarin was not quite correct when he said 'Tell me what you eat and I
will tell you what you are'.

'Tell me where you go to eat and I will tell you what you want to be.'
– *GQ*, December/January 1988-9

6.6 Creative review

To my mind, the most attractive concept in philosophy is the one that Baltasar
Gracian, the Spanish Jesuit moralist, called *desengano*. Literally 'disengagement', it
means that aristocratically aloof detachment from the hurly-burly, a high-minded
and graceful retreat from the scrum, a patrician refusal to confront the grubby
commerce of the here and now.

Gracian was a profound influence on the set of ideas summarized by the word
'gentlemanly'. Through the sway of his *The Art of Worldly Wisdom* (1647), Gracian
defined what we now call manners. He insisted: we should overcome everyday
vanities, we should rise above ambition and self-delusion, we should construct an
interior existence remote from the gutter of life. I don't know how many D-reg
Uno Turbo drivers with an exposed position on sub-woofers have read Gracian.
From my observation of their behaviour on the roads, very few.

The way cars transfer their personalities to their drivers fascinates me. And, of
course, the trade goes the other way, too. Certain cars just seem to beg to be
driven badly and, equally, certain personality types just seem to crave screechy
vehicles to help them project their personality disorders onto the rest of us. We
all know the cars that are driven passively and very badly. Everyone agrees that
Volvo 340s are unequivocally selected by the brain-dead; Nissans are worse. And
Honda Civics also seem to have problems in acquiring owners bright enough to
be able to walk around unaided.

But then there are the cars that are driven actively and very badly. For starters, anything with a badge enumerating the number of valves or the manufacturer's chosen method of fuel delivery or aspiration. Next, previously maintained Uno Turbos or Fords with X or R in their nomenclature are troublesome as company. Astramax vans have a quality, as yet undefined by criminologists, which requires a crippling and embittered form of psychosis to drive them. I've noticed problems with four-cylinder BMWs, too.

The sad truth, of course, is that the more banal or the more wretched and inhospitable the car, the more urgently you wish to dispose of the journey and, therefore, you are inclined to drive as though the clappers of hell are crawling up your inside leg and looking for a spot of lunch. Driving energetically and actively is one of life's great pleasures, but like all exquisite experiences it is rationed by circumstance and best enjoyed in moderation. Occasionally, empty roads and bright weather collaborate to create a sense of outgoing guilt-free optimism when a car can be enjoyed. Other than that, modern traffic conditions make me want to put my head in a sack, or, when that is not practical, crave that experience of disengagement. For most road journeys I don't want a responsive, athletic, nervous car. I want a car that isn't, to adapt General de Gaulle's expression, right or left, but above. I want an aristocratic vehicle, something gentlemanly.

And what would that be? There are a number of possible choices, but I think the car that best approaches a state of grace is a Mercedes-Benz estate. Given the zoology of modern traffic conditions, it's the very nervelessness of the Mercedes wagon that makes it so attractive. It would be a horrible car with a screaming engine, lowered suspension and a manual gearbox. This is a car which carries loads of disengagement. Unless you are of a rare and highly specialized freakishness, unless you pick your teeth with a stiletto or enjoy fire-eating, you simply cannot bring yourself to drive a Mercedes estate aggressively. The stately, but ergonomically perfect, driving position enforces a calm posture. The enormous steering wheel requires polite negotiation rather than violent inputs and the long-travel accelerator pedal assumes that you have an intelligence well adapted to the idea of thinking ahead. Careful but unostentatious ergonomics mean that neither primary nor secondary control functions impinge on your courtly demeanour.

In short, it's impossible to imagine getting into a sweat driving a Mercedes estate. The car's own good manners are projected onto the owner. I sometimes irreverently think I'd like to see a racing series for unmodified estate cars just to find out exactly what can be done – what is, in extremis, possible – but I'm inclined to think that they would have a calming effect even on Eddie Irvine after a session with Ed's Original Cave Creek Chilli Beer. If you had a Mercedes race, the whole think would look like the parade lap. They'd all cross the line together and the drivers would get out and smile at one another bemusedly and give peace and love signs to the other competitors.

You wouldn't want disengagement if someone said you had to drive from Positano to Salerno on the notorious Amalfi coast road at three in the morning; there you'd want a car with the demeanour of a nervous sprinter, not a relaxed noble. But that sort of experience is rare. The most tiring thing about modern driving is that people who would not think of elbowing you in the ribs or spitting

on your shoe if they passed you on the pavement feel licensed to behave disgustingly when they are on the road. For everyday driving, I want a vehicle that behaves with absolute decorum. I want one that turns me into a philosopher, not a brawling lout, a car where D on the selector gate stands for disengagement rather than driving.
– *Car Magazine*, June 1995

6.7 Labour pains and long lunches

Can you tell me how you spell that?'
'It's Stephen with a p-h and Bayley with an a-y: b, a, y, l, e, y.'
'And is he in?'
'This is he.'
'Oh, isn't it a bit odd that you are answering the phone yourself?'
'No, I don't think so. I've been typing my own letters since I was twelve, and if there's a telephone ringing, I'll answer it.'

This curious little exchange occurred about five minutes ago while my assistant was out hiring a costume for a ball she's attending on Sunday. In another minute I'll get up to feed her meter and make some coffee for her return, but in the meantime I am reflecting on how our attitudes to work have evolved as we scroll toward the millennium.

After bed, we spend more time in the office than anywhere else. This is where, if you have an aesthetic, you display it; and if you don't, you show that too. Behind every desk are enough routines and rituals to excite any anthropologist. Here is where daily Jacobean dramas of pride, power, lust and revenge are acted out. Also, long-running comedies of manners, bloody tragedies, huge Hollywood musicals, epics. Compared to the intense passions which are daily currency in the office, home-life is tranquil, tedious stuff.

We live in a world where the frontiers of acceptable behaviour are constantly shifting. Yet the office – outwardly orderly, seemingly composed, with its neat hierarchy of clean and decent furniture – provides a deceptively rigid framework for this volatile situation. Think about the word itself, 'office', and the image it conjures. Even in these days of automation, we still derive our ideas of office normality from our parents' generation: the three-mile journey up the bypass in an Austin Cambridge and a camel-hair jacket, saddle bag briefcase on the floor to the side, to spend the day in a space with frosted-glass windows, a calendar from Rolls-Royce, a desk-set, and a vacant woman, torn between disappointment and sulky pride, as a secretary, her postcards from Brixham and Torbay fixed to the bulletin board above the Dictaphone.

But in today's real life, as man at work evolves from a hierarchical to a more humane creature, these rituals of our parents appear as remote as Elagabalus's child sacrifices to the Syrian god Baal. Rather, the modern workplace, as it actually is, presents a spectacle of role models redefined, work patterns reassessed, and the male as worker/manager naked of everything except his own intelligence and taste. True, you may now and again find dinosaurs representative of the old

155 order, asserting olden-golden-days versions of authority even as they talk in terms of 'space planning', but they are embarrassingly shrill as they do so. Other than punctuality, courtesy and reliability, which remain as necessary to work as they are to all human endeavour, virtually every aspect of office behaviour is now infinitely negotiable.

So, with change as a given, what are the *rules of the game*, the sacrosanct constructs with which work is performed (or should be performed) by the fully evolved man?

First, always attempt to tell the truth. The most persistent, pretentious, semi-literate and ugly lie prevalent in the world of inter-office communication is the secretary's trope: 'I'm sorry, he's in a meeting'. Far better to ask her to say (in order): (1) 'He doesn't want to talk to you now'. (2) 'He's talking to someone else,' or even to tell the whole truth and say: (3) 'He's gone to have a pee,' or (4) 'He's busy reading *Autosport*,' or even better (5) 'He's having an argument with his wife (and he doesn't appear to be winning)'.

But never, ever – not if you want to be respected – allow anybody to say you are in a meeting.

Second, only primitives still think it is necessary to arrive astonishingly early and stay unnecessarily late, irrespective of what work has to be done. Disregard these people, although be aware of the ritual significance accorded to long hours. When I worked in a university I had a friend who knew that considerable power lay with the secretaries and the cleaners. Impress them, he advised and you might acquire real influence. It was his custom to arrive before 8am, go to his study, turn on the anglepoise, ruffle the papers on his desk, put the door ajar, and then leave for the entire day (to play squash or go to the pub), only to return after six, his light still burning, and impress the cleaners and secretaries with the apparently awesome dimensions of his work ethic.

Later, working at a Covent Garden design studio at the beginning of the last decade, back in the days before clamping, I learned a similar cunning. There, every day began with a fearful competition to acquire the space on the single yellow line before either the chairman or the managing director. The rub was that you could only do this by arriving before eight (both the chairman and the managing director being unconverted old-style thinkers). But once done, of course, the day was your own. Your car effectively taking your place as a kind of symbolic presence, conferring by proxy a special status for diligence while you mused in the Penguin Bookshop.

In the same office I picked up some of the rules about lunch. My early experience being confined to universities, I was always influenced by precedent. The first memorable exposure was my marvellous old, Welsh, knitted-tie tutor at architectural school who used to drink a large glass of sherry first thing every morning and who told me that Celts had no use for the puritan work ethic. The second was the master of a college where I was once a very junior fellow. 'What are you doing this afternoon, Dan?' I remember asking him once over a meat pie and bottle of ketchup in the senior common room. 'Thinking about getting drunk,' was the answer.

Since then, I have accepted that the intelligent way to handle the dilemma of lunch is to assess its likely benefits in terms of personal gain or personal pleasure, in so far as they can be distinguished, and make an appropriate judgement about its form and contact. I have one friend, who, inspired by the great line given to Michael Douglas that 'only wimps eat lunch', likes to impose a similar discipline on his staff. Or at least so he told me at La Famiglia off the King's Road one day over a salad and grilled sole, and a bottle of Gavi.

While some people may only require a midday whiff of nitrous oxide and a Swedish taste-free cracker, evolving man has become aware that the civilized pleasures of the table are on the main road of, and not a diversion around, working life. Which brings us to a crucial work rule for fully evolved man (and harkening back to rule one): never lie to your secretary or your wife. Do not pretend that you had a half a glass of low-alcohol white wine if what you really drank was two bottles of a 13 per cent red with a flavour and toxicity that would stun an ox.

Like drink, the telephone also provides a medium and measure for all variations of behaviour, from primitive to evolved. People find the telephone so taxing precisely because the device renders it so easy to lie and so easy to avoid detection. Everybody makes faces when they are talking over the phone. You may sound po-faced, but you are really flapping your hands, rolling your eyes, making exaggerated yawning gestures, hand motions suggestive of enthusiastic onanism. One person I know, dead keen to make his deathly quiet office seem busy, makes fantastic noises-off every time he takes a call. 'Oh, for Chrissake, don't show me that now,' he'll interrupt himself and say to an imaginary party. Or 'Excuse me,' he'll say to his telephonic partner with an I'm-a-busy-man tone, and then mutter only just audibly to an in fact empty room, 'yes, I think we will have to go short on 1994 yen bonds – but don't tell Manfred,' and resume his call with a slight air of melancholy weariness.

Sex is, of course, everywhere in the workplace. Because most of the time we spend in bed we are asleep, it is the office where you rehearse the mechanisms of lust. If you speak to people who do motivational research, they will tell you that the difficulty in public speaking is that fully 80 per cent of any given audience is not listening because they are thinking about sex 60 per cent of the time. This, you will appreciate, provides only a tiny window of opportunity for getting your message across. And it is the same at work.

Most people are thinking about sex most of the time, unless they are critically hungover, in which case they are thinking about sex all the time. Yet the smartest thing is not, no matter how tempting, to talk smut with your secretary, nor to strain yourself too obviously to look down her T-shirt. You may beguile yourself with make-believe monologues which begin, 'Now, look, let's be adult about this', but it is intelligent to keep them to yourself. No heterosexual man is unaware of the pleasures to be had from the subtle – and sometimes not so subtle – brushing of female colleagues' bosoms when passing in confined spaces; but this is a pleasure best left to the imagination where it is enhanced, rather than practised in the corridor where it invariably leads to pain.

A decent restraint and sense of order moderate all fully evolved men's behaviour. Infantile men think it is butch to wallow in clutter, but the essential truth about tidiness is that it is a source of keen pleasure. The rationale for tidiness is not to demonstrate desk-top anal retention but to make your own life more agreeable, to say nothing of others' vistas. The idea that somebody else is available to tidy up for you, to organize your papers, to clear your cups, is unsophisticated. Fully evolved man keeps his desk clean, empties his own ashtrays and knows how to refill the copier, even the fax machine.

Fully evolved man sometimes argues with his wife and always takes calls from his mother. His secretary tells the truth and he makes coffee for her, or even for himself. He is the late-century broker of information. He only wears a suit when it is necessary.

And how do you identify this information-age prodigy in a landscape of normal mendacity and abnormal office crap? Well, FEM has a carrier bag full of vegetables under his desk. Tonight, like every other night, he is cooking dinner for his family.
– *Harpers & Queen*, 1993

6.8 Shaking all over

There's something about intimacy which is like a reciprocal version of Newton's Law of Gravitation about objects attracting and repelling each other. Intimate gestures with those deserving affection or respect provide serene satisfaction. And the opposite applies too. There is always something very remarkable about being touched by another person.

Interestingly, it is the limb beyond the cuff rather than the organs below the belt which are most sensitive in this respect. In his comprehensive study *Les Mœurs Intimes du Passé* (1908), Auguste Cabanès devotes fifty-five pages to the cleanliness of the hands and a scant twelve pages to sexual hygiene. Here is a rare case of digits being more ticklish than dicks. Hands, as any amateur historian of Renaissance art knows, are extraordinarily revealing of psychic states. In harrowing pictures by Dürer, the tensions expressed in brilliantly drafted fingers are more evocative than those in the histrionic faces.

The handshake is not only a deceptively familiar gesture but also a surprisingly complicated one. Children still learn that its origins were in China. The rationale was that by agitating the other person's sleeve you would soon know if he were concealing a weapon. In the long journey from this most functional and discreet of beginnings, the handshake has acquired a deep and enduring structure 4 of meaning, because physical contact impinges on the aura of privacy we all generate: a handshake intrudes on your own definition of self. Although familiarly a greeting, the residual primitive in us recognizes that a handshake is potentially hostile.

We carry with us a mentality that reinforces a belief in our uniqueness and our right to privacy and our possession of an individual self. Meeting people intrudes on that. The first thing you do when you meet someone is to shake their hand. It is a devastating insult to refuse. War may be politics carried on by other means;

here is communication making the same translation. Consequently, styles of handshake are distinctive and provide a cruelly accurate guide to personality.

My accountant is a type. He has the strongest, firmest, driest handshake I have ever experienced. An old Harrovian, he has a splendid booming voice, sparkling eyes and a fixity of purpose that would be depraved, were it not so evidently amiable and responsible for considerable material success. His glance is like a forward-looking infra-red sensor on an Apache attack helicopter. He is totally straight and shakes your hand with a huge pumping motion on absolutely every meeting and departure. Even a committed handshaker such as myself is taken aback by the readiness, ferocity even, of this man's handshake. It conveys, correctly, an impression of absolute probity.

My wealthiest acquaintance, on the other hand, is a different case. Fat, sleek, vain, a bit degenerate, amoral, he does not acknowledge his various ambiguities (although all his other acquaintances – he has no friends – discuss them freely and frequently). Significantly, he dislikes shaking hands, perhaps aware at a basic level that he will betray himself in so doing. Confronted with a situation where a handshake is unavoidable, he avoids your eyes and offers a pudgy hand. The skin is a shockingly soft and there is no strength; it is a handshake which speaks volumes about a man who lacks real conviction as much as he lacks real generosity. It is reluctant, selfish, joyless and damp.

A Jesuit I know, now in pinstripes, offers an alternative. He strides across rooms, sometimes knocking things over. His passions are wine or philosophical discourse – usually both – and his handshake is a double grip. First the conventional engagement, firm and committed, but almost immediately enhanced by placing the other hand on the forearm, equally firm and equally committed. This is an impressive, cultivated gesture of fraternity.

I know an old City man who on first meeting says: 'Nuneham Blakeney never shakes hands with his friends' – a bewilderingly complex statement given the levels of meaning merely hinted at above. I know people in extravagant forms of neurosis about whether they should regularly shake hands with their pals. This anxiety is in itself rich in connotation.

Women now shake hands, although the future of other forms of pan-gender physical contact is uncertain. There is at least one dress designer I know who makes me feel very uncomfortable indeed when it pleases him to kiss me on meeting. I go all Virgin from Surbiton. Those terrible parties and restaurants where lots of table-hopping and kissing happens are now things of the past. No one ever quite gets the kissing-both-cheeks thing right. Do you brush cheeks or make light contact with the lips? Smack or tease? Lips and cheeks are maybe too sensitive to be truly revealing. Certainly, you are on firmer ground with a handshake. Eyes are on the mirror of the soul: hands are its messengers.
– GQ, January 1991

Many long-term husbands are familiar with that grudging, but nonetheless welcome, acceptance of a badly timed amorous advance : 'OK, but be quick, don't sweat and no kissing'.

It is not the speed, nor the sweat, but the kissing that is interesting here. While penetrative sex of the genital kind may be what men are said to think about twenty-six times a minute, sometimes more, it is significant that their familiar partners tend (eventually) to attribute less significance to the rough, predictable motions of the pistons and cylinders in sexual mechanics than to the more subtle and delicate operations of the lips and the mouth. One gathers that prostitutes often charge more for kissing than for how's-your-father on account of it being more intimate. Getting done up against a brick wall to the point where your head's going to explode can pass as a regular commercial transaction, but a peck on the lips…that's not business, that's *personal*.

The kiss is unique, or, at least, unusual, in the repertoire of Eros because it is both affectionate and sexual. Save for the question of the presence or absence of love, there is no ambiguity about copulation. It is an unambiguous expression of Eros, lust made slippery and tangible and compulsive and convulsive. Sex of the sort that operates between the hips and the knees is in and out, up and down. It is literally and metaphorically straight, not susceptible to any interpretation nor to any result other than desire and conquest and satiety. Sex is black or white. Kissing, however, is on a grey scale of infinite variety. We kiss children and grannies one way, same-sex friends another and lovers in a different style altogether.

A form of kissing, or of oral intercourse of some fashion, is common to most birds and quadrupeds, evidence of the significance of the mouth in non-verbal communication as well as in spoken language. Somewhere deep in the thick soup of DNA, kissing may share an original significance with biting: some male animals use their teeth the more firmly to grasp their partners while mating. I haven't tried this myself, although this prehistoric notion may contribute some of its primal force to that suspicion, hardening occasionally into a conviction, among many men that women to whom they are not married are inclined to bite and scream promiscuously, while women to whom they are married are more inclined, while on the job, to sigh in an unerotic style and look longingly at their watches.

Despite the position of kissing in animal behaviour, its significance in civilization seems to be culturally specific. The ancient Greek poets scarcely mention it and while Attic red figure vases show every variation of genital use you can imagine and some you perhaps even cannot, I have never seen one showing a couple kissing with their mouths.

There is, for instance, a cup of circa **480 BC** by the so-called Brygos Painter, now in the Archaeological Museum of Florence, whose decorations (in summary) show a bent-over woman attending orally to an impressively tumid man while she is being had from behind. To the right of this group a kneeling girl prepares to do what kneeling best equips girls for, especially when confronted by a classical dick at 45° to the horizontal, and to their right a naked Greek gentleman is holding a naked Greek lady around his waist while her legs are over his shoulders and a priest-like figure holds what looks like a drip tray beneath them. But a gentle snog? Nowhere. Equally, the old Celtic languages have no word for the kiss, although they may well have had many different words for bardic versions of the foregoing.

But it is the far Orientals who are most ill-disposed to the tongue wrestling and popping-spit exchange we tend to go in for. Reporting from *fin-de-siècle* Japan, that travelling exotic, Lafcadio Hearn, said 'Kisses and embraces are simply unknown … as tokens of affection'. The Chinese regard the European kiss as odious and with its gobbling of flesh suggestive of unwholesome cannibalistic practices; mothers threaten their misbehaving children with a consuming and sloppy white-man's kiss.

But in the nearer east, the *Kama Sutra* and *The Perfumed Garden* accept kissing as one of erotic love's more sophisticated expressive forms. The European Middle Ages saw the development of what we might call the modern kiss, although significantly it is considered a lofty refinement in the act of love, more likely practised by aristocrats rather than peasants. A medieval ballad called the Glasgerion tells the minatory story of a high-born woman who eventually realized she was being bedded by a churl rather than a nobleman because while he efficiently 'got her with child' (as churls do), he never bothered to kiss when either entering or leaving her bed-chamber or, indeed, her. Now, in contemporary Europe, the kiss has become a universal, except in Lapland where they seem to prefer noses, but this may be something to do with ambient temperatures around the Arctic Circle, which tend to discourage the frivolous exposure of mucus membrane.

Cesare Lombroso says the exhilaration of the erotic kiss derives from the oral associations of nipples and motherhood, thus transcending in its meaningful complexity even the rich, dark puzzle of sex itself. Our own slight reluctance to discuss kissing suggests a reticence that is based on something very primitive indeed. Syncopated, mutually penetrative oral sex may not replace the more fundamental sort, but can be a powerfully stimulating prelude to the most effective forms of lubricious exchange whose rhythms and encounters and intimacy it so accurately apes.

Space does not allow even a brief catalogue of the possible variations, although the powerful and flexible and articulate tongue, with its advanced roll, pitch and yaw facilities, is better equipped to explore the whole range of spatial possibilities than the brute and one-dimensional erect penis. Quite literally, a deeply committed kiss (the French call what we call a French kiss 'un baiser très appuyé', a well-applied one) short-circuits those carefully mapped neural paths which link the contours of sex to the heights of taste and, by association, to smell.

The social phenomenon of air kissing – the two or three-cheek mwah-mwah-mwah rituals of restaurant and party encounters – may be derived from ancient olfactory sniffing, the sort dogs do around bitches' bottoms. Swahili folk have an amusing variation on this. It is, one gathers, customary for pubescent boys to raise their garments and expose themselves to society ladies who will then smell the offered member in a charming ritual called 'giving tobacco'.

Smoking is, of course, the one thing that corrupts the pleasure of kissing: Swahili or no, few enjoy the sensation of deep-throating an ashtray. If you want to pass biological matter or foodstuffs from mouth to mouth, I'd recommend a nice old-fashioned burgundy. Just beware next time you visit a Japanese restaurant that tongue sushi is not something you will ever find on the menu.
Erotic Review, 1999

E-mission control
Erotic Review, 1999

I am the first in this neighbourhood to have had virtual sex. Sort of.

There's a school – maybe more accurately a kindergarten – of thought that predicts virtual sex as (and, I'm sorry, I simply can't resist this one) the coming thing. It will require as much bravery, sense of adventure, equipment, taste for strange costumes, technical back-up and emission control as a moon landing.

The nerd's eye view of virtual sex will have us all togged up with bio medical sensors and light-industrial plant where erogenous zones used to be. It will be like Agent Provocateur taking over PC World or Curry's. Ladies, please insert this semi-tumid polyethylene device taking care not to foul the electrical contacts. Gentlemen, position your member inside this stylish and washable SmartFabric™ 256MB sheath. Then you slide on your gloves, switch on the mains, attach the clamps to your nipples, boot up the computer, focus the webcam and wriggle and squirm, pump and grind, puff and sigh until the eagle has landed.

Well, I haven't actually tried that. I'm intentionally malingering at the exchange of body fluids and smell-of-shampooed-hair stage, but something happened recently that gave me an impression of the erotic potential of new media. I was sitting here dolefully checking the e-mail when I found, among the oceanic volumes of electromagnetic junk, a name I recognised from so long ago it was when I was at school. Younger readers, not to mention younger editors, may be interested to know that the Personal Computer dates only from the early 1980s. I was doing educational time even before that. This name came from then.

Her message with a PDT (Pacific Daylight Time) code on it simply said, like hi, remember me? Indeed I did. I remembered her and her tan leather boots and her short pleated skirt and her smile and I remember a number of other things too. Bear with me: they were still making Ford Cortinas in those days and the art of love was at the live axle and leaf spring and push rod stage of its development too. I replied. She returned the bitspit (Californian for e-mail, not an ill-coordinated tongue job). It went on. And then she sent a photograph down the tube, a 50 per cent dot dithered image, which, by the time it had been in and out of some servers, wrung out by AOL, travelled by satellite, been turned into electrons and then recomposed into Apple Mac pixels, was as corrupt as a Syrian mafioso's bar mitzvah. But still, that picture shimmering there on the screen made my groin tingle and my blood rush in a way that http:www//hotwetcunt.com often does not.

What did it show? Not a knees-apart shot of my old friend with a leather-masked carpet-muncher inserting an excited donkey into her bottom while she chewed cheekily on an enormous black penis and winked at the camera. Not my old friend in white high heels and nothing else doing the ironing. Not an airtight job with sex-workers sealing every orifice. No piercing, shaving, masochism, masturbation, coprophilia, buggery or bestiality. Instead, the image showed a pleasant, open-faced fortyish American college professor wearing a simple cotton dress and smiling in her sunny garden with her teenage children. Goodness me, it was a powerful turn on.

So, I am now wondering if there is something seriously wrong with me. How odd is it to be in a condition where pixellated images of fully-clothed Californian teachers give you an unputdownable hard-on without the erotic imagination even *beginning* to wander around the traditional sexual signifiers beneath the simple cotton dress?

Now it is true that my historic relationship with the Californian teacher was not entirely innocent. If the range of sexual activity could be expressed in the model range of the contemporary Cortina, where a 1.3L was holding hands and a 2.0 GLX was whips and thongs and athletically adventurous, we were a 1.6GL, which is to say gratifying to an eager teenager, but when it comes to comparative positions, a Presbyterian Sunday school teacher rather than a missionary of the stature of Albert Schweizer. It was body fluids, red faces and a department-store bra, not *amore*. Heat, fur and elastic; slippery lust, not educated passion.

But something in the transmission of the image, or the revival of the memory, certainly pushed my buttons. Had I bumped into this woman I might never have recognised her. I had scarcely even thought of her consciously for more than a few minutes in the last few decades. She was certainly – unlike, for instance, Princess Caroline of Monaco – not a continuous erotic preoccupation of mine.

I think in fact it's not the image itself that was erotic (anything more chaste could not be imagined), but the transmission technology. Take fax. I know this sounds weird, but there's something suggestive about using a fax. You slip a sheet of paper in here, in an office in central London, and whether the recipient wants it or not, another slip of paper emerges almost instantaneously in a bedroom in Lincolnshire, a great room in Maryland or a hotel suite in Tokyo. Irrespective of the substance of the image, sending a fax is an irresistible act of penetration.

And yet how much more subtle and intimate is the transmission of pictures from computer to computer! Clunky old fax grinds and spits out 90gsm 210 x 297 premium recycled A4 (laser and monochrome inkjet guaranteed), but when one

Sex in-flight
Erotic Review 1999

computer has intercourse with another the experience is much finer: it is not so much crude mechanical penetration, but a much more invasive form of ravishment and the fact that it occurs at the speed of light does not allow demurral. One click and it's there. No fuss, no mess.

They say machines have life, so they must have sex too. The big misunderstanding about virtual sex is that it's the medium, not the message, that is exciting.

Cabin crew, doors to automatic please. There are those who find this familiar announcement a pleasing prologue to the imminent thrill of flight. Others who ignore it, white-knuckled and clenched-jaw, behind their *Financial Times*. Yet others for whom it is the starting point for what is not so much an aeronautical journey, as an imaginative one.

Flight is 95 per cent boring and 5 per cent terrifying. Most of us are difficultly pitched between the three adjacent peaks of, on the one hand, a complacent, bien-pensant, Air Miles-acquisitive, Gold-Card, globe-trotting technophilia and, on the other, a gloomy ironic fatalism (blurring to panic at the first hint of turbulence) induced by self-exposure to the terrible forces of nature in deadly combo with dodgy Boeing wiring and demoralized Air Traffic Control. On yet another hand, there is the other peak of the sheer, seamless, perpetual ennui of jet travel: 'The pale grey wings, the pale blue sky/The tiny sun's sharp shine/The engine's drone, or rather sigh/A single calm design' as Robert Conquest put it.

When it's the ennui that gets the upper hand, the imagination readily turns to sex, or the single calm design of lust. It is well known that being pressurized at altitude has a numbing effect on the taste buds. This is why they serve such soupy Chardonnays and such gloppy sauces with otherwise inedible airline 'food' like the sort I'm eating now. Being pressurised at altitude, especially long haul, seems to have an altogether positive effect on desire ... although it has to be admitted that Bacchus is often in concert with Eros at FL35 (especially after dinner.)

I was much taken by a recent case that filled the tabloids. Here was that stock character of contemporary erotic musings: a respectable Northern business woman, a married mother of four children. Having enjoyed a few brandies, ennui gave way to a mischievous curiosity. By way of introduction to her companion there was not that usual trans-Atlantic in-flight conversational gambit of 'Don't you think the long-term parking at Gatwick is frightfully expensive?' Instead, our respectable Northern business woman, in a memorably sporting gesture, unbidden, took her bra off and gave her grateful and astonished neighbour a blow-job…at least until the rattle of the drinks cart disturbed the business in, as it were, hand.

In my experience, such a pleasingly forward gesture is unusual, although my mind certainly travels to those parts that respectable Northern business women have not yet reached as soon as my aircraft reaches the cruise. The reason that folklore insists there is something called the Mile High Club is because of the universal appeal of uninhibited sex with a complete stranger. The longing is enhanced by the bizarrerie of the circumstances: no matter how familiar you are with flight, the fact is you're teetering on the verge of a disaster and this in itself is stimulating. There's also the sense of complete isolation from other responsibilities. For once in your life someone else – one imagines the captain – is in charge. It is this loss of control that makes egotistical travellers frightened and drives others to extravagant erotic fantasies of ergonomically adventurous sex in the lavatories. Please leave this facility in the condition you found it, the notice says. Throbbing groin? Lascivious leer?

Of course, it never, ever really happens. Without being pedantic, a Mile High is only 5,280 feet above the ground and this is where you find very lumpy air and you'd have to be an acrobat even to find the facility in the first place, let alone any more intimate target once ensconced. Well, at least, it never ever happens to me. Although Kenneth Tynan claimed it did happen to him.

In 1958, Tynan flew to New York to offer himself to William Shawn as drama critic on the *New Yorker*. The meeting was successful. So exhilarating was this professional preferment that, by his own account, it happily resulted in a euphorically stonking hard-on which refused to go away. To explain his delicate condition Tynan took recourse to literature and cited the Tudor poet Samuel Daniel's remark about Bolingbroke entering London in triumph and feeling 'his blood within salute his state'. As I said, he had a very stiff dick.

The first-class compartment on this early Boeing 707 was nearly empty on his night-flight home and Tynan was placed next to an attractive young woman who occupied the window seat. Fuelled by champagne, somewhere over Gander, the in-flight blankets in place, the great critic started a hesitant grope. First a hand on her hip, then the hem of her skirt … Alas, as he reached the armour of her girdle (remember, this is 1958 and tights didn't exist), he found a barrier impenetrable to his literary finger, let alone his literary boner. And, then, the girl leapt up, rearranged her clothes and fled for the loo. If she had been a respectable Northern business woman, and if he had had foreknowledge of the Sun's mythology, Tynan would have known exactly what to do and followed her there, but this was 1958 and, instead, the critic, stiff dick subsiding as if supercooled by Newfoundland air, imagined the headlines 'Goosed over Gander'. 'Critic Charged in Indecent Assault Case'.

The woman returned stiffly, said a quiet 'Excuse me' and reassumed her position: foetal with her bottom to him. The blankets were replaced, the lights redimmed. Time passed and Tynan's blood resumed the salutation of his state. He essayed the territory again. The hem, the stocking top, the upper thigh… and met no resistance. Nearing his destination he found not whalebone and nylon

defences, but lubricious warmth and fur.
Whereupon, up, as Chaucer put it, gan her smock
and in he throng. The recently appointed drama
critic of *The New Yorker* then enjoyed pleasantly
satisfactory sexual intercourse.

I can't make up my mind whether Tynan's story is
a mischievous wind-up: a saucy objectification of
profound, but unrealized, fantasies. Ma si non è
vero, è bellissima è immortale. The thing is, being
in aircraft is to sexual desire what being in a
forcing pot is to rhubarb. Freud and Jung both
knew that sensations of height and fear of falling
were related to the erotic impulse. The
suspension of a plane in flight and which never,
happily, reaches an explosive climax is not
dissimilar in its way to the protracted (and
ultimately deferred) crescendo of tantric sex.
The only thing I don't understand about the
recurrent dream of sex in-flight is how air
hostesses ever got a reputation for being willing
receptacles of imagined lust and its damp
consequences. I may be getting on, but equal
opportunities legislation, the democratization of
air travel, bigger planes, duty free intrusions,
video have made the idea of a pert, solicitous,
sighing nymphet in BOAC uniform with her
freshly laundered white silk knickers around her
ankles nothing but a fading period memory.
But excuse me. Christ! I can hear the rattle of the
drinks cart. I've got to get her bra back on and
do up my zip before it's time to buy…and then
'A calmness settles in/A window seat, an
ambient glow/A tonic-weakened gin'. Robert
Conquest again. Maybe he got it more right than
Kenneth Tynan.

In defence of my opinion
Previously unpublished, 1983

Vox populi, vox dei

*It is never worth a first-class man's time to express
a majority opinion. By definition, there are plenty of
others to do that.*
(G. H. Hardy, *A Mathematician's Apology*)

Foreword
A chaos of confused opinions was how Hugh
Kingsmill defined the first half of the nineteenth
century in his marvellous anthology of Invective
and Abuse (1929). 'The mid-Victorian' he says
'carried within his congested breast a puritan, a
poet, and a pagan'. The consequence of this, at
least so far as it concerned the expression of
ideas, was a lack of clarity and conviction. In 1860
it was entirely possible for, say, an architect to
design a building one day in the High Gothic
style, next in the Greek Revival and then with an
iron exo-skeleton. In an age of turbulent values,
dogma or, at least, comfortable tradition,
provided a refuge. Disraeli has the Old Turk
saying in Iskander (1864) 'I never offered an
opinion till I was sixty … and then it was one
which had been in our family for a century'.

But what is an opinion? The thesaurus offers:
belief, conviction, idea, persuasion, view,
feelings, inclination, sentiment, bias, speculation,
supposition, estimation, judgement. Yes, it is all of
those things. But the commonplace view is that an
opinion is something of your own that you are
entitled to, a concession often granted
grudgingly by people who disagree with you or
who do not share your estimation of your own
opinion's value.

This question of merit constantly occurs in all
discussion of opinions and by metaphorical
suggestion we can move a little closer to a
definition. Few people feel themselves flattered
when told they are 'opinionated'. To be
promiscuous in the acquisition, cultivation and

165

distribution of opinions is in some eyes a bad thing. You have opinions and then you also have something a little bit superior: an 'informed' opinion. People say that opinions are ten-a-penny, even free, but while they may have a value that is hard to define, but they are not worthless. In fact, opinions are the hard currency of conversation, the means of exchange among the chattering classes. To have opinions is one of the great privileges of the modern world: there is no such thing as a medieval opinion. There was medieval philosophy, rhetoric and theology, of course, but their content and scope was rigidly defined. The modern mind with its huge range of reference and its hair-trigger readiness to form opinions emerged from the chaotic confusion of the nineteenth century.

Yet it is astonishing how few people actually have opinions of their own, or know how to acquire them. This essay emerged out of an elaborate joke, or, rather *jeu d'esprit*, intended to make a sardonic contribution to that want. In a career initially spent offering curious journalists and other media badgers informed opinions on architecture and design, I have noticed over the past few years a significant enlargement in their scope of enquiry. While once I used only to be asked technical and specific questions such as 'What was the influence of the Bauhaus?' 'What is the difference between styling and design?', latterly enquiries have included more universal queries such as 'What do you think of Italian *nuova cucina*?' 'What do you think about skiing?' 'Why do all women enjoy wearing black tights?' 'Why is pink a feminine colour?'

I cannot say whether the move away from stock questions about the history and practice of design speaks volumes about that subject's recent, melancholy decline from high public esteem, or, indeed, about my own reputation for being brutally and promiscuously opinionated,

but it is certainly eloquent of a popular demand for interpretative information that is coloured by a personal point of view. There you have a definition of an 'informed opinion'. Here you have a hundred of them.

But while *General Knowledge* may make an evanescent contribution to twenty-first-century dinner party conversation, it has a superb and possibly eternal precedent, a book whose ghosts haunt the twentieth-century imagination. Gustave Flaubert's *Bouvard et Pécuchet* describes two clerks, one fat, the other thin who, tired of routine copying, decide to acquire all the world's knowledge and put it into an encyclopaedia of human ignorance. At the end of the unfinished novel is *'Dictionnaire des idées reçues',* described as *'tout ce qu'il faut dire en société pour être un homme convenable et aimable'*.

Conceived in 1847, it dissects the pretensions and aspirations of the bourgeois, in the sense that to be bourgeois means to want to conform and here was a compilation of conformist opinions. In the sense Cyril Connolly described the book (published posthumously in 1881 and later published again with an ending by Raymond Quenaeu) as 'polymath pessimism ... irradiated by gleams of poetry: slapstick fused with the sadness of things'. Compiling this encyclopaedia of ignorance cost them their health and reputation, which reflects Flaubert's own condition: he read more than 1,500 books in order to compile the *'Dictionnaire des idées reçues (Catalogue des opinions chic)'* which appears as an appendix to the novel, a task said to have accelerated his death.

Here, then is a new catalogue of chic opinions. It is not so bogus as the *Dictionnaire des mots nonexistants* produced in 1990 by two Swiss scholars. It is not as witty as Flaubert's, but nor is it so pessimistic. It is not, I hope, so dull as

Christian Wolff's *Rational Ideas on God, the World, the Soul of Man and on All Things in General* which has some claim to be the most unreadable of books. Of course it is not complete and it could never be: opinions mutate and evolve and too diligent and scientific a pursuit of them all would leave us, like Bouvard and Pécuchet, with their natural curiosity exhausted by nugatory conjecture with the task still incomplete. Harder than beliefs while softer than convictions; sharper than speculation, but more obtuse than judgement: a book of opinions was written to make you think. *C'est tout.*

The Duke of Wellington disapproved of his soldiers cheering as this was too nearly an expression of opinion (a privilege which he would deny the rabble).

Opinions are one example of an informed pattern of thought, although the contemptuous character of the familiar remark 'that's a matter of opinion' shows that opinions are not always respectable.

To change an opinion without a mental process is a mark of the uneducated.

They are in a hierarchy which begins with axioms. Axioms are self-evident truths. Next come epigrams, short witty sayings which are valid in only one particular case and have no general relevance. Aphorisms are short, clever statements, usually of a literary character, which may be said to contain a general truth, but since they concern style and manners rather than science, they are not susceptible to strict quantification. Aphorisms tend to be longer than epigrams and are what Auden described as 'aristocratic' in character since the successful aphorist never feels under any compunction to explain or justify his position and, equally, is convinced of the superiority of his own point-of-view to that of his readers.

But it is a small step from the bright, successful aphorism to the ordinary truism and from the truism to the dull platitude. Opinions are more free and interesting. There was no such thing as a 'medieval opinion' because opinions only flourish when thought is free. As Samuel Johnson said of wit, opinions should be both natural and new. The tepid waters of platitude can be avoided with a cargo of cynicism. The skilled opinion former has something of the aphorist's disdain for the intellect of his audience, but is – by nature of the conversational context which is normally the accommodation of an opinion – more likely to tolerate discussion of, even disagreement about, his pronouncements.

So, an opinion is a lengthy aphorism with a point of view. Aphorisms date from the early history of medicine when the evolution of scientific knowledge in this field was empirical, spasmodic and cumulative. Short, sharp definitions and observations were the most efficient way of recording the progress of knowledge. The word was first found in the *Aphorisms of Hippocrates*, spiritual father of modern medicines which begins with the sententious 'art is long, life is short', which may be described as one of the most influential opinions of all time, perhaps a proof in itself of its own validity.

In his *Advancement of Science* Francis Bacon argues the benefits of arguing in disconnected sentences, or aphorisms, because he says this way of presenting knowledge stimulates further inquiry. Because an aphorism has to be compact and be without elaborate explanation or wearisome footnotes, only those who are what Bacon described as 'sound and grounded' are able to compose them.

As long as man has presented opinions in written form, aphorisms have been known: the books of Ecclesiasticus and the Proverbs of Solomon are just two Biblical sources of aphoristic knowledge. A great deal of modern opinion relies on the maxims and saws of the ancient Greeks who may themselves have been influenced by the hieroglyphic wisdom of the Egyptians. Latterly, of course, the French have brought the aphorism or the *pensée* to the prestige of an art form: the success of La Rochefoucauld (*Maximes*, 1664); Pascal (*Pensées*, 1670); La Bruyère (*Caractères*, 1688); *Vauvenargues* (*Introduction: la connaissance de l'esprit humain*, 1746); Rivarol; Chamfort and Joubert, may be judged by our familiarity with their opinions, centuries after they made them public. Cultivated in the salon of Madame de Sable or at the table of Chateaubriand, the aphorism evolved into the richest currency in the trade of thought.

Often, aphorists found value in detraction. It is too coarse to describe La Rochefoucauld as a cynic, although his great achievement was to illustrate so brightly the laughable hypocrisy and depressing small-mindedness of man. Pascal was not a simple misanthropist, even if his most famous *pensée* (ii. 139) was that '*tout le malheur des hommes vient d'un seul chose, qui est de ne savoir pas demeurer en repos dans une chambre*' and his second most famous one '*plus je vois l'homme, plus j'aime mon chien*', but he did memorialize the crassness and stupidity of his fellows. Vauvenargues ('*tout l'homme qui n'est pas dans son veritable caractère n'est pas dans sa force*') tried to be uplifting, but failed as a successful aphorist, even if today, after a lifetime of relative obscurity, the convention is to regard him as a major influence on Rousseau and the encyclopaedists: a sardonic nature like La Rochefoucauld's is better suited to encapsulating the absurdity of man's ambitions. The wordliness of the French contributed greatly to their free play with wordiness and it is notable that England's great aphorist, Lord Chesterfield, a friend of Voltaire and

Montesquieu, took his inspiration from abroad.

The modern opinion is a bastard form, part aphorism, part conviction, wholly personal, which has been greatly encouraged by an explosion of media. Ever since the rise of the interview as a staple of journalism, it has been increasingly necessary for those likely to be interviewed to have about them a useful set of opinions. Without opinions, personalities seem dull.

While it may be true that opinions can only flourish in times when there is no dominant religious direction, it is perhaps also true that people with strong opinions may be seeking some sort of surrogate religious faith. This is surely the case with the alarming collective mania of political correctness. If an 'opinionated' person is an intransigent, dogmatic individual with scant regard for the nicer sensibilities of other folk, then *political correctness* may be seen to be the collective expression of an opinionated group. But the big flaw in political correctness is that, no matter how difficult or objectionable an opinionated individual may be, he is at least redeemed by being independent and singular in his cussedness. Political correctness hijacks brave opinions and turns them into an unthinking pallid orthodoxy.

The expression 'political correctness' was first used ironically by journalists to describe the reflex responses of fading left-liberal convention, mostly discredited, but still strong in certain areas of the media and on most campuses. PC is a gallimaufry of summer-of-love opinions, supported by a large body of decent liberal equivocation on any matter likely to cause offence to any recognizable group – other than wealthy WASPs or absolutely anybody with a conservative cast of mind, who are always fair game. Political correctness occupies the lower middle ground of ideas, an uncontroversially packaged set of used opinions selected by their users to signal support for everything pseudo-modish in modern life.

An intellectual is someone who enjoys the play and the misalliance of ideas. On the other hand, the politically correct point of view is naive and authoritative. Its intolerance and bigotry mocks rational ideas about genuine 'liberal' thought to which it is often mistakenly compared. The believer in political correctness cannot be an intellectual since he does not believe in the free play of ideas. (At this stage it is necessary to point out how politically incorrect it is to use the male pronoun.) He cannot even be a proper critic, since critics – whatever their politics – have to have intelligence *and* knowledge.

The politically correct world is closed, it represents a fixed body of opinion which has no evolutionary potential. Which is another way of saying that it is dead and irrelevant.

Language was the first victim of the PC adventure in mind control. First expressions of the politically correct mentality came a generation ago with the equal rights and feminist movements, although the vocabulary has been around a lot longer. Equal-rights thinking required familiar expressions, most famously 'negro' to be replaced by 'black', held to be less demeaning (although, of course, semantically identical since 'negro' derives from the Latin root for the colour black). Negroes, especially hipster negroes, have subsequently shown their disdain for the fey PC intervention in manners by insisting on being called niggers. Feminists used the same dungaree-clad, clod-hopping perversion of natural speech to create inelegant nonsenses such as 'chairperson', 'chairman' being held to demean women. Soon, other sceptred minorities were given political correction so as to protect them from the assault

of description or vilification by custom or convention. Thus homosexuals soon sought protection from the stiff and humourless orthodoxy of political correctness and queers became gays. The environment followed.

There is, of course, something queasily Stalinist about political correctness. All dictators, the Church included, detest experts since expertise suggests knowledge *and* opinion. Political correctness cannot tolerate expertise. While political correctness apes the conventions of liberal-thought processes and pretends to support 'minority' 'causes', it in fact represents a massive and complacent body of easily absorbed low-brow, collectivized opinion.

It is an interesting exercise to analyse political correctness. It:

1 Is against any independent or outspoken statement, even if supported by reasonable scientific data.
2 Is against any popular expression of an idea, except when that expression favours a group enjoying the support of the politically correct.
3 Is based on an orthodoxy of the same liberal opinion which has failed so catastrophically wherever it has been applied in economics and politics.
4 Is against individuals and prefers to support groups, from whom it demands uncritical and unfluctuating devotion.
5 Is absolute and embittered. There are no shades or nuances of political correctness.
6 Does not exist to promote enlightened debate, but to impose a stultifying and witless normalcy.
7 Is against humour and free expression.
8 Is for a glum and pallid consensus.

A small analysis of the term itself is interesting. PC is 'political' in that it aims to define a language (and, therefore, an approach) to social behaviour. In this respect it is authoritarian. It is 'correct' only in the most limited interpretation of that term, the one favoured by the grim priesthood whose ambition is to acquire from its congregation a conformity with a rigid set of ideas. To achieve this low-brow religiosity of thought, political correctness imposes a brutally restricted vocabulary on its followers.

So what in the end defines political un-correctness, the subtext of this book? It is a willingness to form outspoken opinions on the basis of information and ideas offered without prejudice. Political correctness is a second-rate plague, a travesty of the intellect. Under political correctness, ideas atrophy and opinions are repressed. Bravery and independence are punished. Primness and conformity are rewarded.

Real opinions, on the other hand, are the stuff of great jokes, of great literature and conversation. No one who was capable of taking political correctness seriously would ever be able to develop an opinion of their own. And nor would they want to read this book.

Part Seven
Our Culture, their Culture

The guilty men: John Betjeman
Blueprint, 1988

Coddled like an egg in its cosy, Britain sits surrounded by the comforting embrace of the past. Hard-boiled and only great in parts, the Land of Hope and Glory is sustained in its decline by an apparatus of nostalgia, ever more effective and effecting as it drifts away from reality. Britain's reaction to the shift in global economic power across the Atlantic and then further west to the east and Asia-Pacific? Britain's reaction to a world containing Matsushita, NEC, Motorola, Daewoo, Hyundai? 'Have another g and t.' 'Don't mind if I do.' 'Antique moulding?' 'Love one.' Fake Sheraton and real ale. Morris dancing in Thamesmead. Ignorant porticoes and whorish details. *Country Living*. Cars full of dead cow skin and old trees. Good intentions and bad roads.

It's like that in the Carlton Club, the St James's fastness where Mrs Thatcher's better-bred desperadoes snuffle Paglesham oysters and sit on battered, structureless – but comforting – sofas, viewed by vicious old Tories immortalized in phoney art. The whistling fires are gas-driven fakes. Nine-tenths of English traditions, according to Lord Snow, were inventions of the nineteenth century. The rest were inventions of John Betjeman.

In clubland you have the hall of fame of English tradition. A Disneyland of snobbery and posture wherein, for instance, genteel Bohemianism and brutish drunkenness can both be sanitized by the bogus distinctions of 'history' and tradition. John Betjeman once had lunch in the Army & Navy Club, the 'In and Out' on Piccadilly. Through gulls' eggs and cutlets he was sweet, charming, generous and amusing. How, then, did his friend, the novelist Evelyn Waugh, come to be writing to him in 1947: 'Blind worm, who are you to lead?' Of what was he guilty?

P. Morton Shand provides a clue. Betjeman was having lunch to talk about this extraordinary figure who, according to Sir James Richards, was the individual most responsible for introducing young English architects to Continental modernism during the 1920s and 1930s. A cosmopolitan, light-travelling, oenologist and gastronome, translator of Gropius, friend of Le Corbusier and Aalto, back in London Shand could put the new architecture of concrete and steel into an appealingly rich cultural context. Many not emotionally disposed to accept modernism under normal circumstances found it palatable coming from a stern Eton-and-Kings aesthete.

Among the people attracted by Shand's meticulous accounts of the new international style was John Betjeman, a young journalist who, after some desultory but amusingly drunken days as a schoolmaster, was enjoying himself rather less working on the *Architectural Review* during that period in the early 1930s when it was a specially serious and influential journal. He later admitted that Evelyn Waugh was 'quite right' to warn him: 'You'll never laugh as much as you do now,' but strong beer in Barnet pubs was swapped for the stern verities of steel, concrete and *Existenzminimum*.

Betjeman's *Ghastly Good Taste*, which concludes in praise of the Bauhaus, was published in 1933, perhaps the *annus mirabilis* of modernism in Britain, what with the founding of the MARS Group at the Architectural Association and the exhibition *British Industrial Art in Relation to the Home* at Dorland Hall. But it was a brief flirtation in an eclectic age: the *Architectural Review* published Georgian details as well as the international style; its editor, James Richards, while an early champion of modernism was also a founder of the Georgian Group.

Richards and Betjeman, along with other popular architectural journalists, could, for a moment, support both the preservation of Georgian architecture and the modern movement. In 1937 each was a struggling minority interest and there was no inconsistency in promoting both. Indeed, the English eclectic tradition encouraged it: for as long as it was rare and exotic, modern architecture exerted an appeal. But as soon as it ceased to be a diversion for dilettantes and appeared to threaten tea with the vicar, Betjeman and his cronies dropped it like hot cakes. The Second World War was the turning point: just as Evelyn Waugh had been moved to write his saccharine and sentimental *Brideshead Revisited* in response to the material and spiritual privations of war, so James Richards was stimulated to write in 1946 a plausible, if rather sickly, panegyric on the suburbs, *The Castles on the Ground*. Shand too became disaffected. His last thoughts about modern architecture were written in a letter to Betjeman shortly before his death in 1960: 'I am haunted by a gnawing sense of guilt in having, in however a minor and obscure degree, helped to bring about … a monster neither of us could have foreseen'.

To Betjeman and his circle, architecture was a pursuit comparable to bird-watching and had nothing to do with either social purpose or avant-garde experimentation. His artistic eclecticism and social snobbery soon got the upper hand over a flirtation with the real world. That snobbery and eclecticism were ever-present, is illustrated by a note in Waugh's diaries made in 1930 after a visit to the Pakenhams: 'John B. became a bore rather with Irish peers and revivalist hymns and his enthusiasm for every sort of architecture'. Betjeman felt safer in a world of trains and buttered toast. He would not have had much to say to Sigfried Giedion.

Curious, then, to find that persistent champion of modernism Nikolaus Pevsner, known to Betjeman as 'Plebsveneer', getting into bed with Betjeman at the founding of the Victorian Society in 1957.

Betjeman scornfully thought art history was much too serious a subject (when he wrote contemptuously of 'doctors' busy classifying everything around us', he was doubtless thinking of Nikolaus), although he did share with Pevsner, but for very different reasons, the conviction that the outer form of architecture was an expression of the spirit of the age.

Betjeman as opposed to Pevsner was architecture as social posture, not purpose. The first meeting of the Victorian Society was in the home of Lady Rosse, granddaughter of *Punch* cartoonist Linley Sambourne. There were blood-lines all over the place. It was her husband, the Earl of Rosse, who had founded the Georgian Group in 1937. Betjeman was vice-chairman of the new society and future historians will emphasize the nice point that this most jealous of conservation pressure groups was founded at the precise moment when Britain was actually experiencing the first bout of mediocre postwar city building that got modern architecture a bad name.

Betjeman was in fact always a conservationist. His dreamworld doggerel was written to memorialize his youth in Highgate, and a vision of a country which had never really existed, but could be evoked with nostalgia when his personal nightmare of 'England … all council houses and trunk roads and steel and glass factory blocks' came about. With the creation of the Vic Soc there was now a club to do it for him. Pevsner could play a part because at first it seemed that an organization dedicated to the better understanding of any sort of architecture must necessarily be a good thing. The great German-Jewish scholar perhaps didn't realize that what was being created was not a Forschungs Institut, but a reactionary clique. Betjeman did.

Throughout the 1960s and 1970s John Betjeman was a familiar figure on television, popularizing his quirky views on architecture, not always to the approval of his friends. In a scornful 1960 comment on Betjeman's autobiography *Summoned by Bells*, Evelyn Waugh claimed that it 'demonstrates how much more difficult it is to write blank verse than jingles and raises the question *why* did he not go into his father's work shop? It would be far more honourable and useful to make expensive ashtrays than to appear on television and just as lucrative'.

But the postwar world provided him with another medium, perhaps more influential in its way even than television. In the 'Nooks and Corners' feature in *Private Eye*, Betjeman was provided with a regular platform from which to condemn 'the drift towards ugliness' which, according to his interpretation, was brought about by the triple united evils of population growth, mass production and loss of faith. Here perfumed high-church values and postures were carried over to the Swinging Sixties, creating a regular critical vehicle devoted to colliding with novelty wherever it might be found. His legatees have done him proud, surpassing in reactionary viciousness and malice what they cannot match in wit and style.

Betjeman never wrote a serious book about architecture, but became its popular champion. He never wrote a decent poem, but became Poet Laureate. An apostate of modernism, anti-intellectual, anti-serious, anti-semitic and antiquarian. John Betjeman was a quaint schoolmaster-type who raised trivia to the level of a great national pursuit. Affectionate, yet perhaps insincere, his relentless glibness and dynamic fluidity of purpose made him the perfect topographer of the English soul. The landscape he described never existed and never could. Thanks in part to his influence, neither could a better, newer alternative.

At what price was Betjeman's persuasive vision of brown garden walls and silvery frosty Sunday nights and St Botolph and 'all the nice things in the world/A cup of tea, a sunny afternoon/A snooze, a cigarette, this comfy chair' bought? At the expense of a positive vision of the future for Britain, where chain stores and council houses might not be sniggered at, where innovation and change would be treated with the reverence now attached to nostalgia and sentiment. A fair poet, a nice man, but a guilty one.

Are the British visually literate?
Design Review, Spring 1991

Wherever British designers gather, a cry goes out. They say their countrymen are visually illiterate, as if this stigmatization of the national character explains lack of commissions, or lack of prestige or whatever woeful state is currently fashionable among the profession. It is a tiresome, ritual observation, and one that betrays a limited conception of design as surely as it displays a misleading view of the national character.

I believe that the supposed lack of prestige that afflicts their profession is one reason why British designers claim that their compatriots are visually illiterate. But this unhappiness over their status comes from false expectations arising from a false reading of history.

Just as there were once designers who, by virtue of their original imaginative genius, achieved a singular prominence in influencing industry – Marcel Breuer, for example, or Harley Earl – there were once architects capable of achieving, or at least hinting at, revolutions. The present generation of designers and architects, however, spend disproportionate amounts of energy aping the *process* of celebrity. In this they are enthusiastically supported by bimbo journalists who would rather interview a fashionable name than read Bruno Taut in the original, or attempt to understand the principles of a heat pump. But the healthy professions are always the least conspicuous; while architecture has never been so prominent, neither has it ever been held in such low esteem. If you ask yourself why, you may decide that the process of celebrity has something to do with it. Certainly, it has nothing to do with visual illiteracy.

Following his lament of British visual illiteracy, the British designer will go on to say how different things are in Italy. The Italian example is routinely cited by those who would blame the shortcomings of their own careers on the failings of their countrymen. In Italy, it is claimed, such is the prestige of the architect that the title is used as an honorific. Meet *Architetto* Sottsass, *Architetto* Bellini. But it should also be pointed out that Italians apply the same honorific system to every profession – *Ingegnere, Avvocato, Ragionere*, for instance. For all I know, you can address a worker as *Artisano*.

The same designer might then refer to Milan as the product of a visually literate nation, and the city centre's fine monuments, Carlo Scarpa underground, coruscating lighting shops and exaggerated regard for the stylish bear this out. Yet, if you go 500 metres further north along Corso Buenos Aires, you will see trashy shops, crass graphics and badly dressed people, and might wonder if the Italians are not visually illiterate after all.

It is also sensible to be cautious about the Japanese achievement. While there is no gainsaying it, none the less it is worth remembering that the Japanese may have an exquisite sense of beauty – most often revealed in scale, detail and texture – but no sense of ugliness. Visually, Tokyo is a hideous place. Nagoya is worse. Nor are Japanese concerns for the realities of urban or domestic design as paramount as you might imagine. Only 65 per cent of Japanese roads are paved; only 41 per cent of the population has mains drainage; only 60 per cent have a flushing lavatory; and only 20 per cent of Tokyo's electric cables are buried underground.

Any question of national characteristics is treacherous and some caution is required. Calling the British visually illiterate is at best a half truth. The culture that produced Constable and Turner in the same generation, with their polar inclinations of truth to nature in the one eye and phantasmagoria in the other, can hardly be accused of discouraging sensitivity in the visual arts. These are, of course, extreme examples, and I would concede that, generally speaking, British painters are of the second rank: Arthur Devis, Lord Leighton and Graham Sutherland are no more than minor figures. Yet the same cannot be said for contemporary graphics and advertising where, without question, Britain leads the world.

If you look at artefacts, too, there is absolutely no evidence that the British are visually illiterate: we have a disproportionate amount of collectors, and the native art trade is without comparison. In the realm of manufactured goods, the British make extremely discriminating choices from imports – BMW enjoys a prominence in Britain which it has nowhere else. In all fields, it is the sophisticated end of the range that is imported into Britain.

To understand what is really meant by the ritual denunciation that we are visually illiterate, you have to look elsewhere. I think the real British disease is complacency, for reasons that go back to a unique attitude to land. In Britain, land is a productive asset which can be traded. There is nothing sacred or mystical about it. Violence is property crime, not vendettas or blood feuds. By Elizabethan times, the British were keeping pets and planting flower gardens. Despite the fantastic achievements and restless energies of Chippendale, Wedgwood and the engineers and ironmasters of the eighteenth and nineteenth centuries – those great men who truly made art popular – the real industrial revolution happened here in the thirteenth century.

The British ceased to be peasants more than seven hundred years ago. Notions of land/property and the insularity of an uninvaded island, combined with a stable political system where civil commotion was generally rare, created a complacent, rather than creative, culture. Free from political terror and the forces of nature, safe in their castles, large or small, the British had little use for community. It is no surprise that the most cultivated of the arts in Britain is the most solitary: literature.

This fundamental complacency and insularity tends to discount research and experimentation. The man responsible for Post-It Notes said: 'If I knew what I was doing, it wouldn't be research'. Einstein explained his breakthrough by saying: 'I simply ignored an axiom'. If these are not characteristically British sentiments, Dr Johnson's attack on imagination in the arts certainly is: 'I had rather see a portrait of a dog that I know than all the allegorical paintings they can show me in the world'.

This is not visual illiteracy, but complacency, a reluctance to experiment. I wonder if architects and designers are not guilty of the same complacency, the same timidity, and the same fear of change, but express it differently. Is there not something patronizing and condescending about the way they blame clients and the public for any malaise that affects their profession? Is not the accusation of 'visual illiteracy' a transference of shortcomings?

While I deplore the slovenliness of so much British life, I think it is often misleading to compare it unfavourably with foreign competition. There is something irritatingly pleasing about the typically British insistence on self-deprecation – a minor vice based on a sense of security. And the fact that it has always been foreigners who notice British virtues, from the great German neo-classicist Karl-Friedrich Schinkel (who was more inspired by Manchester's factories and mills, when he travelled there in the 1820s, than the British Museum) to the Danish academic Steen Eiler Rasmussen, who so admired the modest dignity of London's domestic architecture.

Schinkel and Rasmussen would probably be dismayed by Manchester or London today, and both would doubtless be disappointed to find architects and designers blaming the public and their clients. What impressed Schinkel was the awful majesty of honest industrial building he saw; what impressed Rasmussen was humane, understated domestic architecture and civic planning. These were not products of a visually illiterate culture.

To accuse clients and the public of visual illiteracy ignores the realities, when the same people who, it is assumed, refuse architecture also enjoy the most visually sophisticated advertising in the world and drive the best cars. Perhaps the cure for the British disease is a specially British one: compromise. Designers, I think, should try to meet the public half way.

Paradise lost
Car Magazine, December 1993

Britain is the only country to have had and to have lost a motor industry. Of course, vehicles are still manufactured here, but only zealots and fanatics could regard them as being essentially or meaningfully *British*. A Ford Mondeo is the motoring equivalent of a palimpsest, an ancient document bearing a number of texts, each superimposed on the one before. From these layers of writing palaeographers have to unravel meaning. Check the components and the sources of the Mondeo one by one and then ask yourself whether this product expresses any sort of national identity. It's a multi-cultural alphabet soup of a car. Nourishing and satisfying, perhaps, but culturally authentic? No.

Cars today are more likely to be the result of international component-sharing programmes, currency-hedging deals, and offset negotiations, than the fruition of a dazzling concept sustained by a talented and motivated individual. And it shows. Timorous marketing strategies enforce bland aesthetic conformity where no manufacturer dares lead or inspire, still less take risks, for fear of even temporarily losing market share and then permanently losing his shirt. Computer-aided design and common technological goals ensure that the pallid visions of the marketeers (who inhabit a landscape where the scenery is described in the icy logic of statistics) efficiently and serially bore us to complacency.

If I had been walking for four days in the pouring rain, had worn out a pair of shoes, had blisters, and felt tired, hungry and miserable, I would be absolutely delighted to have the use of a 'British' Carina E, but it is not a machine to exalt the spirits. It is a commodity, not something precious. Romance is wretchedly lacking from today's British cars. The Escort Cosworth might have stupefying performance, but it is an austere, clinical, lifeless thing when compared to a Lotus Cortina, let alone a Jaguar 3.8 Mk2.

Britain's car industry is a closed book. An odd story with a beginning, a middle and an end. It is hermetic. Like rock music, it is over. We have had the best of it. And, as if to prove it, the industry keeps on re-issuing greatest hits: the Mini Cooper and the MGB may be just the first. As we slip neck deep into the swamp of *fin-de-siècle* nostalgia, new compilations or new issues of unreleased material may yet be contemplated. After you with the 1994 Triumph Mayflower. To confirm this national preoccupation with a future connected by very short strings to the past, there is the extraordinary Heritage Motor Centre at Gaydon, Warwickshire, a brand new 150,000sq ft building on a 65-acre landscaped site near the Rover Group's test facilities.

If you can live with the vain, shallow and ticky-tacky daftness of West Midlands neo-late-postmodernism, it's an impressive building. Even if you do have strong views on architectural purity – and I do – there's no gainsaying the fact that the Heritage Motor Centre, with its 300 cars and vast archive, represents a superb historical and cultural resource: it allows us to gain an understanding of what cars mean in the life of a nation. We may have abandoned industry, but we are fighting back with museums.

Anything that is made betrays the preoccupations of those who made it, cars more than most. You can, as Henry Ford knew, read objects like a book if only you know how. The design of a car incorporates all the pride, vanity, folly and hope of human endeavour. Just as great car design can be exalting and inspiring, so poor car design can be risible, or even depressing.

In Italy, there's a whole specialized branch of serious book publishing dedicated to car design.

In Britain, we are still at the workshop manual and garage freak stage of evolution. In Italy, the names of the great designers sound like poetry. Here, the heroes are all but unknown. Perhaps this is appropriate in a manufacturing culture that on many occasions allowed the Pressed Steel Company to finish off the design process, brutally truncating elegant concepts with the stern imperatives of backward manufacturing technology. That is why the 1959 Triumph Herald, whose shape started as an elegant sketch by Michelotti, looks as though it was made out of bent cardboard: the Pressed Steel company did not possess the equipment to express the curves the designer wanted.

Still, there are some heroes: Riccardo 'Dick' Burzi, who sketched the cute little 1955 Austin A30 (half close your eyes and you have a swollen Lancia); his apprentice, David Bache, an extraordinary man now living in seclusion and, one suspects, under a cloud, but responsible for some exceptional car shapes, including the 1963 Rover P6, the 1970 Range Rover and the 1976 Rover SD1. Bache even had a hand in the styling of the Metro, although it is not his fault that early versions looked so straight-out-of-the-shell gawky: late in the day when the new wide body had been committed for production, engineers driven insane by considerations of cost insisted it kept the original-width Mini sub-frames.

And then there are the villains, or at least the jokers. Can there be anyone at any time in the entire, glorious spectrum of Western civilization who is responsible for two more screamingly awful things than the 1975 TR7 and the 18/22 saloons of the same year? Step forward, Harris Mann.

Some may find it too elegiac to consider, and others may just be too squeamish, but the temptation is irresistible: listed here are the six best, and the six worst, Rover Group designs on show at the Heritage Motor Museum.

Through its triumphs and absurdities, its great achievements and its sordid errors, the story of British car design is presented in its entirety by the Heritage Motor Centre. True, even as the low-voltage lights shimmer, the place has something of the feel of a mortuary. But out of this sea of chrome and tinsel and drip pans, rising above the aroma of industrial death, comes one clear message: great cars were made by individuals, not by marketing departments; great companies arose from personal motivation, not from mergers. On show in this museum are cars of which we may feel proud and cars that may give cause for shame, but on balance the achievement is impressive: this funny little island has produced some fabulous machines. What a pity it's all over.

The best:
1948 Morris Minor
The Series MM appeared at the 1948 motor show as a two-door saloon and a convertible. Alec Issigonis's first production car, it had unusual unitary construction, and advanced steering and suspension. Although the Minor later acquired a reputation as a car favoured by schoolmasters and district nurses, its styling – inspired by American designs, and Packard in particular – was as adventurous as its technical specification.

1955 MGA
Designed and made by Oxfordshire *garagistes* to stern no-nonsense briefs, there was never a bad MG before the morbid hand of BMC and BLMH and BL corporatism valued the brand higher than the principles. The lasciviously elegant MGA, a shape both pretty and sharp, was designed by Syd Enever and reached the market just in time to enjoy the California sports car cult. By 1961, 100,000 examples of the MGA had been built.

1959 Morris Mini-Minor
The Mini is one of the very few cars to have defined a type. More than just an innovation, it was a new way of construing the small car, and since 1959 every manufacturer has adopted Issigonis's assumptions about the architecture of the small car. Like all masterpieces of functional design, there is a purity about the Mini that puts it beyond the ebb and flow of fashion.

1963 Rover P6
This was the modern car that gave Rover a mass market, adding bank customers to the established body of bank manager customers. First seen as the 1961 T4 gas turbine prototype, David Bache drew a shape that was elegantly Italianate on the outside and intelligently imaginative inside. Featuring ergonomically shaped controls, sculpted seats and creative use of space, no 1960s car had a better interior.

1970 Range Rover
Like the Mini, the Range Rover gave form to something hitherto indeterminate. Equally, the Range Rover is as near to being immortal as any man-made machine. The austerity and authority of David Bache's bodylines can only be refined, not improved – as the visually awkward Discovery proves.

1976 Rover SD1
Quality problems ruined the reputation of another David Bache design, but in happier times, with brighter management, the SD1 would have become an immediate classic. The body design was influenced by the Ferrari Daytona. With a programme of progressively refined components and serious quality control, the Rover SD1 would still be a strong contender today. That is something that can be said of no other 1976 car.

The worst:
1948 Austin Atlantic
Proof that good cars are made by designers and engineers with conviction, not marketing departments sensing an opportunity. The bizarre Austin Atlantic was aimed specifically at the United States, where it found a mere 350 customers at a time when British cars were coveted imports.

1971 Morris Marina
One of the worst cars ever made, cynically under-engineered and stupidly over-designed. Using running gear, whose lineage could be traced directly back to the 1948 Minor, the Marina (whose name alone indicates the vulgar consumerist affectations of its maker) was available in two body styles: an ugly coupé and an ugly saloon. Somehow, British Leyland persuaded Giugiaro to take on the job of facelifting it in 1980, giving us the Ital. Somehow, Giugiaro survived.

1973 Austin Allegro
After the pleasing Pininfarina 1100 of 1962, the Allegro was an absurd disappointment (although at the time *Car Magazine* praised it extravagantly for its adventurous technology and dynamic competence). If they survive, a complete set of Allegros should be preserved so that design students can study in perpetuity the folly of meretricious adornment: daring, even fair, in its proportions, the Allegro was let down into the sump of hell by its awful detail and execution.

1975 Wolseley 18/22
Nothing better summarizes the fakery of the 1970s than these wedge-shaped atrocities. Conceived during blackouts in the three-day week, the 18/22 was meant to succeed the stately, dignified and decent 1800, the largest version of Issigonis's Mini concept. With all the style and integrity of Gary Glitter, this symbol of the

decade disgraced every known principle of design and engineering. It took them seven years to add a hatchback.

1975 Triumph TR7
When Giugiaro saw the TR7 for the first time, he looked at the extravagantly scalloped side panels and said, 'My God! Have they done that on the other side as well?' They had.

1983 Austin Maestro
The Maestro is depressing not so much for what it is (perfectly inoffensive, if boring) as for what it might have been (an interestingly utilitarian city car of the 1980s). In the outline can be seen ghosts of a rational, excellently proportioned design. However, a bright spark in the marketing department insisted it be kitted out with trim levels to satisfy suburban imaginations – and a car of genuine integrity, which could have rescued Rover years before Honda did, was ruinously compromised.

A nation living at ease with itself
Life and Times, 2 June 1992

The maxim 'Love France, hate the French' is frequently invoked by the British at a loss to understand the totality of the neighbouring culture. France is a totality, much more so than Britain. Of course, the French have as many social classes as we do, but the difference is that the French class system is cohesive, not divisive: Frenchmen of all backgrounds share similar tastes. To separate the people and their country is to admit defeat in matters of comprehension.

The French have a saying '*le style est l'homme*' whose sense betrays a national conviction that form and content are not distinct, but the one the expression of the other. Equally, to speak of *le style français*, that characteristic collection of habits, forms and manners, the sum of the proclivities and customs of the people, is not affectation, but an eloquent expression of a civilization more at ease with itself than ours. The latest evidence of the love-hate schism is Peter Mayle who writes of Provence rather as you would expect of an adman. Mayle loves France and patronizes the French. His Provence is a saccharin confection, glazed and glossy, sanitized and prettified. He has introduced a whole generation who have never got nearer *la France profonde* than a trip to the Calais Mammouth or the local Renault dealer to a dazzling narrative of a *House and Garden* roomset with walk-on parts for the colourful *chauffagiste* and the wily *chasseur*.

But Mayle is only the slickest, not the first. In 1935 Winifred Fortescue published *Perfume from Provence*. Lady Fortescue's style of bemused, beaming, indulgent, patronizing superiority anticipates Mayle's similar confection. She wrote of pre-Mayle Provençals:

They were perfectly maddening, entirely without initiative and quite irresponsible, but they were most lovable.

In the half century between Fortescue and Mayle the British have journeyed through real and imaginary France maintaining visions that are precious and distinctive. The France of lovable, but cunning, peasants, of fantasy breakfasts, lunches, colourful markets and dappled sunshine is no less profound because it is not entirely real. The topography of the countries we construct in the imagination speaks volumes about our own: it is worth saying that the love of France which made Peter Mayle a bestseller is a novelty.

France, as readers of Smollett and Sterne know, was once regarded as risibly dirty and backward, the French as skulking schemers or desiccated, perfumed high-minded cheats. At Marquise, just outside Calais, Lord Nelson was 'shown an inn – they called it – I should have called it a pigsty: we were shown into a room with two straw beds, and, with great difficulty, they mustered-up clean sheets, and gave us two pigeons for supper, upon a dirty cloth, and wooden-handled knives. O what a transition from happy England!' The France of Fortescue and Mayle is not the underworld France of Jean Genet or the suburban France of Robert Doisneau, just as ours is not a particularly happy England. It is the Brits' France, a great imaginative work created to serve our current emotional needs. France represents what we have lost: in particular, this huge, uncrowded country has a pastoral life which is almost real. It has, or so it seems, traditions of cooking and hospitality which are ignorant of portion control and dedicated to pleasure as much as to nutrition or shelter. It has a national style which is borne of natural convictions, not of concepts fabricated by some wally from the tourist authority.

See a picturesque French village and, if you are lucky, there will be someone there who smokes ham, a farmer who makes cheese, a baker who bakes bread. See a picturesque British village and you just sit it out and wait for the Walls, Dairy Crest and Mother's Pride trucks.

Food is the most complete expression of French style. 'Mayonnaise', according to Ambrose Bierce, is 'one of the sauces which serve the French in place of a state religion'. It is not just because we find their food so delicious that we revere France, but because the attention to food suggests sympathy for day-to-day human endeavour: a respect for normality is the basis of the real French style and this is shared by all classes.

In *The Alice B. Toklas Cookbook* (1954) Gertrude Stein's famous companion writes: 'The French approach to food is characteristic; they bring to their consideration of the table the same appreciation, respect, intelligence and lively interest they have for the other arts...I have heard working men in Paris discuss the way their wives prepare a beef stew as it is cooked in Burgundy, or the way a cabbage is cooked with salt pork and browned in the oven'.

France gave us the word élite, but the more you get to know French culture, the more you appreciate that its real quality lies in its ordinariness. 'High' French culture is remote, aloof and cold. There are the starchy tropes of Racine, the frigid classicism of Poussin, or the funeral, marmoreal rhythms of Couperin. According to Horace Walpole 'The French affect philosophy, literature and free-thinking'.

Maybe they did, but we appreciate best the *chanteuse* or Doisneau's charming, warm pictures of street life. It was Doisneau, the Renault factory photographer, who took the famous picture of Picasso with the bread rolls. Here, in Vallauris, one sunny afternoon, the great Franco-Catalan posed in his *pul marin* and lent himself to an image which still speaks eloquently of the French Mediterranean idyll. The madras table cloth, the

stoppered bottle of wine, the expectation
of wit and serious pleasure: Doisneau captured
an encyclopaedia of French meaning in one
clever image.

Of course, there is another sort of self-conscious,
more arrogant, less assured world of French
'design', although it is noteworthy that even today
France has fewer celebrity designers than Italy,
Germany, or even Britain. Like French classicism,
and the culture of the *Académies*, French design
tends to be stilted and aloof (because it is so
removed from popular taste). The few
personalities who do emerge are eccentric
figures. Roger Tallon, for instance, the designer
of SNCF's 'Corail' locomotives and the man who
gave the TGV its distinctive snoot; or Olivier
Mourgue, the polyurethane furniture designer of
the 1960s whose futuristic shapes so impressed
Stanley Kubrick that he used Mourgue's furniture
in *2001*. Or more recently, Andrée Putman. These
are great names, but they are oddities. Design is
not an institution in France.

This is because in France ordinary things tend to
be so excellent that the application of superior
aesthetic intelligence to them is neither
necessary nor possible. You might be very proud
of your Roger Tallon Lipp watch, your Olivier
Mourgue airport furniture, your stylized Starck
toothbrush or Ms Putman's monochrome interior,
but they do not compare in quality or humanity to
the vernacular things which your neighbours
own: a Duralex glass, simple white Apilco
crockery, a Bic pen, a VeloSolex, a Citroën 2CV.
The little Citroën is surely the most complete
single statement of 'le style français': an
automobile designed solely to satisfy certain
demands of functional transport, but one which
does so with great charm and with unforced style.

In contrast to the triumphs of French vernacular,
'high' French design appears absurd, not least

because it is so arch and often so uncomfortable.
A sense of simple luxury is fundamental to the
style of France; even Le Corbusier's most severe
machine-age furniture of the 1920s had, with its
plump leather cushions or its pony skin, a
luxurious character. There is this sense, too, in
Doisneau's Picasso, so powerfully suggestive of
an earthy sort of *luxe, calme et volupté*, the
ingredients of a perfect holiday. For the British,
France means holidays with all the bitter-sweet
associations they have. The very idea of France
produces pleasure because it summons up what
the sociologists call 'anticipatory socialization'.
Think of France and you don't think of HLM
projects in Nanterre or Argenteuil, but of oven-
warm baguettes, fresh basil and delicious, rough
wine. You think of baking in the sun after lunch.
You think maybe Picasso lived like this.

You think, too, of everything associated with
eating and travel. More than anything else the
Michelin guides summarize *le style français*: the
reconciliation of food and motoring is one of the
century's great cultural achievements and one
that is distinctively French. Although France gave
us the terms 'chic' and 'haute couture' these are
only remote, tinselly peaks of French culture.
If you want to understand French style, you don't
want to go to a boutique or a couturier, but to
bury yourself in the Michelin rouge, both a
guide to and a symbol of the country and culture
it represents.

Michelin is based on practical systematic
research presented to the reader in an elegantly
no nonsense way. In this it is characteristically
French. Above all, the Michelin guides are useful.
They employ a symbology which is wilful and
eccentric, but workable. The important thing to
understand about Michelin is that its
recommendations represent a total culture.
Naturally, there are gradations in Michelin's
assessment of restaurants and hotels, but the

meanest little *hôtel de passe* in Toulon is connected to the awesome Crillon by a shared set of values and each has its place on the national spectrum of quality.

Most of all, Michelin conjures up for map-reading voyeurs that special magic of France that creates such an elegiac longing in the British. *Le style français* is not some precious essay in the peculiar furniture of Philippe Starck or the austerely mediagenic interiors of Andrée Putman, or whomsoever *Marie Claire* is photographing this month, but maps, systems and the prospect of a delicious lunch, which is connected to dinner by a journey in a comfortable car. This will be something useable, but also something adventurously designed. Today it might be a Citroën XM, but in the imagination it would always be a Citroën DS.

For the postwar generation, life has very few things more to offer than being in France one sunny afternoon. We have just had lunch, somewhere in La Correze and now there is the prospect of a long drive to a late dinner in La Baule. The sun is shining and it is hot, but our last meal has relaxed us, as fine food always does. The big Citroën lopes along the fast, straight roads. The seats are comfortable, the suspension pliant. In France, real luxury is an everyday thing.

Maybe if someone else is driving we are flicking through the latest Jean-François Revel and musing on what characterizes French style. Michelin rouge and all it stands for, certainly. A big Citroën, without question. French style is like a *bidet*, something at once odd, but also very convenient. *Le style français* is not something narrow, limited and self-conscious. French style is an attitude to ordinary things. Love France, love life.

French lessons
GQ, October/November 1989

Imagine Paris, September 1955. Closer to the end of the Second World War than you and I are to the last days of Vietnam. The streets still have that grimy, beat-up look which photographers like Brassai made famous. On the rue Mouffetard in the Latin Quarter there are still old *bougnats* and other small shops and cafés. The artisans have not yet been displaced by the gaudy Euro-chic. There is a smell of drains and cheap cigarettes and stale garlic; there are *pissotières*, engineered like sanitary guillotines.

But the artisans and Algerians are being replaced. The odour of ordure is being replaced by Gitanes and Vetiver. Litter gives way to *lettres*. The *quartier* is becoming the home of smart intellectuals, including Roland Barthes. It is Barthes, a junior professor celebrated as the author of *Le Degre zero de l'écriture* (1953), presently a research assistant at the Centre National du Recherche Scientific, who leaves his apartment this September morning on an assignment which is going to make him famous beyond the circles of academia. Professor Barthes, one time lecturer in Bucharest and Alexandria, is going to the Paris motor show.

The Paris Salon de l'Automobile in the mid-1950s was quite something. It was not a case of warm gin in plastic cups in some godawful exhibition centre, with scrubbers on the scuttle and bimbos on the boot. It was an extraordinary spectacle which provided, for nearly the last time, an opportunity to look at the latest automobile achievements of the mythic entrepreneurs whose nerve, neck and bankruptcies laid the basis for modern European industry. You still had the likes of Panhard, Borgward, Austin, Morris, DKW and … Citroën.

Professor Barthes was not thinking of this as he strode, head down and collar up, through the *arrondissements* he had made his intellectual stage. He was too busy buffing up the shape of modern European thought to worry about the motor trade. His enemy, he thought, as he picked his way across the traffic clogged streets, was the bourgeois mentality. He called it, with a skill characteristic both of his ability to particularize and to obscure at the same time, *doxa*. He meant popular opinion. In the book he had in his mind, a collection of essays to be called *Mythologies*, he was going to analyse the idols of bourgeois consumerism.

Somebody else was going to the motor show that September morning, but this was not a person, rather a ghost. The engineer Pierre Boulanger had been killed in 1950, while testing his great design, a *voiture de grand diffusion*, for Citroën. A development of his earlier and equally remarkable car, known popularly as the 'Light 15', the new Citroën DS was so sophisticated that, while design work began in Boulanger's lifetime, a prototype was not ready to show the public until five years after his death. So, mounted on a pylon with its wheels removed so that nothing so workaday could compromise the perception of its ravishing shape, Boulanger's DS appeared in Paris in 1955.

When he arrived at the Salon and saw this astonishing car, Barthes was startled out of his academic reverie. Here, he realized, was a perfect four-cylinder symbol of the modern world. Given his self-imposed brief to explain the everyday, here was a car, an everyday object, which so manifestly exceeded the routine disciplines of the here and now that a description and a defence of it could, without embarrassment, contain metaphors and ironic similes which need not constrain even this most energetic exponent of the exercise of the mind. Raising sensitive eyebrows, Professor Barthes declared to the modern world that 'cars are our cathedrals'.

No more remarkable a sentence has been uttered by a modern critic, combining as it does a respect for the past together with an irreverent enthusiasm for the ordinary. For Roland Barthes, the visionary intellectual who saw life as a metaphor, and later as an algorithm, the new Citroën was a gift from the goddess.

But the Citroën was a *grand projet*, and the British, always suspicious of the French and usually of anything that contains an idea above the utilitarian, have always preferred the simple things of France to the elaborate and grandiose ones. The British prefer an infested barn in Normandy to French Renaissance architecture. The British consider Rameau's music to be chilling, but find some old *chanteuse* on the Left Bank capable of exciting a considerable tingle in the loins, if not in the mind. And it is the same with cars. For all the admiration the DS might have aroused, the car which represents France in the British imagination will always be Boulanger's first design, the 2CV. That it was not, by any means, a *grand projet*, illustrates the British preference for the ordinary in French life.

At the same time that Roland Barthes was having his revelation at the motor show, so was the first generation of postwar British tourists experiencing France. Just days after the end of rationing there were Britons taking brave steps to discover France. They didn't visit the Paris motor show, but many of them had read Elizabeth David and had been intoxicated by her almost pornographic accounts of olive oil, lemon and garlic. In search of gastronomic redemption under a John Minton sky, they found little Citroëns, sometimes filled with two priests, always filled with artisans of some sort, wobbling and wheezing down country roads. The sense of simple destiny suggested by the car's slow journey (reinforced by the colour of Mrs David's account of what might be expected on arrival) fixed forever in the British mind a certain vision of France – a vision which was gustatory rather than grand.

Laurence Sterne and Tobias Smollett may have been to France and come home full of lively anecdotes and sardonic accounts of Gallic knavery and that, but the vision of France most influential in Britain is more recent and belongs to Mrs David and the *routes nationales*. It is a simple, slow world, returning to fundamental, 'honest' values. It revolves around food, wine and crafts, and is personified by the Deux Chevaux. And of the DS, the car as cathedral, all the British consider is whether it is true that, because of its lower wheel arches, it cannot be clamped.

There are two versions of France, the French one and the British one. The French like their *grands projets*, whether Haussmann, Eiffel, Maginot or Pompidou is the instigator, whether monuments, public buildings or even complete city layouts are the result. The British are suspicious of this sort of magnificence. The British like their simple view of France; they are wary of the nation's grandeur and vision, even wary of its very modernity. Ask French pundits to sum up the essence of their own country, and they are likely to see it characterized in the grand architectural projects of the past or present, the great roads or buildings or visionary designs. Yet the British version of France remains a pastoral idyll of berets and bicycles, of soft cheeses and rustically unsafe water. Typically, we acknowledge the existence of 'peasant cooking' in their country but not in our own.

Of course, what we identify is a France of our own invention. It is not the France of Professor Barthes. But, then, this is not 1955.

GQ asked a selection of British and French cultural pundits to sum up the essence of France:

Deyan Sudjic, editor, *Blueprint*:
'I think of the French wearing dungarees and driving 2CVs, with baguettes under their arms. But the French hate that view. They like to be seen as technically progressive – they're very keen on the 20th century. So I would suggest the air terminal at Charles de Gaulle Airport, which is straight out of Metropolis.'

Daniel Veruet, editor, *Le Monde*:
'For me, France is all about history, culture, marvellous buildings, cathedrals and theatres'.

Jonathan Glancey, design correspondent, *The Independent*:
'The Citroën 2CV, which sums up that lovely mix the French have between rustic simplicity and great sophistication'.

Romand Leonard, cabaret director, Bal de Moulin Rouge:
'Les Champs Elysées, the most beautiful avenue in the World'.

Rodney Fitch, chairman, Fitch & Co, design consultants:
'The simple, ubiquitous French café chair. No matter that this type of chair is produced worldwide, it always sits at its best for me in a provincial French town'.

Philipe Guillemin, cultural counsellor, the French Embassy:
'My vision of France is not technocratic, but humanistic. France would not be France without its people – the grands projets would not exist were it not for the great variety of French people'.

Agnès B, designer:
'For me, France is a mixture of the past and the future. I. M. Pei's pyramid in front of the Louvre is a very typical example of this wonderful balance between the old and new'.

Our Culture, their Culture

In this sterile diorama, life is but a theme
International Herald Tribune, 9 April 1992

On his first trip to the United States, Charles Dickens was struck by the temporary nature of all that he saw. In Lowell, Massachusetts, he felt that most of the buildings had been erected the day before he arrived. This sense of urgency and immediacy struck other contemporary visitors, from Alexis de Tocqueville to Fanny Trollope, and still strikes people today. A rootless urgency characterizes American culture, which is why the nation has developed such a complicated modern heraldry: McDonald's franchises, Hertz bureaux and Coke. In a vast continentwith a shallow history, people crave and clingto symbols.

Twenty miles east of Paris may seem an odd place to start brooding on American national characteristics, but it is here that Euro Disney (provenance: California 1955, Florida 1971, Tokyo 1983) has landed, and the Old World is presented with all the confident, big ticket flimflam of painstaking fakery that this bizarre campaign of reverse-engineered cultural imperialism represents. Is Euro Disney a good thing?

Only if you enjoy pseudo-events and have a taste for phantasmagoric kitsch. Euro Disney exists because of two major schisms in contemporary culture. One between travel and tourism. The other, between education and entertainment. Calderon wrote a play 'La Vida Es Sueño'. For Euro Disney, life is not a dream, but a theme.

Disney stands for tourism and entertainment, which is to say it is not for the high-minded, but it is for people – of whatever nationality – who are pleased to demonstrate their trade or sporting affiliations by means of logos on trucker's caps. There is a surprising number of these people about.

The statistics of Euro Disney are reminiscent, in their size and horrific suggestiveness, of the awful aggregate of numbers spat out by the First World War. With a total projected size of 5,000 acres (about one-fifth the area of Paris), 5,200 hotel rooms already available and an anticipated attendance of 11 million in its first year, Euro Disney and its shows, rides, themed shops and themed restaurants threaten to shift Europe's centre of gravity. Anyway, it's an ill wind. Maybe the Louvre will be empty after next Sunday.

There is no gainsaying the optimism, commitment and quality of Euro Disney, a brilliantly buffed-up exercise in professional leisure management, but equally the fastidious aesthete is lost for words at the grotesque vulgarity of it all, a vulgarity doubly damaging because it is so effortless to consume. Life is a theme: Camp Davy Crockett, Sleeping Beauty's Castle (43 metres tall), a hotel got up to look like a Rhode Island clapboard mansion (architect: Robert A. M. Stern), Sequoia Lodge ('for a Rocky Mountain high without leaving Europe') and Mainstreet USA (from an original idea by Charles Dickens) are demonstrations of the great Disney machine humming mightily on well-lubricated bearings, extruding seamless and inoffensive themes. It is all so undemandingly mindless, the Prince of Wales might have been the master architect. There is no grit in the mechanism, no flies in the soup, no truculent waiters, no exaltation, no boredom. Forget exploration or hazard; Euro Disney offers a version of culture with the effect of intravenous Valium and elevator music.

This is where the travel/tourism and education/entertainment distinction comes to light. The reason why travel is better than tourism and education better than entertainment is that, ultimately, they are more rewarding for everyone. Such pleasures as there may be in tourism and entertainment are in any case assumed by travel and education. Difficulty enhances pleasure; themed ease may be immediately gratifying but

186

progressively diminishes the potential for delight. The difference is hard work, risk, effort: the things that distinguish worthwhile experiences from the worthless ones. Euro Disney is kitsch; it is bad art. This is not to say that it will not be immensely popular because, as H. L. Mencken knew, no one ever went bust underestimating the public's taste. With its roster of postmodern architects and its seductive catalogue of risk-free themes – no Liverpool dockside or Naples back alley here – Euro Disney takes underestimation to new heights.

But wait a minute. Maybe the synthetic and saccharine easy-listening experience will soon acquire a period charm. Euro Disney has plans through to 2017, but I wonder if new technology will make it redundant before then. You don't have to be a happy-clappy Silicon Valley hippie to see that computer-driven virtual reality is set to upstage Euro Disney before the millennium. The first stage of the separation of tourism from travel may have been to jet in jumbos of credulous, uninquisitive proles to look at synthetic tableaux, board them for the night and jet them back again, but the crucial second stage will be to make them stay at home, strapping on virtual-reality body stockings and having a Davy Crockett experience, complete with wood fires, mosquitoes and chipmunk droppings … in the easeful, unthemed comfort of home. All thanks to high-definition television and some fiendishly powerful chips.

I like to think that by the turn of the century Euro Disney will have become a deserted city, similar to Angkor Wat or Arc-et-Denans: a haunting reminder of a knowing, but innocent, past age. Those hungry for the tourist experience or avid for entertainment will let the fingers of their virtual-reality gloves do the walking. The rest of us can get back to travelling, and here is Disney's greatest opportunity yet. With eye-popping

professionalism, Euro Disney turns the dirt and danger of the American frontier into a cloying, undemanding, perfectly safe, synthetic, valueless, themed sensation.

By about 2001 only real travellers will be moving around the globe. If only Disney's nerveless, competent, entirely safe and thoroughly professional expertise could be applied to the dirt and danger of the world's great airports, then a great service would be done for civilization. Alas, the same cannot be said for Euro Disney.

La Grande Corniche
Le Shuttle Magazine, May 1994

Hollywood made turnpikes and interstates famous, but if you have a taste for romance the best driving roads in the world are in Europe. In Italy there is the Passo di Raticosa, rising to 968 metres on the main road north from Florence to Bologna, near to Modena, spiritual home of the great Italian sports car. The Raticosa Pass was the climax of the Mille Miglia, Italy's great thousand-mile road race, last won by Stirling Moss and Denis Jenkinson in a Mercedes-Benz in the course of one long, long day in 1955.

Further south, the adventurous know the harrowingly beautiful coast road between Amalfi and Salerno. At each turn this amazing ledge cut into the rock reveals two things: a breathtaking view of the bay (which makes you swear that Neptune is still among us) and an uncompromisingly large tourist bus, which blocks out the sun and just makes you swear.

In Belgium you can find the famous Jabbeke highway, between Dunkerque and Veurne, where in 1949 the Jaguar XK120 ran speed trials reaching 120mph, proving it to be the fastest of production cars. Through the Ardennes, the Vosges, or on the thin black top between La Garde-Freinet and Plan-de-la-Tour, people still enchanted by the thrill of controlling an interesting car through demanding and rewarding scenery will find brief but ample compensation for the normal frustrations of driving. But best of all, the road which admits no equals is the Corniche of the French Riviera.

The Corniche (from cornice, a ledge) is not one road, but three (or nowadays four if you count the efficient, but soulless A8 Provençal autoroute which runs in parallel to its ancient predecessors). There is the Grande Corniche, where you negotiate between sky and sea, enjoying tachycardiac kinaesthetic experiences the while; the Moyenne Corniche, a compromise; and the Basse Corniche, which is the clogged coast road, a lovely drive turned into a necessary evil by traffic.

But the Grande Corniche is different. To travel this road is one of life's defining experiences; it is magnificent but, in a purely functional sense, rather useless. This aristocratic lack of utility turns a beautiful road into a journey with no precise destination, but all of which is to be enjoyed. It starts from Nice and goes east up Mont Vinaigrier and Mont Gros, arriving nowhere in particular and passing nowhere of importance before it gets to discreetly faded Menton, its terminus near the Italian frontier.

But like many other pointless exercises, the Grande Corniche is pure pleasure. In between Nice and nowhere in particular is a dramatic experience. The road never rises above 2,000 feet, nor does it have clammy-hand, heart-in-the-mouth, vertiginous corners and fearsome drops (although it makes sense to drive prudently). It can be bleak and barren on a misty day, but it is always an elegant and thrilling road, not a rough and scary one. A drive along it makes you feel a master of this very special part of the world, a region which, like so many of its inhabitants, is at once refined but ruined. Around every bend is a huge vista, the Alps above you, the sea below, thrills in hand.

The best section of the Grande Corniche is between Nice and Eze where it reaches 512 metres. From here you can see St Tropez to the west. A little further east you reach La Turbie at 480 metres. It is touching that the easterly view from here takes in Monte Carlo.

Ironically, after her appearance in the classic film *To Catch A Thief*, with its twisting mountain driving sequence, it was on one of the Grande Corniche's sweeping curves that an old Rover left the road and Princess Grace left this life. Built by Napoleon as a military road in 1806, the Grande Corniche has had a murderous past. In the odd scratchy places where olive groves have survived modern intrusions, there are ghosts of the old Roman Via Aureliana which ran for 1,275km from the Forum to Arles.

It was at La Turbie that the Romans suppressed the aboriginal Ligurians and erected a heroic monument, the Trophée des Alpes, to mark the symbolic frontier of Rome and Gaul. Carefully restored to a state of immaculate ruin, the magnificent structure commands the whole vista of this magical coast. It is as much a relic as the Corniche itself. To drive to La Turbie and stop to think about the futility of earthly ambition is a healthy corrective to the insanity of the coast road.

After the fall of Rome, the area was overrun by hearty ruffians, greatly occupied with pillage, arson and murder. Saracens followed, and some slight remnants of their stay remain in the neighbourhood, but the most important travellers to the Riviera of the Corniche road have been English and American. Tobias Smollett visited Nice for his health in 1763 and wrote about it in his *Travels Through France and Italy*. For those who think that to arrive at the natural style of Mediterranean cooking – *pissaladières, poivres doux* – is human destiny, it is mindful to recall Smollett's feeling about the cooking and the women of the region: 'Most of the females are pot-bellied owing … to the great quantity of vegetable trash which they eat'.

While it was the obscure Burgundian poet, Stephane Liegard, who gave us the name of the westerly Côte d'Azur (a reference to his native Côte d'Or), it was English expatriates who developed the culture of Nice, source of the Corniche roads. Since Smollett, the area has become dense with romantic associations. Nietzsche used to stay in the old Hotel Continental in the rue Verdi. Into the twentieth century with the hurly-burly of Nice you sense the lost days of champagne and caviar.

Nice is a raffish city: the domes of the Hôtel Negresco are modelled on a famous dancer's breasts. Here Somerset Maugham lived on Cap Ferrat at the Villa Mauresque. On the other side of the bay is Villefranche where Jean Cocteau decorated the little fisherman's chapel in the harbour. Michael Arien's *The Green Hat* is set here, and Graham Greene wrote *Loser Takes All* while staying at Hôtel de Paris in Monte Carlo during 1955.

As the lofty Grande Corniche does not really touch villages, let alone towns, there are no remarkable places to eat, drink or stay on the roadside. For that you have to drop down to the coast at Villefranche, Beaulieu, Cap d'Ail or Roquebrune (where the architect Le Corbusier swam to his death in 1965).

Along the Basse Corniche you follow the coast not much above sea-level. There are bars and cafés everywhere, but no restaurants of repute. High above is the new autoroute, but this is only for people in a hurry. If concepts like connecting A and B bother you, you would be wasting your time on any of the Corniche roads. Timeless thoroughfares were not built for clock-watchers.

It is true that there are other corniche roads in France – the Chemin de Corniche, east of Marseilles, and the Corniche d'Or at Cannes – but for the authentic experience, travel east from Nice and go nowhere in particular. Hollywood made great road movies, but the Riviera makes great roads.

Milan: fizz, fun and style
Observer, 17 May 1981

An Italian official did not know whether to call Milan a community of artists or a business city. Of course, it is both and it is the nicely balanced relationship between fine art and commercial practice which makes it the most interesting major city in Europe.

Perhaps because it is the most Germanic of all Italian cities – certainly the only major one with a spiky Gothic cathedral – Milan's character is formed by manufacturing. It is the industrial centre of the new Italy, a country emerging into its own industrial revolution in the period they call the *ricostruzione*, when workers rode the new, democratic scooters and Visconti made his first films.

Yet industry and fashion go hand in hand: the giant conglomerate, Montecatini Edison, is a major shareholder in the chain of Fiorucci boutiques which began in the Galleria Pasarella. So far from hindering the colourful development of Fiorucci's shops, Montecatini actually helped him to expand.

There is a sort of surly vanity about the north Italians which encourages the search for visual perfection. In Rome, they say, you can still hear the rustle of silk on the trams, and men go home in the middle of the working day to have their trousers pressed. In Milan, on the other hand, you can see waiters polishing laminate trays until they glow like their teeth; in the major furniture stores an assistant will buff an ABS plastic chair to a blinding glory as a part of the daily routine.

There is everywhere an attention to detail and an assumption that visual quality is outstandingly important. The temporarily fashionable Plastic discotheque can stand as a symbol of this. Here three dominant features are apparent: much of fashionable Milan's reliance on a consistently invigorating interpretation of 1960s England (Elio Fiorucci, with a touch of irony, still says his main influences are Mary Quant, Biba and Mr Freedom); the talent to make something fresh, bright and new out of what inspires them; and, underneath it all, the ineradicable conservatism of an ancient society.

In the Plastic, where total blackness is relieved only by yellow fluorescent lights, you don't find leggy houris with kohled eyes, but 15-year-old boys strutting, preening and eyeing the cut of one another's cloth. The only woman there the night I went was the wife of the sexagenarian architect who was my host.

Milan is able to sustain its extraordinarily active avant garde not only because there has been a consistently strong artistic tradition in the city, but because official culture is so poor. The industrial revolution came so late to Italy that there is a freshness, an excitement and a challenge about getting involved with making things for industry, in getting industry to work for the designer, instead of the other way around, as we have it here.

Furniture designers are strongly identified with the manufacturers they work for – Castigloni with Flos, Magistretti with Artemide, Sottsass with Poltronova – just as Milan's chief industrial product, the Alfa Romeo car, has a name whose first part is an acronym of 'Lombard Car Factory'. Until it shifted its plant to the under-privileged south, Alfa Romeo badges actually bore the name of the city itself.

At an everyday-shopping level, Milan benefits from the immediacy of designers in industry and in shops. The chic ghetto bounded by the Monte Napoleone, Corso Vittorio Emanuele, Via della Spiga and the Via Manzoni offers to a public arriving in Dino 308s and clad in maroon-dyed minks and silk dresses a range of merchandise whose quality and novelty suggests the notions of art gallery and museum, instead of dress shop and furniture store. The willingness of Italian manufacturers to innovate has encouraged the most stimulating thinking about the culture of products taking place anywhere in the world.

A group of architects has formed itself into an outfit called Studio Alchimia (the name chosen to refute in its entirety the associations of modernism) where their business is to challenge every assumption we make about what furniture should do and be.

Alessandro Mendini, incidentally, editor of *Domus* and *Modo* magazines, invents what he calls 'false furniture', deliberately intended to delight and confuse. He paints a proprietary overstuffed armchair with an imitation Signac picture, calls it 'The Chair of Proust', and then puts it into production to assault traditional convictions. Andrea Branzi has a programme of furniture he calls The Gallery of Copyism, junk exquisitely painted with reproduction Kandinskys and Mondrians.

They talk about 'redesign', but most especially, confronted with international uniformity in product design, they introduce irreverence and irony, delighting in irrational shapes and unfashionable pastel colours and inappropriate decoration. Ettore Sottsass Jr has made a cupboard with imitation leopard-skin laminate and invented a 'trembling table' in pink and eau-de-Nil. There is no doubt that these contemporary Milanese experiments point the way to the design of future popular furniture. It is inevitably the case because Milan is where art and industry meet.

Design capitals
Design, January 1991

Kevin is a style writer. Smoothing his flat top one day in his bathroom mirror he heard a Capital disc jockey drivel on about the tapas bar scene in the Earls Court Road. A jaunt up west convinced him. Bodega Gonzalez is one hip joint. True, no anthropologist would want to be too precise about whether the catering is Castilian, Andalusian, Mexican or Trust House Forte/Majorcan, but two gallons of San Miguel into the evening he was ready for the blandishments of new Spain. A boy in a leather jacket told him about Javier Mariscal and now Kevin is obsessed by Barcelona.

Of course, Kevin already knew about Milan because he'd read about it in *The Sunday Times.* On his way to the Bodega he had popped into the Conran Shop to buy an Alessi cruet. He also picked up a dog-eared copy of *Blueprint* with a bucketshop-style gazer's gazetteer to the new wave bars of Catalonia and Lombardy. Later, he flew to La Coruna then bussed his way east. He practised saying 'tortilla' as perfectly as he could already say Sottsass.

Here he was on confidently firm ground. Once, at a fringe Designers' Saturday mulled-wine-and-Californian-pizza-party on a Rotherhithe barge, Kevin met someone who had once met someone who had known someone who did the PR for Memphis. Not in its early days, you understand, but Memphis nevertheless. Now Kevin is planning a major study, all from tertiary sources, *Spanish Design: Into the Apocalypse.* This is his follow-up to the inexplicably rejected *Five Centuries of the Milan Furniture Fair.*

Kevin gets invited to attend whatever happens next in small home fittings in Corso Venezia or Passeig de Gracia. His latest offer of a press trip was from Artglop, the new Barcelona collective of radical architects whose collection of Unreadable Prose had so astonished the Zagreb Convention on Dissonance earlier in the summer. For the Artglop beanfeast Kevin went on expenses to Adolfo Dominguez in South Molton Street and fitted himself out with a grapeseed and hashish weave suit, similar to the one which the Artglop team had worn to such effect in Croatia.

The Barcelona opening was amazing: Artglop, in conjunction with a cousin of Philippe Starck's, had created a new anguillas and fino bar in the senseless killing district of Barcelona. Every Adolfo Dominguez grapeseed and hashish suit was there, so was every PR gaucho and gaucheta and every style writer in Europe. Find a way of harnessing their collective intellectual or critical scrutiny, discover an equivalence formula and you would have enough raw, powerful energy to light a pencil torch. Kevin thinks he may soon get a break and have an article accepted on the Metro pages of the *Evening Standard*.

Milan and Barcelona are great cities. But it is a travesty to stigmatize them as design capitals, whatever that tawdry expression means. Milan has a magnificent gloominess and a solid, serious power which emanates from real money: the Milanese have trading traditions which go back before the Romans and the sense that the city is the commercial and industrial capital of Italy is profound. It never needs to be overtly stated. You can sense it.

Milan has the only Gothic cathedral in Italy. The food is famously rich, solid and blanched. The people are nearly Germans. A zap around the *tangenziale* in an Alfa 164 should be required for every dimbulb Treasury official. There you see real wealth and real industry. The reason we think of Milan as a place which encourages design is not because it has a lot of brilliant designers (which is true) but because it is a serious city which supports vertically and horizontally integrated industries.

And it is the same with Barcelona. Of course I know that there is an extraordinarily creative atmosphere there at the moment. I know the names of the active architects, designers and the shops and even Kevin's style bars. Spain, and especially Catalonia, is a demographically young country. It has the fastest expanding economy in Western Europe.

Milan is serious and confident. Barcelona is young and growing. Alas, none of these things can be said about London. The reason is people like Kevin mistake cause and effect.

Gianni Agnelli
GQ, June 1995

It would be crass to call someone so
sophisticated a playboy, but through a long and
elegant life Gianni Agnelli has shown a similar
dedication to pleasure as he has to duty. As a
young man in the 1950s he broke a leg while
driving his Ferrari importunately, but
commissioned a custom-made calliper so he
could continue to ski. Last year, at 72, when he
might have contemplated whatever form of
retirement the very rich have in mind, he
extended his demanding contract as chairman of
Fiat, the family firm. At the turn of the century
Agnelli's father, known as *Il Senatore*, had brought
together a group of aristocrats, racing drivers
and industrialists to create the Fabbrica Italiana
Automobili Torino. Now Fiat companies – which
include banking, insurance, publishing, civil
engineering, health care and weapons systems,
as well as vehicles – represent perhaps 10 per
cent of all Italian business. They confer on Gianni
Agnelli a form of prestige unknown in England.
To his enormous commercial power he brings an
exceptional amount of personal style. He has
classic Italian patrician features: expressive,
sorrowful eyes, a magnificent nose and a
complicated demeanour which would be too
simplistically described as languor. Agnelli has
acquired an aristocratic code of conduct,
appropriate to his status. In matters of dress,
Agnelli has two trademark foibles: he wears
button-down shirts, but likes to leave the buttons
undone; and wears his wristwatch over the cuff of
his shirt. In matters of undress, Agnelli retains an
easy superiority. Caught by a *paparazzo* diving
naked from a boat, Agnelli looked superb. He
proves that *bella figura* involves both appearance
and confidence – each of which he has, in spades.

The empire of ideas
New Statesman & Society, July 1991

The Japanese are very different to you and me.
Deliberately so, on many counts. Inscrutability
was Made in Japan. They claim their language is
impossible for foreigners to learn, but – while
certainly it baffles me – linguists say it is not all
that difficult to speak. Writing may present
special problems, but a basic conversation is not
beyond the means of someone who can manage
in Portuguese or Greek.

An ability to speak Japanese well may depend on
having a creative imagination. If you have an
inventive turn of mind, things may be easier:
'Walkman' is only the most famous of the
gloriously awful Japanese coinages in fractured,
made-good but step-ahead English.

Again, some Japanese believe, against all the
most persuasive evidence, that the gestation
period for their children is ten months, as distinct
from the Euro-normal nine. Some jaded *gaijin*
insiders regard this as possible proof that the
Japanese have, in fact, come from outer space,
since so much of their behaviour is contrary to
what the rest of us regard as human nature. The
more rational explanation is that the Japanese
wish to be seen as biologically different. It would
be wrong to call the Japanese a nation of racists,
but they do have a keen sense of national identity.

Never mind that their art and philosophy and
religion were so contumaciously stolen from
China and Korea, that German technicians
installed Tokyo's pressurized sanitation system,
that even their celebrated late-industrial deity of
'quality control' was introduced in the 1950s by a
group of American engineers. Never mind that
the most successful Japanese cars of recent years
have been designed in America by Americans:
the Japanese want to insist on their uniqueness.

And here, of course, is a paradox of world-
historical dimensions. While they are busy

remorselessly dominating world markets, and equally busy consuming established European brands, they want to remain inaccessible and remote. While they are eager to disport themselves with trinkets from Ralph Lauren, Hermès, Dunhill or Gucci, their fundamental taste for exclusion means that, every now and then, the specification for lenses on the stop-lights on foreign cars is changed so as to involve importers in intolerable expense and frustration. They like cute Minis that present no economic threat, but importers offering a product above the level of curiosity value experience real resistance.

Japan is a country of *bi-attitudes*. The culture may entertain a great sense of beauty, but it has no sense of ugliness. If you were expecting Tokyo to be beguilingly oriental you will be shocked at its trashy mid-western hideousness. On the other hand, if you expected to leap into your Rentacar at Narita airport and drive yourself to your destination – forget it, or we may never see you again. Appearances are at best deceptive, and more likely confusing. Years after the occupying American forces told them it would be a good idea to give streets names, most taxi drivers are lost outside their own district.

For every marvellously minimalist *riyokan*, with its ethereal paper walls subtly dividing space with the elusive precision of a haiku, there is a disgusting lacquered Edwardian cabinet. For every austere tea ceremony there is the baroque, noisy, vulgar and interminable *kabuki* theatre. For every Buddhist rock garden there is a coruscatingly garish *pachinko* parlour full of terrifying low-life specimens with tattoos, flick-knives and some very anti-social habits. It is Western wish-fulfilment to imagine Japan as a culture of cool, dignified restraint. When Aldous Huxley saw the Cherry Dances at Kyoto, he said they were 'extraordinarily vulgar and garish'.

Our Western view of Japan is partial and specific. We have interpreted Japan through the eyes of observers who saw only what they wanted to see. They were conditioned in their perceptions by prevailing Western tastes, and the same is true today. There are many awesome things about modern Tokyo, but there are many awful things as well. Japan is not perfect: 35 per cent of roads are unpaved; fewer than 50 per cent of the population have mains drainage; only 40 per cent of the population even has access to a flushing lavatory, and 80 per cent of Tokyo's electrical cables are overground.

All that – and for every 4.7 metres of paved or unpaved road, you will find a motor car. Visitors are frequently dismayed by the suffocating smell of old fish and, as they are jostled by citizens whose culture teaches them to regard interior space as more valuable than external areas, they wonder wistfully about how these people ever acquired a reputation for ruthless organization.

But we comfort ourselves with our myths about Japan. The most familiar and therefore the most misleading is the one about the Japanese preference for copying over invention. Like all myths, this is no better than a half truth. True, the first Toyota exported to America was to a design that critics described as 'melancholy', but this was not because of any inherent lack of talent in automotive engineering. Rather, the Japanese thought it wasteful to duplicate Western market research and instead, produced dire variations on design themes established as popular by American and European manufacturers. They like them with fins and with chrome and with Wurlitzer steering wheels? Then let them have them. Meanwhile, we can invest the money saved on production technology.

They did, and the result has been, thirty years later, that the Japanese are now so endowed with advanced factories, with so many flexible manufacturing systems, with so many robots that work in the dark, that anything that can be imagined can be manufactured.

The Western preference for competitive individualism has, ironically, undermined Western competitiveness. Future cultural historians will marvel at the curiously elegant fit between Japanese religion (with its dedication to detail, miniaturization, discipline, ritual, routine, definition) and the imperatives of engineering for manufacture. Toyota has a test track with a long stretch of perfectly surfaced road: it is utterly flat except that, near the centre, it rises by a few millimetres to compensate for the curvature of the earth!

In motor racing, even Ford and Renault are occasionally dismayed that, between races, Honda is able to develop entirely new versions of its engines. The company issues unsettling press releases that explain that a successful weight-reduction programme has reduced a certain component by just a few grammes. An awe-inspiring capacity for taking pains, which is how Bach described genius, is supported in Japan by softer cultural factors that enhance national competitiveness. The Japanese have not been hindered by any troublesome concepts of fair play, or gentlemanly behaviour.

What will happen in the future, when Japanese industrial standards so exceed Western abilities that Western models no longer count? By the time you get to a second generation of a new type of machine – say an electronic typewriter – it is simply not possible for the opposition to catch up. Sure, you may have made a stonking loss on development of the first generation, but it was a good investment. The costs you incurred have brought you not just market share, but the entire market. You own it. You have created the technical standards.

No longer can we comfort ourselves with thoughts about the Japanese lack of creativity. That only made sense in the quaint, charming, but utterly redundant Western romantic model. Schubert stays up late and writes another symphony. Creativity is now built into the Japanese industrial system, but not in a self-conscious way. It is an inevitable consequence of the process efficiency built into their factories. Just think that Honda has a product life-cycle approaching 36 months, and imagine the levels of creative and technical resources required to fuel such renewals, and you will understand that this is a game not many nations can play.

The extent and completeness of the Japanese conquest of systems and techniques pioneered by the West is humiliating, when it is not simply bewildering. There used to be David Ricardo's old economic theory about the comparative advantage of nations. Japan shocked the world by having few apparent comparative advantages, but succeeding none the less. In this dubious context, there is some hope for the survival of the West. Now that the old relationship between manufacturing and research is loosening, there is reason to believe that ideas will become the chief economic commodity. Kodak, IBM, and DuPont have research facilities in Japan, just as Mazda has a design centre in Europe and Toyota one in California.

The Japanese have made a religion out of manufacturing. As T. S. Eliot knew: 'A religion requires not only a body of priests who know what they are doing, but a body of worshippers who know what is being done'. The next phase of the industrial revolution will depend on whether the Japanese control the future world of ideas as surely as they control the present world of things.

In the Japanese style
Observer Magazine, 2 March 1980

Kimono. Kyoto. Bullet train. Zen. Hiroshima. Banzai. Nikon. Geisha. Sake. Datsun. Samurai. Crowds. Pollution. Rock gardens. Bonsai. Lacquerware. Sukiyaki. Origami. National Panasonic.

This glittering mish-mash of images of Japan, combining stereotypes of tradition and innovation and confronting the crass and the crude with the subtle and refined, just about represents the average European's total knowledge of that remote country.

Being an isolated archipelago, Japan developed an individual character and tradition, and was able to protect them by maintaining, as the national whim pleased, a vigorous economic and cultural isolationism. But in 1853 the American Commodore Perry gave the Japanese a trade-or-else ultimatum, thus starting the process which led to Pearl Harbor and ended with Toyotas cramming the lots on every mid-western main drag. The Japanese have been busy assimilating Western industrialized capitalism into their 2,500-year-old imperial history ever since. Today Longbridge and Cowley await the first deliveries of knocked-down Hondas to save our motor industry, just fifty years since the company we now know as Datsun started in the motor business by building British Austin Sevens under licence.

Japan is still the only fully industrialized non-Western country. The whole process of catching up with and then overtaking the Western industrial system has taken only a century, and this system had to be incorporated into a culture both adventurous and deeply conservative; Japanese life maintains a sophisticated dualism which goes beyond the superficial juxtaposition of Western artefacts and ancient culture. A Toyota executive, looking all day as though he could be drip-dried in his entirety, changes into a traditional kimono at home in the evening. At

Matsushita Electric, to encourage the corporate spirit, employees wearing bandannas with the company logogram do early morning knee-bends, shouting what could easily be the old battle cry 'Tora! Tora! Tora!'

A dualism exists too in Japanese traditional art and modern artefacts. On the one hand is the parched, elegant pattern-making of the print-masters Hiroshige or Hokusai, where nature, while always respected, is bent into decorative patterns; on the other is the fantastic, excessive splendour of a Buddhist shrine. The austere sensibleness of a Nikon camera co-exists with the shockingly vulgar food made of plastic, surreal in its authenticity, which is used everywhere to stimulate the appetites of restaurant-goers, apparently to general delight.

If this plastic food fails to please the aesthete, it is typically Japanese in at least one way, its fanatical dedication to ... effect. There is the same dedication with edible food: confronted with a Japanese meal of raw tuna served on a wooden block with little pyramids of horseradish and a cucumber sliced to translucence, you don't know whether to eat it or contemplate it.

Simplicity, in food or interior design, is a source of inspiration for all Japanese. It is no paradox that the familiar Spartan interiors of Japan were favoured not by unworldly monks, but by the warrior classes.

Rather before they started beating us at our own game, the Japanese had already had a significant influence on American and British design through their influence on the crafts revival. The Cornish potter Bernard Leach trained in Japan, and lovingly documented articles on Japanese skills appeared in the influential American magazine *Craft Horizons*. But the material objects of modern Japan most familiar to the West are its universal consumer durables. The high-tech glow of the light-emitting diode and the sybaritic sheen of satin-finished stainless steel have become the frankincense and myrrh of a generation which, from Fifth to Shaftesbury Avenues, prizes well-packaged baubles and bibelots.

Why do the Japanese succeed in product design? It is not only because they make things no one else can – at any price – but because their design has an appeal which transcends cultural differences. Miniaturization and compactness are qualities which people everywhere seem to find fascinating. The Japanese taste for compactness finds poetic expression in the condensed forms of the *haiku*. It is also expressed in combining, with bewildering virtuosity, a radio, television and cassette recorder into a box no bigger than a twin lens reflex camera, or by getting a six-cylinder motor-bike engine into a space where Triumph and BSA used to manage engines of only one.

It was of course motor bikes which, after cameras and before stereos and cars, became popularly associated with modern Japan and introduced the West to the patterns of marketing and design philosophy which have since become familiar. Too familiar, some would say.

Honda is now considered a softer less raunchy competitor to, say, Kawasaki in the field of motor bikes with pumping stations for engines. But it was Honda that blew apart the complacent British bike industry of the late 1960s with a highly developed, innovative design. This *machina ex deo*, the famed 750 Four, had a then unheard-of multiplicity of tiny, endearing cylinders, sophistications like an electric starter and engineering features like a front disc brake (which British manufacturers thought could never be incorporated on a motor bike). Wiping out the opposition with this awesome brute, Honda was

soon able to name its own terms in a market it now completely dominated.

This pattern recurred: hot-shot marketing that made Madison Avenue look like basket-weaving at play school was combined with a Japanese tradition of fanatical attention to detail and devotion to the exquisite and tiny. The Honda engineers who designed pistons the size of pepper pots also carried around in their pockets little Buddhas in lacquer boxes about as big as a halfpenny piece.

Cars followed the bikes. At first they appeared to howls of derision because they had names like gastric disorders, but their attractiveness in a market which could not get enough Cortinas was soon apparent.

Japanese cars are the most difficult of modern products to assimilate into a model of Japanese culture. They do *not* on the whole have a reputation for engineering inventiveness, but they do have one for reliability. Won over by this, the public is often helplessly seduced by the curious visual interest some Japanese cars possess. The baroque and entirely extraneous mouldings on, say, a Datsun suggest a culture struggling to develop a familiar form for an as yet unfamiliar machine. But sensitive international markets demand blandness, and it seems unlikely that Japanese car designers will be able to develop their own repertoire.

It is in audio equipment, where, because of their almost total dominance of the amateur market the Japanese do not have to consider the competition, that the manufacturers have been able to invent a vernacular style of their own: stainless steel, simulated hard-grain wood, a Krakatoa of knobs, dials, VU-meters, flick switches, tumblers, LED read-outs, coiled coaxial cable and, latterly, a disturbing trend towards marshy green militarism in the AM/FM portables … all these arranged in a pattern to make the player of a Mantovani disc in Bromley feel more like Captain Kirk than Jimmy Young. That's symbolism.

Yet … in the postmodern age, when Design Council 'if-it's-geometrical-and-primary-colours-we'll-take-six-dozen' no longer holds effective sway over the hearts, minds and credit cards of men, designers are beginning to acknowledge that the complex mayhem of a Panasonic tuner more accurately reflects the real nature of the electrical gubbins within than does the admired, cool, sleek, self-conscious minimalism of Bang & Olufsen or Braun.

Time was when the West operated a kind of industrial imperialism in the East, a commercial adventure reflected in our culture when *Madame Butterfly, japonisme* and weird expatriate writers like Lafcadio Hearn charmed us with Japanese folklore. Latterly, apart from Resnais's *Hiroshima Mon Amour* and James Clavell's best-selling novel *Shogun*, Western culture has shown less interest in Japan.

Now, while astute Western minds ponder the trade gap, the Japanese are engrossed in our culture. The enthusiasm is genuine, but it often has comic results. Western script and the English language are considered chic. The fashion designer Issey Miyake chose his own first name because, to him, it sounded authentically Western.

Although so many of its products are familiar to the point of invisibility, Japan itself remains tantalizingly remote to Europeans. The industrial capital and the country are very different, another aspect of its dualism. Tokyo is not Japan. Maples still grow in temple grounds in Shiga Prefecture; Buddhist priests still meditate in moss gardens; moon viewing rituals take place; cranes still fly; carp kites billow in the mountains.

Meanwhile… another BL dealership fell to Datsun.

On the shifting sands of Californian design
Design, June 1990

Reyner Banham was something of a rarity – a design writer of pedigree. Banham, even his best friends would agree, could be waspish, but in his writing he combined a level of articulate wit with a depth of hard-won knowledge rare in any age and unheard of in our own.

Banham was a genius who had met everyone and if he hadn't, knew someone else who had. I once said we should set an exam question about 'Less is More' and Banham said to me 'Aw, come on, sonny, everybody knows that was Philip Johnson not Mies'. I corpsed, but went back to look it up in the archives and found Banham himself quoting it in the original as *'Wehniger ist mehr'*. I'd been had.

Banham himself was had by California. He was seduced by it. The last time I saw him really properly was ten years ago in Santa Cruz. Disappointed by life at University College London and still inflamed by the American Dream, Banham left England for good not so long after he had published *Los Angeles: The Architecture of Four Ecologies*.

He eventually got a longed-for position in the University of California at Santa Cruz. It was a happy time, but the sad thing was that the California Reyner Banham was longing for no longer existed. Here was this great man in lonely Santa Cruz at Christmas 1980, arriving at the party when everybody else had gone. Seeing him there reminded me of nothing so much as that terrible wall-scrawl: 'As soon I find out where it's at, they move it'.

California is a vacuum which designers abhor and they rush to fill it. Ever since 1911 when the Horsley brothers rented an abandoned Los Angeles tavern at Sunset and Gower and used it to film actors, most of them drunk, with Edison's new moving picture machines, California has

been a laboratory for images. This must be the precise reason why it fascinates: it is like a perfect market, open to any influence, drawing them in.

It was in California that Harley Earl, who was a neighbour of Cecil B. DeMille, set up his custom car shop which subsequently reversed into General Motors and, from 1927, laid the basis for American car styling. On Chautauqua Boulevard 1948-9 John Entenza, editor of *Arts and Architecture* magazine, sponsored 'Case Study Houses' by Charles Eames (from prefabricated industrial components), by Eames and Eoro Saarinen (International Style) and Richard Neutra (redwood and brick). Eames's house, in particular, exerted a very particular influence over the history of architecture during the next twenty-five years. Similarly, it was in the 1950s that the Sports Car Club of America helped to create the sports-car cult. Sure, Britain was already manufacturing TR2s, Austin-Healeys and Jaguars, but there was something about the magic realism of Californian light and sunshine that made these cars look more at home in the San Fernando Valley than in Barnet. California has a scale and an appetite for mythologizing that translates ordinary events into legends. It was in California that a straightforward car crash helped to create the Porsche fable. The driver of the car which hit the pick-up was James Dean.

California takes people and things, magnifies them and as a consequence distorts them. Los Angeles is a terrible place: *Architectural Record* found in 1973 that 'without its people and its cars and its activity' the city 'will make a lousy ruin'. The only real monuments Los Angeles has are the ones where people, cars and activity get together: on the freeways. Banham was almost obsessed by the San Diego-Santa Monica intersection which he lovingly described with the visitor's sense of wonder as 'a work of art, both as a pattern on the map, as a monument against the sky, and as a kinetic experience as one sweeps through it'.

Marilyn Reese, the resident structural engineer responsible, was a little more sober: 'Our objective was to supply specifications that would conform to the engineering standards of a 50mph curve, while making it as pleasing as possible'.

Detroit executives used to go to California to discover what people were buying because it has always been so open to influences (it was in California that Japanese cars were seen for the first time in the West). Detroit's problem was that by the time the executives got back to Michigan, they had forgotten what they had learned.

But since they had also left behind the hallucinatory reality of the desert and the ocean, it probably didn't matter.

An office you can't refuse
GQ, February – March 1989

Once you accept that gestures have meaning, that there is no such thing as a mute or inarticulate choice, then you are locked into a dialogue with things which our education ill equips us to understand. Mugs with dead biros; dog-eared Post-It notes; stress-fractured paper clips; yellowing cuttings. All that dross on your desk is eloquent, if not benign. Your desk itself says something about you, the wastepaper basket even more. These things speak. That much is certain and undisputed, but the territory for exploration and speculation commences with the deadly questions: 'What is it saying?' and 'What does it mean?'

The top of your desk is an altar where the rituals of the professional work ethic are celebrated. We all know the dizzy individuals who make a downbeat virtue of untidiness and the office Nazis who like clear desks and empty bins (or, failing that, the stationery aligned orthogonally). But, as with so many other things, the meaning here is quite the opposite of what it appears to the uninformed.

The desk lout is disingenuous: chaos in the office is, in fact, an arrogant demonstration of a tidy mind. No organism other than a well-drilled and disciplined brain could find its way through a mess. Only those whose minds are in turmoil need to have their desk and their office display the regularity and retentive neatness of a Swiss nuclear medicine research lab. But these are mere details, and what concerns us here are larger ideas, a broader canvas.

Like other religions, the work ethic has its instruments. You, as the officiating priest, must jealously guard them. It is this powerful mixture of personal symbolism, professional status and primitive territory which makes people so possessive about their desk tops. This is why one of my most memorable moments was when I saw for the first time the chairman of a large company go into his chief executive's office (with the man *in situ*) and start rearranging the papers and knick-knacks. In psycho-social terms such an intrusion compares with rape. The chairman still does it, although the executive has been demoted and has taken to drink.

This intrusion is a devastating form of the 'I know better than you and I'm not afraid to show it' phenomenon. It demonstrates that the office is a battleground where the major conflicts of status are rehearsed and then fought. Like every other instrument of status in the contemporary world, the office cannot be fully understood outside the context of consumer society. The modern office is a product of industrialized capitalism and was simply not known in the age before Adam Smith. Only when the division of labour occurred was there any need for certain functionaries to be separated from the workforce and here, in this epochal distinction between capital and labour, was the missing link created: the factory manager and all his unique trappings (Bakelite desk-set, car firm, girlie calendars, metal filing cabinets).

In the earliest stage of the office, there were only middle-men; the owners stayed at the big house on the hill, beat their wives, played the piano, had incest and counted their money. It was only with the maturation of the joint stock idea that offices developed internal hierarchies, just as big fleas have little fleas. Of course, this development occurred first in the United States and was described and damned by Sinclair Lewis in *The Job* (1916). The dominant forms of the office are named after those heroes of American capitalism who gave the different phases in the history of wage-slavery their characteristic form: the Frick, the IBM (sometimes known as the DuPont) and the Boesky.

It was in 1913 that Elsie de Wolfe, the pioneer interior decorator, performed one of the most memorable acts in the history of modern material culture when, by spending three million dollars on antiques, she introduced Henry Clay Frick's new American money to a lot of her chums' old French furniture. Ever since, WASP America has tended to validate it status at work with the support of antiques. Even beyond the East Coast Frick, Carnegie, Mellon and Vanderbilt culture, a craving for status through the acquisition of olden-days furniture supported generations of 'executives'. In England, the same taste finds expression in sporting prints and framed photographs of the chairman's daughter eventing.

Readers of John Z. DeLorean's ghosted autobiography *On a Clear Day You Can See General Motors* know that as late as the 1960s things had not changed too much in Detroit since Alfred Sloan made the world's biggest joint stock assemblage out of a car boot sale of hand-me-down chickenshit companies. Up on the fourteenth floor of the celebrated General Motors building, while the Pontiac plant was turning out the wild tyre-melting, street-racing GTO, DeLorean and his cronies were ensconced in office environments whose wood panelling and ancient plush made New York's Plaza Hotel Oak Room look like a *pachinko* parlour. Their minions, in their thousands, were established in bullpens. Their minions, in turn, were in typing factories.

And, of course, a reaction was established. IBM was later on the joint stock game than GM, and necessarily peaked a decade later. The GTO notwithstanding, GM's peak years and the climax of the Frick style were the 1950s. IBM's was the 1960s. But the influence was again European. While the lumbering and inefficient GM was the inevitable consequence of the Frick, Carnegie and Mellon coal and steel culture, so IBM was of the postwar baby boom and the electronic systems which supported it. Thomas Watson Jnr, the son of the founder, knew that mahogany and 'Looey Cans' furniture was not appropriate to the information age, so he asked a Harvard architect called Eliot Noyes to help him out. Noyes had been taught by Walter Gropius, who had by both nature and nurture learned a few things about how to flush out your psyche. In one of the most epigrammatic bits of consultancy never yet to feature on business-school syllabuses Noyes, after a depressing survey of IBM's Frick-style offices and Rube Goldberg consumer products, said: 'You would prefer neatness'.

And neatness had a European name. From the leaden brownness of Frick and sporting prints and fire tongs and console desks and blotters came a Blitzkrieg of flexible partitions and storage systems and tasklights and free form space called Burolandschaft. This 'office landscape' was the handiwork of a new breed of designer, the space planners, experts whose relationship to architecture may be compared to that of the McDonalds' marketing team to the *Michelin Guide Rouge*. They were in rebellion against not only the crepuscular Frick but also against the rigidity of early modernist interiors with their suspended ceilings and grid patterns.

But the IBM style itself fell victim to the inevitable technological progress which the company had created, rather as if Armonk, NY, were translated into the setting for a classical tragedy. By about 1985, with Apple coming from the West and the Japanese coming from the East, IBM and its office style was as flabby as General Motors had once looked. What is more, with life insurance companies in Swindon and Dundee easily parodying the style of a corporation that once looked as if it was about to rule the world, the IBM lost its status as the ultimate executive office.

By liberating the office plan from the structure of the building, these wild-eyed space-planners had

set in train a revolution which other forces soon joined. Suddenly, corporate raiders called Perot, Icahn and Boesky looked more powerful than Fortune 500 companies like IBM and DuPont and, simultaneously, the neat architectural style of Eliot Noyes and the space-planners, which had once conveyed effortless corporate power and the hum of an efficient capitalist engine, stalled. During curative maintenance its specification was discovered to be last year's model's. For as soon as Ivan Boesky began to be photographed with two phones in each hand scanning a mission control of VDUs, the loose corporatism of Burolandschaft looked quaint.

Marshall McLuhan predicted that in Boesky's electronic village we would all work at home, even if home has bars on the window. This technological storm is upon us and it has come at the time when another fine new concept has entered the world of commercial ideas. Look at PLC letterheads and you will often see the rubric 'From the Office of the Chairman'. This chairman is not in the house on the hill, nor even minding the shop, but on the highroad of enterprise culture. With faxes available in cars (if not yet in prisons), the bricks and mortar of The Office of the Chairman have never had less real purpose.

In 1984 two Italian designers, Vincenzo Iavicoli and Maria Luisa Rossi, proposed a 'walking office', a hybrid between jewellery and technology rather like a miniature, chromium-plated version of a military communications system. It is too early to say, but Iavicoli may yet join Frick, IBM and Boesky.

**Part Eight
Museums and Monuments**

Cars for cathedrals
New Society, 23 May 1985

Britain is shortly to have the world's first museum of design. It will be a unique venture which will benefit anybody who has either a professional interest or a personal curiosity about why things that are made look and behave the way they do. Located at Butler's Wharf, near Tower Bridge, in London's Docklands, the project has been made possible by a gift of £4 million from the Habitat founder, Sir Terence Conran. There is only one problem: what to call it.

The launch took place in March, at a dinner hosted by the Prime Minister in Downing Street. Ever since she was Minister of Education, Mrs Thatcher has had a keen interest in design, and she endorsed the venture with characteristic passion. Her only reservation was the name 'museum'. She said it sounded antiquarian and insisted that anything concerned with design must necessarily be *progressive*.

The Conran Foundation had no argument with that. Design is the business of change; if you are involved in design – of packaging, the environment, information, products – the assumption is that you know how to do something better than your predecessor. You know how to make a bucket more durable, more attractive, more profitable; you can sell more cars, add more style, add more value, give the consumer *and* the manufacturer tangible benefits, receipts for their money. So, yes, design necessarily should be fresh and new, so perhaps it is absurd to shackle so bright and thrusting a thing of the future to so weary a vehicle as … the museum.

But what *is* a museum? To understand the museum of the future, you have to understand the museum of the past. Not least because of what the critic, George Santayana, said about those people who are ignorant of history: they are condemned to repeat it.

The word itself, of course, is Greek. A *museoin* was the home of the Muses, a pre-classical arts centre. Look it up in, say *Larousse Universel*, and you will see that museum with a capital M was the portion of the Palace of Alexandria where they had the library and where the celebrated savants and philosophers gathered. It was the rediscovery of classical values during the European Renaissance that brought the museum as an institution into being. The Renaissance necessarily entailed an awareness of the past that was entirely novel, the perception that history was not static or cyclical (as the Greeks themselves had thought), but linear and progressive.

From the beginning, with the architect Bramante fitting out the niches of a Vatican cloister with sculpture, the museum has been associated with an idea of progress because the Renaissance revival of classical values depended on the idea that you could only make better art in the future if you studied the best art of the past. To this idea the eighteenth-century Enlightenment brought scientific order; not only did scholars like Winckelmann rationalize the papal and aristocratic taste for collecting antiquities, but a democratic influence was actually brought to bear on the collections themselves.

Throughout Europe, in spasms of pre-revolutionary munificence, the collections of antiques and curios gathered on the grand tour were available to the public: Schiller remarked that the famous collection of antique casts at Mannheim gave 'Every inhabitant ... and every stranger ... the unlimited freedom to enjoy the treasures of antiquity'.

In Britain, a new generation of middle-class consumers who could not afford to go to Italy to collect authentic antiques had their aspirations satisfied by artist-merchants – men such as John

Cheere and Josiah Wedgwood. Cheere ran a sculpture yard at Hyde Park Corner (illustrated on the frontispiece of Hogarth's *Analysis of Beauty*) to provide reproduction lead 'antiques' so that middle-class customers could create little museums of their own. Wedgwood did the same with ceramics.

It was in France that the museum as a modern institution became properly established. In 1792 the Assemblée Nationale decided to turn the old royal palace, the Louvre, into a museum so that Napoleon could have somewhere to store the loot confiscated on his trawls through Europe. The incidental advantage of this was that so magnificent a collection of art appeared to offer the *arriviste* from Corsica the sanction of the past. Elsewhere in Europe, this same desire to give cultural credentials to new nation states was the inspiration for the creation of many a famous museum. In Munich, the Wittelsbach family, raised to the Kingship of Bavaria by Napoleon, created the Glyptothek (or sculpture gallery) both to advertise their own credentials and to offer lessons in taste for their new citizens.

More immediately practical rationales for the creation of museums were found in Britain, where a long continuous history of stable government gave no cause for the creation of museums on the Munich model. In Britain, museums had to be created to help with *exports*. A parliamentary select committee report on Arts and Manufactures (or what we would call 'design') was published in 1836 and, then as now, pointed out that British industry was failing with respect to the competition because neither the manufacturers nor the consumers had the right sort of models to educate and inspire them. One of the host of expert witnesses called in to give advice was from the new Prussian museum in Berlin. He said that Britain should be creating 'collections of the most beautiful models of furniture and of different objects of manufacture,' and putting them into buildings where the public might see them and, at a stroke, the toiling masses of Coventry and Birmingham could be translated into new patrons of the industrial arts.

It was this report that led indirectly to the creation of what is now the Victoria & Albert Museum, that great nineteenth-century institution, committed by its zealous and over-active creator, Henry Cole, to reforming arts and manufactures. With all the moral certainty characteristic of his age, Cole knew exactly what to do: he created a 'chamber of horrors' where he displayed manufactured goods which displayed what seemed to him 'false principles' in design, thus wittily reversing the accepted role of the museum in offering not paradigms for imitation, but shocking examples to avoid.

Design, by its nature, is a dynamic subject, but the civil service exists in a large part to resist movement and change and so, when Cole's museum was progressively institutionalized, the original irreverent and reforming spirit which created it was driven out to make room for bureaucrats and keepers, instead of leaders and critics. The V. & A. continued its magnificent way and became the world's outstanding custodial museum of the applied arts; the price it paid for this status was to lose its dynamism and replace it with a vast collection of treasures.

There has been nothing much to replace it during the twentieth century. Certainly, there have been museums in our own age, but they have all been created with one or other version of the animus which made an obscure Bavarian family build a sculpture hall in Munich. The Museum of Modern Art in New York, which began with a reforming zeal somewhat like Henry Cole's, soon became institutionalized. Instead of beating the drum to the rhythm of the convictions of its founders, it

evolved into a temple of preciousness as exquisite and as irrelevant as the pedimental sculptures of the Temple of Aphaia at Aegina, chief ornament of the Glyptothek. The Museum of Modern Art has to flatter the tastes of its wealthy patrons, whose collections would be severely devalued if the museum were ever to adopt the causes of doubt, criticism or revision.

Similarly, in Paris, the Centre Pompidou is a heroic symbol of the *dirigiste* economy gone funky, while in Germany, the new museums in Stuttgart, Moenchengladbach and Frankfurt demonstrate only that the children of the *Wirtschaftswunder* are determined to obliterate memories of the Third Reich with beautifully detailed repositories of *Kultur*, bought with the surpluses of Daimler-Benz and BMW.

This leaves Britain with the option and the opportunity to create a truly modern museum, one dedicated to the explication and reform of the modern world. Just as nineteenth-century culture demanded collections of antique statuary to edify and educate its citizenry, our century demands that its own monuments – the Citroën 2CV, the Boeing 747, the Vespa, Pentel, Olivetti ET111, the Doyle Dane Bernbach Volkswagen campaign – be understood. The real culture of the twentieth century is out there on the street, as Roland Barthes once remarked (echoing Moholy-Nagy and predicting Tom Wolfe): 'Cars are our cathedrals'.

There is a familiar and convincing argument that during the twentieth century, technology has replaced art in its ability to exalt and astonish us, but this does not mean that the new design museum will make the mistake of treating the fruits of industry exactly as if they were strums of the Muses' lyres. There will be a permanent collection of the excellent, successful and astounding products, but they will not simply be on tastefully lit plinths. They will be surrounded by the marketing and technical data which allows an object to be understood in context. Together with this permanent collection there will be a continuously changing international review of current products, as well as a space for temporary, thematic exhibitions which can also be used for presentations of new designs.

Design is going to be ever more important in the future, but by that I don't mean that it will be more than ever important to wear bow-ties or carry a brightly-coloured plastic briefcase. Design is a catch-all term which means both the process and the product of *material culture*. Economic changes in the nineteenth century created the 'right' and the 'left' in politics. One expression of this was focused manufacturing and the transfer line. That economic system brought with it certain assumptions; for instance, that modern products have to be the same because in order to be cheap they have to be produced in high volume. Long lead times, long runs, identical products are now a thing of the past.

The new technology will actually become our politics because it is all about the reorganization of work. The new information and communications systems will change the shape of the world as certainly as electricity and radio once did because they shift the primary creative challenge from merely tinkering with the look of things, to an opportunity for moderating all of experience.

The old museums were created to control and administer and impose standards on the last industrial revolution; the new design museum is going to help provide some of the creative resources for the next one. There is the prospect of creating an electronic version of what André Malraux once memorably called a 'museum without walls'.

The best designers, the best manufacturers and the best retailers will be better still with more ideas, images and information at their disposal. It is an old idea, but one with a lot of promise.

We don't need our history packaged by this Trust
Evening Standard, 27 February 1995

It's often said that the National Trust is an authentic expression of that idiosyncratic British talent for doing odd things extremely well. Like narrow-gauge steam railways, double-decker buses, black cabs and Scout huts, it is a unique national institution.

Nowhere else on earth does such expertise and commitment go towards preserving and displaying the remains of a patchy national architectural history. And it is extremely successful and popular, with more members (its supporters eagerly tell you) than all the political parties combined, as if this proves a point. But 'successful' and 'popular'? So are Pop Tarts and *Blind Date*.

With its portfolio of civilized-sounding concerns about preserving natural and man-made places of beauty, criticizing the Trust is not for the timorous. Critics risk being demonized as destructive philistines, whingers, knockers or whatever personality defect is assumed to attach to those odd small voices who speak up against the morose imposition of 'heritage' on to everyday life.

But with its dominant position in our imagination, only the dullest person can resist asking searching questions about exactly what the Trust does and why it does it.

Agreed, in the business of tarting-up old piles and merchandising them to an eager, if dimly uncritical, public, the National Trust has no equal. Nowhere else outside Anaheim, Orlando, Marne-la-Vallée, or wherever Disney strikes next, can such glibly consumerized packages of stylized history be found. Yes! Elderly drivers of Rover 214s in quilted jackets and harassed parents in Japanese estate cars and leisure-suited grannies on coach trips find the National Trust offers 'a good day out'. But does not life offer any higher goals? At what cost to our national morale are these days our being provided?

The National Trust was established exactly 100 years ago by a group of well-meaning Fabians, contemporaries of Bernard Shaw and the inventors of rambling and cycling. Before modern town-planning legislation, its enlightened purpose was to preserve wild coastlines, heath, forests, marshes and commonland for the invigorating use of Everyman.

Only in 1936 did it begin to change its character and direct itself not towards the democratic preservation of open spaces, but towards a far more divisive policy of preserving decrepit country houses and, indeed, their decrepit owners. Its character, purpose and direction were immediately transformed and in all essentials this is the National Trust we have today, trapped in its obligations to a distorted version of history which is the inheritance not so much of antiquity as of a more recent twentieth-century taste.

The National Trust was hijacked by a single individual: James Lees-Milne, who in 1936 became secretary of the infamous Country House Scheme.

Between the wars when the continued presence of old established families in their old established houses, the energetic and ambitious Lees-Milne saw the National Trust not as a means of allowing the dispossessed of Plaistow to have a breath of fresh air, but as an institution which might secure in perpetuity the homes of his cronies and of those would-be cronies whose social peaks he was yet to climb.

Lees-Milne bicycled hither and yon, having tea with a bewildered Lord-this, staying the night with a confused Lord-that, and, after negotiations, passed on to the rest of us an extraordinary catalogue of more than 200 fine old houses.

As anybody who has read his elegant architectural essays and his waspish diaries knows, Lees-Milne was not only an opportunist and an aesthete, but an excruciating snob as well. But it is wrong to see the National Trust as an upper-class conspiracy, even if random paragraphs from Lees-Milne's accounts of his National Trust years read like competitive entries in some sort of Trivial Pursuit name-dropping combination.

No, the funny thing is that while Lees-Milne and his Country House Scheme are guardians of an exclusive and restrictive sort of privilege, today's National Trust is not an élitist organization. Its problem is that it is so bourgeois; an atmosphere of suffocating complacency and unquestioning smugness surrounds the staff and its members, all caught in a collective delusion fabricated fifty years ago.

Of course, there are worse things than wanting to preserve eighteenth-century houses, but there are better things as well. The absurdity of the National Trust is that, having convinced aristocratic owners to hand over their houses 'inalienably' and 'in perpetuity', it is now incarcerated in a prison of its own making. Despite the odd limp attempt to acquire an Art Deco cinema or a modernist house in Hampstead, the personality of the Trust is still dominated, even overwhelmed, by its inheritance. It is locked in an unbreakable, self-sustaining cycle of middle-brow gentility.

Ignoring the smelly presence of potpourri and rubbishy knick-knacks in the Trust's atrocious shops, there are two other reasons why this is a bad thing.

The first is that once the National Trust acquires a house it then primps and polishes it to a state of fanciful perfection which devastates its spirit.

True, these old houses are popular with visitors, but they are seeing a mausoleum. Buildings are living things which change and evolve: preserve something living and you kill it. The experience which National Trust visitors have is a diminished one. Never mind the absurdity of his superannuated lordship living in a staff flat while the crocodile of grannies titters at the nudes, the important aesthetic point is this: to look at something you believe to be beautiful and to fear that it may be gone tomorrow is an intensely moving experience. But to look at the same thing and know that it's inalienably protected in perpetuity is a bit of a dead loss.

But worse than the dead loss is what the National Trust does to the national spirit. It tells us that the best is in the past, that the worst is yet to come. Any reader of James Lees-Milne knows that his attitude to the here and now is at best one of barely tolerant scepticism. It is depressing that someone so privileged and talented should see such little value in the modern world. His inheritors share this view. The National Trust turns us into unresponsive custodians of culture rather than active participants in it.

It would be foolish to say that the National Trust is a cause of that nostalgic malaise which has so affected British life in the twentieth century and so hobbled every attempt to come to terms with modern life, but it is certainly a symptom of it.

Fine buildings will look after themselves, it's the people that are the problem. Do let's have a National Trust, but let it be as radical and original as it was meant to be. 'There are,' said Beatrix Potter, an early Trust supporter 'some silly mortals connected with it, but they will pass'. Let's hope so.

A haven for modern muses
Weekend Guardian, 1 – 2 July 1989

The achievements of civilization can be measured by the naming of its parts. In fact, degrees of civilization could be quantified by the number of discrete human activities that have been identified: primitive societies have few; sophisticated cultures a lot. Progress affords us a reflective distance from the hurly-burly of survival. In this way religion becomes separated from magic, art from work, industry from science.

But at what stage in the evolution of a subject should a museum be created to cultivate it? The west and north wings of the British Museum were built in the 1830s to house a growing collection of classical antiquities. The Natural History Museum is a product of the 1870s, when a new biology was ready to radicalize the idea of evolution. Applied art was separated from applied science when the Victoria and Albert and the Science Museum were created, out of the old Department of Science and Art, in the first decade of this century.

And now, nearing a millennium, we have a Design Museum. There are cynics – quite a lot, I'm afraid – who will say that, after a decade of flashy materialism, commodity fetishism and the brightly coloured froth surrounding designer-this or designer-that, the best place to put them is *in* a museum. But that would be to misunderstand a subject that goes back to Vitruvius and to devalue an institutional idea that goes back to the Muses. Design existed long before bored editors of colour supplements discovered the Milan Furniture Fair.

Design has a history at least as important as literature and the fine arts and, since it involves both commerce and culture, a future that is perhaps even more promising. Similarly, museums – while antique in origin – are only at the infantile phase of their development. With an eye on the future rather than the past, I'd say the two were made for each other.

If you look at it etymologically, design comes from the Italian word 'drawing'. Drawing was the first means by which ideas about the visual character of things were communicated. From this usage came its subsidiary, but significant meaning 'intention'. Put communication and intention together and you have a subject so huge that it potentially embraces the entirety of human endeavour.

Design is what gives meaning and quality to the products of industry. Designers emerge in any economy which has raised itself above the solemn rituals of subsistence. The first museum was the home of the daughters of Zeus and Mnemosyne; Erato, Terpsichore and Calliope among them. But the modern muses are industry, commerce and technology. The Design Museum is their home. But what will be in it, and what else is it for?

The Design Museum limits its scope by looking at design for mass production, specifically excluding craft at one end and pure technology at the other. The concept was originally Terence Conran's. At the height of a career devoted to bringing better merchandise to the marketplace – and thereby covertly educating the public – Conran was able by the late 1970s to create an educational body to provide for students and the public 'something as useful for today as the V. & A. was for me'.

The first plan was to create a high-tech building in Milton Keynes where robot stacker trucks would whizz up and down aisles retrieving 'masterpiece' fridges for scrutiny. This reverie was interrupted when Sir Roy Strong discovered our plans and, with a characteristic gesture mixing flair with audacity, suggested that whatever we were doing we should consider starting doing it in the V. & A.

Since the ghosts of Prince Albert and Henry Cole had been looming around Conran's and my conversations, this seemed especially appropriate. Thus we were busily distracted by the Boilerhouse Project and its exhibitions about Taste, Coke, Bags, Sony, and the Ford Sierra. That it became London's most popular gallery of the 1980s confirmed our conviction that design was a sufficiently important subject to deserve a museum of its own.

And of course, it is not going to be a museum in any conventional sense. The unwritten epigraph of the Design Museum is: 'You can't win souls in an empty church'. The building is a landmark, an ingenious reconstruction of a Thames-side warehouse whose uncompromising neo-modern style and touches of 1930s parody admit that the best design usually contains elements of wit.

Within the dazzling white box the visitor will find a marble hall where Perrier has sponsored continually changing exhibitions about graphics; an international review of new and speculative projects; a revival of the original Boilerhouse; and a major study collection, as well as a library, lecture theatre, restaurant, and bar. Unlike most museums where education is too often an afterthought, it is the sole intention of the Design Museum.

As a body it is international in scope and critical and evaluative in purpose. It is not concerned with technical education nor with trade promotion; nor does it exist to validate any particular version of modern design. But it is dedicated to the proposition, originally Conran's, that a better educated *consumer* will be able to make more discriminating choices, thus forcing up standards from retailers to manufacturers. In short, the Design Museum addresses the question: what does 'design' mean in a nation retreating from manufacturing *things*? The answer is simple: it means *visual education*.

I don't expect the Museum will be an empty church. It will be active rather than passive, using all available resources to realize its educational purposes and in doing so extending its concept. First there will be television. The process of organizing an exhibition is much the same as making a TV programme, you get an idea, write a script, do a storyboard and interview people. Only at the last stage does the process differ: in exhibitions the resolution involves medieval technology like glue and nails, while TV does it electronically. The Design Museum will turn its exhibitions *into* television, creating a far wider constituency.

But having industry and commerce sponsoring exhibitions and programmes does not mean the Design Museum is going to be merely a slick agent for the multinationals. Engaging commercial interests in the educational process proves that at this stage of civilization industry does not need to *buy* culture because industry *is* culture.

Eventually the Design Museum and its public will become involved in new product development. Say we have an idea about a green diesel motorbike; we find a third party to sponsor a design; we make this process into an exhibition and invite visitors to comment. The idea evolves so that this product which has been test-marketed, can be passed to a manufacturer. This involvement of the public with designers and industry is surely *culture* in the purest sense.

When the Design Museum opens on Thursday, it will be the beginning, not the end. Its contribution? To remove the distinction between art and work.

Bauhaus on Thames
Blueprint, 1989

Now the whole world and its marketing directors know about 'design', it is becoming urgent to decide what it actually means before it gets junked along with a lot of other words that have got separated from their meanings. Sometimes it seems a very fugitive subject, a vagabond in the visual arts. There are academic departments of 'art and design', or journals – like this one – of 'architecture and design', but design itself seems to resist precise definition, as you would expect of any subject which can accommodate both hairdressers and aerospace engineers.

When the word stands alone, as it does on the radio blanking plate in certain cars, where it says, meaninglessly, 'Whatsit Design', it seems trivial and meretricious. Alternatively, seeking a broader definition, a term which can be applied to almost any aspect of human endeavour during the industrialized centuries must inevitably be so flexible of definition as to be useless. Since it is often said that 'everything has been designed', then surely it follows that almost everyone is a designer? But Edmund Burke knew that a clear idea is another name for a little idea. Clearly, design is a big one and the new Design Museum, at last becoming a reality ten years after the idea was first hatched, has been created to cope by bringing clarity to a popular, but elusive, subject.

The Museum is housed in a 42,000 square foot building and will present a range of exhibitions of different durations, treating mass-produced consumer design in different ways. There is a study collection of remarkable design on the top floor, containing more than 400 different objects, some well known, others less so: this is the Museum's point of reference. Below is a revival of the Boilerhouse, which, with its provocative exhibitions, will be comparable to the features pages of a newspaper. In front of that, on the same floor, is a review of new and speculative products, intended to offer a shop window on innovation:

the news and current affairs part of the Museum. But with all this design on display, how are we to understand what it means?

In that distant civilization before industrialized production brought about what Dostoevsky, in all his lonely suffering, despised as 'cheap happiness', 'design' meant something similar to intention. Sir Christopher Wren interpreted it as skill in composition, detail and massing, and used capitalization to illustrate it: 'The duly poising of all Parts to equiponderate; without which, a fine Design will fail and prove abortive. Hence I conclude, that all designs must, in the first place be brought to this Test, or rejected'.

To the cultured dilettante of the eighteenth century, 'design' was certain qualities – say, wisdom and propriety – in the mind of the artist, it merely requiring 'genius', exemplified for instance by Wren, to give them form. But the first age of mass production brought popular choice into play and while a century before, privileged virtuosi had debated taste in their salons, by the middle of the nineteenth century all the material world was on display in museums and department stores. Here was a nationalized culture, waiting to be rationalized by design.

The way to particularize any meaning of design was not now to declare it an example of genius at work equi-ponderating, but to attach moralizing qualifiers. 'Design' has always meant something special, but it was in the Victorian age of moral certainties that the curious notion of 'good' design was born. 'Good' design was like a state of grace: a formal quality which objects might attain if they avoided the pitfalls of what Henry Cole, with all the certainty a mandarin could muster, called 'false principles'.

From this arose a notion that design had something to do with *redemption*, that a moral cause was supported in the use or acquisition of it. This was neatly symbolized in Gropius's choice of Feininger's woodcut cathedral as the image for the first Bauhaus manifesto, but was given more persuasive form still when transferred to the United States by these same men, now refugees from Germany. Here, with his placement of key staff at the Museum of Modern Art, Gropius helped to turn the democratic Bauhaus ethic into mainstream metropolitan chic. Tom Wolfe was not the first to point out the irony of the architecture and design of worker housing becoming the style of corporate capitalism, only the funniest.

By selecting certain merchandise for special attention, a process begun the century before by Henry Cole, the Museum of Modern Art had the damaging effect of making design seem exclusive and rare, when, of course, the very best in design is always available and popular. For a while, it was something which others – notably the Finns, Danes and Swedes – all had, but something which, at least according to West 53rd Street, was altogether absent in Detroit or Kenosha. Thus, instead of being a means of redemption, the 1950s found design an object for emulation, at a price. It was known to exist, but it was out *there*, not here.

It was in Europe, busy reconstructing itself after the Second World War, that similar ideas also became public. Here the chief event was the opening in London of the Design Centre in 1956. Asked to comment on the occasion, visiting professor Gropius was coolish, saying little more than that he had never seen anything of its sort that was quite so good. But by this time Gropius was no longer a utopian pedagogue and builder, but a Harvard academic with a private client list.

Despite Gropius's coolness, the idea that a distinguished council would select certain merchandise which met its standards was a good one: in those days when Britain had horizontally and vertically integrated industries, a selection of excellence put on display had a prospect of being influential on doltish manufacturers. But the damaging effect was that the very same process suggested that design was extra special, that it existed only in rare merchandise, which needed to be identified by experts. By definition, it seemed that design was hard to find.

And, of course, at the time it was, but the 1960s, 1970s and 1980s, with their interest in pop and celebrities, helped turn design into a fashionable cause. The inevitable extension of making celebrities out of objects was to make celebrities out of the people who designed the objects. It was once thought that when factories replaced studios as sources of cheap happiness, the idea of the artist would be redundant. Suddenly, her name appliquéd to her denims, Gloria Vanderbilt's 'designer' jeans, c.1979, became a landmark in the history of authorship, even if of a rather base sort.

Designer jeans, indeed designer anything you care to name, are evidence both of a materialistic age where social advancement is a function of consumption and of another direction which the fugitive design has taken in its flight from meaning. Ms Vanderbilt did not actually *design* those jeans; she merely lent, or rather sold, her name to the people who manufactured them. If design's alliance was once with morals, by the early 1980s it was firmly with trade. Thus 'design' became a marketing tool.

Cultural anthropologists of the future will marvel at the way in which governments and huge industries were captivated by turbo-charged operators from Soho and Covent Garden, whose golden words led to the curious sight, at any time during the 1980s, of bewildered PLC chairmen at photocalls with a PMT of their new logo on polyboard, explaining to analysts how a puce and apricot squiggle would increase investor value. Certainly, in the best circumstances, this grail of the decade might be achieved, but it tended to enhance a suspicion, still strongly held in some quarters, that design is by definition superficial.

It did not take long before the influential and sardonic Lex in the *Financial Times* began to claim that the only entrepreneurs to survive the harsh passage through enterprise culture entirely intact, have been those who have had least to do with making things. While this deplorable state is as much a reflection of the philistinism of the money-grabbing institutions and their distrust of anything you can't put in a bank, it is a dolorous consequence of the 'design decade' that it will be a long time before someone who has the word 'design' prominent in their business plan will feel confident about showing their face in the City.

So is 'design', now stigmatized in some quarters as a questionable asset in any business which does not already have its fundamentals in good order, just a minority activity, restricted to shoppers for branded polo shirts in Brent Cross and the readers of *Blueprint*, intent on discovering another impossible chair, more new puce squiggles and another Japanese geegaw? If design is to mean more than shopping, those responsible for its supply and demand, as well as those in the middle, must establish it for what they know it to be: an interdisciplinary subject whose broad relevance to the economy and to culture will increase as post-industrial culture places an ever higher value on ideas.

The Design Museum exists to provide a venue where designers can meet their clients and the public can articulate its desires. It is a museum of ideas as much as of objects, intended to dignify a subject which has sometimes recently been given rather a false gloss. The Design Museum will emphasize the practical aspects of design, but not at the expense of the aesthetic ones. Rather, it will stress the unique importance of design, which, when handled well, can enhance both business and art. Most importantly, it will stress the obligation of designers and manufacturers to be in the service of the public, rather than at odds with it.

But the idea that design should be truly responsive to popular need is not new, only ignored. One very healthy aspect of the recent deregulation of architectural history is that we now have a fresher perspective on what does and does not have value. But when people say that modernism has been discredited, they reveal a limited conception of its meaning. In his book, *The Scope of Total Architecture* (1956), Walter Gropius presents the conviction, essential and unique to modernism, that quality is separate from preciousness, that with good design, 'cheap happiness' is potentially available to all. This is the essence of the modern movement ethic and the challenge of design – a challenge and adventure repudiated by the City, smug in its cocoa futures and Japanese trusts. In his *apologia*, Gropius was at pains to explain that modernism is an idea, not a style, the idea being that quality is potentially available for everybody and does not need to be expensive. Despite a decade of new fascia boards and low-voltage lighting, design is not solely about celebrity knick-knacks, the next new thing, but – as Walter Gropius knew – about searching for quality: 'no longer must the isolated individual work continue to occupy pride of place, but rather the creation of the generally valid type, the development towards a standard'.

It is crucial that designers understand the opportunities and problems facing them in the remains of the century, when rapidly changing technology threatens to change the meaning of their business in the same way as rapidly expanding production did a century before. Technology and expert systems are now going so quickly in one direction, that design will soon literally be separated from them. Because no designer is ever again going to have the same sort of influence over a corporation that Eliot Noyes had over IBM, Mario Bellini has recently said that industrial design is redundant. It would be naive to miss the element of irony in what Bellini says, but his point – that the shamanistic role of the designer is a myth, and always was – is a sound one. Technology is now very nearly independent: what 'creativity' it needs could soon be satisfied by expert systems. No longer a glass of water in the desert, the notion that the sole purpose of design is to save ailing businesses has no more substance than a mirage.

But overselling design-for-industry was always underselling its real value. Design can now be in the service of people, rather than huge corporations, though, of course, it is the shrewdest corporations who will realize this. The Design Museum wants to recover for its subject some of the roundness and dignity lost after ten years of remorseless hype, when a subject which occupied Leonardo, Michelangelo and Edison was reduced to a paragraph in a company report.

There is no doubt in my mind that the work of the greatest designers can be compared to the work of the greatest artists, in that both have given us forms and ideas by which to measure and judge the world at large. But for the prototype of the designer of the future, I think you have to look backwards. Vasari and Burckhardt have given marvellous accounts of Leon Battista Alberti. With his feet together he could jump over a man's head, or throw a coin so that it hit a cathedral roof. As a matter of course, he could tame wild horses and 'in three things he desired to appear faultless to others, in walking, in riding, and in speaking'. Painting, sculpture and architecture he

practised by the way, and he also wrote a funeral oration for his dog, which all who heard found unforgettable. But most of all, it was the sympathetic intensity with which he engaged in life as a whole which made him remarkable.

After a century of design as redemption, followed more recently by a decade of design as a saver of businesses, it is encouraging to think that ever more effort can be put into that most familiar, yet demanding, of human tasks: the art of living, and in particular, the art of living in a home. The next mission for design is one aborted earlier: a search for standards. It was Le Corbusier who, thinking of something rather different, but in essence much the same, said just before the last war: 'I believe we are now entering a period infinitely more serious'. Goodbye squiggles. Hello, intelligent typography; thoughtful furniture; dignified packaging; safer appliances. Design is intelligence made visible and now you have the Design Museum to help to prove it.

So, who is the most stylish of them all?
Evening Standard, 25 July 1995

Never have there been two better candidates for an epic public spat than Sir Roy Strong and Sir Terence Conran. The funny thing is, the two have a lot in common, including me, as I know and like them both. They came to my notice at the same time, when I was at school. I admired Strong for being the first person in Britain to believe that museums could be exciting, popular places. In the days when museum directors were as stiff and desiccated as their exhibits, Roy Strong established the flip, sonorous soundbite and the cheeky pose. He was a great popularizer. And so, of course, was Conran.

A more sophisticated, perhaps more cynical, world may have wearied of any attempt to impose taste, but if, like me, you grew up in the dreary north of England and believed that good modern architecture and design were something they had on the Continent, but not at home, the stylish optimism of Conran's local Habitat was a revelation, a genuine inspiration.

There's no doubt that each has a genuine passion for the visual arts, but while Conran is intuitive, Strong is intellectual. Conran is a patchily educated public-school boy with a vivid appetite for the shape, feel and smell of things, including lunch, cars, chairs and women. Strong is a highly educated grammar-school product who tends to be bookish. He neither drives nor womanizes. Each likes gardens, but while Conran will show you his vegetable patch with those little Japanese artichokes which, he always says, make you fart uncontrollably, Strong will more likely tell you he early history of the parterre in the southern Netherlands.

Conran is a robust Bohemian, with a brilliant eye; Strong has a nervous intelligence. The distinctions are obvious in their physical presence and their dress. Roy Strong has a bird-like frame and used to wear Tommy Nutter clothes with a perhaps too marked tendency towards the sharp (although latterly he has mellowed towards Paul Smith and the Italians).

Conran is a bearish type whose generously cut bespoke suits, by David Chambers, look as though they're being tumble-dried even while he's wearing them. I suspect Roy never lets go of his wardrobe while, at home, Terence wears those blue trousers favoured by French garbage collectors. Of course, each style is highly self-conscious in its way, but then both Conran and Strong are in every sense self-made men, to rather different designs.

In the late 1970s, when Habitat was still a private company and discussion of design in newspapers was restricted to descriptions of hanging baskets on the women's pages, there was some agitation in the sleepy world of museums to have the subject taken seriously. At the time I was a young and pushy academic, writing a book for The Design Council which, I see with hindsight, set the agenda for the commodity fetishism of the following decade. Conran asked to meet me and said something like: 'I've made a lot of money out of design and I want to do something educational with it, I'd like to provide for future generations what the V. & A. provided for me'.

With Conran's financial backing I was immediately transformed from a very skint lecturer with a backpack, at the rear of the plane, into something rather smoother with a cocktail nearer the front. I travelled the world, checking on design in museums, and came back to Britain to sell the idea of a design museum to the leaders of national life, and ultimately to the Prime Minister herself. It was only when I arrived at the V. & A. that Roy Strong had the vision (and perhaps opportunism) to say, 'Why not get started here?'

This got him out of a hole and got us into one: in the fetid basement of the old V. & A. we built the Boilerhouse Project which, between 1982 and 1986, became the most popular gallery in London with one exhibition, about Coca-Cola, attracting more visitors to our small underground space than to the rest of the V. & A. in its entirety. The very success of the Boilerhouse put Roy Strong in a deliciously awkward position with his rebellious staff, who were jealous of its popularity and energy.

Although he admirably declined to interfere, his remote posture changed in nuance over the years. At first it was a sort of arm's length pride that he had pulled off a terrific coup in getting massive external sponsorship for the V. & A. and made it take notice of modern design.

Later, as we became more confident and successful, Strong had to deal with his petulant and tiresome colleagues who did not believe that, say, a car could be a work of art, or that a carrier bag could be an object worthy of intense aesthetic scrutiny.

His attitude evolved into an unhelpful indifference and he refused when we attempted to negotiate an extension of our lease to build a genuine museum of modern design in the V. & A. The result of this failure of nerve was that the V. & A. lost perhaps £8 million of external investment, a fabulous source of popular and professional interest and left the actual Design Museum we built in Butlers Wharf struggling to get by without the resources or prestige of a national institution.

I don't know whether this lost opportunity was the source of the acrimonious ordure which Roy Strong smeared across *The Saturday Times* in his already notorious review of Conran's biography. This was a ferocious and apparently embittered patchwork of *ad hominems*, half-truths, innuendoes, selective quotation and bilious opinion which moved Conran and most of his children to protest so strongly this weekend.

But there's an anecdote which illustrates the differences between the two men. One day the V. & A. acquired a new medieval illustrated manuscript. As a trustee, Terence Conran had been shown it. He picked it up, felt it, turned the pages and admired it. I recall Roy Strong telling me this in horror. Conran's physical contact with the precious object tested his later reserves of curatorial *amour propre*. There were, he seemed to be saying, limits to how much one might admire and enjoy design.

Still, Roy Strong was the best postwar director of the V. & A. and Terence Conran has always been passionate about this most quirky of museums ... to the extent of being prepared to invest millions in it. It would be going much too far to blame the fall-out from the botch as the course of the recently exposed acrimony, but shortly after we left the V. & A., Strong resigned. And Conran, disenchanted with the stuffed shirts of the City, left corporate life.

Thanks to the influence of Conran and Strong shops and museums are coming together as commerce and culture grow less distinct. It's a pity the same happy phenomenon has driven the men apart. And who is right? The sense of bitterness in Strong's attack was acrid and tangible. Conran, on the other hand, expresses dismay and bemusement from his terrace in Provence. Each would agree on one thing: *le style est l'homme.*

Curators of poor taste
Evening Standard, 5 August 1991

The cars chosen by museum directors are of special interest to those of us who, like Henry Ford, are anxious to wring as much meaning as possible out of the banalities of everyday life.

If you saw, for instance, the individual responsible to his trustees for the conservation and display of, shall we say, the Elgin Marbles travelling to Great Russell Street in a full-race Shelby American 427 Cobra with 14-inch Hallibrand wheels, twin Holley four-choke carburettors, a chrome-moly roll cage and open exhausts, it would require two things of our interpretation: that the Cobra may, despite initial misgivings be worthy of serious consideration by fastidious aesthetes and that the director of the British Museum may not be such a dry old stick after all.

Again, if it were known that the director of the ICA was pleased to use a 1962 Bentley Continental with special bodywork by Mulliner Park Ward, that too would require reinterpretation of both the character of the car and the identity of the individual.

I started thinking on these lines some years ago when I saw Nicholas Serota, the basilisk-featured and icily uncompromising director of The Tate, pootling out of the car park of the Nine Elms Sainsbury's like an Eastbourne psycho-geriatric in a vile Volvo 340.

Both at the Whitechapel and subsequently at Millbank, Serota has been a stern champion of conventional modernism, a slave to aesthetic absolutism, a vigilante on the cutting edge. No one in London, surely, was in possession of more persuasive data to support the argument that the twentieth century has democratized art, that there is an endless source of richness in exploiting contemporary possibilities, that frontiers are there to be crossed?

Finding him in a Swedish-badged, cynically under-engineered, pig-ugly DAF tended to undermine my sense of conviction about the credibility of the foregoing. How could someone who could date a Cy Twombly or attribute an Yves Klein even bear to be seen in such an awful crapbucket? I never took the Turner Prize seriously again.

At the V. & A., the excellent Sir Roy Strong was less hypocritical, although bafflingly resistant to the aesthetic, if not the practical, blandishments of the automobile.

Sir Roy, whose passion for the arts is genuine and profound, always, like the great Sir Nikolaus Pevsner, refused to learn to drive and, while he can discourse learnedly and amusingly on Elizabethan court ritual and the *Hypnerotomachia Poliphili*, he nevertheless made no objection to being driven around in a creaking Ford Escort, dulled by age not to an agreeable patina like a Coardstone urn, but irretrievably tarnished to a light absorbing matt by accretions of birdlime.

Sir Roy's contemporary successor, Alan Borg, is altogether different. Borg has chosen an Audi estate, shorthand for 'I'm a scientific rationalist', a car with a character and a carrying capacity appropriate to a museum director who's going to need a lot of new brooms.

Across the road from the V. & A. is the Science Museum. Once the same institution, parliamentary fiat separated them ages ago into a place which has things that work and a place which has things that don't. Few museums have made more progress in closing the gap, some would say blurring the distinction, between education and entertainment, although it is a melancholy testament to the lack of technical awareness and diurnal perceptiveness suffusing the place that Sir Neil Cosson's secretary had, when we phoned, absolutely no idea what car he used. (It's a Rover.)

Far more impressive was the elegant Charles Saumarez Smith, the energetic and stylish director of the National Portrait Gallery. Saumarez Smith, who for a while was a frequent sight on a postman's bicycle, now uses a Saab, a car that has acquired a reputation for being responsible and hygienic, but ever so slightly raffish. With these credentials safely established, Saumarez Smith confided that he didn't actually know what precise model he owned, but was fairly confident it was red.

At Oxford's Museum of Modern Art, David Elliott also chose a Saab, but significantly gave me the exact designation: a 9000 2.3i. Elliott is responsible, hygienic, raffish, but also in possession of important technical data.

At the Serpentine Gallery, Julia Peyton-Jones has a very well-used Peugot 205, whose insouciant condition articulates an avant-garde disdain for the motor trade and its rituals of service.

Rosa-Maria Letts of the Accademia Italiana uses an ethnically correct Lancia Thema, the preferred car of all functionaries in Milan and Rome, while the Design Museum's Paul Thompson has a modest Fiat Cinquecento, a poetic expression of style combined with an essential modesty.

Professor Eric Fernie, the new director of the Courtauld Institute, does not have a car and had to hire one to move his books from Edinburgh.

An exhibition of museum directors' cars would contain few exciting surprises. Some would say this is exactly what's wrong with London's museums.

**Part Nine
Design Elements**

On corporate identity cowboys
Design, 1991

Jack Smythe had had a terrible night, but he felt certain he was going to have a wonderful day. It had been a black-tie dinner for a home counties Chamber of Commerce and Jack had been the guest speaker. Since the publication of his book, *On the Make*, Jack received lots of after-dinner invitations. He never turned them down no matter how humble since, as he had written in the epigraph to his own Masters' dissertation ('The Role of Opportunism'), chance always favours the mind that is prepared.

Chance on this occasion came in the form of the placement at dinner: the owner of the south-east's largest chain of franchised battery, clutch and silencer depots was sitting on his right. Jack's well-prepared mind spooled-up like the mighty engine it was and over lots of cheap port convinced battery, clutch and silencer that he should diversify into Portuguese fast food and that the Scavenger Pack, as Jack's consultancy has been called since it joined the USM, should be expensively retained to design its every aspect.

So, the evening had not been without its rewards. But Jack was certainly going to have a better day, because this was the day of his most important ever presentation to a major city institution. Five years ago, before the Scavenger Pack had gone public, Jack had picked up his first tranche of work for this most important of clients and had transformed serious letterheads with a bracing version of what seemed modern in 1985. Some of the conservative board members to whom Jack had first presented all those years ago had timidly expressed reluctance to scrap what Eric Gill had designed for them half a century before, but Jack had the zeitgeist, the high-street revolution, market forces, a seminar at number ten and about a thousand kilowatts of chutzpah working for him and reluctantly, the board conceded the Scavenger Pack's proposals,

Metropolitan lines
Independent Saturday Magazine, December 1997

implemented the design and paid the enormous bills that Jack sent their way.

But Jack's problem now was that the market demanded growth, and he was going to have to tell his client that it was time for a change. He had to persuade the board that what they really needed was to get back to basics, to rediscover the original identity so rudely abandoned, to banish confusion from the public mind ... and reinstate Eric Gill.

Of course, all that is fiction, but the following is fact. I was called into a very large public relations company and asked to recommend a firm of designers. The man on the other side of the desk looked exquisitely uncomfortable and said, 'Quite frankly, we don't want someone to tell us what we are all about, what we *mean*, where we have been and where we are going. We just want a new letterhead'.

After centuries of effort to get design taken seriously in our literary-biased culture, people like Jack Smythe discredit it for a mere 15 per cent. Unless self-dependent values are rediscovered, design will be consigned to the same bin that used to accommodate planned obsolescence. Think of John Ruskin: 'Things ... are noble or ignoble in proportion to the fullness of the life ...they themselves enjoy', or Daniel Burnham: 'A noble, logical diagram ... will never die, but long after we are gone will be a living thing, asserting itself with ever-growing intensity', or Ettore Sottsass: 'Who tells them to produce warplanes instead of lukewarm showers of rosewater for defeated old fathers or springtime lawns for old arthritic mothers already wearing black as they approach the portals of the Houses of Dust?'

Of course, each civilization gets the design it deserves. We get Jack Smythe.

Can you design an entire city? This is the subject of Richard Rogers's new book, a development of his 1995 Reith Lectures. Our word 'civilization' is a semantic extension of the word 'city'. No doubt, the great cities of the world are among mankind's most representative achievements. Think of what makes us proud to be human, and images of Venice, Manhattan and Paris come to mind. While musing, some might even catch an imaginary glimpse of the San Diego and Santa Monica freeways, or Chelsea Reach, or Regent's Park – if not, perhaps, Vauxhall Cross.

The great thing about cities is not how awful they are – with their crisp packets, dog shit and diesel – but how wonderfully well they work considering that putting 10 million aggressive hominids into close proximity and inviting them to engage in serial acts of competitive individualism, whether for jobs, schools or parking spaces, could not be considered a reasonable idea. Put rats in claustrophobic circumstances and they become homosexual, murderous and cannibalistic in no time at all.

Instead, humans find ingenious solutions: underground car parks, Chinese take-aways, one-man buses, cycle lanes, tall buildings. I love cities because of the way their subtle, dense and complex structures merge power with style and function and beauty. To see a busy traffic intersection from the air is exhilarating. The formal beauty is breathtaking and the fact that, in the general order of things, the traffic flows so freely and so reasonably without grave interruptions or efforts is a thrilling testament to human fastidiousness, ingenuity and decency. As Le Corbusier said of New York, the modern city is 'a magnificent catastrophe'.

But it would be stupid to ignore the problems which Lord Rogers addresses. Half the world's population now lives in cities and by 2005 it is estimated that that fraction will have risen to three quarters. And while it is true that every midtown Manhattan resident longs for a place in the Hamptons as surely as every *Independent* reader probably pines for Wiltshire, our need to escape the gravitational pull of the city is simply evidence of our urban maturity. On the other hand, be warned that the entire rural populations of India and China, give or take a recalcitrant 100 million or so, are just waiting to slip the surly bonds of subsistence peasantry and go live in a high-rise with an office job and a parking space.

If you factor in some alarming statistics, sourced by Rogers from Herbert Girardet of Middlesex University, the future prospect becomes positively apocalyptic. Every year, London, to give an example, consumes 110 supertankers of oil, 1.2m tons of timber, 1.2m tons of metal, 2m tons each of food, plastics and paper and 1bn tons of water. London's digestive system then dyspeptically exhausts 15m tons of rubbish, 7.5m tons of sewage and 60m tons of carbon dioxide.

While Metro London covers less than half a million acres, it draws on the resources of 50m acres. Imagine similar figures applied to Shenzen and Calcutta, then Rio and Jakarta, and you can see that the planet will soon be overwhelmed by a necrotizing plague of garbage, toxic waste and general-purpose crap.

Richard Rogers's solution is well-mannered, classic, humane, Euro-modern. *Le stile*, after all, *è l'uomo*. Rogers is one of the great creative figures of the second half of the twentieth century, a unique hybrid of hedonistic Italian heritage with cool British professionalism. His own buildings – the Centre Pompidou, Lloyd's, the Court of Human Rights – are among the most significant monuments of contemporary civilization. Their audacious concepts, meticulously engineered

and detailed, have given a unique spin to their particular urban locales. In the case of the Pompidou, it was the stimulus for the rebirth of a vast and sordidly neglected quartier of Paris and can probably claim to be the most popular modern building on earth. Thrilling stuff.

What Rogers wants to see in the cities of the future is more beauty and less waste, more intelligent use of natural resources (the slovenly neglect of London's river is a personal obsession), resource-efficient buildings, advanced public transport, public spaces and free exchange of information. He seeks city-planning which undermines traditional assumptions about rigid hierarchies, replacing them with structures that positively stimulate diverse, democratic systems.

Of course, like Peace and Love, it's hurrah for all of that. No reasonable, no *civilized*, individual could deny allegiance to Rogers's insistence that to survive with decency we have to be more responsible about the built environment and, whatever our political style, altogether less short-termish and money-grubbing. But wisdom, they say, is not knowing what we should do, but what we should do … *next*. How, then, to reach a position where our cities are no longer vast, anarchic, dirty, expensive and frightening engines of filth?

I'm a little wary of Rogers's belief that much can be gained from consultation and from pedestrianization. All the evidence I know about great buildings and great cities is that they do not come about following plebiscites at the Drop-In Centre nor from excluding traffic. Great buildings, including Rogers's own, tend to arise from the dogmatic perseverance and bloody-minded commitment of talented individuals possessed of the unfaltering conviction that they know best.

As for traffic, while there's no question that the use of the private car should be stringently controlled by eye-watering taxes and made to look ridiculous in contrast to sublimely efficient public transport, these longed-for changes are some way off. Besides, moderate volumes of traffic give animation to city centres. Does anyone believe that Oxford's Cornmarket has been improved since it was shut to traffic?

My preferred route to the ideal city of the future is suggested not so much by Rogers's theories of planning in general, but his attitude to building design in particular – something almost neglected in this book [*Cities for a Small Planet*, Faber and Faber, 1997]. While the culture which formed Rogers was firmly based in the deterministic modernism of the 1930s, his own philosophy has rapidly evolved. He admires the anti-rational but exhilarating architecture of Will Alsop, Zaha Hadid and Daniel Libeskind.

Rogers now sees that modernism is not a style; it's an attitude. He writes that: 'We must build cities for flexibility and openness, working with, not against the now inevitable process whereby cities are subject to constant change. As homes, schools, entertainment and work-places become less defined by their single function, one basic structure, linked to a common network, can accommodate learning, work and leisure. Aesthetics are all but freed from the association with the function that the building encloses. The building system itself – its craftsmanship, responsiveness and beauty – is fast becoming the dominant criterion. The aesthetics of response, change and modulation have replaced the fixed order or architecture'.

In other words, let's keep on redefining modernism and continue to build better buildings which make the most of all contemporary possibilities. Better cities will inevitably arise from this careful and responsible process of continuous renewal.

I'm not a *laissez-faire* planner. Town planning is one of Britain's great contributions to world culture. I am also a great admirer of Rogers's architecture and achievements, not to mention his personal style. I want to see better designed, cleaner, safer, more vital – most of all, more modern – cities. I'd certainly like to see more Richard Rogers buildings wherever I go. But I'm cautious about holistic city design.

Certainly, more than 100 years ago, Camillo Sitte's *City Planning According to Artistic Principles* was a benign influence on the Garden City Movement, but it was a short step from Letchworth to the less delightful Wolfsburg and then Mussolini's hilarious EUR, Sabaudia and Latina. The ideal city has forever been a preoccupation of civilized thought and Richard Rogers now takes his place in a list of opinion formers which includes Plato, Cicero, St Augustine, Dante, More, Francis Bacon, William Morris and H. G. Wells. I'd personally like to live in a world designed entirely by Richard Rogers (and especially so if his wife were in charge of catering). But while we contemplate with delight the coming of this utopia, let's not forget that litter is a sign of vitality and wealth; while a G-reg Escort is, for many, a means of individual liberation.

Design Council: facing the scrap heap
Daily Telegraph, 17 December 1993

William Morris said you should have nothing in your home which you don't know to be useful and feel to be beautiful. Combining beauty with utility is exactly what designers do. It is a noble calling, so it is surprising to find the Design Council in such a bad way.

Today's Design Council is a leaderless, muddled, directionless quango facing massive cuts in its grant of £7 million from the Department of Trade and Industry. It looks as if its main role – advising industry about design – will be taken away and given to a network of offices called Business Links. Overmanned and underloved, the Design Council is a cruel parody of its ancestor organization, which led the world out of darkness into the bright lights of design promotion.

The history of its decline can be traced in the personalities of its four directors. In 1934 Sir Gordon Russell founded the original Council for Art and Industry in response to a Board of Trade fiat. Russell was a furniture maker and designer of immense character and prestige, a living link with the dignified Arts and Crafts movement. He chose as his successor a dapper, articulate newspaperman, Paul – later Lord – Reilly.

It was Reilly who in 1956 opened the Design Centre on the Haymarket, giving design a shop window in the days before colour supplements. Under Reilly's subsequent directorship, it enjoyed its greatest influence and prestige. Its awards – with their memorable black-and-white swing tags – were prized. Its magazine was noticed and it was copied all over the world.

But, like many successful men, Reilly was reluctant to be outshone by his successor, and when he retired in 1977, his replacement was Keith Grant, a cautious committee man with few communications skills. Grant's own successor was Ivor Owen, a chippy ex-industrialist who has

presided over the Council's decline. Just a few weeks ago he agreed to 'stand down'.

Yet it was during the period of its greatest success that the Design Council began to lose its sense of direction. In its early years it was immensely influenced by the Scandinavian example, where small heterogeneous populations had a uniform demand for well-made, thoughtful merchandise. But this idea of 'good form' could not accommodate the explosion of eclectic values which 'pop' culture brought about in the 1960s.

Equally, the Design Council could not deal with commercial success. It would have been unimaginable, for example, for the Design Centre to display the most popular car of its type – the chromed, pearlescent, snarling, *American* Ford Mustang. As a result of this fatal narrow-mindedness, successive Design Council awards represent a catalogue of well-meaning disasters.

The problem has been that the context – both stylistic and commercial – in which the Council was conceived has changed in ways which Russell could not have imagined and which Reilly did not accept. In 1956 British manufacturers made a wide variety of goods in every category. When, say, someone in Wolverhampton was making a vilely ugly vacuum flask, it made sense for a design 'council', marshalled by Russell and Reilly, to impose its polite liberal aesthetics on a coarse industry. 'Look, you chaps, this is what we educated fellows think it should look like. Run along now and get on with it.'

But our manufacturers have been unable to satisfy domestic demand for consumer goods. As a nation we have retreated from the manufacture of office machines, consumer electronics, optical goods, trucks and buses and our activity in white goods and automobiles is sustained only by massive technology transfer from abroad.

The Design Council's problems became most acute in the 1980s, when a retail boom and a rash of avaricious consumerism turned a practical discipline into a notorious subject. The Council's reaction to the designer decade was to create an ingenious, but ill-starred, 'funded consultancy scheme'. This, memorably described by Sir Peter Parker as an outboard motor strapped to a drifting raft, offered financial support for industrial first-time buyers of design.

The mistake here was that it made design look like an optional extra, when it is essential at all stages of the business. Instead of connoting elegance, precision, quality – what Le Corbusier called 'intelligence made visible' – design came to suggest the flashy, the superficial ... and the unnecessary.

Worse, with the decay of manufacturing, the Council's insular promotional policies made it look, latterly like a desperate Made-in-Britain centre. A narrow brief to promote 'design in British industry' could not work well in an age of multinational companies, global products and planetary movements of capital. This led to embarrassing absurdities: stalls full of fluorescent gonks, the Design Centre selling oven gloves and marmalade.

By the late 1980s the Department of Trade and Industry was already becoming restive over the Design Council. At a private lunch, I had the chance to talk to Kenneth Clarke, then still a DTI minister. I began, 'Look, I don't want to say anything *against* the Design Council ...' but he cut me short, looked me in the eye and asked: 'Why not?'

There is a role for a modern Design Council, not as a dinosaur with a staff of 200 foraging for something 'British' to put on display, but as a small, expert, articulate and influential bureau.

There is not a single aspect of public life in Britain which could not be improved by the intelligent application of design. For instance, Manchester's Olympic bid was not helped by the anile crassness of its stuffed-lion mascot. The Council should have been advising. Our cities are squalid with ill-considered street furniture and intrusive signs. The Council should intervene.

But best of all, the Council just might have a part to play in that longed-for renaissance of manufacturing which would provide such a boost to national morale. A new Design Council should establish the standards for the manufacture of simple goods for which there is an existing domestic demand – glass, ceramics, furniture and so on – and use every incentive to get them made. This would not only provide a stirring rationale for its continued existence, it would also help provide useful – maybe even beautiful – work for the vast numbers of well-trained, highly motivated and sorely disappointed young designers in Britain. We have an unrivalled art education system; creating genuine opportunities for them to find work would be the best possible reason for binning the not-to-be-resuscitated tag presently dangling ignominiously around the neck of the once-proud Design Council.

4

ON THE DECLINE OF PRODUCT DESIGN
Design
AUGUST 1990

I can remember the precise moment – if not frankly, the exact date –
when I realized my interest in design. I suppose I was about ten and I
was reading one of my father's copies of *Motor*. In it I saw a picture
of a handsome, daringly modern sports car and standing by it was a
handsome, daringly modern man. His name was Raymond Loewy
and he was wearing, as I recall, a white suit and spats. This seemed
terrific. The caption said he had designed the car and I thought, Wow.

Later I discovered other great designers, notably Charles Eames and
Eliot Noyes, who today still seem to me paradigms of what design is
meant to be about: a cultivated activity concerned with applying
intelligence and – dare I say? – taste to the creation of everyday
things. Later still I discovered Ettore Sottsass and, to my satisfaction,
even got to know him a little. Here was someone capable of adding a
genuine spiritual dimension to a subject that in Loewy's hands looked
brash, in Eames's and Noyes's earnest and serious.

My accumulated knowledge about the life and work of these characters made me absolutely fascinated by product design.

The idea that a single controlling mind could have a decisive influence over the form and content of a contemporary object, whether a
motor car or a chair, fascinated me then just as it fascinates me now.
But I wonder if Loewy, Eames and Noyes and the people like them
were ever quite so influential as I once believed, or was I the gullible
dupe of Mephisthophelean PR?

The reputations of Eames and Noyes are probably impregnable, not least because there are still a lot of people around who knew them well. Still, a little mild revisionism might be refreshing. Are those Eames chairs really that great? I see them now as period pieces, charming but irrelevant. Anyway, he did them for a furniture company that knew how to hustle. Noyes did an absolutely terrific job on IBM, but wasn't it relatively easy to do so then when the entire computer industry was horizontally and vertically integrated and, at least in IBM's case, under the total control of its chairman? Isn't it misleading to look to the example of Noyes, or Loewy, or Eames to provide a model for the product designer of today?

I thought this while I was helping to put together *Design 1990*, the magazine published with this year's BBC Design Awards. Going through the entries it was noteworthy how weak product design appeared. Environment was full of gutsy stuff by talented mavericks, graphics contained some really strong and imaginative material, but products! My God, products looked like a car-boot sale in northern Sweden. 'What', I thought to myself, 'do these people think they are doing?'

A similar thought came to me when I looked at some of the product design in the various college degree shows: 'What are these people being trained for?' Product designers at work in Britain are lost and bewildered remnants rather like those Japanese soldiers they still keep finding in the Sumatran jungle who think the war is still on.

I'm no conservative, but I find the ceaseless quest for superficial novelty which we see in so much product design tiresome. If I see another silly 'solution' to a problem no one has I shall scream. I shall scream even louder if it is purple with knobs on.

It is humiliating to look at an electronic gadget like a currency converter, when you know all the clever bits are oriental, and hear it said that someone in the UK 'designed' it. We mean 'drew the box'. Product designers seem to draw a lot of boxes nowadays. So many product designers, particularly the ones who make the most portentous claims, seem to be operating at a level of unreality. What do they think those Japanese with AF cameras you see at every show and exhibition are doing? I can tell you: working on an expert system which will make European product designers redundant.

So, these are strange times. Product design in Europe brings to mind that medieval expression about *lacrimae rerum*, the sadness of things. Japanese products optimistically approach perfection because they are driven by unbelievably efficient production and process technology. Day-Glo blobs are depressingly irrelevant. The majority of product designers lead lives of quiet desperation. Meanwhile, panel gaps in Japan are down to 4mm.

5

CLASSIC STATEMENT
Design
AUGUST 1990

Some things have an essential rightness. There is not a great deal you could add to the Parthenon to improve it; while changing its proportion and details would diminish its serene beauty. It's the same with wellingtons … or brogues, teddy bear coats and hacking jackets. Each has a just-so stability, timeless and four-square. This is what we mean by a 'classic' – that handful of designs which seem to have permanent value outside the ebb and flow of caprice.

The enduring appeal of classic designs makes them the province of both the department store and the museum. In an age when commerce and culture are coming closer together, it's instinctive and amusing to watch the brief passage of tinselly trash, while demand for the durability of classic design has never been so strong. After decades of uncertainty in matters of taste, simple truths have become very alluring.

You could gather up a gang of Sorbonne intellectuals and other people who take these things seriously, fire at them the question, 'What does a classic design look like?' and you'd find no very serious dissension among them. Make a pile of their choices on the floor and you'd come up with those perennial hacking jackets, grey flannels, brogues, those Jean Muirs, polo-necks, cashmere blazers.

Classics are not necessarily expensive or rare. A generously-cut Brooks Brothers T-shirt, Levi's, Dunlop tennis shoe and a Lacoste shirt are all cheap and mass-produced indeed. They are not overtly startling, or exclusive; as William Morris said of all well-designed furniture, any good piece will most likely mix with any other good piece. (Those Levi's would look terrific with an ankle-length black sable coat.) Classics are not precious: the best are understated rather than loud. A Chanel dress of '47 doesn't make you wince the way diamanté hot pants of '71 do.

The mystery of making a classic is a central question in aesthetics; it is also a grail which few designers ever discover. The goal is design that cuts across the ephemeralities of fashion and taste. Design is a practical activity which combines creativity with control. Fashion is the way designs look at any given moment (last year's safari style, this year's Empire line). Taste is the mechanism with which you respond to fashion and to a great extent is modified by time. Fashion historian James Laver described it nicely: responses to any design, he said, went from indecent to beautiful, by way of shameless, outré, smart, dowdy, hideous, ridiculous, amusing, quaint, charming and romantic. The great appeal of classic design is that it transcends all this.

So what is the essence some designers have which gives them permanent value in a changing world? The qualities they all have in common are not far off the definitions of design so hard-won by the pioneer modernists. The polemical Adolf Loos, the high-minded Walter Gropius and the maverick Le Corbusier were searching for some sort of order in the modern world to replace the academic principles which got lost when twentieth-century doubt and utopianism replaced the moral certainties of the nineteenth. They came up with ten commandments which as easily apply to classic modern clothes as to buildings.

> Always pay attention to the intended function of a piece which will offer a key to its ideal form.

Never force unnatural forms or contrived patterns.
Ornament is crime.
Look to nature and industry for inspiration.
Never do anything bogus.
You should respect the nature of the materials you use.
Wherever possible use the simplest materials.
Don't ape the past.
Express your intentions honestly and clearly.
Try to ensure that the details harmonize with the whole.

The modernists also noticed that very often things designed for purely functional purposes, say, a revolver or a boiler-suit, had a simple elegance missing from the fussy, contrived merchandise styled to catch the eye.

These elemental rules of design provide the framework for a classic. Like all simple truths they never date. On the contrary, like the hacking jacket, flannels and brogues, they actually improve with time. In fact, you get close to Ruskin's idea that inanimate objects have a sense of spirit when you start defining classics. You find yourself coming up with evaluative terms which could apply as well to a decent person as a decent design: in both what we admire is honesty, integrity, guts and good manners.

6

A BIRDS-EYE VIEW OF AUTOMOTIVE AESTHETICS
Car Magazine
FEBRUARY 1998

For me the very greatest moment in the history of styling was this. By the mid-1950s Harley Earl's programme of lengthening and lowering General Motors' cars during successive annual model changes had the result that the roof now became visible to a person of average height. (Earl himself, being a six-foot-four banana-munching giant in a cinnamon linen suit, had had privileged early warning of the approaching problem of roof aesthetics.)

The Chevrolet Nomad show car was the first to get the treatment. This was a glorious confection of Corvette and wagon, the triple distillation of Futurama, the pure spirit of styling. Butt-naked vulgarity. It could stun an aesthete at 100 yards. The only problem was that the roof was a plain plane, virginal sheet-metal, a desert of vast artistic eternity. Nature, and stylists, abhor vacuums. Harley Earl saw the roof as a challenge. He munched on his banana, and soon had the solution: 'We groove it'. Thus the Nomad became the first car with a styled roof, and non-structural corrugations took their place in mankind's great aesthetic adventure.

You could write an entire (if somewhat perverse) history of styling by considering roofs alone. The next landmark was in Italy. In anticipation of Lancia's lovely 1967 Fulvia Sport, Zagato proposed a coupé whose rear windows ignored conventional demarcations between sheet-metal and glass. Italian styling is philosophically contained by a strict vocabulary which names every part of a car body, but Zagato's innovation of glass curling over the header rail required a new entry in the dictionary. It is true to say that the Zagato stylists were not able to resolve with entire success the conflicting artistic and practical demands of this innovation, but it was nonetheless remarkable, creating a distinctive signature for Lancia and offering back passengers in a coupé something entirely original: a view.

Next came Abarth's 'double bubble', the dual blips in the canopy to accommodate helmets. Internally, Raymond Loewy's landmark Studebaker Avanti was the first car to have a roof-mounted console and then we get the interesting pagoda roof on the Mercedes-Benz SL, a device to invite more light without compromising structural integrity which gave this beautiful car its distinctively taut aspect. Bizarrely, we then get the van-in-drag Matra-Simca Rancho whose many functional shortcomings cannot disguise its significant place in the story of consumer psychology: Rancho anticipated funky 'sport-utes' by a decade and offered groovy glazed roof lights in its raised pavilion roof.

The Japanese then sensed that the top horizontal surface was something you could manipulate in pursuit of the customer's cupidity, his yen and his dollars, so the high roof became a desirable and expensive option on big 4x4s. Twin sunroofs on the Renault Espace were additional evidence that this unclaimed territory was becoming to designers what Brillat-Savarin said the chicken was to chefs: an empty canvas. Now BMW was at it too. The outgoing 5-series estate had the marvellous option of ingeniously engineered twin metal sunroofs so that the people in the stern travelling economy class were suddenly upgraded. Alas, with a characteristic lack of joy, BMW later dropped this delightful feature.

And since then not much has happened, except for the Mercedes A-class, whose sunroof is a novel formulation of large chord louvres, like an over-sized venetian blind. (Tasteless wags might say this was especially clairvoyant for a car whose roof has, so far, played a disproportionate role in its public performance.)

Given modern traffic conditions, 50 extra horsepower is going to get you nowhere at all. Aesthetics are more important than dynamics. I spend most of my time staring at my headlining, although I can sadly tell you that the designer did not give the banal swathe of grey felt nearly as much attention as I do. The roof is the last frontier of styling. I promise you: watch this space. I do.

7
ON THE DEADLY MONOGRAPH
Design
JULY 1990

The gods often commission monographs on those whom they would destroy. A published study seems ruinous, even murderous. Pre-emptive ones might even form interesting elements of hostile future business strategies.

One of the best books in the modern genre of writing about design was Wolfgang Schmittel's *Design, Concept, Realization* (Zurich, 1957), containing well-illustrated accounts of corporate design at Braun, Citroën, Herman, Miller, Olivetti, Sony and (a sop to national vanity) Swissair. It is interesting to reflect on these companies' subsequent fortunes.

By the mid-1980s, Braun, so much under the thumb of its owner Gillette, itself under threat from *arbitrageurs*, speculators and other pin-striped trash, had lost the entire plot. Refinement and subtlety, hitherto a hallmark of Braun design, became things of the past and Braun's curiosity value nowadays is as provider of collectors' pieces.

At the same time, Citroën, manufacturer of many fine but unprofitable vehicles, having tried Michelin's patience for too long, was sold to Peugeot and the erosion of a carefully nurtured, if eccentric, engineering policy began. Herman Miller has been unable to sustain its position as an exemplary manufacturer in its use of design. Olivetti, with a reputation for product design which was rightly second-to-none, has become a service industry. Only Sony is in better shape, like for like, although it was not long after the publication of Schmittel's book that it wobbled, as the stream of characteristically innovative products looked as if it was running dry.

In the mid-1980s *In Search of Excellence* was a popular collection of business case studies, but less than two years after its publication, Forbes and Fortune were dolefully recounting how many of the hitherto excellent companies had succumbed to pressures unanticipated at the time of publication. While IBM, often cited in *Excellence*, had for decades enjoyed the prestige of a market leader apparently invulnerable to predators, its own inability to learn the lessons it had taught the world made it seem a likely target for break-up. Similarly, Philips, for so long number one or number two in most of its chosen markets and sectors, and treated to a lavish adulatory design monograph less than a year ago ('The resurgence of design at Philips has enabled the corporation to maintain and develop its market share'), astonished the business world with a spectacular profits collapse announced in May.

What's wrong? Is it the monographs or the manufacturers? Or is it our notion of business? Any answer has to be seen against a backdrop of western manufacturing in seemingly terminal decline. As soon as a recovery is made on one front, there is a relapse on another, apparently caused by a monograph.

The problem is that we are still applying a model of 'design', formed years ago during the infantile period of industrialization, onto modern circumstances which are entirely different. Once it was possible for designers of real stature and rare vision – one thinks of Peter Behrens and Eliot Noyes – to walk into big corporations, have lunch with the boss and institute dramatic changes in corporate direction simply as acts of aesthetic will stiffened with moral purpose. Unfortunately, this attractively primitive scenario has since passed into the history of art.

What is wrong with one-dimensional design management monographs is that there is a fundamental mismatch between form and content. In their limited vision of their subject, they refute the very idea of integrity which makes the study of a huge and complex organism such as manufacture worth attempting in the first place. They are rarely a disinterested historical analysis, nor a workable professional handbook. I have never seen one which contains the precise statistics on market performance necessary to confirm the more wacky or self-serving assertions.

Too much of what has been said about design for industry has been about presentation rather than substance. We have been given description rather than analysis. This has been reflected and enforced by monographs which look only on the superficial. It is deceptively simple to write about the design of surfaces which is why the 'art historical' monographs of the past 15 years have provided a seductive model – but have been so misleading.

8

FUTURE OF GRAPHIC DESIGN
Design
NOVEMBER 1990

You don't need to work for the Henley Centre for Forecasting to real-ize that the solutions to the products of tomorrow are not going to be found by the people we identify as designers. For good or for bad, the initiative has gone elsewhere. Even as far as the economy is con-cerned, the vale of manufactured goods is less and less significant. The great economies of the future are going to be the ones best able to transport their citizens efficiently and to communicate information among them. That is why Matsushita wants to buy MCA.

It is also why there is a great future for graphics and packaging. The British economy is strong in consumer packaged goods, especially food, drink and personal or household products. It is also strong in chemicals, pharmaceuticals, petroleum products, leisure and enter-tainment. In short, exactly those areas which have the highest demand for graphic design and packaging skills. In the few areas of manufacturing where Britain is successful – mainly aerospace and defence – the industries suffer from what the business school demotic likes to describe as lack of depth in the clusters. Since the national economy is specially weak in machine-based industries, it is no won-der that product designers spend a lot of their time sucking pencils and thinking about moving to the country.

Specialists in graphics and packaging, on the other hand, are working in an interesting landscape, although it is one in which some of the landmarks are moving. The past ten years have seen a lot of changes in the geology of the business and now it is time for the long-term view to take over from the tendency towards firefighting. Some people and businesses which used to look like fixed points are now more clearly seen as passing clouds. A whole generation of professional designers has had the benefit of being trained in the big studios and can now service clients without the burden of the overheads which sent a lot of the big studios the way of the dinosaurs. The shrewdest clients realize this and are now prepared to use a small, professional and very efficient team, or even an individual, rather than a brontosaurus with account handlers possessed of brains the size of a pea. This happens without any compromise to the quality of the end result.

But what are the shrewd graphic designers going to be doing in future? I think in terms of style we are due for a change. The eternal bull market of the eighties produced a great deal of excellence, but it produced rather a lot of the other thing as well. Upward spiralling demand from hectically competing retailers solicited a lot of very adventurous – not to say audacious – work from a lot of new designers. So audacious that sometimes you felt you had trodden in it. On occasions, there was brilliant novelty, but on just as many occasions – sometimes more – there was also a lot of painfully over-stretched contrivance.

I have this belief – so innate that I'm tempted to regard it as instinctive – that clarity is something to do with quality and that, in terms of business, what you see is what you have paid for. Believing that form and content are one, indivisible and expressive of each other, it does not surprise me that the last Next catalogue was one of unexampled fussiness – hard to look at and worse to read – and contrivance and lack of clarity. The results have spoken for themselves.

I think we have seen enough pastel flourishes on supermarket yoghurt pots, enough humourless wit, enough wasteful use of inners and outers, enough Glyn Boyd Harte illustrations on bottles of so-so olive oil. I detect a demand – although I also concede that this may be simple naive longing on my behalf – for unpretentious illustrations, literate typography and a stylish economy in resources. This may put a few of the new studios out of business, but that alone will provide a stimulus for the others. If this argument sounds conservative, is not that what we are told the nineties is all about?

9

EXHIBITION DESIGN
Design
OCTOBER 1990

The exhibition is a very crude, but powerful, communications tool. It is not well understood and consequently is very inefficiently developed as a medium. Perhaps exactly because the exhibition is so volatile and full of potential, it confounds designers hither and yon. The basic problem of display and explanation is, on the face of it, a primary task in information design, but the extra dimension of space where that information has to be articulated proved the undoing of so many of the designers who worked in the Boilerhouse.

Looking back, it seems remarkable that the best exhibitions, the ones with the cleanest presentation of image and object, the most dramatic or interesting aspects and the ones to excite the curiosity of the public, rather than its dismay, were often designed by architects, one of whom it is sobering to remark had been in practice (and in much the same style) since the fifties. The exhibitions designed by designers, by which I mean that self-regarding stage army which came to prominence a decade ago and is now busily preoccupied in rescheduling loans and appointing receivers, betrayed the shortcomings of this oversold 'profession'.

I was continuously dispirited by the lack of evident creative imagination, something you'd think was a stock-in-trade. Granted, it was illusion that the Boilerhouse, being a square white void, offered the 'neutral' provision of an empty canvas. Clearly, empty white spaces are extremely assertive, so much so that the tiny minds of some of our 'designers' were overwhelmed. I used to say: use anything you want. Try paper or string. Don't be inhibited. This is theatre. I showed them pictures of the great Fascist air exhibition. They blinked. Be adventurous with type and graphics and colour. They said yeah. All you have to do is make the visitor look and react. I also used to say that such-and-such is the budget, but that was routinely ignored until executive intervention put things back in order.

I'll never forget the day that the team of designers, the same ones who had specified the permanent downlighters in the first place (average bulb life about 100 hours) installed a huge muslin dropped ceiling over the entire lot for an exhibition scheduled to last six weeks. The consequent effect was like Haydn's Farewell symphony where all the instrumentalists, each holding a candle, leave one by one and put the hall into darkness.

Furthermore, it was a matter of routine that text and labels were set too small; that monstrous panels of ponderous MDF were expensively fabricated offsite and clumsily manhandled into place where a few sheets of newsprint, Magic Marker and a notepad would have done nicely; that elementary aspects of circulation were ignored so that more often than not the public, amiably bewildered, was directed around an exhibition whose argument more-or-less demanded sequential consumption. Elizabeth David's best design aphorism was 'a bad meal is always expensive'. Exhibition designers were always afraid to do things modestly, lest the simple materials show up the modesty of the concept.

No doubt many of these problems were the fault of an ambitious or sloppy client, but it is equally certain that they betrayed the lamentable lack of discipline in all my dealings with 'designers': that very few of them had any idea how to use colour or light to good effect. The distinction between size and scale was meaningless to the majority and the notion that there should be an intelligent, but variable, relationship between image, text and object, depending on the context, was mere sophistry.

So, perhaps because it uses medieval technology, the exhibition is troublesome to execute. But I have no doubt that it has a great future, like a lot of other things from the past. There has never been so much demand from the public for intelligently presented and well-packaged information about art, manufacturers and the environment. By virtue of its inherent simplicity, the exhibition is cheap (at least when compared with a supersite on the Great West Road or 30 seconds in the break during News at Ten). Similarly, it is adaptable. Museums and galleries worldwide represent, I would say, about 10 per cent of the potential opportunities for exhibitions. People like them. There remains a special – almost religious – magic about the experience of consuming object, image and text first hand in agreeable spaces.

10

GORDON RUSSELL
The Listener
4 JUNE 1981

I was lucky enough to meet Sir Gordon Russell a number of times and he impressed me, as he did everyone else, by his thoroughgoing integrity, good humour, honesty and vision. He was a remarkable man, all of a piece, just like the furniture whose manufacture he so lovingly supervised from 1919 to his death last year. It was impossible not to like him: a large, but very gentle, person with an open and cheery face, rather like some species or other of benign forest creature. Besides furniture, he loved nature and fine wine, combining his affection for both by building in his magnificent Gloucestershire garden an enormous wall, made out of empties from the old family hotel. At the very end of his life, despite the progressively disabling affliction of motor neurone disease which cruelly deprived him first of the use of his hands, he remained confident, optimistic and inspirational. I heard him talking at 87 about the future.

Gordon Russell did not actually create the Design Council (then the Council of Industrial Design), but when he became its second director in 1947 it was scarcely three years old, and he was still able to formulate its original policy and its continuing character. His successor, Paul (now Lord) Reilly, maintained the tradition with equal panache. The achievement was to bring discussion about the nature of material culture, of *design*, before the astonished gaze of the state.

Russell's father had been a banker who became a rural hotelier, and it was in the antique restoration shop in Broadway, while at an anticlimactic loose end after World War One, that Gordon became interested in the process of making things. By 1922, he had his first exhibition of furniture designs in Cheltenham, and thereafter mortise mated with tenon and his life was filled with a whole succession of official successes, including chairmanship of the Board of Trade's utility furniture panel, playing a formative part in the creation of the Festival of Britain, a knighthood, the creation of the Design Centre and a fine autobiography, *A Designer's Trade*, which appeared in 1968. So how did the lad from Cricklewood with, as he freely admitted, no very special manual skills, manage to become during the middle years of this century a decisive influence in British design? It was all a matter of thinking and of method: the economic necessity to install machinery in the early Broadway workshop, where medieval craft practices still were routine, brought Russell face to face with the need to accommodate individual craftsmanship to the exigencies of the modern world. It was the eloquent and attractive solution he found to this problem which provided him with a lesson (still not fully learned) that he happily repeated throughout his working life. While respecting the traditions and the techniques of the craftsman, Russell used machines either when they saved a workman from repetitive and boring tasks, or when they could provide a finish or an effect which could not be achieved by hand.

Although Sir Gordon could, if he had wished (which I doubt), trace his intellectual and cultural inheritance back to the curious idolization of the navvy advanced by Carlyle and by Ruskin, and even though he had an almost mystical admiration for 'skill' (the title of his last public address), he had no delusions about the division of labour. He was the boss and the workers were there to execute his designs. It was the direct experience of this sort of delegation which helped Sir Gordon to formulate his lifetime policy which he summarized by saying that 'all my drawings started from the workshop, not the studio,' meaning that he studied the technique and process of design rather than rushing to a premature visualization of the finished product. This conviction, and his love of the country, allowed him to describe, say, a bridge which he liked as 'the structure Nature had been waiting for' and gave him both modi operandi *and* vivendi.

The book about him just published by his son-in-law and daughter, Ken and Kate Baynes (*Gordon Russell*, Design Council), has the agreeable vice of being more touching than objective – because it has to be said that the design of Gordon Russell Ltd furniture was never actually inspired, nor ever entirely in touch with the realities of the popular budget or the dreams of advanced taste. Although always fine, conscientious and, in fact, desirable, most of the furniture was and happily remains a version of sophisticated repro. Only with the cabinets made for Murphy radios during the Depression, not long after Henry Ford visited Broadway, did the firm design for the mass market, and then not for long.

Yet this is not the point. Sir Gordon Russell helped to bring the idea that making things is a professional business to public and official notice. Nowadays, with everybody's taste vacillating, his reconciliation of machine production and applied decoration is a provocative and stimulating one. But most important of all, his reassuring belief that the acquisition of skill is its own reward provides an age where the work ethic has gone adrift with an idea which is as much an inspiration as the example of the man himself.

II

ON A FUNDAMENTAL MISUNDERSTANDING OF ITALIAN DESIGN
Design
SEPTEMBER 1990

In Britain, a generation was taught by suggestion that 'design' was something monopolized by Scandinavians and inherent in crystal-owl paperweights and 1930s chairs made out of 'natural' materials. The implication by omission was that Italian design was not quite proper. Perhaps this was because of its continuously fashionable content.

Perhaps because of its direct links with futurist and therefore Fascist ideology. But most of all, I suspect, because of its close association with manufacturing industry. The relationship of design to industry has been something which the British are better at talking about than achieving.

In New York, the mistake was somewhat different. An Italian icon was for a long time prominent in MoMA's design collection, a fabulous Cisitalia of 1947, but it was there solely because its body was designed by Pininfarina. No one bothered to explain – or, perhaps, no one actually realized – that the reason, then as now, that Pininfarina had been able to create such a lovely shape was because his own artistry was able to flourish in a hierarchy of mutually supportive trades. This economic structure, a survival of Etruscan trade practices, still distinguishes northern Italy from anywhere else in Europe.

The Italians have so much brilliant design not because they are such brilliant designers, but simply because they have the capacity *to make things*. When Ettore Sottsass spoke at the V. & A. in 1981, someone asked him why Italy flourished without art schools. 'That's exactly why' was his laconic response. In this, as in everything else he has done, there is a strong element of irony, but you know what they say about many a true word. There is no gainsaying the amount of ironic genius invested in the early days of Memphis, but the phenomenon was just as much the evidence of Lombard and Piedmontese workshop traditions as it was of free artistic spirit.

It is the same with car design and this is where MoMA misunderstood the Cisitalia. Certainly, Pininfarina's original shape was one of rare beauty, but by concentrating on the purely visual aspects of industrial production, MoMA short-changed design. Any of the 'cars' that have emerged from the great *carrozzerie* are not so much darlings of *bella figura* designers, but a liaison of panel-beaters, pattern-makers, die-cutters and foundries. Efficient little workshops exist everywhere in Italy and this means that there is inevitably a production-based reality about what would otherwise be merely indulgent flights of fancy. Small factories set genius free.

And yet, as ever in awe of the superficial at the expense of analysis, we still celebrate the object and the personality. To know Italian design simply from what's in the shops is like preparing for a season's hunting merely by a visit to Swaine, Adeney and Brigg.

It seems that just as the Museum of Modern Art once misinterpreted Italian design, so we do today. Yet, as anybody fortunate enough to have seen a Ferrari 275LM in the same vista as Brunelleschi's dome knows, design – least of all in Italy – is not a one-dimensional subject.

12

FRENCH ÉLITISM
Design
MARCH 1991

The last decade saw the glorified putrefaction of the designer phenomenon, most especially in France where luxury goods form a significant part of the economy. In 1989 the Comité Colbert, a trade association of 70 merchants of expensively useless things, had sales of $5.4 billion. But now we have a recession and a crisis in retailing. The Avenue Montaigne does not yet look quite so blighted as Sloane Street and Bond Street, but it is going that way. The flamboyant couturier Christian Lacroix has toned down his latest collection and Balmain has abandoned *haute couture*. Louis Vuitton Moët Hennessey now does its ads in-house and 10 per cent of the US market for perfume is replicas.

Almost forever the French have made money out of quality, but is this period now over? I don't think so. Real French quality is distinct from exclusivity (whose prominence in retailing was just one of the more noticeable aberrations of the 1980s).

The very word we use to describe an élite is French. There is no English equivalent for *hauteur* or *froideur*. A sense of quality and an inclination towards stylishness affects all French life and did so long before anybody dreamed about niche marketing. The single thing about French culture which distinguishes it from British is its unity. A textile worker from Lille would be more likely to share the values – in, say, food, cars, clothes and education – of an *antiquaire* in the Rue Jacob than would the UK equivalents. That is not to say there are no distinctions in French society – there are – but it is a matter of distribution rather than intention. It is simply that the rich art dealer has more of what's available than the artisan. His tastes are not so different.

Frances Trollope, whose most famous work trashed American civilization, wrote her *Paris and the Parisians* in 1835. Just as the restive coarseness of American life repelled, the French love of doing things correctly attracted her: 'The manner in which an old barrow-woman will tie up her sou's worth of cherries for her urchin customers might give a lesson to the most skilful decorator of the supper table'. It is exactly this quality which makes French things special. Strange to say for a nation so avowedly élitist, it is often the ordinary things which work best. French vernacular architecture is marvellous; French official building frostily vacuous. You admire Starck for his skills at self-promotion, but see another uncomfortable chair designed to be photographed. Small French cars – the Renaults 4 and 5, the 2CV – are among the best ever made; their big cars invariably less successful.

A reason for this may be that the low culture is constantly supported by daily contact still with peasant traditions. More important still is that every *manif* of low culture has its own style: Paul Poiret memorably described Coco Chanel's achievement in using handkerchiefs and workman's clothes as '*misérablisme de luxe*'.

At a higher level, the French *esprit de corps* is famous. This is supported by a fantastical higher education system. The rollcall of the haughty *grandes écoles* (and the fascinating dates of their foundations) is like mankind's own journey of discovery, from design to shopping: École nationale des ponts et chaussées (1747); École polytechnique (1794); École nationale des mines (1783); École nationale supérieure des arts décoratifs (1795); and the latest, the École supérieure de commerce et d'administration des entreprises at Amiens and Nice

(1962). These institutions have given form, content and direction to French élites and we have nothing like them, except maybe Aston Business School.

The English have a distaste for evolving any theories in advance, whereas for the French it is an inclination so effectively cultivated you are tempted to regard it as natural. The French are at home with opulence, yet they maintain a genuine peasant culture; the English do not.

A more realistic economic environment in the 1990s may cool demand for XSOP brandy, sequinned cocktail dresses and luggage to carry bullion, but it will not alter the facts of French superiority in matters of design whose source is a preference for quality – at any price.

13

THE NEW
Creative Review
1996

At its best, industrial design is one of the most distinctive cultural achievements of the century. Along with the movies and rock music, it has provided symbols by which our civilization's aspirations and achievements may be defined.

While so many traditional art forms, including fine art, opera and even the novel, appear to me to be exhausted – at best derivative, at worst shrill in their pursuit of elusive shock value – design looks vigorous and honest.

At some point, although it is notoriously difficult to say exactly when, painting on canvas ceased to be the chief form of expression favoured by talented artists. This is not to say that painters of genius do not exist today – they do – but they are practising the relic of a once-proud craft.

One consequence of the death of painting as a leading medium has been the appearance of dead animals in London's Serpentine Gallery; another consequence has been the growing belief that industrial design may be the most legitimate artistic endeavour of the late twentieth century.

It is to the credit of painters, however, that we owe this perception. Francis Picabia, Fernand Léger and the pop artists are only random examples of taste makers who saw in the products of industry a poetic relevance that painting could not match. Technology routinely affords us examples of physical beauty and intellectual astonishment on a daily basis. Watch a plane landing or use a computer and you soon get the idea.

Industrial art has upstaged fine art, providing many of the sensations of aesthetic delight, awe, exhilaration, and images of the idea that were hitherto the province of painting. But it is a mistake for designers also to imitate the process of celebrity that has so contaminated fine art.

Human affairs demand that we can attribute great works of art to individuals, be it *The Divine Comedy*, the Portinari altarpiece, or Damien Hirst's dead lamb in formaldehyde. This idea of authorship works with fine art and is just about viable with a car such as the 1957 Chevrolet Bel Air, which tells you at least as much about American civilization as a novel by Jack Kerouac; but it disintegrates when you consider, say, a Boeing 747 which is so complex that no single individual could ever claim responsibility. The plane, however, remains a paradigm of industrial design.

The great achievements of design recall the medieval cathedrals: universally appreciated and created by legions of anonymous artisans engaged in a selfless quest. But today, because of the symbolic power of successful design, the intoxicating thrill of creating something admired and desired by *millions*, a new generation of designers is being misled by the lure of celebrity.

A substantial amount of what nowadays postures as design is in fact second-rate artistry in disguise. The Coke bottle is a perfect unity of form and function that makes the ultimate package; by comparison, the limited-edition bowl by Gaetano Pesce seems pitiful and preposterous because it will not in fact hold water.

In this country, the status of industrial design is further complicated by local economic factors. What is presently unclear (because Britain had no predecessors in its journey into industrialization) is to what extent a healthy design function can be maintained in a culture that has all but foresworn manufacturing in favour of post-modern activities such as financial services and tourism and Lord Gowrie's arts. Saying you want to be a product designer in 1994 Britain is rather like wanting to be a surgeon in a country without operating theatres.

The dangers inherent in the pursuit of celebrity are illustrated in the new edition of *The International Design Yearbook*, a substantial catalogue of new products from all over the world. Its content is somewhere between one of those infuriating catalogues of gimcrack novelties (a potato clock, a heated letter-opener) and an excitable guide to a student exhibition.

I did not notice any relevant consumer or performance data in more than 500 product entries. So much for '*Vackrare Vardagsvara*' ('more beautiful everyday things'), the motto of the Swedish design movement. So much for wanting to give everyone a better salad bowl, art dealer John Kasmin's affectionate jibe about Terence Conran. In *The International Design Yearbook* you have joined an exclusive club of wacky initiates with addresses in Soho and Covent Garden.

A generation ago, 'design' was a screwball subject … and sometimes I wonder what has changed. In the text of this volume, you get 'sea changes', 'benchmarks' and 'barometers'. Answers 'lie in' things and there are 'struggles to reassert creative supremacy'.

There are some marvellous individual items in the yearbook (I particularly liked Konstantin Grcic's beechwood coathanger with integral brush: a small work of genius), but the overall effect of any annual survey is to encourage novelty and, therefore, to reduce a worthwhile endeavour to sophomorish triviality.

There is more to design than *The International Design Yearbook*, which covers only furniture, lighting, tableware, textiles and products such as computers, telephones and cameras. It omits graphics, packaging, signage, illustration, fashion, vehicles, interiors, street furniture and information design. Significantly, it is in these neglected areas that Britain is strongest. As we watch the dust settle on the touching ambitions of the 1980s when industrial design promised to be the glue that would bind industry, commerce and culture into one fabulous wealth-producing entity, there has never been a better moment to make stirring statements about the meaning of design in a rapidly de-industrializing culture.

There is not a toot of this in *The International Design Yearbook*. It does not represent any coherent philosophy of design (unlike the pre-war Bauhaus movement), nor even display the stylish venality of America's pioneer industrial designers.

To be fair, this is not all the fault of the editors and the publisher. 'Design' is such a huge word that its use betrays the poverty of language. If to you 'design' is shorthand for a search for aesthetic and practical standards in an overcrowded world, if it is – to use Le Corbusier's memorable phrase – 'intelligence made visible', then you will find *The International Design Yearbook* disappointing.

If, on the other hand, you are the sort of person who needs to keep up with the very latest development in track lighting, or you have a restless curiosity about yet another slightly new chair by an ambitious young Belgian, this book is full-colour heaven.

When the great artists and architects of the early century discovered the beauty and poetry of machines, their conviction was that the future held a prospect of stability and purity, that well-designed, mass-produced goods would make beauty and practicality universal. To see what a far-fetched and unworldly vision this was, just look at the gallimaufry of novelty and warmed-up semi-innovation that passes for design today.

The future of design must not be one of restless innovation, but one where existing standards are refined. The public does not want to be mugged by successive novelties, but wants to enjoy more of what it already appreciates to be excellent.

So what is the mission of the industrial designer? He or she should be applying creativity to the challenges of our age, namely designing information rather than twiddling about with the shape and colour of a desk lamp. The designer will be involved with experience, not just appearance.

David Kelley, the Californian who created Apple computer's first mouse, a design that changed the way the world thinks and works, put it this way: 'I used to think creativity was designing a product to solve a problem. Now I think it's deciding what problem to work on'.

Part ten
Design politics

I

ROCK BOTTOMLEY
Harpers & Queen
APRIL 1994

Just what is it that makes the Secretary of State for Health so abominable? Quite a lot, as a matter of fact.

Let's start with the idea of 'public service'. Reading through the hillocks of press which 'Golden' Virginia Bottomley has received since she entered Parliament in 1984 requires both a gorge with a reliable disinclination to rise and a steely concentration, lest the mesmerizing effect of cliché piled upon platitude turns even the astutest sceptic into a doe-eyed sissy. Yes, the cuttings are boring, but in an indifferent patchwork of warmed-up banalities, one idea remains adamantine. It is this: Virginia Bottomley, by virtue of established family tradition and an acquired, yet inflexible, sense of moral superiority, is dedicated to 'public service'.

One form which public service takes is hospital visiting. A *Sunday Express* journalist, not known as a raving Trot, was once appalled to see Mrs Bottomley intrude into the solemn and private bedside rituals of a dying man's family, all teeth and smiles and jolly hockey sticks, in pursuit of a favourable hospital photo-opp. For a certain English caste, of which Mrs Bottomley is a prim and typical example, 'public service' is a well-greased career path with a huge pot of honey at its destination.

Mrs Bottomley's genes repay investigation – she comes from one of those sprawling English families which, if not precisely the great and the good, are certainly the bourgeois and the busybody part of our intricate day-to-day governing network. Her grandfather wrote a book called *Education and World Citizenship*. Her uncle by marriage, Lord Jay, was in politics. Peggy Jay, Virginia's aunt and matriarch of the tribe, was a Greater London Councillor and a prominent campaigner to preserve Hampstead Heath. Her cousin is, of course, Peter 'Mission-to-Explain' Jay and her brother, William Garnett, is a solicitor in one of the country's leading practices. Then there is Lord Hacking, a cousin by marriage who is a barrister. All solid, worthy know-betters.

Like Mrs Thatcher, Virginia Bottomley (born Virginia Garnett, Dunoon, Scotland, 12 March 1948, the year the National Health Service was founded) radiates sexual power. Although I myself think there is something aesthetically wrong with her knees, she is certainly the only woman in the House of Commons about whom it is possible to entertain and even develop pleasing erotic fantasies. Never mind that the competition is not fierce – indeed, the roguish Sir Nicholas Fairbairn once said that women MPs tend to look like the grim members of a Soviet motorized machine-gun corps – Mrs Bottomley has a special allure. Deadly.

Kick-arse, tough-but-sensitive, strong-but-sexy women are disconcerting to most men, but I believe much of her terrible power comes from two other stereotypes of women-in-British-life which she has adopted into her coruscating and indefatigable ego: the head-girl and the nanny. The aroma of merciless do-gooding is as suffocating as the scent of white hyacinth soap.

Although she has a fine academic record, not everything is exactly as it seems in the matter of Virginia Bottomley's secondary education. Although well qualified for the post – bags of energy and the depressingly telling admission 'I was an exhausting child. I was very serious' – she did not become head girl of Putney High, the south

London school with a richly deserved reputation for turning out girls who are Lorena Bobbitts of the male intellect. Later, she also failed to acquire the longed-for place at Somerville, accepting Essex instead. Here, again, is a misleading clue.

Although Virginia Garnett was famously married as a student only some months after the birth of her first child, it would be going too far to cast her as a feckless hippy-dippy or a rebellious campus radical. Essex University c.1966 was comfortably middle class, not a hotbed of Maoism, and her pregnancy was attributable not to a heterodox assault on bourgeois conventions, but to her being 'a little slow to cotton on to the realities of life', as her personal tutor Peter Townsend adroitly put it. It was at Essex, while others were listening to Pet Sounds and furtively reading copies of *International Times*, that Mrs Virginia Bottomley (BA Hons 2:1 Social Science) joined the Conservative Party. Whether despite or because of this early testament, she did not impress staff at Essex very favourably. Her sociology tutor, Professor Peter Abell, pronounced himself amazed that his student had risen to Cabinet rank, something which he said he never imagined would happen in 'a million years'.

Still, Virginia Bottomley went on to the London School of Economics and for the next fifteen years pursued a career of immaculately left-liberal credentials. In the 1970s she housed a Ugandan-Asian family for eighteen months and has correctly shown an interest in seals, toxic waste, litter and lead-free petrol. Her first job was as a researcher for the Child Poverty Action Group and then for eleven years she was a psychiatric social worker at the Maudsley Hospital.

If the clock had stopped in 1981 Virginia Bottomley would have been preserved as an educated, attractive, 33-year-old upper-middle-class working mother of three, the brilliant wife of an amiably eccentric MP (he once broke off a conversation about drink driving with journalist Henry Porter to ask the frequency of Radio One). At the beginning of the 1980s it looked as though she was prepared to bury her political ego in her social good works and be a fragrant Tory wife in her spare time: you can imagine a vanguard environmentalist in a Saab with muddy paw marks on the rear windows. That much brighter and smarter than most, but a Tory wife nonetheless. But then something happened. Virginia Bottomley decided to release herself into the community and become a Member of Parliament.

First time out she failed to be selected as candidate for Richmond, in November 1981. Second time out in 1983 she failed again, this time in the Isle of Wight, very likely because of her appalling slogan 'Turn Wight Blue'. This rejection by the voters was a particular snub as, through four generations, the modern Bottomleys and their ancestors had come to look on Seaview, IoW, rather as the Kennedys had Hyannis, MA. That the Isle of Wight failed on this occasion to turn blue, despite Virginia telling it to do so, was also a mistake costly in terms of personal stationery and one horribly predictive of behavioural disorders to come: such was her confidence in being elected in a territory she regarded as her own, she had had business cards printed with the legend Virginia Bottomley MP before the count.

The gods will not be mocked, but being reasonable divinities, having extracted humiliation and a cheque for the printer for the hubris of the IoW, they rewarded the persistent Mrs Bottomley with South West Surrey the following year. With Haslemere and Farnham within the boundaries, this constituency is the humming epicentre of the Home Counties, the scriptural home of middle-class values. Here Virginia Bottomley felt comfortable. Immediately, one of the most remarkable of modern political careers – measured not in coffee mornings but in fixed smiles, a firm hand and well-prepared speeches – began. It just goes to show how wrong Essex sociology professors can be.

When in 1988 Mrs Thatcher offered the job of Under Secretary for the Environment, Virginia accepted without demur. She has always insisted 'I was approached', since this gives the effect of her acceptance being a humble response to the call of duty ineluctable for someone of her background and ambition. Of course she was, but the 'I was approached' mantra which has been chanted to every inquiring journalist is characteristically opportunistic. It suggests a state of innocence quite out of character with the certainty of Her Way.

The curves of ambition and fate soon crossed: since the accident of birth the National Health Service has been Virginia Bottomley's coeval and, perhaps, her destiny. The one now a tough, self-possessed, 46-year-old careerist in brazenly rude health, the other a rather dear but worn-out old thing. The two are an odd fit and a dramatic one. The NHS has been a graveyard for Tories who find it both suspect and awe-inspiring. None of them has ever really got to grips with it.

When Mr Major 'approached' Virginia Bottomley with the smouldering health portfolio he was doing two things: one, providing the Cabinet with a token woman of highly agreeable appearance and, two, putting the last and most terrible of the Thatcherite blitzkrieg of market reforms into the capable hands of a politician who, in the view of many, allowed ambition to overcome what personal reservations she might have had about compromising the nation's welfare for doctrinaire political reasons. The Health Service is for Virginia Bottomley just like 'New York, New York' for Sinatra: if you can make it here, you can make it anywhere.

Before confronting the issue of what exactly is going on at the National Health Service, it must immediately be said that Virginia Bottomley's personal record of social responsibility is a legitimate one and makes her, at least in theory if not, alas, in practice, absurdly ill-equipped to impose the latest and greatest of monetarist reforms on to the creaking and leaking flagship of welfare. It does appear that Mrs Bottomley cares and I don't just mean the Ugandans and the seals; her uncompromising you-must-eat-your-greens pronouncements are, in a sense, honourably liberal, since they contain the faint echo of older ideas about a command economy and planning.

As incontrovertible as the fact of Virginia's genuine concern for health is the fact that the National Health Service needed reform, although this has not been a sufficient basis for a happy relationship. No reasonable person could deny his allegiance to the idea that 'free' health care for all is an attractive idea, but equally by the 1980s no reasonable person could deny that Britain could no longer afford it. Here was a £40 billion monster with more employees than the old Red Army. And, besides, everyone knew that there was profligate waste and inefficiency in state hospitals.

Never mind that the United Kingdom was spending less on health in both absolute and real terms than other advanced countries, the NHS had the effect on Mrs Thatcher that Holy Water used to have on the devil in Dennis Wheatley novels: the mere mention of it would cause spasm. She sacked John Moore from the job of Secretary of State for Health when he had the nerve to hint to the three Presidents of the Royal Colleges who petitioned him for more money that he might be sympathetic. According to C. J. Dickinson of the Wolfson Institute of Preventive Medicine: 'The concept of any public service that was free to people who had not made identified financial contributions was deeply offensive to one whose obsession with money and self-reliance was overwhelming'. What better than to expose the old system to the thrilling blast of market-place efficiency?

But the problem with health is that it is not a market place in the icy logic of the profit and loss account. Something as huge and ambitious as a National Health Service for a population of 60 million people could never be wholly efficient and successive governments of various complexions have continued to chip away at it: the provision of prescription charges was just the beginning of making the public aware that the Health Service was not 'free'. The health market being imposed by grin-and-bear-it Bottomley is the reduction to absurdity of this principle. Its structure is fabulously complicated and could only have been devised by mandarins of elevation so lofty that their view of reality became blurred, but it goes something like this: now that hospitals are enjoined to make a 'profit' they have to do so from ECRs, or Extra Contractual Referrals made by fund-holding GPs who act as agents in matching up the supply of expertise to the demand for treatment. They disburse funds previously held by local health authorities. The problem here is that the dynamics of human illnesses do not conform to balance sheets. Enoch Powell has said that systematizing health in a way a dim accountant could understand cannot work, because it is 'measuring the immeasurable'.

The area for wheeling and dealing now being explored by fund-holding GPs creates a 'market', but only in a limited sense because, unlike a real market, opportunities for growth and expansion do not exist. Any hospital's contractual funding for such-and-such a medical service is limited. Irrespective of any continuing demand for routine operations, when a hospital has fulfilled its contract it has to stop performing them because in the logic of the system it is doing so for the hated F-word ('free'). In this version of efficiency, skilled people sit around doing nothing useful, sick people remain sick. The market also means that in practice patients are shuttled from one region to the next, so that 'demand' chases 'supply' up and down the motorways of Britain. This arrangement suits the poor, the homeless and non-drivers very badly. Worse, profit-making activities include glamorous technical operations (hearts and brains), but do not include long-term continuous health care provision such as geriatrics. Reformed hospitals dread receiving someone disabled by a stroke since the cost of caring for him or her will exceed the provision of funds available for such a service. When wards in NHS hospitals become empty, they can be privatized.

The arbitrary forces of the market-place make rational planning of health care provision impossible. This crazily inefficient quest for efficiency is the source of the grievance about the two-tier health system. The grievances come both from suffering patients and from frustrated doctors, one of whom described the present circumstances as 'utter chaos'. One consultant in a London teaching hospital, a normally phlegmatic individual who asked not to be named, someone who works daily with the chaos and absurdity of the new 'efficiency', says of Mrs Bottomley's claims to be improving the Health Service, 'She looks sensible and intelligent, but I know she's lying'.

With the NHS farce, Virginia Bottomley is trapped between public outrage and the despair of the medical profession, but as far as her career is concerned she is probably more concerned about the suspicions of the Tory Right who see her, rather implausibly, as a wishy-washy liberal who lacks the nerve to see these reforms through. John Redwood, Welsh Secretary, Fellow of All Souls, one of the Prime Ministers 'bastards', was openly and damagingly critical of the mountains of paperwork generated by the newly 'efficient' NHS. Recent figures show that over ten years, managers are up 32.6 per cent with an increase in nurses of only 1.1 per cent. Worse, many of those nurses have had to become managers. Almost as ruinous to national morale has been the ugly spread of MBA psychobabble: it does not help intelligent discussion of the future of the nation's health care when hospitals are called 'provider units'.

But it is perhaps not Mrs Bottomley herself who is abominable, although many would support the proposition that she is a provider unit of lethal amounts of abomination. Maybe it goes with the horrible job of being a modern minister, especially one who is an individual torn between idealism and careerism, but who appears to be prepared to sacrifice personal convictions and objective truth on the altar of ambition. It is like the knees, not a pretty sight. Still, all correspondents note Virginia Bottomley's smile and many are favourably impressed. In every encounter with the press, every good deed is presented as iconic, or revealing of a modest yet positive personality trait, but there is a horrible pride in the way she insists she is the 'world's worst cook'. Cooking requires only simple disciplines like planning, care, patience and a desire to please, so there is not much to boast about at being bad at it.

What she is very good at, however, is cooking up photo-opps for herself, of which the annual event recording the Garnett/Bottomley family gathering at Seaview on the Isle of Wight has become a fixture in the Fleet Street calendar. Here Mrs Bottomley takes the carefully staged opportunity to push her paid-up membership of middle England, her 'traditional' but not grand family – and her starring role in it (for she is always at the centre of the picture). Year follows year and there is Mrs Bottomley sucking an ice-lolly in a deliberately distressed straw hat. She's just like us really, the carefully staged picture seems to say. Like us? With 40 members of a family dragooned into a group on the Seaview seashore facing the telephoto lenses of Fleet Street? Hardly. There is something faintly ridiculous in all this. It just doesn't work, because it works too hard.

Is Virginia Bottomley a monster? Maybe she is unlucky in the way she is reported, or maybe she just has a fabulous ability to be misunderstood, a talent for making reasonable propositions sound sinister, or hilarious. Remember the business of Marks & Spencer when they opened the store specially for the Secretary of State, just like Elton John at Versace? As if the two-tier health service was not enough, we had two-tier shopping at Marble Arch, something which outraged the Shopping Hours Reform Council. But her rationale was soundly based on a democratic principle. She said, 'Women in public life are looked at, and it's nice when people can say they saw me coming out of Cabinet in something they've got too'. Then she ruined the effect by adding, 'At least it wasn't Harrods'.

When this January the *Observer* ran a headline saying: 'Put single parents in hostels' it was merely reporting a Bottomley initiative to provide on-site babysitting as she was anxious about young mothers being lonely. Alternatively, her opinions on sex are risibly similar to the sloganizing of the Red Guards. You feel the following are better suited to a stern political officer in a washing-machine factory at Hang-Chow rather than someone who lives next door to Penelope Keith in Milford: 'Good personal and sexual relationships can actively promote health and well-being' and 'Sexual activity can sometimes lead to unwanted pregnancies, ill-health or disease'.

Withal, the horror of Virginia Bottomley is that she is a do-gooder. Certainly, this is a more desirable condition to the do-badder, but the assumption of superiority it entails fits uneasily with public service where humility and a taste for listening are attributes at least as valuable as priggishness and case hardened convictions. A journalist once explained to Peter Bottomley that she did not want to make his wife sound too worthy. To his credit Bottomley said, 'I think you will find it very hard to make her sound anything else'.

Encouraged by Thatcher as a telegenic antidote to her own brand of Victorian values, brought on by Major as a token woman, detested by the medical profession, scourge of slackers and recidivists, drinkers, smokers, fornicators, doctors and patients, Virginia Bottomlz pursues her father's grail of 'work, service, cooperation, sacrifice'. Another relation, her uncle, Lord Jay, father of Mission-to-Explain, may have influenced her in this soaring justification of social engineering when he said, 'In the case of nutrition and health, just as in the case of education, the gentleman in Whitehall really does know better what is good for people than the people themselves'.

There can be no doubt that Virginia Bottomley's estimation of her own worth confirms her nannyish conviction that she knows best, even in the face of a dismayed medical profession. She says, 'It may be that nanny isn't always wrong'. Possibly, but in a *Daily Telegraph* poll of September 1993, 59 per cent thought nanny … insincere.

2

A BRAND-NEW MORRIS MARINA
Newstatesman & Society
18 JANUARY 1991

I rode shotgun on a vehicle that sped through the decade of enterprise culture. At first, the ride was exhilarating then increasingly futile. Out of control, the vehicle crashed. Now that Mrs Thatcher has picked her way out of the wreckage and her successor is directing the traffic, what are we to make of the apparently vast, but, in reality, so fragile, achievements of the 1980s?

Howard Brenton wrote a remarkable piece in *The Guardian* last month that, if it had been parody, would have been hilarious, but, since I think it was intended to be serious, was, in fact, rather quaint. With a righteousness grown huge, but limp, born of many evenings in the pub, alienated from the circus of consumption where almost all of us enjoyed ringside seats, Brenton described the eighties as 'malevolent'.

He presented himself and his subsidized cronies as emerging from the saloon bar, dusting themselves off after a decade of intoxicated hibernation, to offer themselves and their 'art' to a public that, gorged on West German cars, Japanese videos and Sainsbury's Côtes du Rhône, now wants, or so it imagines, to return to the thrilling blast of socialist-realist playwriting. This is like saying: 'Would you like to buy a brand-new and unused Morris Marina?'

I think Brenton has got it wrong. There is not a huge audience waiting for him. People actually seem to *like* Audi, Sony and Jaboulet, and are now better able to appreciate these excellent product than ever before.

This arose from that terrible period when malevolent GTIs and 911s patrolled the streets, and cell phones, brasseries and gyms made it unsafe for socialist dramatists to unfurl their placards. People, on the other hand, became better dressed, ate better and took more care of their health than ever before, but this is by-the-by.

That Mrs Thatcher 'politicized everything' is absolutely true, but this was, for a long time, an ambition of the hard left, which failed to politicize anything, apart from its own absurdly narrow agenda, because it used blunt and unattractive tools. So the crypto-Kropotkins are lamenting the fact that now that people have a choice, they are rejecting clapped-out avant-garde thought. It is a beguiling paradox that, nowadays, there is nothing quite as dull and dated as the avant-garde. As Gore Vidal once asked: 'Avant to what?' The squeals can be heard from Kentish Town to Chalk Farm.

Life and art are closer now than at any time since the urban revolution. Now that everything has, indeed, been politicized, there is no place for a politically conscious art. Real politics nowadays is about taste and the environment, not about political dogma. In his 1953 essay 'Communism in Power and the problem of Art', Alberto Moravia – long a Communist sympathizer – acknowledged that the only valid art was that produced through a direct commercial transaction between artist and consumer. Quite so. This not the law of the jungle but the theory of the market place.

The problem with Mrs Thatcher was always her aesthetics, rather than her ideas, which were really rather libertarian. Mrs Thatcher's notion, which I believe is quite correct, that there is no such thing as society, only individuals and their families, is not a sentiment that can serve the cause of authoritarianism. I don' know whether Howard Brenton has read Hegel's *Vorlesungen*, but it's worth pointing out that the MP for Finchley did not invent the *Zeitgeist*, she was an expression of it. If her interpretation was occasionally vulgar, and too often shrill, then this is what must be expected when mere politicians – especially ones with no professed taste for culture – are entrusted with the philosophy of history.

The 1980s were an extraordinary adventure whose coruscating

absurdities only serve to emphasize what deep structural changes occurred. At their beginning, I witnessed one of the flotations that, together with the sequence of acquisition and mergers that followed, characterized the business life of the decade. The sense of confidence, ambition and certainty was mesmerizing. It was only when, about six years later, I saw all the long wheel-base 'S'-Class Mercedes-Benzs lined up for a Guinness do at the National Gallery that I realized quite how much had changed forever. Recently I went to a performance of *Un Ballo in Maschera*, sponsored by Fiat, whose guest I was. I met a friend in the bar and commented how fine corporate entertaining was becoming. 'Yes, sure,' he replied, 'but the food here is nothing on last week's BMW B-Minor Mass'.

The intrusion of business into art and education was astonishing. I went to a meeting where Ralph Halpern's number two was explaining, in between spastic intrusions from his beeping portable, how Burton was planning to create an artworkers' community in the north-east to rival Darmstadt or Worpswede. Rodney Fitch sponsored scholarships at the Victoria & Albert Museum and Jocelyn Stevens, a Fleet Street publisher of bloodthirsty notoriety but considerable accomplishment, became Rector of the Royal College of Art. Most famously, Sir Terence Conran built a Design Museum.

Design was, of course, the token and talisman of the decade, its significance best understood by anthropologists who know about sympathetic magic. I was involved in the museum and, when it opened in summer 1989, it caused me to wonder 'at what stage in the history of a subject does someone build a museum to cater for it?' I came to the conclusion that the answer was 'somewhat late in the day'. Not because it was the end of 'design' in any sense. Design is a term that unites all the disciplines involved in the planning of material things and, as such, will clearly always be with us. But, by the late 1980s, it was becoming clear that 'design' was being stigmatized as a glossy cure-all for a more fundamental malaise.

It was not mere opportunism that led entrepreneurs to design, but the status temporarily achieved by some of the big consultancies (all now much smaller) was evidence of something disturbing, and at the source of British decline: our baffling inability to understand the nature of true competitiveness. Even as Mrs Thatcher was preaching the gospel, she was ignoring the basis of the problem in education. It is not true that Britain has an education system that does not recognize the entrepreneurial spirit. On the contrary, people like Gerald Ronson and Terence Conran were spotted immediately – and expelled. Sir Clive Sinclair was not expelled, but, like Sir Ralph Halpern, he never had the benefit of higher education.

Only the frivolities of the 1980s were absurd: the Sinclair C5s, the gallerias and the bloated art market. What really happened was the consolidation of art into life, or commerce into culture, but not without disturbing implications for the future of Britain, which even socialist playwrights have not anticipated. The future is not going to be an absurd tussle between the ghost of the philistine Thatcher and the reborn Bohemian Brenton. Britain's manufacturing industries were horribly damaged by daft, politically motivated, industrial and investment policies. The last pretence that Britain might remain an independent manufacturer of consumer goods disappeared. Even the famed cultural industries have vanished: recorded music, so long a focus of national pride, is now located almost exclusively in Burbank and Hamburg.

So many of the losses were real, so many of the achievements dubious; but two outstanding features do characterise the era just past. The first is the individual's relation to consumption, whether of goods, services or art. We now accept that there is nothing venal about the marketplace, since this is just a word to describe a place where people make choices. The second is industry, and its relation to culture. During Mrs Thatcher's years, industry began to acknowledge that it had a role in education and in art. Helping to create the climate of opinion that made the Design Museum possible, I recognized this sense everywhere.

Now, like so many industrial lessons from the past, the case has been argued here and won elsewhere. Look to Japan and you will see that, just as Nissan learned to build cars from a licence granted by Herbert Austin, so now a huge popular lesson in design education has been transplanted east, for subsequent export here. Mazda has its new M2 building and Toyota its Amulux centre. These extraordinary ventures are not only dramatic architecture in their own right, but curious hybrids between showroom, museum, convention centre and think tank. Their existence confirms the public's engagement in the products of the future.

The conceit that a bunch of dusted-off socialist playwrights is now about to redraft the cultural agenda is as naive as it would be unwelcome. The market is the best judge, and that market is now global. Fancy local flashes of the commerce-and-culture phenomenon might have been misleadingly bright and disappointingly short-lived in Britain, but their influence remains. Sponsored television, once unthinkable, is now inevitable. The fragmentation of the media means not more manipulation by communicators or advertisers, but more popular choice, expressed in terms of consumption. The communicators and the advertisers are at the mercy of the public.

But what a tawdry old Manichean conflict the visitor of some left-versus-right drama conjures up. People are not left or right; they are consumers. Politics is no longer about what politicians think and do, but about what people want to acquire and consume. Dr Edzard Reuter, chairman of Daimler-Benz and its aerospace subsidiary DASA, quietly acknowledges this. Daimler-Benz now has a deliberate international strategy to place itself beyond political influence. Meanwhile, the sad old lefties stumble blinking into the light.

3

DISPOSABLE ATTITUDE TO AESTHETICS
Spectator
17 JANUARY 1998

ASSOCIATED PRESS, London. *A SWAT team working for the Minister without Portfolio is suspected of being behind the mysterious disappearance of the design guru …*

Well, of course, that's not actually true. And nor is the stuff about voodoo sacrifice. But, as they say in Italy, *si non è vero* ... The Mount St Helens of silly coverage last weekend was caused by a leak of resignation correspondence followed by mysterious off-the-record briefings to various journalists designed to damage those parts of my reputation which even my own baroque flair for self-destruction cannot reach. The result was that my house was surrounded for the entire weekend by intrusive journalists. There is something scary about aspects of this government.

A few weeks before I first met Peter Mandelson, *The Guardian* ran a profile with a headline describing me as 'The Peter Mandelson of aesthetics'. This rather amused me, the implied diabolical mastery of my own subject being flattering. So much so that when we were eventually introduced, I mentioned the description to the minister. He offered the very thinnest of smiles, engaged in a brief pause, dipped his head and asked if I was pleased. I didn't at the time have a response, although it is noteworthy that Mr Mandelson has not since taken up the seemingly attractive option of describing himself as 'The Stephen Bayley of politics'.

As a politician, it is inevitable that Peter Mandelson has a disposable attitude to aesthetics. With someone like myself, who regards typography as far, far more important in the general run of things than politics itself, there is potential for conflict. Alas, while it would be absurdly self-dramatizing actually to believe what the papers say, it does seem that the Minister without Portfolio and I had a doomed relationship, such as it was. Thus, despite my enthusiasm for the Millennium as a whole, Peter Mandelson's recent and much photographed trip to Disneyland prompted my final resignation from a major project which fascinates me.

A covert mission to Florida to experience at first hand Disney's supreme professionalism would have been one thing, but a formal audience with Mickey Mouse for inspirational purposes was, I felt, misjudged. Disney has been doing Disney since 1955 and has acquired a peerless repertoire of deep, deep expertise in crowds management, entertainment systems and computerized data capture. Even if it were desirable to attempt a thin replica of Disney in

Greenwich (which is a mere few hundred kilometres from the local Disney in Marne-la-Vallée), the time available simply does not allow it. I believe that the Millennium Experience should be an elegant and economical exhibition about the world of the future, designed by the greatest architects and designers available. Accessible to the public, comprehensible to the media and with technical collaboration from the world's great industries who would be involved as creative partners, not arm's-length sponsors.

Of course, in a government-funded project, it's inevitable that there's a political dimension. It would be naive to expect otherwise. But in Millennial Britain, politics is not about real vision or commitment. Politics is not about brave, statesmanlike convictions. Politics too often depends on bobbing and weaving to intercept public opinion. Our executives are like the nightmarish agency account man who simply wants to know what time of day would you like it to be. You cannot use focus groups to test creativity. To be excellent, the Millennium must be daringly creative in style, execution and content. Yet this sort of daring is incompatible with New Labour. Creative people like to think the unthinkable. New Labour encourages a dim political correctness. Creative people, like me, are pig-headed and unreasonable. With New Labour you have, in the awful, stilted jargon, to be 'on message' or you are off the job.

Take two well-publicized examples of Millennium Muddle: the Union Jack and Christianity. These are perfect examples of how the unreasonable creative impulse can only with difficulty work with the more pragmatic political one. Now, I happen to be extremely proud of being British and don't take second place to anybody in my argumentative advocacy of Britain's superiority in many of life's refinements. I think it is sensationally interesting and stimulating that the world's biggest Millennium event is happening in London. Our capital is the most exciting city in the world not only because the ethnically British happen to be good at what the Department for Kultur, Media und Sport would call the 'creative industries', but because every Spanish film-maker, Argentinean architect, American photographer and German designer wants to work here. The Millennium is a superb advertisement for Britain's huge contemporary competitive advantage. Union Jacks, notwithstanding my admiration for the timeless graphics, are redundant in this context.

Christianity is more contentious, but the creative argument would be that, of course, Judaeo-Christian theology has established our moral and justice systems which are the most decent in the world. However, a narrow denominational approach to the Millennium which involved the Established Church may alienate Jews, Hindus, Parsees, Muslims, Catholics, Vegetarians, Scientologists and Voodoo priests. Far better to construe religion as an integrated part of a healthy culture and to ensure that Millennium activities reflect and generate the highest aesthetic and moral principles. However, we creatives may have lost this one. The last time I checked the scoreline it was Conran and Bayley nil, Mandelson and the General Synod, one.

How odd, then, that when I was talking to Bettina von Hase about the Creative Industries Task Force, she just said, 'But this is pure East Germany'. Karl-Marx-Stadt, 1964. Just think of it. That's what politics did for creativity. And morals.

4
MANDELSTEIN'S MONSTER
Observer
NOVEMBER 1998

What is People's Britain going to look like? I think you can forget Betjeman's village green as a model, just as you can forget the alternative vision, which the Poet Laureate so reviled, of a Britain full of council blocks and bypasses. Something else is being prepared in Professor Mandelstein's laboratory.

Not since the elaborate refinements of Byzantium has a civilization cared so much about the nuances of iconography, the heraldry of nationhood. This obsession with style may be the distinctive feature of our *fin de siècle*. Harold Macmillan cared so little for the look and taste of things that he thought it ungentlemanly actually to notice what was on his plate. Yet you imagine *The River Café Cook Book* is more prominent in Tony Blair's library than Walter Bagehot or John Ruskin. In New Britain, *The Stones of Venice* might be mistaken for a new north Italian polenta dish. Probably seared.

Style and packaging have become two of the greatest activities of the State. I'm rather surprised we haven't actually got a Ministry of Corporate Identity, with Departments of Emblematic Constructs and Cognitive Dissonance, busy working on mad Professor Mandelstein's brief to rebrand Britain.

There is already some work-in-progress. We are told it is People's Britain, which for this person at least sets alarm bells ringing. Last time we saw a new European government so determined to do things in the name of the People, the word they used was Volk. Totalitarian governments almost always accord special significance to architecture and design as expressions of power and authority. There are, for instance, only imperceptible shades of difference between the bloated classical style favoured by Stalin and the bloated classical style favoured by Hitler. Nor is there a world of difference between the Soviet 'party line' and Professor Mandelstein's wince-making neologism, 'on message'.

This preoccupation with style is all-pervading. Donald Dewar MP, not a noted aesthete, has lifted his kilt and shown a bit of leg to the Prince of Wales, suggesting His Royal Highness become involved with the design of the new Scottish Parliament, because he enjoys architecture. This is as misjudged and incongruous as inviting the Queen to do a spot of mucking-out at Lambourn because Her Majesty enjoys racing. Despite his avowed interest in architecture, there is very little in the Prince of Wales's record to suggest a genuine knowledge and enthusiasm for building. The catalogue of complete works prepared under his enlightened patronage is a thin one. No matter, Donald Dewar's necessary emblematic gesture has been made.

New powers have often sought an expression of their purposes and personality in heroic building. When Napoleon installed the

Wittelsbach family as Kings of Bavaria, they set about an ambitious programme of city-building which still defines the character of Munich. Nineteenth-century beer and soap barons built themselves castles. Industrial power gave us enduring symbols such as the Mies van der Rohe and Walter Gropius buildings in New York, for Seagram and Pan Am.

Today, US corporate architecture is designed as a symbol to be seen from the freeway. It is this version of corporate identity that has inspired Professor Mandelstein's proposals for a rebranding of Britain. Which is to say: a rather dated version. The recent Demos pamphlet, 'Britain – Renewing our Identity', reads like the transcript of a Highgate dinner party circa 1983. The paradox about New Labour's People's Britain is that it is acquiring a flavour that is both inappropriately corporatist as well as half a generation behind the curve.

Just as Professor Mandelstein is ordering up his design proposals for an entire nation, the big corporations are abandoning any attempt at universal identity. Ford is more advanced than most in its plans for global production, but its products will be different in all territories. Ford's conviction is to think global, act local. The modern economy, with instantaneous data transfer and planetary movements of capital, makes a nonsense of traditional ideas about nationhood. The chairman of BMW, Bernd Pischetsrieder, declared that real value lay in saying 'Designed and engineered by BMW' rather than 'Made in Germany'.

In a world where e-mail undermines frontiers, too self-conscious an approach to national identity is surely misguided. In physics, the Uncertainty Principle says you can never understand sub-atomic particles because the mere act of investigation distorts their behaviour. National identity is just as sensitive and fugitive.

Which brings us to the Millennium Dome, the Colosseum of Blair's Information Age Empire. It is already the most familiar new building in Britain: a genuine repository for our unease about the present and our hopes for the future. While Richard Rogers's design is truly audacious, it is, like the rebranding campaign, curiously dated.

Architectural fashion calls for a more flexible, intuitive, anti-rational design such as Frank Gehry's £60 million Guggenheim Museum in Bilbao. Rogers is undoubtedly an architect of genius, but the Dome is what he wanted to build rather than the building the Millennium needs. Thus, as a solution which existed before the problem was properly stated, the Millennium Dome perfectly represents a culture where almost everything is sacrificed on the altar of presentation.

In off-the-record briefings in his subterranean lab, Professor Mandelstein explains that the Great Exhibition in 1851 and the Festival of Britain in 1951 had their detractors. True, but there is a difference. In 1851 and 1951, the philistines were on the outside.

5

COOL BRITANNIA
Labour Camp
1998

What more compelling symbol of transformation can there *ever* have been than the one that changed Reginald Kenneth Dwight (b.1947) into Elton Hercules John (b.1967). Here was inspiration of an extremely high order. It predicts and reflects with hypnotic accuracy the transformation of Old Labour (b.1900) into the sleek, heroic New version (b.1994) where Reg and Ken are not welcome, need not apply. And to support the metaphor, each transformation has its supporting characteristics of shiny, brittle, petulant vanity to replace the more homely (but 'old') traits of its predecessor. The rich semantic dissonance between Reg and Hercules transcends mocking comment.

It is not surprising that rock music has been appropriated as the chief expression of the people's art in the magic kingdom of cool Britannia. A radical 'New' government finds it incredibly, sloppily convenient to bypass the tiresome and time-consuming business of earning respect and building up credentials by enlisting council household names to represent New Britain. But even in this wonderland, the preferment under New Labour of Elton John has been astonishing. Bryan Appleyard, a noted cultural commentator, calls John 'the worst popular musician ever'. In *Faking It* (1998), Anthony O'Hear made the memorable observation that to have Elton John playing at the funeral of Diana was as absurd as having Vera Lynn singing at the funeral of George VI. But in New Labour's magic kingdom, it actually happened.

This so-so one-time pub pianist has become the chief sentimentalist of the New Labour regime, although I must concede that cool he is not. But knighted he is. We cannot say whether this honour was designed to divert the passions of the Diana cult into votes for New Labour or to acknowledge services to export. The records may be dodgy, but the record is awesome: a generation of low-to-middle brows has grown up to *Your Song* (1971), *Rocket Man* (1972), *Crocodile Rock* (1972), *Daniel* (1973), *Candle in the Wind* (1974) and *Don't Go Breaking My Heart* (1976). Elton John is suburbia amplified: he is to the true story of rock what Barry Norman is to the *Cahiers du Cinéma*. Since 1971 he has had countless number ones and sold millions of albums, each one golden. His Diana Dirge is the bestselling record of all time, easily out-sentimentalizing *White Christmas*.

He is a popular phenomenon, therefore it is irrelevant and élitist even to wonder if he is actually any good. He is emphatically middle of the road. He is classless. He is clean, dried-out. He has seen the dark side, but has come up smelling of Versace. His gayness is not frightening, at least not in public. His career was just about ready for a valedictory 'yet more greatest hits' when fate intervened and he relaunched himself. Whoever would have thought you could relaunch Old Labour? Whoever would have thought you could relaunch Elton John? As I say, the parallels of the transformation are remarkable.

Late May 1988, Elton performed at Stormont in NI. It was, they say, immensely moving, a clear recognition of what can be achieved when popular culture works in the cause of cool Britannia. It was, according to Mo Mowlam, the NI Secretary, a 'truly historic occasion'. She went on to praise Sir Elton for his consistent dedication to the Irish (to coin a truly memorable phrase) 'in good times and bad'. It was an epiphany, was Elton in Ulster. Real cool. The singer of *Crocodile Rock* did not, on this rare occasion, shed crocodile tears. He had been clasped to the bosom of Ulster. And what, a *Times* reporter asked the Secretary of State, is your very favourite Elton John song? She didn't know. Couldn't answer. Had a memory lapse. Perhaps couldn't care.

Curiously, although archaeologists of jargon are not exactly agreed on this, 'cool Britannia' seems to have been an invention (or, at least, an opportunistic discovery) of Virginia Bottomley's regime at the Department of National Heritage. Cool Britannia has become a hot issue, as quickly disavowed by embarrassed ministers as it was earlier accepted with credulous enthusiasm. Cool Britannia was the inevitable (although, it seems, temporary) destination of a journey that began with the branding of Britain.

If you ask me, there's a big problem with the idea of 'cool'. First, it's a period label so antiquated that its only effective use is an *ironical* one. No one in their right mind ever refers to anything as cool, other than ironically. The origins of the term are instructive. From the vicarage tea party term 'as cool as a cucumber', meaning unflustered and composed, there was an easy (if surreal) conceptual leap to describe the stoned and groovy composure of jazz musicians Charlie Parker and Miles Davis (whose *Birth of the Cool* was released in 1949). That locates the idea somewhat distant in time. And in space. We are talking of New York in the 1950s. 'Cool' is a quaint archaism.

To find a contemporary government, let alone a contemporary government that styles itself as 'New', showing such a witless interest in the most gormless forms of neophilia is embarrassing. Of course, the actual expression 'cool Britannia' is an unsophisticated pun, which has its own origins in the 1960s. To be momentarily fair, the term has never been officially endorsed by the government, but on the other hand, discounting current hasty disavowals, never has it been energetically rejected. In so far as it's a lazy cliché that evokes a rather dopey concept of style, it is characteristic of a camp regime, which insists on appearance over substance.

Cool Britannia mugged the intellectuals. After so many years of positive anti-aesthetics – if she thought about art at all, one imagines Mrs Thatcher thought it wet – a government that said it was interested in style appeared to be a very good thing. To appropriate an expression of Mrs Thatcher's, architects, designers, filmmakers and artists thought that they could do business in a New Britain whose government did not repudiate art, but positively wallowed in it. But what quality was that wallowing? And in what intellectual depths did the wallowing take place? Shallow is the answer. In the breathless rush to have all symbols of modernization in place and shining very brightly, the PM has provided eloquent and damaging evidence of superficiality. He does this at media tie-in parties at Downing Street where the guest list looks like what Sir Roy Strong scornfully described as 'sweepings'. It is much, much easier to be seen and, more importantly, to be photographed hugging Mick Hucknall of Simply Red than it is to radicalize intellectual property law or reinvent music on the National Curriculum.

Here the problem changes again. I don't, I'm glad to say, know what Mick Hucknall thinks, but I don't want rock stars – even middle-of-the-road housewives' choice, first-time caller, greatest-hits, in-car-CD-player rock stars – enrolled as the consorts of politicians. The relationship is doubly damaging, coarsening one party and neutralizing the other. As Picasso knew, authentic art is always seditious. Explaining the invention of Cubism, he said 'We didn't any longer want to fool the eye, we wanted to fool the mind'. And later elaborated:

> The point is, art is something subversive. It's something that should not be free. Art and liberty, like the fire of Prometheus, are things one must steal, to be used against the established order. Once art becomes official and open to everyone, then it becomes the new academicism... If art is ever given the keys to the city, it will be because it's been so watered down, rendered so impotent, that it's not worth fighting for... Every poet and every artist is an anti-social being. He's not that way because he wants to be; he can't be any other way. Of *course* the state has the right to chase him away – from its point of view – and if he is really an artist it is in his nature not to want to be admitted, because if he is admitted it can only mean he is doing something which is understood, approved and therefore old hat – worthless.

The paradox is that governments do not like subversion. The pursuit of coolness, either explicit or unacknowledged, is a self-denying ordinance. It is just like the nightmare individual who comes up to you at a party and says 'I have been told I have an exceptionally interesting personality'. There is nothing so depressingly ordinary as the desire to appear exceptional. Wanting to be cool immediately and irrevocably disqualifies you from ever being so. Miles Davis did not need this explaining to him. So far from being cool, the New Government's position is timorous and unprincipled. It is sweaty and tacky.

Even if it were an intelligent and attractive policy (which calls for a nationwide suspension of disbelief), a notion as crude as cool Britannia is pitiably thin and one dimensional. William James gave readers of *The Principles of Psychology* an interesting definition of 'self':

> The sum total of all that [an individual] can call his, not only his body and his psychic powers, but his clothes, and his house, his wife and children, his ancestors and friends, his reputation and works, his lands and horses and yacht and bank account. (vol. 1, p. 291)

Which is to say that William James knew that anybody's self, notwithstanding the relative rarity of the horses and the yachts, is complex, various and eclectic. And, rather as Picasso insisted, that, just as creativity cannot be managed or directed, a national identity, still less a self-consciously cynical and self-promoting cool national identity, cannot be managed or imposed. As soon as you become self-conscious about any aspect of national identity, it becomes an onerous embarrassment.

Significantly, just as the major corporations are examining the validity of monolithic corporate identities (Ford says it must 'think global, act local') a new government is taking them on. As in so many of its initiatives, this idea is now a generation out of date. Simplistic notions of identity cannot survive the Darwinian struggle for survival in the densely nuanced information age. It is true that brands are increasingly important in the marketplace, but it is also becoming difficult to ascribe to them a particular national identity.

    The realities of world business with instantaneous transfers of data
and capital and global manufacturing make a mockery of olden-days
nationalism. The radically designed Ford Ka is no doubt a very cool
product, but is it British? Not in any very credible sense, is the answer.
The Ford Ka is manufactured in Spain by a US corporation using components
sourced from Basildon, Belfast, Bridgend, Dagenham, Enfield, Halewood,
Leamington, Treforest, Berlin, Cologne, Saarlouis, Wulfrath, Genk,
Bordeaux and Valencia. It was designed in Essex and Cologne by a team of
individuals sourced from more than twenty different countries.

    The branding of Britain in general and cool Britannia in particular
is as misconceived as those crude notions of branding that preoccupied
business in the 1980s. You cannot create brands. You can only create
excellent products and support them consistently. Then, after time, your
brand values may evolve into something recognizable and attractive.
Intangible, maybe, but detectable, most certainly.

    Cool Britannia is a fundamental misunderstanding of the
relationship between product and brand. Genuine brand value depends on
substance, on associations and expectations established over time.

    It is deeply uncool to be cool. It is even more uncool for a prime
minister to take time out from a Middle East tour, as he did in April 1998,
to attack the critics of cool Britannia. The rhetoric here was much the
same as that used when Blair told the nation two months earlier to shut up
and stop whining and enjoy the forthcoming Millennium experience. Cool
Britannia is a generation out of date. A little late in the day, this
pseudo-event is being busily disavowed by the very image-builders who so
opportunistically promoted it. A government that wants to run the country
via pseudo-events will eventually leave behind a litter of such
communications catastrophes.

THE DOME - AN OPEN LETTER TO PIERRE-YVES *GERBEAU

    Dear Pierre-Yves

    The New Labour of Hercules

    I don't know whether you're keen students of the classics over there
in EuroDisney, but the situation at the Dome - the one they've asked you to
fix - reminds me of one of the messier labours of Hercules: clearing out
the Augean stables. These had become rather grubby because they
accommodated an incontinent herd of oxen. Imagine the smell.

We don't have exactly that problem, although people do tend to use
the word 'crap' quite a lot in Dome conversations, but we've developed
this stables thing into a metaphor of anything that needs a bloody good
sort out. Hercules' solution was to evacuate the mess by diverting the
course of a river. I thought it might be helpful and comforting to know
that the River Thames is close at hand.

I gather things are rather more spick and span and orderly at
Mauschwitz, but you'll feel at home in Greenwich. Indeed, the Dome has got
something of a *faiblesse* for Mickey Mouse and his colleagues. I well
remember that weekend back in '97 when Peter Mandelson, at the time, the
minister in charge, nipped over to Walt Disney World in Orlando to seek
inspiration in the magic kingdom. Call me a fastidious aesthete, but I
thought Peter's little trip was, at best, misjudged. When I say 'poor
duck!' I don't mean Donald: I just thought silly Peter. Did he really think
he was going to acquire more than forty years of Disney's proprietorial
expertise on an away-day? No. Hence the call to you.

It made me a bit cross because, while Peter was always going on and
off about his 'messages', I thought the Florida message was the wrong one.
I had rather hoped the cultural reference points for Britain's millennium
celebrations might – how can I put it? – be more sophisticated. But Peter
was very against élitism and rather felt the public should be treated like
complete morons and given a themed leisure experience. (He likes
'experiences', even though he was told that this word is what grammarians
call redundant amplification: it's lunch, I mean, not a lunch experience.
Same with the millennium. I told him the name he thought up, the New
Millennium Experience Company Limited (NMEC), rather needed focus-grouping
and didn't fit in the window of a standard DL-size envelope. But then he
never listened to me.)

So, I flounced out and we got this poor imitation of Disney. I am
afraid what you are going to discover in the stables, I'm sorry, I mean
Dome, is a spectacle that looks like a Baltic communist state had been
shown a blurred photograph of Orlando or Anaheim and asked to knock it off
on a limited budget. I know what Disney should be like at its best. In
particular I recall a description by my old friends, the US cultural
historians Jane and Michael Stern, who said 'Disney is to fun what
Velveeta is to cheese: pasteurized, processed, smooth, neat, bland,
square, loved by children'. W-e-l-l. I'm sorry to say it's not even that
good. It's not Velveeta. At least Velveeta is consistent and
unhypocritical. It's a dog's *petit dejeuner*.

I know you're good at changing the light-bulbs and all that, but the
first thing you're going to have to look at is not the inept signage or the
entrance arrangements that are like an Estonian ferry terminal, or the
stench of extended-life cooking oil (no garlic here, *mon brave*!), or the
pitiful attendances that make the far perimeter of the Dome look like
Gatwick North Terminal at 3 a.m., but the management structure. I'm sure
your INSEAD MBA will come in terribly handy here, although you can always
borrow Bob Ayling's axe if you need one. I'm afraid mine's been worn out by
grinding. Goodness only knows, I'm no management expert. I'm a wacky

creative type and I've always enjoyed Voltaire's belief that it's better
to be ruled by one lion than a hundred rats. The Dome, to bend a metaphor
to the point of distortion, might be a sinking ship, but I'm afraid there
are still hundreds and hundreds of rats on board.

In fact, I'm going to recommend that INSEAD makes the NMEC a case
study in its bad-practice classes. There is a *mille-feuille* of management
layers, none of them much good. No one will make up their mind about
anything until it's too late and then everyone wants to interfere.
Retrospective vision is 20-20. You've got the government behaving like a
disgruntled shareholder at an AGM that never ends. You've got the
Millennium Commission that frets pompously about cultural value and then
condones rubbish. You've got a lot of angry sponsors. And you've got a long
history of weak management. That poor Jennie Page used to harrumph and
fuss about 'finding a balance' between all these conflicting interests. I
think that was a total misunderstanding. It wasn't 'balance' that was
needed, but authoritative and clear direction. Anyway, I'm sure you
dirigistes will be able to fix the flummox. Do you have friends in the CRS?

Another big problem you must contend with is the atrocious media
relations. I'm sorry to say that the NMEC's press office was really rather
sleazy and nasty. I mean, they would have done a very good job for Beria's
KGB, but I felt they lacked the lightness of touch, the gaiety and the
optimism that this particular task required. Instead of enthusiasm and
open-handedness, they preferred to threaten journalists and strangulate
dissent. As a result, you will find it very difficult to find even one
journalist with anything positive to say about the Dome and all who sink in
it. Theirs is a culture of furtiveness, corridor whispers and sleazy
manipulation, not communication.

And in the same way that journalists feel hostile, you will also
find that London's huge community of architects, designers, filmmakers,
artists, musicians, writers, photographers – perhaps the most
extraordinary collective of talent in the world – feels alienated. No one
has ever actually bothered to explain to them why they have not been
employed in the Dome. Don't misunderstand, but when there are perhaps ten
thousand people here already who are well able to do your job, there are
going to be calls on your diplomatic as well as your management skills.
Maybe one of the white-knuckle rides you are promising could follow the
career path of senior NMEC staff.

But my real concern is what it is you are actually going to do when
you've finished rolling your sleeves up. I mean to say, it's all very well
being billed as Captain Fantastique, but I hope you didn't mind me saying
on the telly yesterday that I thought the circumstances resembled an
invitation to a leading cardiac surgeon to resuscitate a dead tabby cat.
What are you going to work with? We are not talking *carte blanche*, we are
talking three-quarters of a billion's worth of nanny state tack already in
place. I know it's a temptation to do a New Labour of Hercules, but where
exactly are you going to find the money and the time?

I know you'll need all the support you can get, but I've got to

----

pre-empt any invitation you're thinking of making. The history is too
depressing. Most projects like these are bedevilled by a shortage of cash.
This wasn't so in the beginning: there were shedloads of the stuff. The
funds were originally available to allow something truly excellent to be
made. Personally speaking, I had had great art, architecture and design,
literature, technology, history, culture, futurology and music in mind.
Alas, Mandelson and Page established a direction that led to a depressing
'Millennium Experience', which is more like a school project than it is
like the Getty Center. When you have time, do ask them both why, when the
possibility of excellence existed, they consciously elected to go for
mediocrity. And then not even with heroic commitment.

But I *do* have an idea that I will give you for free. The Dome's
contents lack the respectful awe and veneration that great art and great
ideas generate, the sort of thing people crowd into the National Gallery
to inhale and enjoy. At the same time, the heritage lobby is disgruntled
that the Dome is not more like a museum. I think you can appease them *and*
save money. Just relaunch it as a time capsule. I've always believed in
that idea of Henry Ford's that 'you can read any object like a book, if
only you know how'. Greenwich really is a Domesday Book: in all its
flatulent bravura and intellectual vapidity, its grossness, triviality and
high-handed carelessness it is, in fact, a deadly accurate portrait of
Britain 2000.

So forget about clearing it out: it is a genuine museum of today.
Project it as such. Let's make it a Museum of Mediocrity. Keep it there
forever, unchanged. *Le style*, as they say in EuroDisney, *est l'homme*. Over
here, *Le style est Le Dôme*.

So! *Courage, mon brave!*

*gerber is French slang for to vomit, from gerbe meaning a bilious
yellow sheaf of corn. Hence, *gerbeau*: a bit of sick.

(*The Independent*, 8 February 2000)

URBAN SHAMBLES

Politicians, alas, are rarely aesthetes, or even practical men.

The PM is pleased to provide photo opportunities that have him
domestically slurping from sad mugs. A great many of the Dome's problems

derive from Peter Mandelson, while he was there, being incapable of distinguishing between volume of activity and the quality of it. The results of this shortcoming are now well known.

London's mayoral competition confirms that our politicians take themselves more seriously than they take the world. They are, to adapt Lord Falconer's resonant distinction, VIPs who patronise ordinary people. There's Steve Norris, the amiable cove who cheerfully admits that he has more money than taste. You can check this out too in the at-home photos. Ken Livingstone has a charming antiquarian conceit about reintroducing the Routemaster, without seeming to be aware that the factory responsible for making this much-loved bus was shut down a generation or so ago. As for Dobbo, even fertile imaginations struggle to accommodate the sublime spectre of awfulness that might be the Dobson aesthetic.

Here is someone who thinks like a Camden Council ring-binder. When this newspaper recently put to him some amusing ideas about renaming Heathrow, his response was not intuitive and welcoming; instead he called for a business plan. Someone still in possession of the lazy, puerile archaism 'toffee-nosed' may well have difficulty appreciating art. If, one imagines, he thinks about it all, art, architecture and design are, to Labour's official candidate, the province of arty-farty pooftahs.

This is rubbish. You don't have to be a limp-wristed faggot to take aesthetics seriously. It doesn't even help. London is presently the creative capital of the world. Paris seems provincial. Berlin is a mess and no one wants to speak German. Tokyo is surreal. New York remains New York, but anyone in book or magazine publishing, broadcast media, advertising, new media, art, architecture and design needs a major presence here because, global electronic village notwithstanding, this is where the people are and the buzz is. People who need people are not just the luckiest people, they tend to be Londoners of all nationalities. Ford recently announced that it will build a new international design centre in London because this is where it can recruit the most interesting and able talent. The mighty BASF, a symbol of German industrial pride, has decided to move its operational headquarters to London, retaining a token presence only in its historic base at Ludwigshafen. The world's leading old-media publisher, Bertelsmann, conducts board meetings in English. It would only be a short conceptual step actually to move here. Back to Ford: the Detroit company, recasting itself as the world's leading consumer products manufacturer, already has the intellectual HQ of its US Lincoln, Mercury and Swedish Volvo divisions in Berkeley Square. Building a Design Centre here may be just the beginning. There are seductive arguments for all multi-nationals to be in London: the world's outstanding financial, communications and creative centre also just happens to be a fascinating place to live.

But London is also filthy, lawless, crowded and overpriced. Naturally, it is these very discomforts and hindrances that help to make it so stimulating. And there you have the human predicament in miniature: if London weren't so bloody difficult, it wouldn't be so seductively interesting. A new mayor must be someone not only with the vision and stature to sense the subtleties of balance required here, but also one who sees that the fabric of the city is the most valuable asset it has…and London's is deteriorating fast and out of control. Aesthetics is not effete. Aesthetics is about not wanting to step in dog shit. Aesthetics is having a true belief that the way things look and work is of primary importance. In this sense, aesthetics is more important than politics since, if you get the man-made environment right, then, the argument goes, humane disciplines follow. A politician who does not care about the look and the meaning of things will, ultimately, care about very little else. I am talking litter and roadworks, not art criticism.

The architect Le Corbusier once said that good design is 'intelligence made visible'. London's atrocious catalogue of excrement, burger boxes, diesel particulates, double-parked laundry trucks, insolent roadworks, hucksters, cynical souvenir peddlers, aimless tourist buses and vigorously free-enterprise street crime are depressing testimony of something other than applied intelligence. It is true that, in a contrary sense, litter and congestion are evidence of prosperity and vitality, but I am not convinced that they are actually necessary for the fulfilled life. All Londoners know that dirt, traffic and the wrong sort of people can ruinously tip the balance so that the colourful Darwinian struggle for competitive urban advantage occasionally becomes a farcical, tragic and expensive agony.

To improve London, the new mayor will have to start with the roads, the health of which is the clearest indication of the state of a nation (think Rome circa 100 AD, think California 1955). London's roads are very sick indeed. London actually has a Director of Traffic, although what he actually does is unclear (unless his occupation is to rota streams of angry white vans and dirty red buses from his infernal bunker in order to circulate and frustrate, frighten and demoralize Falconer's ordinary people). The routine response to road problems is pedestrianization. This is as sensible as saying the solution to eating disorders is to stop eating. We don't want pedestrianization since cities need traffic, which adds a dimension of human vitality.

What we want is a reduction in traffic volume. Everyone knows it's commuters and not local residents who cause congestion. These are what in Manhattan they call BNTs: bridge 'n' tunnel folk. On weekdays you can recognize the local variety here: grim pushy men in Toyotas and shirtsleeves; on weekends, shell-shocked provincials more than two up in a car. A transit tax of £50 rather than £5 per day for visitor's rights seems about right. At the same time, office parking should be taxed to extinction so that only commuters who could afford helicopters would even think of driving in.

A further refinement in the new mayor's perfecting of the capital would be that the emergency medical teams from gas, water, electricity and cable dealing with the rotting and disabled infrastructure of the city should be charged rental while they excavate to encourage efficiency and coordination. In whose interests is it to leave those ditsy little bits of rubble and cones and barriers?

Next, litter. A McDonald's tax could readily be applied to other culprits: the onus of responsibility for litter should be shifted from the retards who drop it to the complacent and greedy suppliers who make the dropping of it possible. It wouldn't be difficult to frame legislation requiring deposits to be paid on Styrofoam boxes or ring-pull cans and thus there would be an incentive for returning them, even among the very stupid. Equally, modern methods of data capture can identify the source of litter and the original supplier could be punitively fined. If you made so cost-conscious an organisation as McDonald's financially responsible for litter, you can be confident they'd find an effective solution. McDonald's would say 'This will effect our business'. The new mayor should reply 'Fine. Suits me. Any diminution in McDonald's business is a stimulus to urban civilization'.

An aesthetic mayor would also believe that virtually every manifestation of organized tourism has a melancholy effect. It is deeply offensive to find huge coaches parked all day with their diesels turning over simply to power the driver's on-board TV while his passengers throw McDonald's wrappers on the pavement and clog the Tate. Why are these same buses allowed to park, along the Embankment and along Park Lane, obscuring Londoners' views of London for the convenience of a busload of listless anoraks from Nijmegen? Tourist buses should be required to terminate at depots adjacent to the most remote underground termini. And then turn their engines off.

These are just easy targets, but there are plenty of others. Londoners should have some sort of privileged access to their own museums: at the moment, the National Gallery is all but inaccessible. There are few more economical sources of pleasure than lighting buildings and bridges at night. And bridges? We need more pedestrian ones. Even in sleepy Paris, street cleaners and washers are on ceaseless vigilant watch against ordures.

Are these things too fine and exclusive for the cast of the mayoral farce? I don't think so. Ford and BASF like London because it is civilized. Just think: civilizations are remembered and valued by their artefacts and their fabric, not by their bank rates or their PSBRs.

It is not a voice that London needs, but a pair of eyes.

(Observer, 23 January 2000)

```
**************************************
*  INDEX :                           *
*                                    *
**************************************
```

A

Addison, Joseph 17
advertising 7, 47, 76, 124
aesthetics 16-17, 21, 86
Agnelli, Gianni 193
Agnelli, Giovanni 31
air safety 148-9
Albert Memorial 14-15
Alfa Romeo 84, 98-102
alloy wheels 43
Americans, 6
Amstrad 89
aphorisms 167-8
Apple 110, 248
Arad, Ron 60
architecture 6-7, 9-11, 14,
        58-61, 172-3
Arnold, Matthew 22
        art 13-16, 36, 74-80
        neo-classicism 28-9
        pre-raphaelites 26
        romanticism 26
        surrealism 83
art history 7-8, 18
art posters 79
audio equipment 197-8
avant-garde 35-41, 80-2

B

Banham, Reyner 7-8, 199
Barcelona 191-2
Barthes, Roland 24, 71, 84, 93-4,
        183-5
Bartle, Bogle, Hegarty 76
baseball caps 64-5
Bass, Saul 144
bathrooms 44, 53-5

Bauhaus 16, 48, 83
beauty 13, 15-16, 26, 28, 83, 223
behaviour 24, 32, 74
Beatles, The 6, 45
Behrens, Peter 70, 233
Bel Geddes, Norman 16, 123
Benetton 113
Benjamin, Walter 79
Bertone 84
Betjeman, John 171-4, 265
Bich, Marcel (Bic) 68
Biedenharn, Joseph August 117-18
Blomfield, Sir Reginald 38
Boilerhouse 236
Borg, Alan 217
Bottomley, Virginia 249-57, 270
Brand, Stewart 10
brand values 128-9
brands 125-7, 135, 137
Braun 232
Britain 52, 87-91, 174-6
        cars 71-3, 177-80
British Airways 131-6
British Leyland 93-6, 125
British Telecom 124
Brucciani, Domenico 78
Bulthaup 57
Burberry 63

C

California 199-200
Capek, Karel 107-8
Car (magazine) 126-7
cars 5, 19, 83-6, 102
        aesthetics 5, 93-6, 229-31
        brand values 128-9
        British 71-3, 177-80
        colour 70
        cult objects 63

French 183–5
Italian 98–102, 241
Japanese 102–6, 197–8
manners 152–4
museum directors' 217–18
taste 42–5
traffic 222
Chanel 46–7, 66, 73, 243
change 9–11
Cisitalia 241
cities 11, 220–2
Citroën 94, 184–5
Clark, Kenneth 14–15
class 22, 51
classics 227–9
clothing 46–8, 64–5
sport 47–8, 66
Coca-Cola 5, 52, 115–23, 126, 137
Cole, Sir Henry 33–6, 51, 205, 211
colour 23, 44–5, 54, 69–71
Conran, Terence 8, 43, 56–8,
96–8, 203, 210, 215–16, 260–1
Conservative party logo 125
consumer durables 11
consumers, definition of 30–1
Cool Britannia 268–73
Corbusier, Le 29, 38, 49, 51,
56, 58–9, 80, 83, 182, 189,
228, 278
corporate identity 124, 131–5,
136–8, 219–20, 272
crafts revival 196–7
Crichton, Michael 91–3
crosstrainers 48
cult objects 62–73
culture 10
customer loyalty see good will

D

David, Elizabeth 27, 56–8,
115–16, 151, 184–5
deadlines 144–5
decoration 42
decorator, the 60
Demos 138, 267
Descartes, René 106
Design
modern industrial 16
quality of 16
'good' 19–20
mass-produced 79
popular 29–30

Design 1990 (magazine) 226
Design Council 8, 223–4
Design Museum 203, 209–14, 260
designer labels 19–20, 212
Dewar, Donald 266
distribution 113
Dome, The (see Millennium Dome)
Dorfles, Gillo 40
Dreyfuss, Henry 116, 123
Dunne, Dominick 139–43

E

Eames, Charles 60, 112, 114,
199, 225
Earl, Harley 83–85, 199
Eastlake, Charles 32–3, 60
eating habits 23
Eco, Umberto 23–5
editorial 7–8
education 6, 261
El Greco 14
elitism 242
Elton John 268–70
estate agents 44, 130–1
Euro Disney 186–7
exhibitions 236–8

F

Ferrari 5
Flaubert, Gustav 24, 49, 166
flying, fear of 147–9
food 23, 181
fountain pens 67–8
France 49, 180–5, 188–9, 242–4
Freud, Sigmund 12–13, 24, 37, 112
function 228–9
furniture 29–30

G

Galbraith, John Kenneth 18–20
Gandini, Marcello 84
Garibaldi cult 26
gas fires 61
Gehry, Frank 267
genius 8–9
Gerbeau, Pierre-Yves (letter) 273–6
Giugiaro, Giorgio 84, 180
Glaser, Milton 79

globalization 52
good will 126-7, 137
Gothic revival 15
Gracian, Baltasar 17, 152
Grande Corniche 188-9
graphics 126, 234-5
Great Exhibition (1851) 33-4
Greenberg, Clement 39, 41
Gropius, Walter 51, 56, 59, 202,
        212-13, 228, 267
Guggenheim Museum 267

H

Habitat 52, 75-6, 82, 96-7
handshakes 157-8
Heathrow Airport 138
Hepplewhite, George 29-30, 114
Hirst, Damien: 242
Hobsbawm, Eric 42
Hume, David 17-18

I

IBM 201-2
In Good Shape 8
industrial design 83, 214, 244-8
The Industrial Design Yearbook 246-7
intellectual property 126
Italy 25-7
        cars 98-102, 241

J

Japan 60, 91-3, 193-5, 193-8
        cars 102-6
Jones, Owen 42

K

Kant 18
Keats, John 15-16
Kelley, David 248
kissing 159-60
kitchens 56-8
kitsch 37, 39-40
knowledge 74

L

Labour, New 268-9
La Mettrie, Julien 106-7
landscape 10, 25
La Rochefoucauld, François 17
Lampedusa, Giuseppe di 9
Landor Associates 133
Laura Ashley 75-6, 82
Lees-Milne, James 207-8
Levi-Strauss, Claude 23-4, 46
Levitt, Theodore 52
literature 15
Liverpool 6-7
Loewy, Raymond 83, 85, 112, 114,
        116, 120-3, 225
logos 123-5
Lombroso, Cesare 24
London 276-9
Loos, Adolf 36-7
Lubbock, Jules 7-8
lunch 155-6
luxury 48-50, 182

M

Macintosh 110
magazines 74
Malraux, André 13
Manchester 7
Mandelson, Peter 263, 265-7, 276
manners 23-4, 144-5, 152-4
manufacturing 70, 87-91, 113-14
        in Japan 104
Marx 18, 20, 22, 24, 26, 86
mass-production 83
Matsushita 87, 234
Mayle, Peter 180-1
mayoralty race 276-9
Memphis 41
Mercedes-Benz 76, 85, 96, 103, 105,
        121-2, 137, 153
Michelin 182-3
Milan 190-1
Millennium Dome 9, 267-8, 273-6
Mini 45, 88, 95, 179
miniaturisation 105, 197
Mitford, Nancy 13, 28, 42, 52
modernism 20-1, 38-9, 49-51, 222
monographs 231-3
Mont Blanc 63, 68
Morita, Akio 103-4, 125